Introduction to Organizational Behavior: A Situational Approach

Robin Stuart-Kotze

Reston Publishing Company, Inc.
A Prentice-Hall Company
Reston, Virginia

Library of Congress Cataloging in Publication Data

Stuart-Kotze, R.
Introduction to organizational behavior.
Includes index.
1. Organizational behavior. I. Title.
HD58.7.S78 658.3 79-20916
ISBN 0-8359-3259-1

A Prentice-Hall Company
Reston, Virginia 22090

10 9 8 7 6 5 4 3 2 1

Printed in the United States of America

Dedication

To Bill Reddin who got me started on all this, and to Lynn and Don, who got me through it.

Contents

Preface

> *"All theory, dear friend, is grey, but the golden tree of actual life springs ever green."*
>
> *Goethe*

That's a daunting thought to any would-be author. But some books are greyer than others, and this one is hopefully on the green end of the scale. I have tried to write this text so that it is easily read and easily understood, so that it is relatively enjoyable to read, and so that the reader can learn the theory and see its applications without having to learn a new language at the same time. I have purposely tried to stay away from technical terminology and jargon. My ideal would be to have readers say that they learned from this book, and they enjoyed the experience of learning. I hope you do.

We learn best by experience. I have built some cases right into the chapters that allow you to try your hand at applying the theory in the book. I urge you to make the effort to analyze them and to apply the theory you have learned up to that point in the text. The more you get involved with this book, the more you'll get out of it.

It often helps, in embarking on a new course, to know where you come from. Organizational behavior's roots are traced briefly in the appendix, and if you're interested in the development of the field, you might read it prior to starting the rest of the book. However, the chapters are designed to build on one another, and it is recommended that you read them in the order they've been written. Material from earlier chapters is constantly being tied in with current material.

There are a number of cases at the end of the book as well. They are primarily there for classroom discussion. It is difficult to analyze the cases and apply the theory for them without some means of feedback as to how well you're doing. Tackling the cases on your own may not be too rewarding. If you can find two or three other individuals who are interested, a discussion of the cases with them would be far more fruitful.

A lot of people reviewed this manuscript as I was writing it, and I owe them a real debt of thanks. A lot of people also commented on what they felt should be included in a book of this type, and what should not be included, and I followed their guidance in large measure. It's a bit different writing a book that way—rather like starting at the end and going backwards—but it was both interesting and enjoyable. (Of course, if anyone says they don't like the book, I can now say it was someone else's fault—''rationalization,'' Chapter 4.)

Thank you, Ben Wentzell, for the effort, the encouragement, and the unflagging optimism. I just hope your editorial career at Reston doesn't hinge on this book. And thanks very much, Diane Freed, for the painstaking and professional production job. You're in the clear, Diane. And thanks to Jaye Foley and Louise Pick for typing all that nonsense over and over again. I know you never thought it would come to anything.

Just a last note. If you have any comments on the book, any suggestions, any criticisms, please write to me and let me know about them. Apart from being deeply interested in knowing how to do it better if there is a second time, I'd just like to get the mail.

Robin Stuart-Kotze
Grand Pre
Nova Scotia

1

Introduction

OBJECTIVES

When you have completed this chapter, you should:

- know what is meant by "organizational behavior";
- recognize the importance of theory as an aid to understanding the behavior of people in organizations;
- have formed an initial opinion as to the payoffs of studying organizational behavior;
- have made some behavioral analyses and predictions that you can return to and evaluate after further reading and thought;
- know, in general terms, the approach the book is going to take, and our objectives in writing it.

WHAT IS ORGANIZATIONAL BEHAVIOR?

If we are going to make a study of organizational behavior, we should clear up, at the start, what we mean by the term. "Organizational behavior" is the study of how people behave in organizations. We will argue that they tend to behave differently when they are in an organizational setting than they do when outside that setting. This is not a book on the general behavior of people—that is the purview of psychology, sociology and anthropology—but rather a more narrow examination of how they tend to behave when they are members of formally organized entities such as businesses, hospitals, governmental or social agencies, or whatever.

In order to give you a feel for what we will be talking about, here are two short situations which involve the behavior of people in an organizational setting. Read each one and see if you can predict the type of behavior that the people involved are likely to exhibit. (You will probably think that this is a ridiculous thing to ask of you, given the tiny amount of data presented in each case, but give it a try anyway. We will be coming back to these two situations as we work through the book. We will provide you with additional data as the situations unfold over time, and, of course, we will also be presenting concepts in the various chapters which will allow you to see what is going on, and make your predictions more accurate.)

HOVEY AND BEARD COMPANY

The Hovey and Beard Company manufactured wooden toys of various kinds: wooden animals, pull toys, and the like. One part of the manufacturing process involved spraying paint on the partially-assembled toys. This operation was staffed entirely by girls.*

The toys were cut, sanded and partially assembled in the wood room. Then they were dipped into shellac, following which they were painted. The toys were predominantly two-colored; a few were made in more than two colors. Each color required an additional trip through the paint room.

For a number of years, production of these toys had been entirely handwork. However, to meet tremendously increased demand, the painting operation had recently been re-engineered so that the eight girls who did the painting sat in a line by an endless chain of hooks. These hooks were in continuous motion, past the line of girls and into a long horizontal oven. Each girl sat at her own painting booth so designed as to carry away fumes and backstop excess paint. The girl could take a

*Abridged from Alex Bavelas and George Strauss, "Group Dynamics and Intergroup Relations," *Money and Motivation* by William Whyte, pp. 90–94. Copyright © 1955 by Harper & Row Publishers, Inc.

toy from the tray beside her, position it in a jig inside the painting cubicle, spray on the color according to a pattern, then release the toy and hang it on the hook passing by. The rate at which the hooks moved had been calculated by the engineers so that each girl, when fully trained, would be able to hang a painted toy on each hook before it passed beyond her reach.

The girls working in the paint room were on a group bonus plan. Since the operation was new to them, they were receiving a learning bonus which decreased by regular amounts each month. The learning bonus was scheduled to vanish in six months, by which time it was expected that they would be on their own—that is, able to meet the standard and to earn a group bonus when they exceeded it.

HOVEY AND BEARD—PREDICTIONS

Make the following predictions, based on what you know about the situation in the paint room. Jot down your reasons for each of the predictions so that when we get back to this case, you can recall why you said what you did.

1 Production

Will the rate of production

- **a** exceed
- **b** equal
- **c** fall short of

the levels predicted by the engineers?

2 Job satisfaction

Will the girls be

- **a** highly satisfied
- **b** have no feelings either way
- **c** dissatisfied

with their jobs under the new production system?

3 Attitude to supervisors

Will the girls' attitudes to their foreman (and management in general) be

- **a** favorable?
- **b** neutral?
- **c** unfavorable?

4 Interaction

The job, and the changes that have been made in it, may either be a popular topic of conversation among the girls, or they may pay relatively little attention to it. Do you think the interaction among them concerning the job will be

a high?

b low?

*DANIELS COMPUTER COMPANY**

Daniels Computer Company's Memory Engineering Department was composed of four sections: magnetic, electronic, mechanical, and electrochemical. The customary development work undertaken by the department involved well-known principles of memory design. Each section carried on its phase of development in logical sequence, using the results of the previous section as a starting point. The members of each section were expert in their own fields. The sections were close-knit socially. The manager of the department left technical direction to section supervisors, reserving for his own responsibility the securing of essential services and maintenance of the development schedule. The department rarely failed to meet its schedule or technical requisites.

In July 1962, the Memory Department was assigned the development of a memory incorporating several new design concepts which had never been experimentally evaluated. The functioning of the special computer which was to incorporate the new memory depended upon the most advanced memory device possible within the limits of the new concepts. Development time was one-half the length of more routine developments.

The Memory Department manager selected the four most competent project engineers from the four sections to work on the special project. Each project engineer was directed to select five engineers and five technicians to work with him on the project. Because of time limitations and the unknown aspects of the new memory concepts, the four groups were to work on their own aspects of design simultaneously. Each team, remaining in the geographic confines of its home section, but independent of its former supervision, commenced immediately to test design schemes and components relevant to its own division of the technology. The project group members quickly became enthusiastic about their new assignment. The department manager left technical supervision to the project engineers of each group.

 This case was prepared by J. Barkev Mihran Kassarijan under the supervision of John A. Seiler.

DANIELS COMPUTER—PREDICTIONS

Make the following predictions based on what you know about the situation in the Daniels Computer Company. As you did for Hovey and Beard, jot down the reasons for your predictions. We shall be coming back to this case as we progress through the book.

1 **a** The four project engineers will work closely together to coordinate the output of their respective sections.

b The four project engineers will keep their sections apart from the others and will work largely on their own.

2 The members of the four sections of the project group will

a become increasingly enthusiastic about the project, as it progresses.

b maintain their original level of enthusiasm for the project.

c become disenchanted with things as the project progresses.

3 Progress on the overall project will tend to be

a smooth, and as planned.

b uneven, although generally as expected.

c slow, and well below expectations.

4 The members of each of the four sections involved in the project will

a spend a lot of time talking with people from other sections working on the project.

b tend to close ranks and discuss things only with other members of their own section.

The two situations described in the *Daniels Computer Company* and *Hovey and Beard Company* provide the meat of the study of organizational behavior. We are not interested in them specifically because they deal with manufacturing firms, computers, or different types of technology, but because they describe *people at work*. The predictions we asked you to make were concerned with the *behavior and feelings of the people* involved in these situations. We want to know how they will act, and why.

As you progress through this book, we will present you with a number of theories that will help you understand and explain behavior. We will also encourage you to try these theories out on *Daniels Computer* and *Hovey and Beard*, on some other cases, and against your own experience. If the theories help you to understand the behavior of people in organizations, they will have done their job and be good. If they fail to help you understand behavior, then they will *not* have done their job, and you may decide to classify them as "useless," or at least "of limited use."

The study of organizational behavior involves the examination and testing of a wide variety of theories about what makes people act as they do, and what results when they interact with others. The term *theory*, however, should not intimidate you. When we think of theories, we immediately think of such things as Einstein's Theory of Relativity, or Darwin's Theory of The Origin of Species, both of which are somewhat forbidding to the uninitiated. You should not find the theories covered in this book difficult to grasp or to apply, however. In fact you will find them clear, logical and applicable.

What is the purpose of theory? What should a good theory do? Kurt Lewin, a pioneer researcher and writer in the field of human behavior, remarked that "There is nothing so practical as a good theory." The job of a theory is, without getting technical and complex, to *explain* a class of phenomena, and thereby make these phenomena easier to understand. A good theory takes the highly complex and seemingly unrelated happenings of the real world and provides a pair of spectacles through which these happenings can be seen as organized, patterned, and logical. You, no doubt, have some theories of your own about behavior. Our culture is full of "Granny's Laws," popular theories which purport to explain the behavior of people. The problem with many of them, however, is that they have not been well tested, and they tend to reflect personal biases rather than behavioral facts. For instance, all the following statements are theories, of a kind, about behavior:

- You can't trust people with big ears.
- Fat people are jolly.
- Your personality depends on your astrological sign.
- All people are basically lazy.
- Man is basically competitive.
- Man is basically cooperative.

All these statements may apply to *some* people *sometime*. But who, and when? When the chips are down, theories like these are not very helpful at either explaining or predicting behavior. We shall try to do better.

WHY STUDY ORGANIZATIONAL BEHAVIOR?

We live in an organized society. A university is an organization; government departments are organizations; so are baseball teams, local sports leagues, church groups, the students' union, and the local supermarket. It is virtually impossible to escape organization of some shape or form, other than by becoming a hermit.

A large part of our lives is spent in organizations of one kind or another. To begin with, we can spend a dozen or so years in school, perhaps three or four more years in college (or up to ten years for graduate study or some professional degrees). After all that we are prepared to enter a different series of organizations where we will work for the next 40 or more years of our lives. As well as having to work for a living within certain organizations, we will probably spend much of our leisure time in others, such as community groups, Boy Scouts, church groups, the armed forces, and so on. Simply on the basis of having to live within organizations for such a large percentage of our lives, it would seem reasonable that we learn a bit about how they operate.

We all have to work under other people, with other people, or as supervisors over other people. It is therefore very important that we understand what makes these people tick (as well as having some idea of what makes us tick ourselves). The physical scientist takes pride in being able to perform the four basic functions of a science: to *describe, explain, predict* and *control* the phenomena with which he deals. The behavioral sciences have not advanced to a stage of precision which matches anything that physics, chemistry or biology can demonstrate. But we can and do describe behavior quite well. We can, with the use of a number of theories, explain it to a degree; and, if the theory we use is adequate, it even allows us some measure of accuracy in predicting future behavior and controlling it. *The study of organizational behavior attempts to enable us to describe, explain, predict and control the behavior of individuals and groups in organizations.*

As a member of an organization, you are often confronted with incidents which perplex you, anger you, and frustrate you. Understanding why people do the things they do in organizations does not change the fact that they do them, but it may enable you to react in such a way as to modify their behavior and yours. You may become better able to avoid escalating conflicts, and you may be able to channel the behavior of others into constructive effort, to build on the strengths of those around you, and to stay clear of their weaknesses. In doing so you will not only be able to increase their effectiveness, but become more effective yourself.

But there is a second reason for wanting to know how organizations work, and that is that their effective operation forms the basis for our whole *way* of life. If all our organizations are inefficient, we must forego our present standard of living and put up with something worse. Every nation's welfare rests on the effectiveness of its organizations. If municipal government is poor, then towns suffer; if state or provincial government is inefficient, then we all pay too much in taxes in return for too little. And the same thing applies to the business sector. If we cannot manufacture textiles, washing machines, automobiles, computer circuits, furniture, or telephones at a reasonable price, then these businesses will disappear. All the people they presently employ will be out of work, and all the money they would have earned and spent will not be spent, and so a large number of other goods for sale will remain unsold, etc.

We cannot claim that the study of organizational behavior will bring about the effectiveness of all of our society's organizations, but we can point to two facts: (1) all organizations are run by people, and (2) by far the greatest number of problems in organizations are people problems.

AN EXAMPLE

In order to demonstrate the pervasiveness of people problems and their effects on organizations, a short case situation, The University Audit, is presented in Box 1-1. The comments which follow the case point to *some*, but by no means all, of the behavioral aspects of this situation. This is an actual incident.

BOX 1-1

THE UNIVERSITY AUDIT*

In the years immediately following World War II, returning veterans flooded State University. Later, student enrollment sustained this growth as more high school graduates poured in to fill the places vacated by the veterans. But starting about 1955, student enrollment fell off relative to other private and state universities in the region.

The university administration was unchanged from 1941 to 1958. During these years, the president, the vice-president, and one favored college dean developed a palace guard. Favors passed back and forth; promotions and other academic honors went to the members of the palace guard. A closed system of communications developed; only those in the know, knew. Academic departments not favored by the three in command carried on as best they could with little funds, slight recognition, and no encouragement. Many qualified faculty members left because they were incapable of making the intellectual surrender required by the prevailing standards of a "good" organization man. Their replacements, who were mostly new-degree men, had a high rate of turnover, except for those few who "fitted" the specifications for inner-circle membership.

In late 1958, the president retired for reported reasons of health. His successor was chosen from the outside; State-House pressure on the university's Board of Trustees forced the Board to bypass the crown princes. The new president, who had extensive experience in university administration, began a routine program of administrative audit of individual colleges and departments. The uneven findings of the initial audit made each succeeding audit more clinical.

Finally, in early 1960, the university administration blew apart. The old guard closed ranks, shouting charges of unsound administration; the audits were becoming increasingly critical. The new president was bewildered by this reaction to his program of administrative improvement. He was forced to take a stand.

He announced to the public press that a functioning top management for the university had to be developed and that he was recommending to the Board of Trustees a university-wide administrative audit. He said that the citizens of the state had a right to know the conditions of their university and that the university was not dedicated to a cult of personalities.

*Reprinted with permission from ***The Management Experience***, by Arthur L. Svenson, Prentice-Hall, Inc., Englewood Cliffs, N.J., 1968.

COMMENT

Organizational behavior is not restricted to business alone. Organizations include such things as universities, hospitals, government departments and agencies, prisons, summer camps, and law firms. *The University Audit* demonstrates that lack of understanding of how people behave in *any* organizational setting can lead to trouble. All of us can see that what happened here was that the "palace guard," as they are referred to, ran things purely their own way, and that when the scales tipped against them, they became upset at the prospect of losing control. We can acknowledge that the old system was unfair to some people, that the high turnover of faculty was probably bad for the university, and that things needed to be changed. But what changes to make and how to go about making them were the difficult issues.

The new president's job was to make his university effective. The major resource of all universities is their people. Therefore the president needed to get all the members of his university performing to their highest potential; he needed to recruit the best people he could; he needed to make sure that each department was provided with the resources they required to do a good job; and he needed to ensure that everybody agreed on the overall goals of the university and was committed to working towards achieving them.

Easier said than done. Unless the president was able to understand how the people in his university ticked—what made them behave as they did; why some of them were committed to change and why some others were highly resistant to it; how they defined their jobs; how they perceived themselves as people; what they valued in their jobs; what turned them on or off; what allegiances they had, and what boundaries they had set up within the system; and so on—he had little chance of avoiding a huge blow-up.

The problems here are basically *people-problems*. A blow-up was *not* inevitable. There are ways of dealing effectively with this situation—ways which would allow changes to be made relatively smoothly, which would increase commitment of faculty to the goals of the university, and which would allow individuals and groups to achieve the things that are important to them to do a good job and live a worthwhile life. We will examine how all of these things could be done. That is what organizational behavior is all about.

HOW TO STUDY/LEARN ORGANIZATIONAL BEHAVIOR

There are, of course, many different ways you can learn about organizational behavior. If you are reading this book you probably have opted to learn within the structure of a course offering of some kind. But the study of how people behave in work settings certainly is not limited to classroom situations. There are many individuals who have a deep understanding of human behavior and yet have never been near any classroom study of the subject. A discussion of how to study/learn organizational behavior ultimately comes down to some decision as to the degree to which *theory and content* are important, as opposed to *experience and process*. These two approaches can be represented as being at the ends of a continuum, as in Figure 1-1.

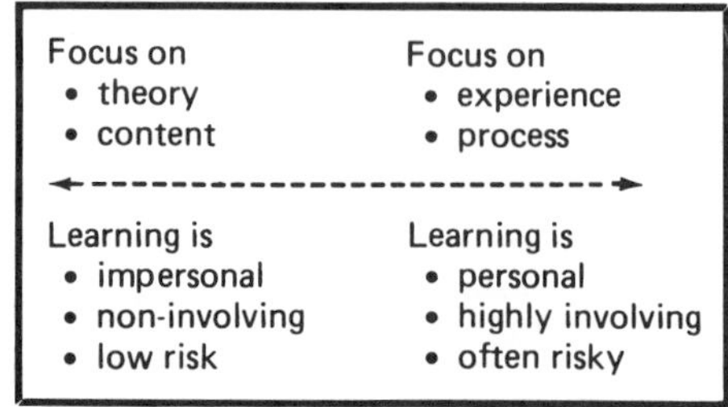

FIGURE 1-1: APPROACHES TO TEACHING/LEARNING ORGANIZATIONAL BEHAVIOR.

One set of options in teaching/learning organizational behavior is centered at the left of the continuum in Figure 1-1. The focus is on the presentation and discussion of theoretical findings and hypotheses about human behavior. For instance, the individual can read about, listen to lectures on, discuss various theories, and examine them on the basis of their conceptual foundations, their descriptive and predictive power, and so on. When the study of organizational behavior is conducted at this end of the continuum solely, there is little demand for involvement on the part of the student. You don't feel behavior in your guts, you think about it in your head. You stay clear of emotion, and focus on rationality. Theory is kept at an impersonal level and you are not asked to risk any part of yourself in an attempt to test it personally.

At the other end of the teaching/learning continuum, the focus is on *experiencing* behavior. You are asked to immerse yourself in situations where you observe and engage in behavior *personally*. You get to test theories right then and there. You are less rational and more emotional in your response to what is going on around you. You are highly involved, and you must take the sort of risks inherent in putting your behavior on the line. There are others around you who will react to you, and to whom you must react, and you can do things well or not so well. At the right hand end of the continuum, you are much closer to reality, even in a classroom situation. While the situations presented to you may be contrived in some sense, they are nonetheless very real and involve you and some other very real people. Many teachers of organizational behavior believe strongly that the subject can only be truly learned at the experiential end of the continuum. But every teacher behaves differently and thinks differently, just as every student thinks and behaves differently, so we cannot predict how you will use this book in your course. We can only make some suggestions.

As we see it, there are four basic options in studying organizational behavior:

1 You can read the theory and/or listen to lectures on it and discuss it with your fellow students and your instructor.

2 You can take the theory and apply it to situations in which you are not personally involved—cases—and test it for its explanatory and predictive powers.

3 You can take the theory and apply it to situations in which you *are* personally involved—your present job, student tasks, experiential exercises, and so on—and test it.

4 You can immerse yourself in various working (organizational) situations and develop your own theory on the basis of your observations and experiences.

Our bias, in teaching organizational behavior at an introductory level, is towards a combination of approaches two and three. We believe that you must have a working knowledge of the theory of human behavior, if only to use as a checklist of what to look for and what relationships to expect. But theory is hollow without practice, so we recommend that you test your knowledge of theory on various situations. Depending on the degree of involvement that you and your instructor want to experience, and the degree to which you both want to risk the give-and-take of reality, you can decide how much you are in favor of a case approach or an experiential approach. We like both. We believe in starting off at the level of cases and building up towards higher and higher degrees of involvement. We believe you really cannot understand organizational behavior unless you have experienced it yourself. The experience is exhilarating. We urge you to try it.

THE GENERAL APPROACH OF THE BOOK

In our talk about theory and experience we may have given rise to a misconception about organizational behavior: that there are universal rules that always apply. We do have some general statements that can be made about behavior, which are true more often than not, but there are no immutable laws. As Berelson and Steiner remark, "Nothing is true in the behavioral sciences (or in life) except 'under certain circumstances'."

The phrase "under certain circumstances" reflects the basic approach of this book. We call it a *situational* approach—"it depends on the situation." Others refer to it as a *contingency* approach. Call it what you will, an underlying assumption of this whole book is that *the behavior of people in organizations depends on the situation*.

We will describe what we mean by "the situation" as we proceed through the book. Such aspects as job complexity, rewards, and technology will be examined as part of "situations." The essence of a situational approach, however, is based on the realization that *there is no one best way to manage people*. People are different and organizations are different. The effective management of people depends on taking into account the specific characteristics of the organization in question, and blending these with the characteristics of the people involved. Managerial effectiveness is concerned with the matching of people, jobs, rewards, status, motivational needs, and other related factors.

A second underlying assumption of this book is that organizations operate as "systems." A system is simply a whole made up of interacting parts, but there are several important corollaries to that statement. If an organization can be conceived of as a system with a number of subsystems (divisions, departments, sections, etc.), all of which interact with one another, then we must be prepared for the fact that changes in one subsystem are likely to bring about changes in other subsystems. At this stage, perhaps this process can best be illustrated with the use of a mechanical model.

In Figure 1-2, assume that the four objects A, B, C, and D are attached to each other and to the frame surrounding them by rubber bands. A, B, C, and D are subsystems in an organization (maybe departments), and the rubber bands connecting them represent relationships between the subsystems and the organization's external environment. (This assumption of a rigid, unchanging external environment is, of course, false, since there are constant changes in the environment within which organizations operate. But it helps simplify the model at this stage.)

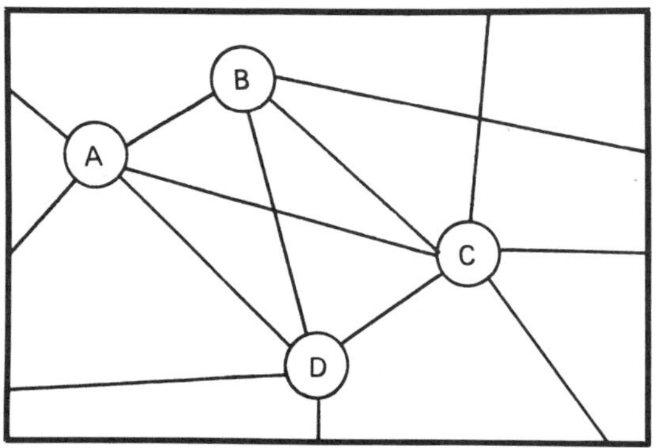

FIGURE 1-2: THE RELATIONSHIPS BETWEEN A, B, C, AND D REPRESENTED BY A SERIES OF RUBBER BANDS CONNECTING EACH WITH EACH OTHER AND AN IMMOVABLE FRAME. (Adapted from: Henderson L.J., *Pareto's General Sociology*, Cambridge, Mass.: Harvard University Press, 1935.)

To grasp the dynamics of a system, imagine that department A is moved closer to department B for some reason (maybe the two have to work closer together to solve some specific customer complaints). Immediately a number of strains are placed on all the rubber bands (relationships) in the model. Both the length and the direction of the rubber bands have changed. In real terms this may take the form of a change in the degree of interaction between the other departments (they may coordinate their activities more or less) and in the type or direction of interaction (they may find it more difficult to get certain information from one another, but easier to get other information. Old established working relationships between people in the departments may be disturbed, and so on).

What we see in this simple illustration is a set of interacting parts varying in relation to one another as a result of change in one specific part. It is this sort of relationship that we imply when we talk about a system.

SOME INITIAL BEHAVIORAL PROPOSITIONS

Viewing organizational behavior in systems terms, we can put forward several important propositions that you can test as you work through the book:

1 *No behavior takes place in isolation*. The behavior of any individual or group takes place in some context, and the meaning or explanation of the behavior can only be found in relation to this context. *Everything is done for a reason*. Even the most bizarre acts are done for what seems like a good reason to the actor. We often fail to see the rationality of certain acts, and describe them as senseless, stupid, or inexplicable. But that simply means they are inexplicable to *us*. We are applying a different frame of reference to the act; we have failed to see it in the context in which the individual involved sees it.

2 *No behavior can be traced to a single cause*. We have a tendency to explain behavior in simple one-cause-one-effect terms. For example, we say things such as, "Sue is upset because she has to take her vacation in June." If we assume a simple cause-and-effect relationship between these two things—Sue's dismay and an enforced June vacation—then we might be led to believe that telling Sue she must take her vacation in August would solve things. Of course, we are now assuming something else. The fact of the matter may be that it is not *when* Sue takes her vacation that matters, but *how the choice is made*. The source of her dismay may be tied to feelings that the organization over-controls her, undervalues her, is insensitive to her needs, and so on. She may also have had some personal plans that involved others and are thwarted by a June vacation period. We could speculate forever on reasons for her being upset. But jumping to single-cause-effect explanations won't help us.

3 *Every action sets off a chain of reactions*. If we take the simple example of Sue and the vacation, we can see a number of things happening. Her boss may change his attitude towards her, the organization, himself, or others. Her performance may change; her satisfaction with her job may change. She may interact differently with her boss, or others.

Conclusion and Summary

Armed with the three behavioral propositions just presented, we are now prepared to launch into the study of organizational behavior. We have tried to point out that in order to operate effectively in organizations, you should have some understanding of how and why people behave as they do. Since organizations are made up of people, we can safely assume that many of the problems they encounter center around people. The skill of management is deeply involved with getting people to do things—getting the girls in Hovey and Beard to paint a certain number of toys; getting the engineers and technicians in Daniels Computer to design a new computer memory; getting the faculty and administration of State University to work together to provide the best education possible for its students at the lowest cost to the state taxpayers. If management is successful, we would like to think that everybody benefits: the individuals who work in the organization, the organization as a whole, and the society, which consumes its products or services.

There are many ways in which you can learn about organizational behavior. You can study the theory, discuss the concepts, and evaluate them on their validity and applicability. You can take this theory and try to apply it to cases, using it to explain and predict behavior. Or you can relate it to your own experiences and test it out against "real life" as you see it. The ultimate test of the theory and concepts presented in this book is whether they enable you to describe, explain, predict, and control behavior of people in organizations. The degree to which they allow you to do this really determines their usefulness. Some may enable you to do all of these things, others only some. The behavioral sciences are still very much in their infancy, and what we know is not, unfortunately, precise.

Part 1

The Context of Organizational Behavior

2

The Organizational Basis for Behavior

OBJECTIVES

When you have completed this chapter you should:

- understand the underlying reasons for having organizations in our society;
- understand the basic functions of an organization;
- be familiar with the concept of rationality and have weighed its importance as an aid in the understanding of the behavior of people in organizations;
- understand the concept of a system;
- be able to apply the concepts presented in the chapter to the analysis of actual, specific instances of organizational behavior;
- have reconsidered, and perhaps refined, the predictions you made concerning the Hovey and Beard Company and the Daniels Computer Company at the end of the last chapter.

ORGANIZATION AND PEOPLE

A common denominator of all organizations is that they are made up of people—IBM, the Red Cross, the Little League, the PTA, the Student Council, the Army—and all these people behave in one way or another. But one of the striking facts about various organizations is the relative similarity of the behavior of their members. This is not to say that the employees of IBM act like the members of the Students' Council or the Army, but rather that people in the Army act a lot like other people in the Army, and the behavior of PTA members, while often vocal and sometimes acrimonious, tends to remain within certain boundaries. There is a degreee of predictability to the behavior of people in all of these organizations.

What causes these similarities? Are people categorized at birth to be tinkers, tailors, soldiers or sailors? Or do organizations, when one joins them, perform some sort of transformation which changes people into "organization types"? Strange as it may seem, both of these processes occur to some degree. Our personalities do tend to steer us towards certain types of occupations and organizations, and organizations themselves do tend to mold their members' behavior. A great deal will be said about both of these processes, but perhaps even more basic to the issue of why similarities occur in the behavior of people in organizations is the very nature of the organizations themselves.

Organization is a product of evolution. Man, along with certain other animals, bands together in order to overcome the threat of his harsh environment, in order to survive. Certainly organization is not unique to man. Among insects, bees and ants form highly organized societies. The structure of a beehive, with its clearly defined roles for different bees, is a model of organization. It allows the bee to survive in an otherwise hostile environment. Ants provide a similar example of organization among insects. Anyone who has watched the industry of an anthill and has broken it open to reveal the myriad chambers, all of which have specific functions, cannot help but admire the energy and organization of its inhabitants. Primates, other than man, also have organized societies. Baboons structure the roles and relationships of the members of a troop very carefully. Certain baboons perform certain functions, and there is a distinct social hierarchy, from the dominant males to the infants.

By banding together, animals *and men* are able to defend themselves against the dangers of their environment, either in the form of predators or other hazards. *Organization, then, is a result of a need to band together in order to overcome external threats and uncertainty.* The world is a hostile place, and facing it alone, with no help, is a dangerous and often short-lived experience.

THE PURPOSE OF ORGANIZATION

As man bands together for survival, however, he encounters another problem: other men. His relationships with his fellows are difficult and fraught with danger. How does he know his mate won't be stolen, his children slaughtered, his possessions destroyed? Clearly, the potential dangers of living in proximity with other men require organization to be imposed on the band. Like the baboon, *man has to order his relationships with his fellows;* individuals have to adopt certain roles. There must be a *sense of continuity* to the organization; a feeling that once things are agreed upon, they will stay that way, and people can go on about their business without the threat of sudden change.

Organizations continue to perform these two basic functions in society today: they reduce uncertainty (all organizations have rules of one kind or another which tend to make the behavior of their members more predictable), and they provide continuity and stability (organizations tend to last for some time; they are *expected* to be there tomorrow).

People cannot operate in a climate of complete uncertainty. We all need some fixed reference points. We need to know that some things remain constant and that we can "touch" them and know they are there. Experiments in sensory deprivation, where the subjects are removed as much as possible from being able to sense their environment, show that individuals begin to experience psychological breakdown very quickly. Not being able to feel, smell, hear, or see anything is very unsettling. At a more mundane level, imagine how difficult life would be if you had no idea of which side of the road people were going to drive on tomorrow. Or whether the policeman at the corner would wave at you in the morning or shoot at you. Or whether your school or your job would exist tomorrow, or what would be expected if you turned up and they *were* operating. How difficult would it make life if you could not determine what behavior was considered acceptable by the people around you? How would you feel if you didn't know when they would like you, reward you, hate you or punish you?

THE BASIC PROCESSES OF ORGANIZATION

Man "organizes" his environment by doing three types of things:

- Structuring relationships between the people involved;
- Setting goals for the organizational unit;
- Coordinating the efforts of the individuals and groups towards achieving these goals.

All organizational units reflect these three basic processes. The members of the organization must have some idea of who is to do what, to whom, how, when, how often, and so on. They must have a conception of what they wish to achieve from their efforts; and there must be some means of making sure that they act in a complementary fashion rather than at cross-purposes. We can see, therefore, that man acts to some degree in a rational manner. He can sense a problem, divine a solution, set goals of performance, and organize his activities to achieve these goals.

HUMANITY OR RATIONALITY?

The *concept of rationality* lurks constantly in the background of any discussion of organizational behavior. We tend to think of organizations as being rational and people as being emotional or "human." We see organizations as cold, impersonal, intent on achieving their goals, and not too concerned with human values along the way. And while we profess to like individuals who have some human failings, when it comes to running an organization we prefer the clear, rational thinker, and disdain the individual who can't stay cool.

But organizations are often criticized for their failure to take into account the "human factor." Charlie Chaplin's *Modern Times* presented the definitive caricature of the insensitivity and callousness of big business. And a description by an automobile worker of his job on the line lends support to the inhumanity of some work:

> You don't achieve anything here. A robot could do it. It doesn't need any thought. They tell you that. 'We don't pay you for thinking,' they say. Everyone comes to realize that they're not doing a worthwhile job. They're just on the line. It's a relief when you get off the moving line. It's such a tremendous relief. I can't put it into words. When you're on the line it's on top of you all the time. You may feel ill, not one hundred percent, but that line will be one hundred percent.
>
> (Beynon, 1973)

Not all organizations are run this way. In fact, few organizations operate on a purely rational basis, devoid of any concern for people. But there is still a very strong current of opinion which would maintain that when it gets down to the crunch, emotion and feelings have to be thrown out of the window and hard thinking of a logical, rational, objective kind must take its place. Make no mistake about it, human relations, organizational behavior, manpower administration, or whatever you choose to call it, is considered soft-headed by many people. All this talk about understanding the motivations of workers, communicating with them openly, being sensitive to their feelings and perceptions, and treating them as responsive human beings is still seen by many people as the pipedream of academics and do-gooders. The underlying model of organization that exists in our society is still largely one of rationality.

INTEGRATING PEOPLE AND ORGANIZATIONS

What is needed is a *balance* between concern for people and concern for getting the job done, between emotionality and rationality. Organizations which are completely people-oriented and show low concern for productivity tend not to last in our competitive, fast-moving society. On the other hand, organizations which are solely task-oriented and treat their people as numbers or machines tend to develop severe problems as well.

The television series *Star Trek* captured the essence of this balance between emotionality and rationality. One member of the crew was the Science Officer, Spock, who, having one non-human parent, had the characteristic of being absolutely logical in all his actions and decisions. The series very neatly explored the interplay between the consistently logical and unemotional Spock and his emotional colleagues. The point was made that without the "interference" of emotion, feelings and sentiment, the starship Enterprise operated at less effective levels. The delicate blend of rationality and emotionality on the bridge of the starship was put forward as the formula for its continued success in the face of monumental crises.

The point to be made here is that rationality is not *the* base on which organizations should be built. *Man is not a purely rational animal. We are all affected by emotions*. We perceive things through a screen of emotion and sentiment and we transmit things through the same screen. It is important that we do not ignore this fact. The insensitivity of individuals and organizations is *learned. We can just as easily learn to understand and utilize emotions and feelings*. The movement towards understanding and dealing with feelings which has grown up over the last 15 years is recognition, at last, of the inadequacy of reliance on a purely rationalistic basis for decisions and actions.

WHAT ORGANIZATIONS DO

From a behavioral viewpoint, organization does a number of things for us. We know that it serves to reduce uncertainty and provide for stability. It also helps us grapple with complex problems that require the energies of more than one person for resolution. The world is full of such problems. Churches are founded because the job of spreading the faith and gaining converts is too much for an individual to handle. Just the question of how to go about doing these things is so complex that it requires the input of many minds. How to provide for a variety of student needs and to act as a representative body for student opinion is a problem that Students' Unions have to grapple with. How to make a living out of manufacturing jam in the garage workshop is a problem faced by the Jones Family Jam Company. All of these problems require organization, and all organizations engage in a series of activities aimed at achieving their objectives.

All organizations have the following processes in common. Some perform some of these activities better than others, and some emphasize certain aspects more than others. But all organizations must come to grips with the following issues:

- *Goal setting*—Every organization must have some overall goals and objectives.
- *Communication*—These goals and objectives must be made clear to all members, and information relevant to their achievement must be channelled to the right people at the right time.
- *Division of labor*—The organization must decide who is to do what, and who is to be a boss, who a subordinate, and who peers.
- *Motivation*—Once the roles have been sorted out, the people involved must be inspired to do the job.
- *Coordination*—Dividing up the jobs is a starting point, but many jobs depend on the activities of more than one person. The organization must then facilitate the coordination of relevant groups of people in order to get work completed.
- *Leadership*—Effective division of labor, coordination, and motivation all require that leadership is exercised by certain individuals in the organization.
- *Decision-making*—All sorts of decisions have to be made. Goal setting, division of labor, design of information networks, etc., all require decisions. Leadership, motivation, and coordination are all needed in the making of these decisions.
- *Control*—Standards of performance must be set and actual performance measured against these standards. The organization must have some idea of how well it is faring.
- *Recruiting*—People must be found to do the jobs. Relevant abilities must be decided on and people must be selected with these abilities. They must be trained and placed in appropriate jobs.
- *Planning*—There must be an orientation to the future in any organization. Planning and forecasting are essential for survival.
- *Adjustment to the environment*—Organizations must exist within the larger society and must be sensitive to changes in society that will affect them. All the various internal activities of the organization listed above must be evaluated in the light of these environmental changes.

If you glance back over this list of essential organizational processes, you will note that they all involve *people*. Whether we talk about goalsetting, communication, division of labor, motivation, control, or planning, people are always an integral part of the scene. And they aren't all rational, logical thinkers. And they don't all do what we expect them, or want them, to do all the time. They are human beings first and organizational members second. It is important that we recognize and remember that when we refer to "organizations" or "managers" or "employees," as we will throughout the book, that we are talking about *people*—

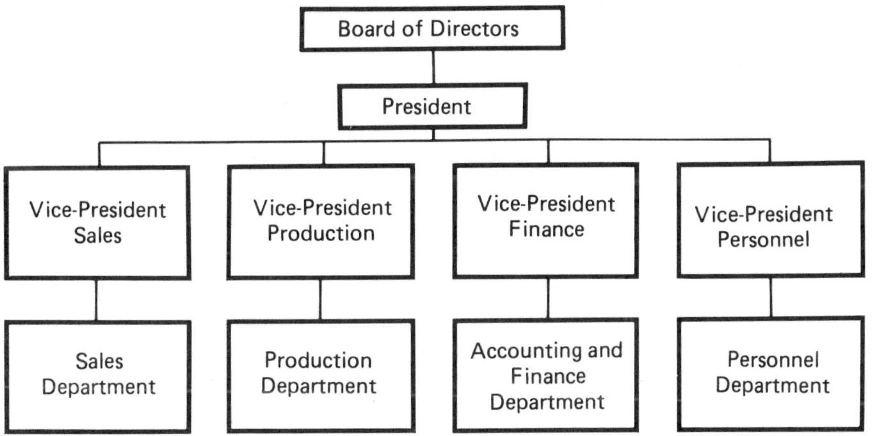

FIGURE 2-1: A SIMPLE ORGANIZATION CHART.

ordinary human beings who just happen to occupy some role or other in a large, formally structured group.

Organizations are traditionally represented by a set of interconnecting boxes, as in Figure 2-1. These boxes represent either individuals in specific jobs, or groups of people performing similar or related jobs. The organization chart in Figure 2-1, which is a highly simplified one, contains both types of data. The lines which connect the boxes give an idea of *some* of the interconnections between the various people and groups. It is very clear that nobody, or no group, operates in isolation. They are all dependent in some way on others in getting their jobs done.

By the same token, the *functions* of the organization listed above, such as goal-setting, communication, division of labor, and so forth, are all related to one another. Goals cannot be set without some communication, and they cannot be accomplished without division of labor, coordination, leadership, motivation, and the rest. An organization is a set of interrelated parts, people, jobs and functions. In the jargon of the behavioral sciences, an organization is a *system*.

THE ORGANIZATION AS A SYSTEM

The term *system* has some special meanings. First of all, it describes a unit which is made up of *interdependent subparts*. A manufacturing company fits this description. It has interrelated subparts called departments—marketing, engineering, production, finance, research, and so on. These departments, in turn, are made up of interdependent subparts called sections. For instance the production department may contain a quality control section, a design section, a maintenance section, and so on. And each of these sections may be further broken up into work groups composed of a small number of employees who work together on similar tasks or related tasks.

The definition of a system is *any set of mutually interdependent elements*. The human body is a system. It is composed of a number of subsystems such as the digestive system, the respiratory system, the nervous system, the reproductive system. Each of these subsystems functions in concert with the others. For instance, when food is eaten, the digestive process requires muscle action, which in turn requires blood, which in turn requires oxygen from the respiratory system, and so on.

The aspect of mutual interdependence in a system means also that *changes introduced into one part of the system will bring about changes elsewhere*. While this point may seem obvious, it needs to be stated, since it is of real importance with regard to organizations. Often managers overlook this point and are surprised when something seemingly simple like a change in working hours introduced in the plant affects morale, job satisfaction, production, materials waste, absenteeism or any number of other factors. Like the human body, changes in one area of an organization can have profound effects in other areas.

A second characteristic of systems is that they seek to maintain some level of equilibrium, or balance. Once again the human body serves as a good example. Running causes muscle contraction and expansion, which in turn brings about an oxygen deficit and a rise in body temperature. Immediately the body reacts to these changes and breathing becomes faster in order to ingest more oxygen; the heart pumps faster to supply the oxygenated blood to the muscles; and surface pores open up to give off moisture to reduce the body temperature. A few minutes after mild exercise has been completed, these processes have brought the body back to its normal equilibrium.

Organizations, too, seek an equilibrium. When new automated equipment is introduced into a manufacturing company, production workers are expected to change their output per man-hour. The actual output is often less than expected, to the dismay and puzzlement of the management. One of the factors at work in this type situation is a resistance on the part of the production workers to move away from an equilibrium, or balance, between a "fair day's work" and a day's pay. The individual and the group have a concept of how much work they are willing to give the organization in return for a day's pay (or a week's pay, or whatever). This equilibrium is set seemingly regardless of the advances permitted by new equipment, and so on.

In order to maintain its equilibrium, a system must have *feedback. Feedback mechanisms are a characteristic of all systems*. The body must know when temperature is increasing, just as it must know when it is returning to normal so that the appropriate mechanisms can act. A good example of a system which utilizes feedback to operate effectively is a home heating system. The thermostat is set at a certain level, which can be defined as the equilibrium level. As the temperature in the house drops, the thermostat signals the heating mechanism (feedback), to turn on. The house temperature rises until it reaches the equilibrium level. If it goes above this level, as it might in summer, the cooling system receives feedback and goes into action. All parts of the system are in touch with one another and act interdependently.

In defining a system we talk about its *boundaries*. An organization has boundaries, either in terms of the physical space it occupies or the people it employs. Within the organization, departments have boundaries of authority and responsibility. Sales is not held responsible for production, which is outside of its boundaries. In some fashion, we can draw limits to each of the subsystems. The issue of boundaries of systems is important when we look to see whether they are *open* (to influences from outside their boundaries) or *closed* to these influences.

Open systems are responsive to changes from outside their boundaries. In the case of the home heating system, the thermostat receives feedback from the environment (the air temperature) and feeds this into the system. This aspect of responsiveness to the external environment is most important for the effective operation of systems. Those systems that are *closed* to their environments run the danger of going awry when unnoticed environmental changes occur. When the thermostat breaks down and the heating system gets no feedback from its environment, either no heat is delivered to the house and the people in it get cold, or the heating unit fails to turn off and they roast. By the same token, organizations that are shut off from their environment tend to go off track and become ineffective.

Finally, systems can be looked at as having three parts; *inputs, a transformation process*, and *outputs*. Given the case of a manufacturing company, inputs may take the form of raw materials, machinery, people, skills, etc. These are employed in the transformation process, turning the raw materials into some sort of product (output). Mining companies take ore from the ground, refine it into pure metal, and then pass it on to fabricators who turn it into manufactured goods.

The reason it is useful to think of open systems in these terms is that one can see change occurring in a system as a result of feedback from any of the stages. For instance, if the ore being mined changes in makeup, or costs of mining change, or some other change occurs in the inputs to our mining company, changes may have to be made in the transformation process or the outputs. The ore may have to be refined differently (transformation); costs of the refined metal may change (output); or profit margins may get narrower (output). Changes in any of these processes are likely to bring about changes in the other two. If the product is too costly, then changes will have to be made in the transformation process, or else other sources of raw material will have to be found. If the transformation process is inefficient, the product will be sold at less of a profit or even a loss. Money (an input) will become scarcer for the organization, and we all know what that does! *Change in any aspect of an open system will bring about change elsewhere within the system*. Beware!

THE PROBLEM OF AUTONOMOUS SUBPARTS

Does the systems model apply in all organizations? Are there some companies or institutions which do *not* function with interdependent subparts? The government, for example, divides itself into a number of departments such as defense, health, foreign affairs, and so on. Are these subsystems of the overall government bureaucracy? If so, then they should be interdependent, feedback should flow from one to the other, and the total system, as well as its subparts, should attempt to maintain some equilibrium level of operations. Such things as changes in foreign policy should bring about traceable changes in policies in health administration, welfare, energy or even law enforcement. But often it seems that there is little coordination between government departments. Some are run effectively and others are run poorly and there does not seem to be any spillover from one to another.

In the same vein, what about a pharmaceutical firm that has had a poor record of research developments over the past ten years, but still generates high profits from a product developed 15 or more years ago? Does the poor performance of the research group affect the organization adversely? If the company as a whole is still making good profits, how can we make this sort of assertion? Is it enough to argue that if research could develop more products, profits would be even better?

In the government example, we could argue that a change in foreign policy that increased foreign aid would bring about changes in other government departments and agencies in terms of their budgets if nothing else. The only problem is that governments seem to have an inexhaustible supply of money and nothing seems to deter them from spending it freely.

The fact of the matter is that not all organizations operate as perfect open systems. Some are able to continue to operate profitably in spite of changes in their environment to which they haven't responded. Some have departments or divisions which operate poorly, but which are effectively isolated from the rest of the organization and are thereby prevented from adversely affecting the performance of other areas. The department that operates inefficiently can be avoided. In effect, it is surrounded by an insulating barrier and cut off from the rest of the organization so that the effects of its inefficiency are minimized. Its outputs may be ignored. Its inputs may be severely limited so that it has less to mess up with. Or it may be transformed into a closed-loop operation and cut off from the rest of the system entirely (that is, its outputs may be fed directly back into its own system, thereby closing it off from the environment and letting it continue to feed on itself, regardless of what it produces or does).

Some organizations do have autonomous subparts, or at least semi-autonomous subparts. *But relatively few*. The rules of systems apply in most organizations. There is generally a heavy interdependence between organizational subparts.

WHAT DOES A SYSTEMS APPROACH DO FOR ORGANIZATIONAL BEHAVIOR?

How does systems theory fit with behavioral theory? Is it just another set of theory that perhaps has equal weight with motivation theory, perception theory or personality theory? The answer is no. Systems theory does not explain behavior *per se*, but it does provide a framework within which to envision the interrelationships inherent in a study of organizational behavior.

The systems approach does not change any of the existing theory or knowledge of management or organizations. What it does is change the *applicability* of our present theories, rather than their content. For instance, the concept of span of control (the number of people who can effectively be supervised by one boss) is still a valid one, but if we adopt a systems framework for examining the operation of an organization it becomes clear that the span of control in various segments of the organization is affected by a number of other variables. We can no longer say that we have a *principle* stating that span of control should never exceed six, but rather, that span of control depends on certain variables such as job complexity, physical proximity of workers, degree of job similarity, leadership style, and so on.

What a systems approach to organizational behavior does is erase many of the so-called ''laws,'' or principles, of management and organization and focus attention on the relationships between organizational variables.

A systems view supports the propositions put forward in Chapter 1 that,

- No behavior takes place in isolation;
- No behavior can be traced to a single cause;
- Every action sets off a chain of reactions.

The one major fallacy of behavioral explanation that a systems view dispenses with swiftly and sharply is the concept of the single-cause assumption. As John Seiler (1967) remarks, ''Stated simply, we humans have a tendency to think that the effects we observe are rather simply caused; in fact, that effects often have single causes.'' Seiler explains this propensity as being partly a result of the fact that life is extremely complicated and we, of course, have a great deal of trouble understanding our own motivations and behavior. Therefore, in order to avoid the feeling of helplessness that this inability to understand ourselves and others brings on, we assume that explanations are simple and may be easily discovered in single-cause relationships.

To some extent, then, a systems view presents us with a rather rude shock. It serves as an annoying reminder that the single-cause explanations which we constantly bring forth to interpret events involving ourselves and others are inadequate, and are really simple forms of self delusion. We are forced to realize that everything is related to everything else and that changes in one variable bring about changes in all the others. But how, one might ask, does this harsh removal of a set of ''simple'' explanations and its substitution with the unmanageable idea of ''everything'' help us understand organizational behavior?

Fortunately, systems have one property which makes all the difference to our understanding; they are *hierarchical*. That is, each system is composed of a number of subsystems and we can therefore separate the component parts and examine their relationships more easily than at first appears. We can decide the *level* at which we want to examine systematic relationships. For instance, do we want to look at the relationships of the various system components of the *individual* (the nervous system, the circulatory system, the psychological system, and so on), or of the *work group* (interactions, sentiments, values, perceptions, etc.),or even of the *depart-*

ment (inter-group), *the division* (inter-department), the *organization* (inter-division), or the *culture* (inter-institutional)?

Seiler (1967) makes the point well:

> Since we seek a way of thinking about human behavior which permits us to account for multiple causes without being overwhelmed by infinite complexity, the idea of a hierarchy of subsystems first permits us to look at the relatively limited number of events taking place within a particular system and between the relatively limited parts of that system . . .
>
> Second, in order to act effectively in response to what is going on, we do not have to know all that *can* be known about every potentially relevant system, all about everything which has a conceivably important effect on what we are interested in. . . . Instead, we establish who we are, what our role is, what our competence is, and what our goals are. Then we choose to analyse the internal workings of those systems whose internal condition is something we can and want to do something about. . . .
>
> The hierarchy-of-systems idea, then, allows us to concentrate on understanding one internal system at a time without becoming immobilized by infinite complexity; it allows us to treat some systems as external environment, some as the producers of internal effects and some in the full complexity necessitated by the nature of our goals, responsibilities, and skills.

AN ILLUSTRATION OF AN ORGANIZATION AS A SYSTEM: THE HOVEY AND BEARD COMPANY

Chapter 1 started off with two short cases, one of which was the Hovey and Beard Company. If you recall, it concerned a group of girls engaged in the painting of wooden toys. Take a minute or two now to read the case over again. It is reproduced here for the sake of convenience. This is Part I of the case. As we progress through the book we will continue to add data so that you can see how the theory in the book may be applied to a specific situation.

Up to now, what we have discussed, in terms of theory, is the systems concept. How might that apply to what we know about Hovey and Beard?

> *The Hovey and Beard Company manufactured wooden toys of various kinds: wooden animals, pull toys, and the like. One part of the manufacturing process involved spraying paint on the partially assembled toys. This operation was staffed entirely by girls.*
>
> *The toys were cut, sanded, and partially assembled in the wood room. Then they were dipped into shellac, following which they were painted. The toys were predominantly two-colored; a few were more*

than two colors. Each color required an additional trip through the paint room.

For a number of years, production of these toys had been entirely handwork. However, to meet tremendously increased demand, the painting operation had recently been re-engineered so that the eight girls who did the painting sat in a line by an endless chain of hooks. These hooks were in continuous motion, past the line of girls and into a long horizontal oven. Each girl sat at her own painting booth so designed as to carry away fumes and backstop excess paint. She could take a toy from the tray beside her, position it in a jig inside the painting cubicle, spray on the color according to a pattern, then release the toy and hang it on the hook passing by. The rate at which the hooks moved had been calculated by the engineers so that each girl, when fully trained, would be able to hang a painted toy on each hook before it passed beyond her reach.

The girls working in the paint room were on a group bonus plan. Since the operation was new to them, they were receiving a learning bonus which decreased by regular amounts each month. The learning bonus was scheduled to vanish in six months, by which time it was expected that they would be on their own–that is, able to meet the standard and to earn a group bonus when they exceeded it.

The Hovey and Beard Company (Part I): The Beginnings of an Analysis

To begin with, we can define the company as a *system*. And it clearly has a number of *subsystems*. The first level subsystems include the wood room (where toys are partially assembled), the shellacking section, and the paint room. (We might also assume other sections, or departments, in the company, such as purchasing, packaging, sales, accounting, etc.)

The sections are *interdependent* in that the number of toys assembled in the wood room or shellacked in the dipping section depends, to a large degree, on the speed with which the paint room can finish them. The work put through these two earlier stations will approximate the productive capability of the paint room. The system will attempt to have neither too few toys going into the paint room, nor too many (there are costs associated with building up stacks of half-finished toys).

We should decide, before we go too far with our analysis of the case, at which *level* we would like to examine the situation. For instance, we could look at behavior from an *individual* standpoint: how does each girl's personality, motivation, knowledge, values, and so on, affect her behavior? Unfortunately, we do not have enough data to analyze behavior at this level in any detail. We don't know enough about the girls, or their supervisors.

We could examine the *work group*. We know that there are eight girls in the group. We know that they are expected to work as a group, since their bonus plan is designed to reinforce that type of behavior. We also know how they used to work in the past: they did the work by hand, and probably did not sit in a line (assumption) or at painting booths with exhaust fans in them. We could make some assumptions about how pleasant or motivating the work of painting toys would be under the two sets of circumstances, but let's remember that we would be making assumptions, and not stating facts.

We could look at the system at the level of the *department*—the paint room. We can see that the paint room has a *boundary*. This is defined by its function; the toys come into the paint room from the shellacking section and leave it presumably to go to packaging and shipping. But the boundary of the paint room is also defined by its members. The eight girls know one another and identify themselves as painters rather than sanders or shellackers. When all is said and done their primary concern about how things go is confined to the paint room. They, like all of us, are concerned with themselves first. The paint room is theirs, and they would tend to resist pressures from other groups or sections to change things within their own boundaries.

However, they must be responsive to *feedback* from the rest of the organization. The system will have to be *open*. They can't be painting more toys than are required by the firm; nor can they paint so few that huge backlogs of unfinished toys build up. At the group level, the girls will have to come to some sort of agreement among themselves as to the level of production that they are willing to achieve. They will have to find an *equilibrium level* of production where they feel that what they are producing (a day's work) is *fair* in terms of what they receive in return (a day's pay). Management may wish to move this level by altering one side of the equation or the other—i.e., changing the work level, or changing the reward level.

At the level of the department and the organization, we might note that *change in one part of the system will put pressure for change on the other parts*. If the productive capacity of the paint room is increased, there will be pressure to increase the output of the wood room and the dipping section to keep up.

Once there is an increase in productivity in one area, the others will be adjusted and brought into balance (*equilibrium*) with one another. (These balancing changes will move out into other areas of the company not mentioned in the case, such as sales, which will now have more toys to sell, or packaging, which will have more output to handle.)

Feedback will be required from each subsystem to the rest of the system so that this balancing can take place. Each segment in the organization will have to know about the changes taking place in the paint room so that it can adjust to them. Bear in mind also that the original impetus for change in the production system came as a *result* of *feedback* from the marketplace—"to meet tremendously increased demand."

The system will have to remain *open* because it will need to have access to continued feedback from the market as to how the toys are being accepted (quality, variety, price, etc.) and whether the company can sell more or should cut back its production.

A final consideration which you might want to make in your analysis of the Hovey and Beard case concerns not systems theory, but the concept of rationality.

Management, on the basis of feedback from the market, sees a need for increased production of these toys (and perhaps a need for a decrease in the cost of producing them). They are adopting what appears to them a rational, logical approach to the solution of these two problems; they are installing a more sophisticated production method and training the girls in how to work with it. To motivate them, management is offering a group bonus. It is assumed (based on a rational approach to performance) that the girls will see the need for the increase and for the new methods, and will accept these. It is also assumed that they will find the idea of the group bonus attractive enough to motivate them to learn the new methods in the set time and to produce at, or above, the required levels. These assumptions seem *logical*. They are based on a concept of rationality. Are they valid? Will they hold in this situation? Why, or why not?

Learning/Understanding Organizational Behavior

In Chapter 1, we talked about various ways in which you could approach the study of organizational behavior. Our feeling is that it is best done within the framework of application to specific situations (cases) and to your own experiences. A book can't do the latter for you, but it can help you with the former. It is our intention to help you take the theory that is presented in the book and apply it to the situations presented in actual cases. You can evaluate the theory on the degree to which it helps you understand the behavior in these cases. As we said before, if it doesn't help, then you can rate its usefulness as low. We think the theories presented here will help.

Perhaps you would like to go back to the predictions you made at the end of Chapter 1 and see if you want to alter them in any way. If you do, then make a note of your reasons for doing so. We are still not finished with this first part of the case.

Are there any other predictions you feel you would make about how the people involved are going to react and how the organization or any of its subparts, is going to react?

How about Daniels Computer Company? Does any of the systems or organizational theory help you make the required predictions?

Chapter Summary

1 Human beings organize themselves into various groupings for a number of basic reasons:
   - a to overcome external threats,
   - b to order their relationships with their fellows,
   - c to overcome uncertainty in the environment,
   - d to achieve some sense of continuity of life and relationships.

2 We organize our environment by doing three types of things:
   a structuring relationships between the people involved,
   b setting goals for the organizational unit,
   c coordinating the efforts of individuals and groups towards achieving these goals.

3 All organizations have the following processes in common. Whether they handle them well or not is another matter, but sooner or later the following issues must be engaged:
   - goal setting
   - communication
   - division of labor
   - motivation
   - coordination
   - leadership
   - decision-making
   - control
   - recruiting
   - planning
   - adjustment to the environment

4 Organizations are based on a concept of man as essentially a rational and logical being. Organization charts define formal relationships and focus on jobs or roles. However, the people who occupy these jobs or roles operate on an emotional as well as rational level. One of the tasks of managers in organizations is the integration of emotionality and rationality to achieve effective operation. This is the "Starship Enterprise" principle.

5 Organizations can be viewed as systems. A simple definition of a system is "any set of mutually interdependent elements." All systems have the following characteristics:
   a they are made up of interdependent subparts,
   b changes introduced into one part of the system bring about changes elsewhere in the system,
   c they seek to maintain some level of equilibrium, or balance,
   d in order to maintain this equilibrium, or to move to a new equilibrium, they require feedback,
   e they have definable boundaries, set either by their physical limits, function, or membership,
   f they are either open or closed—i.e., they either accept feedback from the environment or not,
   g they are hierarchical,

h in terms of their operations they can be looked at as having three parts: an input phase, a transformation phase, and an output phase. We can examine their operations and affect changes at any of these phases.

6 A systems view provides us with a framework within which to examine the interrelationships between organizational and human variables. It destroys the single-cause-effect explanation of behavior in organizations and emphasizes that behavior does not take place in siolation, but is the result of a complex set of interacting variables.

3

The Key to Effective Behavior: A Situational Approach

OBJECTIVES

When you have completed this chapter you should:

- understand the concept of managerial effectiveness and its importance;
- be aware of the interaction between the organizational system, the individual system, and the work group system as they affect the behavior of people in an organization, and in turn are affected by it;
- understand what is meant by a "situational approach" to management and organizational behavior;
- be aware of the major situational variables that affect managerial behavior;
- be able to make a "situational analysis" of a specific case.

"Begin at the beginning," the King said, gravely, "and go on till you come to the end; then stop."

–Alice in Wonderland

Easy for the King to say! But sometimes it's useful to know where we're going as well, and a little peek at the end may help to keep us on track. Robert Mager (1975) relates a story about a sea horse that helps to make the point.

> Once upon a time a Sea Horse gathered up his seven pieces of eight and cantered out to find his fortune. Before he had traveled very far he met an Eel, who said,
>
> "Psst. Hey, bud. Where 'ya goin'?"
>
> "I'm going out to find my fortune," replied the Sea Horse, proudly.
>
> "You're in luck," said the Eel. "For four pieces of eight you can have this speedy flipper, and then you'll be able to get there a lot faster."
>
> "Gee, that's swell," said the Sea Horse, and paid the money and put on the flipper and slithered off at twice the speed. Soon he came upon a Sponge, who said,
>
> "Psst. Hey, bud. Where 'ya goin'?"
>
> "I'm going out to find my fortune," replied the Sea Horse.
>
> "You're in luck," said the Sponge. "For a small fee I will let you have this jet-propelled scooter so that you will be able to travel a lot faster."
>
> So the Sea Horse bought the scooter with his remaining money and went zooming through the sea five times as fast. Soon he came upon a Shark, who said,
>
> "Psst. Hey bud. Where 'ya goin'?"
>
> "I'm going out to find my fortune, replied the Sea Horse.
>
> "You're in luck. If you'll take this short cut," said the Shark, pointing to his open mouth, "you'll save yourself a lot of time."
>
> "Gee, thanks," said the Sea Horse, and zoomed off into the interior of the Shark, there to be devoured.
>
> From *Preparing Instructional Objective,* 2 MD ED., by Robert F. Mager, Fearon-Pitman Publishers, Inc., 1975. Reprinted with permission.

The end result of understanding how people behave in organizations is hopefully being able to manage them better. We believe that the skills taught in a course in organizational behavior go a long way towards making managers effective in their jobs. That is where we're heading: towards increased managerial effectiveness, not just out for a ride like the sea horse.

THE MANAGER'S TASK: EFFECTIVENESS

Bill Reddin (1970) says that a manager has only one job, and that is to be effective. By that he means that the manager has certain outputs, or results, for which he is held accountable; achieving these results is what his job is about.

In talking about managerial effectiveness, Campbell, et. al. (1970) focus on three aspects of the problem: the *person*, the *process*, and the *product*. What sorts of people are effective managers? What *is* effective managing (the process)? And what are the results (products) of effective managing? Our answers to these questions demonstrate the overall viewpoint of this book: a *situational approach*. There are no cut-and-dried answers to the questions of who, how and what is effective in every organizational instance. *It depends on the situation*. Some effective managers are hard-driving, tough, aggressive people who like to do everything themselves. But there are also a lot of effective managers who are warm, open, and friendly, and who let their subordinates take a lot of authority and responsibility. Which is the more effective process? Doing as much of the work as you can, or delegating as much of it as you can to others? If you look at a lot of different organizations and managers, the answer is clear. But it is also frustrating, because it comes back to "it depends on the situation."

Summarizing the research of a number of writers, Campbell et. al. (1970) present a list of personal qualities thought to be necessary for managerial effectiveness:

Able to sustain defeat
Alert
Ambitious—achievement oriented
Assertive
Capable of good judgment
Competitive
Concrete
Creative
Decisive
Dedicated
Dynamic
Emotionally stable
Energetic
Extraverted
Fearful of failure
Group-oriented
Honest
Intelligent
Mentally healthy
Optimistic and confident (as a cover-up for fear of failure)
Pragmatic
Predictable
Reality-oriented
Self-controlled but defensive
Tolerant of frustration

If you think that is a long list, an exhaustive study done by one of the foremost researchers on leadership (Stogdill, 1974) looked at 43 characteristics of effective leaders, in 163 studies on the subject. These characteristics were divided into categories such as physical characteristics, social background, intelligence and ability, personality, task-related characteristics (e.g., initiative, persistence), and social characteristics (e.g., tact, popularity). The overall conclusion reached from this summary of research studies into traits of effective leaders was that individual traits, or characteristics, bear little relationship to effectiveness. There may be certain clusters of characteristics which aid in effectiveness, but these are also very much a matter of the situation.

Looking at the ''process'' aspects of managerial effectiveness, as Campbell et al. define them, lists of effective behaviors include such things as delegating, making decisions by consensus, cooperating, coordinating, setting realistic goals, communicating, behaving consistently, and stimulating action in others. But once again this sort of list smacks of ''motherhood'' statements. How can one argue *against* setting realistic goals, communicating, and enlisting the aid of others in decision-making? The fact of the matter is, however, that some managers do none of these things, or, at least, do them minimally, and are highly successful. Goals are often set arbitrarily, without discussion with those involved (and the reward for achieving them is getting to keep your job). Communication is often downwards, from the boss to the subordinate (and no backtalk, please). And decisions are often made unilaterally and simply passed on to subordinates. All of these tactics can be observed in relative abundance, and all work very well from time to time.

It is only when we get to the final category of ''product'' that we begin to get a grasp of the concept of effectiveness. The effectiveness of any manager or any employee can best be measured by what he *produces*. Giving points for effort is not a sustainable custom in any sort of competitive environment. Lawyers are rated on the basis of cases they win, not how hard they work on their research. Doctors are judged by the number of cures they affect, not how hard they try; engineers by whether their bridges stay intact, not how beautiful the design is; artillerymen by whether they hit their targets, not by how quickly they make their calculations; fishing captains by whether they catch fish; baseball players by their batting averages; typists by their speed and accuracy. What makes it any different for managers? Every job must, or should have, some reason for being; that is, it should have some required outputs or results. If the job incumbent fails to get the results, he is not being effective. This does not necessarily mean that he is not a good worker, intelligent, or diligent. It may mean that the job is poorly defined, that he is not getting the help he needs, or that other conditions have made the accomplishment of the task impossible. Focusing on *product* or output is not a means for assigning blame, it is a means of getting some idea of what constitutes effective performance. It is the only way, when all is said and done.

ACHIEVING EFFECTIVENESS

Looking at jobs from an output standpoint means that there is more of a focus on the *ends* achieved rather than the *means* taken to achieve these ends. This is *not* a suggestion that ends justify means or that actions taken by people in organizations do not need to conform to some standards of ethical and moral conduct. But it does mean that there may be a number of different ways to achieve the same end; that there may be different ways of doing the same job.

Why do automobiles have to be manufactured on a long, moving production line? There may be alternate methods of car manufacture. In fact, Volvo of Sweden is experimenting with radically different methods.

Do sick people have to be treated in hospitals? Why can't they be treated at home? There is some data that hospitals prolong illness because the atmosphere of the hospital reinforces the idea of being sick for the patient. The question arises as to when patients should be admitted to hospital, and when they should be treated at home or released early. The answer would appear to be based on the individual involved, his illness, the type of treatment needed, and so on.

If we can borrow a concept from the field of systems theory, we can begin to see the problem as being open to situational analysis. Systems people talk about "equifinality". What they mean is that specified final results, or ends, may be achieved with *quite different starting points*, and by using *quite different methods*. As Kast and Rosenzweig (1974) put it, "this view suggests that the social organization can accomplish its objectives with varying inputs and with varying internal activities." We cannot assume a simple cause-and-effect relationship between the starting conditions of an open system and its end condition. This, of course, is due to the fact that it will *change* as a result of its transactions with the environment; it will adapt.

This is not "All roads lead to Rome," but it certainly suggests that managers and organizations may start off on many different paths and may utilize many different processes in the quest for effectiveness. Perhaps it should be called the "different strokes for different folks" approach.

Reddin (1970) remarks that, "the effectiveness of any behavior depends on the situation in which it is used." But what do we mean when we talk about the "situation?" Bear in mind that our focus of interest is on how and why people behave as they do in an organizational setting. Figure 3-1 illustrates the complexity of the "situation" in an organization. Behavior is influenced by a number of factors.

A SYSTEMS MODEL OF ORGANIZATIONAL BEHAVIOR

The *organizational system* is made up of such things as *rewards and punishments*, the *structure* of the organization (what are the reporting relationships, who is boss over whom, who gets the resources, the money, and the people, and what are the sources of power?), and the organization's *goals and priorities* (what achievement is expected, and what is seen as important?). These factors clearly affect how people act, and what they produce.

An organization also has some expectations of output—a required set of results. But these may or may not be achieved by the people involved. Expectations may be exceeded or they may be badly missed. Getting something done is far more complex than simply ordering it done.

In technical terms, we talk about the *required* system of behavior. The re-

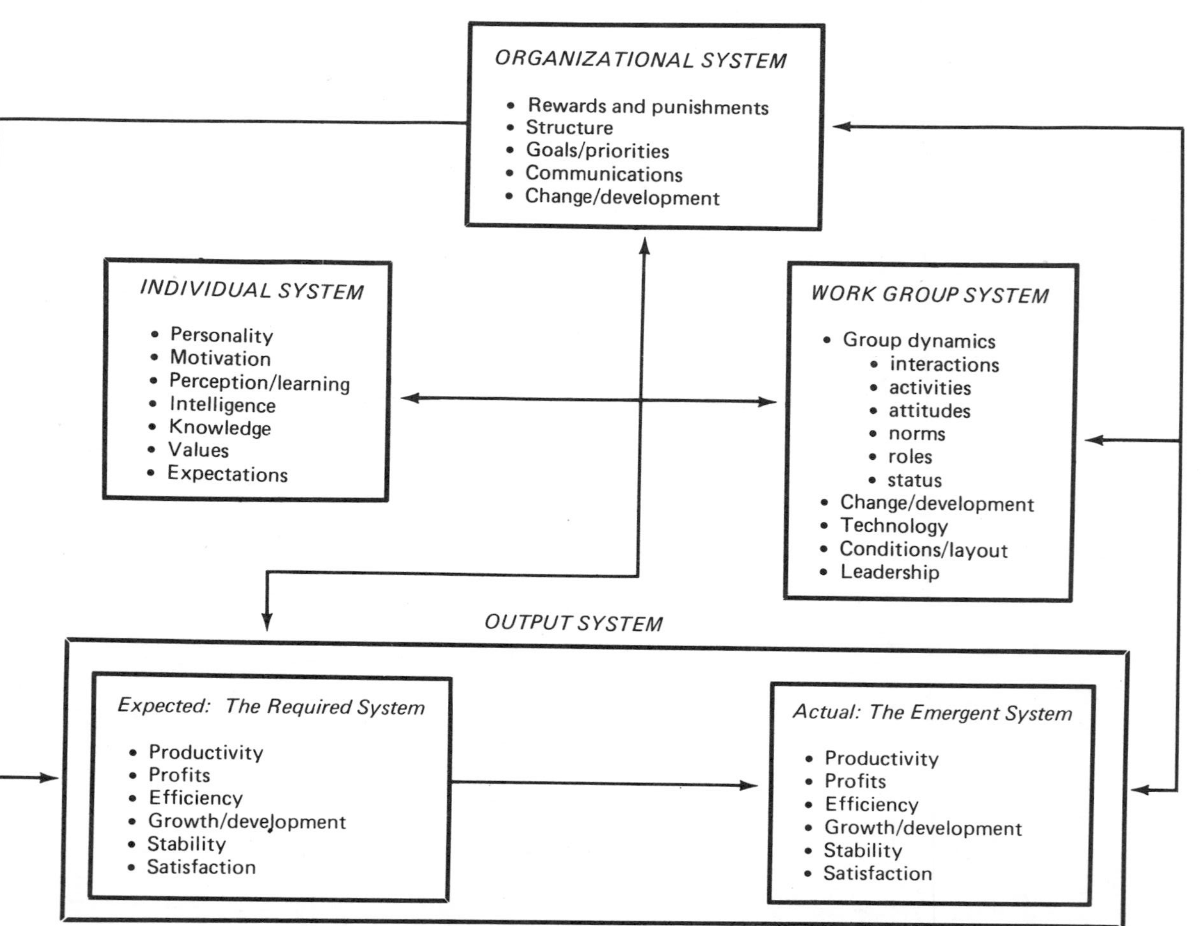

FIGURE 3-1: A SYSTEMS MODEL OF ORGANIZATIONAL BEHAVIOR.

quired system reflects what we would *like* to have occur, while the emergent system is what actually *does* occur. If it appears strange to you that these two things are not identical, read on, because they seldom are.

In Figure 3-1, the arrow from the *organizational system* to the expected side of the *output system* illustrates the process whereby the organization's rewards, structure, and goals are designed to coax, enable, and stimulate behavior that will result in certain levels of productivity, profits, and efficiency. The fact that there is a right-hand side to the *output system* area, labelled ''actual,'' indicates that there is some intervening process that upsets ''the best laid schemes o' mice an' men'', to quote Robbie Burns. This intervening process is heavily involved with our field of interest: people.

While the model illustrated in Figure 3-1 is made up of a series of separate boxes, do not be misled. The *organizational system* is implemented by people who are represented by the *individual system* and the *work group system*. Figure 3-1 is *not* an organizational chart. It is a systems representation of the various influences that affect the behavior of individual people in an organization. The basic unit of study in organizational behavior is the individual. If we are to understand why he behaves as he does in certain circumstances, we must be able to understand (a) what he brings to the situation *as* an individual (his *individual system*); (b) what influences he is subjected to by the group of people with whom he works (his *work group system*); and (c) the influences he is subjected to by the culture of the organization (the *organizational system*). These three sets of behavioral influences interact with one another to produce some sort of behavior on the job. Our task, as managers or fellow employees, is to sort out the relationships between these variables and understand *why* others act as they do (and why we act as *we* do).

As our systems model indicates, and we know from experience, it takes people to make an organization go. To begin with, the *organization system* of rewards, structure, goals, communication, and developmental plans is the product of a group of people at or near the top of the organization. There may be some deep disagreements over the design of this system. Some members of the top group may feel, for instance, that different rewards or goals would be more appropriate. Their feelings are bound to be sensed lower down in the structure with some effect on the required output system. If one vice-president feels that the growth and development of his subordinates is more important in the long run than the productivity of the company, while another vice-president feels just the opposite, we can expect variations in the act *actual*, or *emergent*, system. Productivity in some areas of the firm will be higher than in others, and satisfaction will vary, as will profits, efficiency, growth and development, and organizational stability.

Even if the top group who are the owners of the organizational system are in full agreement over its design, and in full agreement over the required behavior of members of the organization, there are still two very important screens through which these requirements must pass before they become actuality.

The output of the system is the result of the efforts of the people in it. All of these people first of all bring their *individuality* to the organization. They all have different personalities, different motivational needs and drives, different perceptual sets and learning patterns, different levels of intelligence, different stores of knowledge and experience, different values and different expectations for their jobs and lives. Needless to say, they will tend to react differently to the various elements of the organizational system, and will tend to interpret the required output system differently. One individual may feel that rewards offered are appropriate and worthwhile, and that required levels of output are reasonable. Another may feel that expected output levels are unreasonable, and the rewards offered for achieving them inadequate. Needless to say, these differences will be evident in the actual outputs that emerge from these two people.

A second major source of variation between required and emergent outputs is the *work group system*. As employees work together, they form opinions about their jobs, their bosses, and the organizational system in general. There tends to be a strong convergence of opinion over these issues within the work group (for reasons which we shall go into later). There is a very strong interaction between the individual and the work group. Each individual works as part of a group, and his individuality must somehow be tailored to fit the confines of the group or else he suffers severe consequences. The work group "socializes" the individual, taking the sharp edges off him, and making him conform more to its set of values and attitudes. If you want to live peacefully and happily amongst a group of people, you had better not be *too* different from them, and you had better hold to *some* of their more cherished beliefs and values if you want to have them support you. This is not an argument for conformity. It is a simple statement of fact. There are other options, of course, but few of us wish to take them. Not many people are suited to the life of the true loner.

Of course, this influence also works the other way. Individuals can and do influence the behavior of the groups to which they belong. But research has shown that an individual cannot take a group where it really does not want to go. Leaders in groups perform the function of articulating the group's goals and facilitating their accomplishment. It would be exceedingly difficult for a leader of a group of Hell's Angels to get his followers to spend 50% of their time working as volunteer hospital aides. Any leader who tried would find himself ejected from his position of authority rapidly, to put it mildly.

As Figure 3-1 indicates with its maze of arrows in various directions, there is a good deal of interaction and interdependence between the individual system and the work group system. These in turn interact with the organizational system (which is the product of people, too, only higher up the ladder), and there is a constant "bargaining" or negotiating process which takes place between the various systems, bringing about changes in each other. The required outputs of the system are set down by top management. The organization system is designed to reinforce the achievement of these outputs. As various outputs are achieved, this information is fed back into the overall system at different levels. Individuals assimilate the data and decide how to adjust their behavior. Work groups interpret it and decide how to act. Individuals and work groups in positions of enough power to do so, decide whether they wish to change either the required outputs of the system or the "reinforcers" (the organizational system).

In Chapter 2 we looked at the concept of a system and how it might be applied to the analysis of organizational behavior. Here we have begun to be more detailed, looking at a specific systems model of the people, process and products of organizational behavior. We have also made the point that *effective* behavior depends on the situation; certain behavior is appropriate at some times, but not at others. By looking at an organization as a system we are able to erase many of the so-called "laws" or principles of management, since they tend to reflect absolutes, and to focus on the relationships between organizational variables. In other words, a systems approach allows us to *focus on the differences between various situations*, and to examine how the interrelationships between subsystems act to mold behavior. We can now talk about a *situational approach* to organizational behavior.

THE SITUATION AS THE FOCUS FOR MANAGEMENT ACTION

Managers have suddenly become aware that many of the traditional methods which have worked so well in the past are no longer effective. Change is so much a part of life today that those organizations which do not make the effort to adapt constantly become the targets for takeovers, mergers, and reorganizations, or else they go bankrupt. Is this a phenomenon of our age? Has everything changed so radically that the old methods are no longer applicable? In large measure, the answer to these questions is yes.

The situation has changed drastically since World War II. There has been an incredible advance in technology, particularly in computers; there has been a dramatic shift in attitudes of much of the world's population, partly as a result of improved communications. The economy of the world has become inextricably enmeshed with government both on national and international levels.

Peter Drucker (1968) calls this the "Age of Discontinuity." He points out that such large scale changes are upon us that it is impossible to predict the future by looking at trends. We cannot expect a continuity with these major changes being injected into the system. We must *analyze the situation* and make plans based on our findings.

There is still a lot of attention paid to traditional organization theory. But the fallacious assumption behind the "principles" approach to management is that they apply equally well to all situations. What we have failed to recognize is that the principles and techniques of management are effective only when they are applied in *appropriate situations*. It is the situation which determines effectiveness. The manager or organization that wants to be effective must first analyze the situation. Only after that can effective action be taken.

Wilfred Brown (1960), practicing manager and management thinker, puts the case clearly: "Only by *understanding* can managers have a mastery of the situation. If they do not understand, the situation masters them instead."

WHAT IS "THE SITUATION?"

What do we mean by the term *situation*? The word is used a great deal and the meaning is usually unclear. In managerial terms, the situation is *all those factors which affect the outcome of a set of alternative actions or decisions*. Every time a decision has to be taken, there are a number of alternatives. For instance, if a manager is experiencing trouble in getting the work of his unit done, he might consider hiring a new man to add to his staff. Some other alternatives might be to reorganize the work of the unit so that the existing staff could handle it more easily, to work overtime, or to let production slip. An examination of the situation will tend to give an indication of which of these decisions is best. For instance, if the overload is expected to be temporary, hiring a new man might be unwise. If the union is militant, reorganization of the work might be a long drawn-out process. If cost is paramount, overtime might be out of the question. These are just a few of the situational factors surrounding this managerial decision.

THE BOUNDARIES OF THE SITUATION

How can we define the boundaries of a managerial situation? Are they contained by the limits of the specific organization or do they extend out into society? Do such situational factors as the changing levels of education in a country greatly affect the job of a middle manager concerned with production control, or is his situation better thought of in terms of a system of interpersonal relationships?

We have talked about systems concepts and have made the point that an organization as a system exists within the larger cultural system and is made up of smaller subsystems such as divisions, departments, sections, work groups, etc. The concept of systems is most useful when we begin to talk about the managerial situation. The characteristics of a system largely define the elements of the situation. When we are describing a managerial situation we must take into account all the elements (or subsystems) in the situation and must consider their relationships with one another. It might be a fair statement to say that the management theorist talks about systems while the management practitioner talks about situations; each uses his own terminology, but each is considering essentially the same variables.

One of the first questions which arises when we talk about managerial situations is, "What perspective are we looking at the situation from; the situation relative to whom or what?"

The issue is whether to take a micro- or a macro-approach to the analysis of situations. A micro-analysis ("the close-up picture") examines the functions and relationships inherent in the manager's immediate job. It is most appropriate for the individual manager in a specific situation. It provides him with an "on the ground" picture of those aspects of his job which are most important or are placing the most pressing demands on him. It helps him to become more effective personally, within his own area of influence, but it may overlook some of the wider factors affecting the organization as a whole. On the other hand, a macro-approach ("the big picture") which looks at such things as economic conditions and trends, political changes, social values and attitudes, and the changing competitive picture in an industry, is most appropriate for decisions made at or near the top of the organization. But it tends to overlook the relationships between individuals and groups and such things as motivation, leadership, attitudes, and communication. It is also removed from the realities of the budgetary limitations and technological problems which middle and lower level managers face every day.

Most decisions require an analysis of the situation at *both* levels: an examination of factors both *within* the organization and those *external* factors which make up the environment in which the organization functions. Both sets of factors affect the outcomes of alternative actions or decisions. Both can be considered as situational elements.

A FRAMEWORK FOR ANALYZING MANAGERIAL SITUATIONS

Clearly a managerial situation can be analyzed at two levels: one level reflects the situation the manager faces within the firm, and the second level concerns those environmental factors outside the boundaries of the organization which affect the outcomes of decisions made within it. There is an interrelationship between these two levels; changes in one level affect changes in the other level.

The major situational elements with which a manager has to deal *within* an organization are:

- finances
- technology
- organization structure
- people

The major situational elements with which a manager has to deal *within* an sions made within an organization are:

- economic conditions
- the nature of competition
- social values and attitudes
- the political/legal climate

These two sets of situational elements can be thought of as *surrounding* the manager in his job. He lives and works within the constraints they set up, and he makes his decisions in consideration of their effects. This view of a manager's situation is pictured in Figure 3-2.

Each of these eight situational elements can be analyzed separately in order to determine its effect on the outcome of a particular decision. They are also *related to*

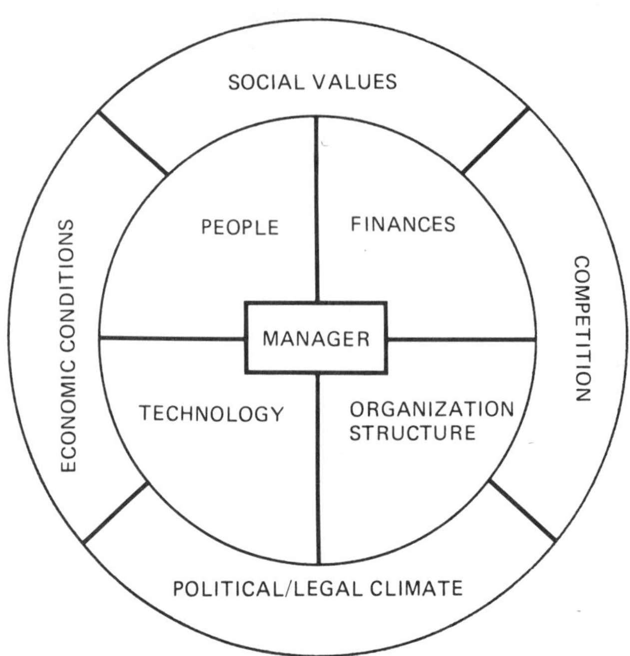

FIGURE 3-2: THE MAJOR ELEMENTS AFFECTING A MANAGERIAL SITUATION.

one another in any particular situation. For instance, an organization's finances may depend in large part on the general state of the economy, its organization structure on the nature of competition in the industry, or its technology on prevailing social values and attitudes.

"INTERNAL" SITUATIONAL ELEMENTS

Finances

The financial element in a manager's situation can be reflected in his operating budget, in his unit's budget, in the cost controls placed on him regarding spoilage, leakage, or machine downtime. At higher levels, it can be reflected by the restriction or freedom allowed by cash flows, profit margins, or the organization's ability to raise funds in the open market. The manager's financial situation reflects the availability or lack of funds which affects the outcome of a particular decision he must make.

For instance, during the initial development stage of a new product, there may be little concern with spoilage, but when the new item is being produced for the commercial market, tight controls may be imposed on wastage, spoiled parts, and so on. The manager concerned has to change over from operating under a rather flexible budget to working within the constraints of a carefully costed production process.

Technology

Technology can be thought of simply as *the way the work is done* (Reddin, 1970). For instance, a manager has different technologies available to him to implement control or information systems. He can use computerized data collection systems, he can rely on manually operated paper systems, or even a system of verbal reports; these are three different technologies which can be used to do the same job. Clearly the way the work is done affects the outcome of certain managerial decisions.

The effects of differing technologies on the structure of an organization and the way in which its people are managed have been noted by a number of research studies. Certainly the way in which an internal auditor manages his unit is different from the way in which the supervisor of the creative art department of an advertising agency manages his. The way in which an internal audit is conducted, with strict procedures, and attention to detail, is very different from the "let it all hang out" approach of creative designers, artists, and writers.

Organization Structure

The structure of the organization in which a manager works, or even the specific unit of the organization in which he works, often affects the outcome of his decisions. The structure of an organization or work unit is *the way in which the work is divided*. It concerns who does what, who reports to whom, who has what responsibility, who has what authority, and so on.

A manager with a span of control of forty subordinates can hardly think of approaching his job the same way as a manager with only three subordinates. Especially if the forty are spread across the breadth of the country, and the manager's budget does not allow him to visit them continually. A line manager who has the responsibility to make certain decisions *without* the express agreement of a staff (advisory) group is in a very different position from the manager who *must* obtain the agreement of a staff group for certain things.

People

Of course, the people in an organization represent a very important element in the situation. Their actions, attitudes, values, perceptions and motivations have a very real effect on the outcome of a manager's decisions. They represent the most complex element in any organization and also the most potentially productive element. As Peter Drucker (1954) says, "Business is a human organization, made or broken by the quality of its people."

The expectations, values and preferences of a manager's superiors, subordinates and coworkers all contribute to the makeup of his situation. He has to operate somewhat differently under a boss who likes to follow procedures closely, than he does under one who delegates a large measure of authority and responsibility and is concerned only with results and not with the methods used to achieve them. A manager is faced with different operating conditions if he has an older, stable, well-trained group of employees, or a young inexperienced group with high turnover. Depending on the strength and militancy of the union, a manager may institute change in various ways. People are clearly a very important part of any managerial situation.

This book is largely about the people dimension of an organizational situation. We will want to know how individual motivation and perception affect behavior, how work groups communicate, how they determine roles for their members, how they set standards and norms, how they relate to the organizational suprasystem, etc. We will examine interpersonal dynamics, leadership styles, communication patterns, value sets and motivational patterns, all under the general label of "people." While "people" is represented as just one of a set of situational elements it must be recognized as being a *dominant* one in most cases.

"EXTERNAL" SITUATIONAL ELEMENTS

Economic Conditions

Economic conditions may be gauged by a number of indicators. Of basic concern to the manager is whether the market for his goods and services is likely to increase or decrease over the short, medium and long term. General economic factors such as levels of disposable income, consumer spending, gross national product, and the balance of trade have an effect on the outcome of many managerial decisions.

For instance, the recent downturn in economic conditions (basically worldwide) has had a major effect on the operations of most organizations, from charitable foundations to consumer goods marketers. Inflation has meant a rise in costs across the board. Prices have risen to meet demand, and wages have risen to keep up with the prices. As interest rates have risen in an attempt to contain inflation, borrowing has become more expensive and therefore spending has been curtailed. The implications of this are profound. Firms have refrained from capital expansion; individuals have shied away from building or buying new houses, cars, and so on; companies have cut back on costs, often translated as reducing their workforce, and therefore adding to unemployment; and the shortage of disposable income has been felt by charitable organizations which depend largely on public donations for their support. Any manager overlooking the major economic trends surrounding his organization will find himself in serious trouble.

Until quite recently, many managers saw the economy as having *some* effect on the overall operations of their organizations, but, in general, conditions tended to improve at a fairly constant rate, and adjustments to economic fluctuations were made relatively easily. With violent changes suddenly taking place in the price of fuels, and formerly "silent" areas of the world entering into the free-for-all of world trade and monetary wrangling, however, the state of the economy has been subjected to some sudden twists and turns which have brought its significance as a situational factor for both the private and public sector into sharp relief.

The Nature of Competition

The nature of competition in an industry affects the outcomes of managerial decisions as well. For instance, in industries such as steel and paper, which are, in economic terms, oligopolies, price changes made by one large producer are likely to be followed by a rapid realignment of prices throughout the industry. Little or no competitive advantage can be gained by changing basic price structures in this type of competitive atmosphere. However, in other industries, price changes can bring about dramatic changes in profitability and competitive strength.

Managers in organizations where there is little competition, either because of an artificially created monopoly position, or because of dominant market share, tend to operate differently from managers in fiercely competitive situations. The latter are keenly responsive to any changes in the marketplace, and they adjust their behavior accordingly. To them, the competition's actions represent a very important situational element.

While competition, *per se*, does not exist for managers in the public sector, they must be aware of what other government agencies, perhaps in other jurisictions or even other countries, are doing to provide certain services to their client populations. As new systems are tried and developed elsewhere, the manager in the public sector must be aware of their potential benefits or drawbacks and attempt to maximize their application in his own area, adapting them to local conditions.

Social Values and Attitudes

Social values and attitudes can have a marked effect on the outcomes of managerial decisions. Examples are found in the changes which have been made in industry as a result of environmentalist groups, the women's liberation movement, or minority racial or religious groups. Social values pervade the entire organization and are reflected in the attitudes and motivations of the workforce at all levels.

A striking example of changes in social values and attitudes that brought about dramatic changes in an organization is presented by the new approach to automobile production of Volvo of Sweden. The old assembly line concept has disappeared. Instead, teams of workers are made responsible for assembling an entire section of a car—the electrical system, steering and controls, instrumentation, brakes and wheels, etc. They decide how the work will be done (the technology), who will do what jobs (the structure), and when and how to rotate jobs.

The basic reason for this radical approach to making cars, given by Volvo's president, Pehr Gyllenhammar, is a change in the *social values and attitudes* in Sweden. "In Sweden today," he says, "we spend more *per capita* on education than any other country in the world, and towards the end of this decade we estimate that about 90% of our youth will go through college education. It's from these people we have to recruit our labor force. These people have different views and different values, even from workers of the previous generation."

The Political/Legal Climate

The political and legal climate in which an organization functions has a clear impact on the outcome of certain managerial decisions. The recently published memoranda of ITT concerning the situation as they saw it in Chile under Allende presents a stark example, albeit a rather bizarre one.

National energy policy has sweeping effects on how organizations can or must operate. The automobile industry is facing estimated expenditures of about $25 billion to meet legislated fuel consumption and emission standards by 1985. Antitrust action and legislation can also have dramatic effects. Consider the implications of the recent FTC action to consider the breakup of General Motors, or current efforts to break IBM's dominant position in the computer industry. Either of these decisions will affect the lives of thousands of people and the operations of thousands of organizations. We can hardly ignore what government and the courts are doing to change the rules of business and organizations.

Obviously also, legislative changes in such basic areas as tariffs and trade agreements affect many organizations. And governmental reactions to economic fluctuations cause wide situational differences; government spending affects many areas of both private and public sectors.

A SITUATIONAL MODEL

The situational model presented in this chapter is only a framework through which we can view organizational behavior. It is an attempt to bring a degree of order and simplicity to the analysis of an otherwise wildly complex phenomenon. Whether the model is "correct" or "accurate" is not the relevant issue. Its objective is to simplify and clarify thinking about behavior in organizations. We will use it as a frame for our subsequent discussions concerning behavior. If it helps to tie concepts together and to make some sense of the varied and odd collection of facts and theories concerning behavior which will be presented, it is a good model; if it does none of these things, it is a waste of time.

The Daniels Computer Company (Part I): Applying a Situational Model

As we did with the Hovey and Beard Company at the end of the last chapter, we are going to take a look at the applications of the theory and models presented in this chapter to an actual case situation. We had a look at a systems model of organizational behavior (Figure 3-1) that showed the interrelationships between the organizational system, the individual system, the work group system, and the system of outputs that result. At this stage we will not attempt to apply this model to the case, because, as you noticed, we did not look at the *components* of each of the subsystems in the model. We still do not know enough about organizational, individual and work group variables. But we will.

The second model we considered was one which represented the *situation* facing a manager (Figure 3-2). This was made up of two sets of factors: internal factors (those within the organization), and external factors (those which make up the environment). The point was made that each of these factors, both individually and interactionally, affect how a manager must perform in his or her job to be effective. Let's take a look at the Daniels Computer Case (Part I) to see if we can apply the model to any degree, and if it is helpful in analyzing the situation depicted in the case. Part I is reproduced here for your convenience.

DANIELS COMPUTER COMPANY (PART I)

Daniels Computer Company's Memory Engineering Department was composed of four sections; magnetic, electronic, mechanical and electrochemical. The customary development work undertaken by the department involved well-known principles of memory design. Each section carried on its phase of development in logical sequence, using the results of the previous section as a starting point. The members of each section were expert in their own fields. The sections were close-knit socially. The manager of the department left technical direction to section supervisors, reserving for his own responsibility the securing of essential services and maintenance of the development schedule. The department rarely failed to meet its schedule or technical requisites.

In July 1962, the Memory Department was assigned the development of a memory incorporating several new design concepts which had never been experimentally evaluated. The functioning of the special computer which was to incorporate the new memory depended upon the most advanced memory device possible within the limits of the new concepts. Development time was one-half the length of more routine developments.

The Memory Department manager selected the four most competent project engineers from the four sections to work on the special project. Each project engineer was directed to select five engineers and five technicians to work with him on the project. Because of time limitations and the unknown aspects of the new memory concepts, the four groups were to work on their own aspects of design simultaneously. Each team, remaining in the geographic confines of its home section but independent of its former supervision, commenced immediately to test design schemes and components relevant to its own division of the technology. The project group members quickly became enthusiastic about their new assignment. The department manager left technical supervision to the project engineers of each group.

To begin with, we don't have much data concerning the environmental factors affecting the Daniels Computer Company's Memory Engineering Department. But we do know that development time for the new memory was one-half the normal length of time given to developmental projects in the firm. This may be an indicator of *competitive pressure*; Daniels may have to have the memory completed in time to submit a tender, or to fulfill the terms of a contract. Whatever the situation, the shortened time dimension strongly indicates that the crunch is on. Will this affect the behavior of the people involved?

As far as the *structural* dimensions of the department are concerned, we can note a change that has taken place as a result of the new memory development project. Prior to July 1962, the organization structure looked like this:

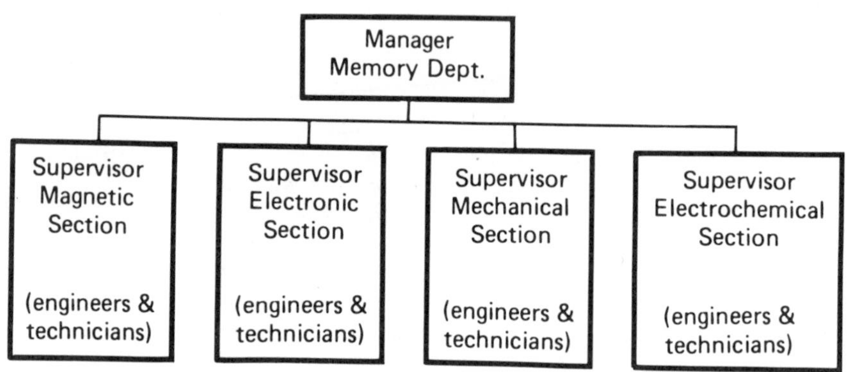

Each section had its own supervisor. Each worked rather well on its own, with the work flowing from one section to the next, as the preceding section had completed its work (much like the sequence in Hovey and Beard). The manager of the department left the section supervisors in charge of technical direction. The department manager occupied a coordinator's role, securing essential services for the sections, and planning and maintaining the development schedules (making sure that work flowed as planned, and on time). Essentially, then, we had four separate sections, keeping largely to themselves, and in charge of how they did their own work.

After July 1962, the structure changed. It now looked something like this:

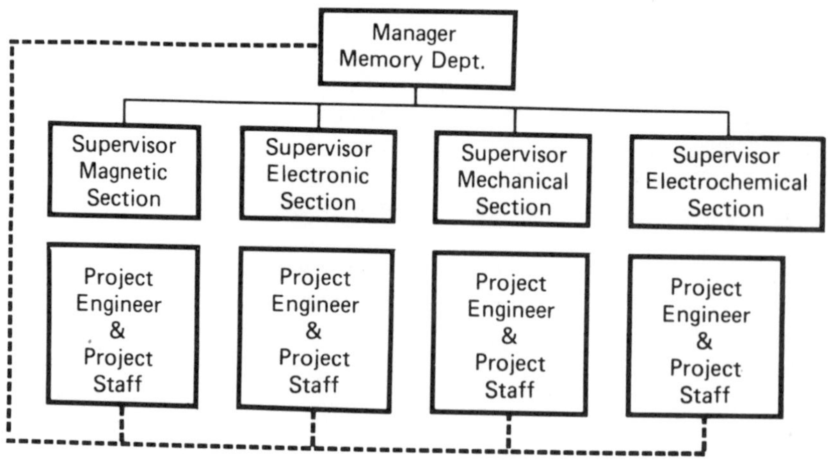

Note that now there are four independent project groups staffed by people from the four sections. Note also that the members of each project group have been drawn from a single section; there are no cross-sectional project groups. Also, the project engineers no longer report to their section heads; *they* are in charge of the technical aspects of their own project groups. But they do report (see dotted line) to the Manager of the Memory Department who maintains his coordinating role, as he did with the sections in the past. In fact, he is in charge of the new project as a whole.

Presumably this change in structure is intended to do two things: first, to free teams in each of the sections to concentrate solely on the development of the new memory without being bothered by other sectional work; second, to promote coordination between the sections of the project group. In essence, there is only *one* project group, and that is headed by the department manager, with the four project engineers and their staffs reporting to him. This is the *intention* of the structural change (it sets out the *required* behavior), but whether this behavior will, in fact, take place (''emerge'') is something for you to question.

Let's take a look at the *people* in this situation. We know they are experts in their fields. We know that each section is close-knit socially. We know that within sections they are used to working on their own, as far as technical matters are concerned. After July 1962, while the structure has been changed somewhat, the people still work in the same geographical areas, still see the same people each day, and still define themselves as experts in their own fields, and continue to work in these fields. We might question whether the structural change is powerful enough to change the behavior of the people involved, given the above.

And finally, we might consider the *technology*. Prior to July, 1962, the work was described as being concerned with the application of ''well-known principles of memory design.'' While it was not routine work, it was not experimental either. *After* July, 1962, the work of the project group was concerned with ''several new design concepts which had never been experimentally evaluated.'' The product was to be ''the most advanced memory device possible.'' The technology had changed dramatically; the work was much more innovative and untested.

How did this affect the behavior of the people involved? Did they continue to operate as they had in the past, or did they adopt new patterns and new methods? If we are to believe our model, then a major change in technology might call for a major change in behavior.

This ''analysis'' has raised more questions than it has answered. Has it changed your concept of the situation at Daniels Computer? Or at Hovey and Beard? Would you change any of the predictions you made at the end of Chapter 1 (and perhaps revised at the end of Chapter 2)? Take a look at those predictions now, and if you wish to make any changes, make a note of why, and what you feel will be different.

Chapter Summary

1 It is the manager's main job to be effective. This implies a focus on the people involved (the "person"), the methods of managing/working (the "process"), and the results achieved (the "product"). Effectiveness is best measured by focusing on results; an individual's effectiveness is determined by the degree to which he or she achieves required results.

2 Organizational behavior can be viewed usefully through a systems perspective. Results (the actual, or "emergent," system) can be seen to be the product of an interaction between the overall requirements of the organizational system and the various elements of the individual and work group systems.

3 Managers work within a system of forces that define their *situation*. In order to be effective, a manager must act in a manner that is appropriate to the situation he finds himself in. It is the situation which determines effectiveness. As Wilfred Brown puts it, "Only by *understanding* can managers have a mastery of the situation. If they do not understand, the situation masters them instead."

4 We can define the situation as "all those factors which affect the outcome of a set of alternative actions or decisions."

5 From a manager's point of view, the situation has two sets of boundaries. One is the boundary of the organization itself, those factors which are *within* the organization: its finances, its technology, its structure, its people. The second boundary extends to the organization's environment. This includes factors such as economic conditions and trends, the nature of competition, values and attitudes in the society in which the organization operates, and the constraints placed upon it by political and legal forces. All these elements interact with one another to form the situation confronting a manager.

Part 2

The Individual System

4

Building and Maintaining the Self

OBJECTIVES

When you have completed this chapter you should

- have a basic understanding of the concept of the "self";
- know how the self concept is developed, maintained, and changed;
- understand the pivotal function of the perceptual process in building and maintaining a self concept;
- be aware of some of the basic defense mechanisms we tend to employ to avoid changing our self concepts;
- recognize that there are also certain mechanisms which can be employed to widen and change our concepts of ourselves;
- have a basis on which to build an understanding of the individual system.

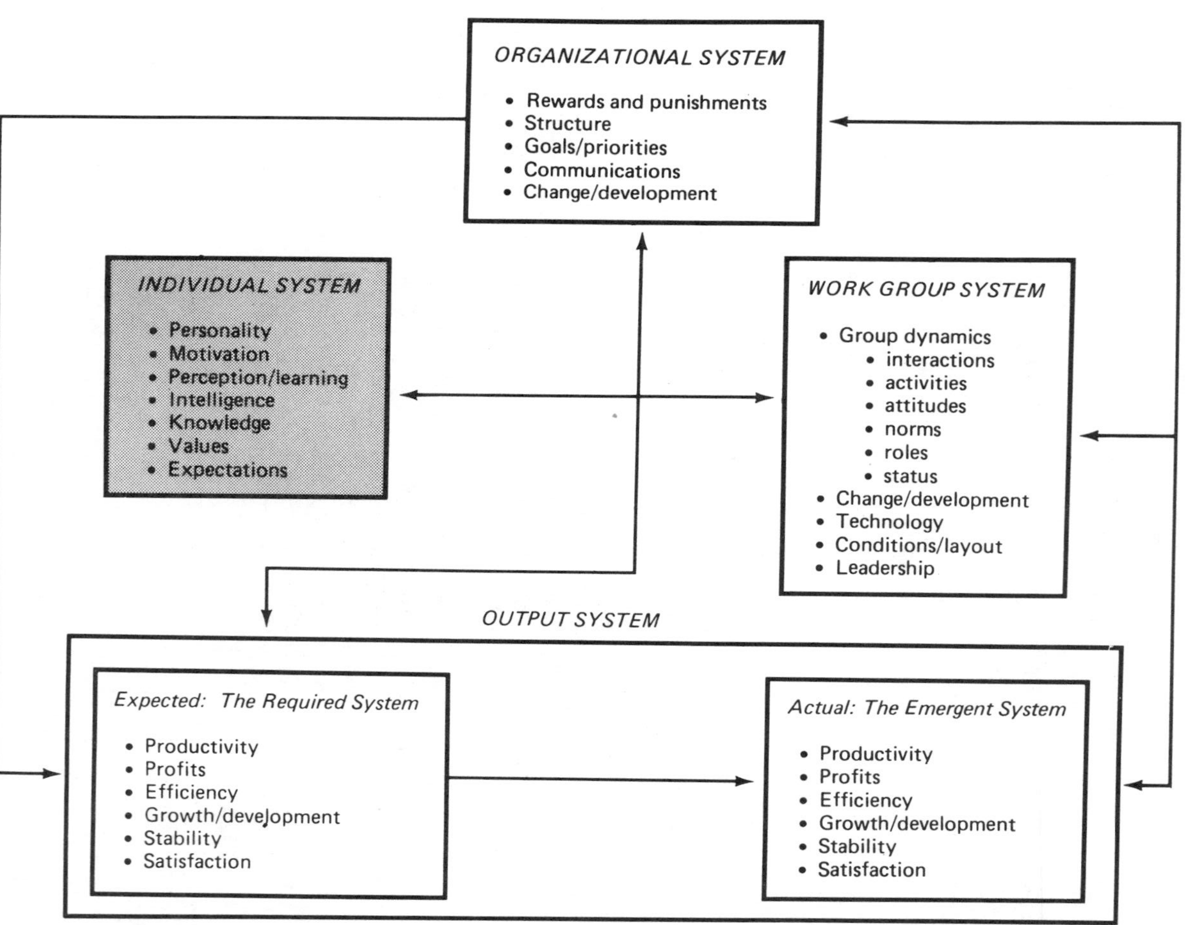
ORGANIZATIONAL SYSTEM
• Rewards and punishments
• Structure
• Goals/priorities
• Communications
• Change/development
INDIVIDUAL SYSTEM
• Personality
• Motivation
• Perception/learning
• Intelligence
• Knowledge
• Values
• Expectations
WORK GROUP SYSTEM
• Group dynamics
• interactions
• activities
• attitudes
• norms
• roles
• status
• Change/development
• Technology
• Conditions/layout
• Leadership
OUTPUT SYSTEM
Expected: The Required System
• Productivity
• Profits
• Efficiency
• Growth/development
• Stability
• Satisfaction
Actual: The Emergent System
• Productivity
• Profits
• Efficiency
• Growth/development
• Stability
• Satisfaction

"If anthropology has succeeded in proving any one thing, it is that people and races are fundamentally very much the same."

(Ralph Linton, 1936)

"In an important sense it is true to say that it is not the individual but the primary group which is the basic unit of society."

(J.A.C. Brown, 1954)

"No one who does not understand individual behavior can fully understand group behavior or behavior in large organizational units."

(Harry Levinson, 1976)

JIM WATSON (A)

On Thursday morning, the 21st of July, 1960, the 20 students who were employed during the summer by the Western Manufacturing Company appeared in the shed to wait for the assignments of the day. They were dressed and acting in a way which had a close resemblance to the idiosyncrasies and habits of James Watson, an old regular worker who had been supervising the work of the students for the last two summers.[1]

The students were wearing old flannel lumberjack shirts, with ill-matched gaudy ties tucked in between the second and third button of the front. Each student carried a notebook and a pencil, some as many as six or seven pens and pencils. Some of the students wore high-cut boots in recognition of Jim Watson's preference for jack boots. They were carrying out a plan they had conceived a few days prior to have what they called a "Jim Watson Day."

This performance immediately attracted the attention of the regular workers who were going to their jobs. They laughed and joked with the students. When Jim Watson appeared he seemed to take it well, but when he caught sight of several students studiously writing down their duties and then briskly marching off, his expression changed. He reminded them of the seriousness of the job and finally started threatening them by saying, "I will take any one of you on." The students gave up their acting after that, and while they did not remove their apparel, they went about their business in the customary manner.

The day was just beginning for Jim Watson, however, as he had to take jibes and kidding continuously from the regular workers, including the foreman, Don Johnson. Within a short time the news of the incident had spread to most of the 12 buildings of the Western Manufacturing

Company and Jim could not go anywhere without hearing laughter and snide remarks such as: "Is that a student or Jim Watson?" "Will the real Jim Watson please stand up?" "Has anybody reported you lately, Jim?"

Nobody asked the students to abandon their "uniforms." Everyone seemed to enjoy this performance by the students. The supervisor, Ron Brown, also joined Don Johnson in his obvious pleasure at the sight. Mr. Robert Morrison, the department superintendent of works, met a group of students on an elevator and gave them a smile. The students believed that the "Jim Watson Day" had been a complete success.

[1]There were two classes of hourly paid employees at Western Manufacturing Co: regular and summer only. Copyright 1962 by The University of Western Ontario. Reproduced by permission.

What do you think was Jim's reaction to "Jim Watson Day"?

Before you continue with this chapter, take a few minutes to consider the different kinds of reactions that Jim could have had and decide which was most likely. Jot down your predictions as to what happened with Jim and make as detailed a list of reasons for your prediction as possible. We will return to the case at the end of the chapter.

Where should we start looking at organizational behavior? Should we start with the smallest unit of behavior, the individual, and then work up through pairs to small groups to large groups, and finally to full scale organizations? Is it in groups that all the action takes place? Should we begin there and then work back towards the individual and outwards to the total organization? Where *is* the beginning? As our model of organizational behavior illustrates, all parts of the system are interdependent, so there is no real beginning or ending.

Harry Levinson, who argues that we must understand *individual* behavior first, makes the point that we must adopt a systems approach. He points out that psychologists have tended to look at people without taking their environments into account, and on the other hand, sociologists have tended to study environments without taking individual variables into account. Levinson makes the point that:

> We cannot really understand people and their behavior unless we take the system into account, too. Thus, as we talk about how men and women are motivated, we must necessarily also talk about the circumstances which have shaped them as well as the conditions under which they function.
>
> (Levinson, 1976)

PERSONALITY

Put yourself in this situation: you are talking with a friend about someone you know, whom he doesn't know. Your friend asks you, "What is she like?" You could describe this third person's appearance (her physical characteristics), but there may be a follow-up question, "But what is she *like*?" In other words, can you describe how she acts? How would you characterize her behavior? How *do* you characterize the behavior of someone? How *do* you describe what someone is "like"?

Essentially, descriptions of what a person is "like" are descriptions of his or her *personality*. The word personality is used in everyday conversation with quite a different meaning than when a behavioral scientist uses it. People talk about others (or themselves) as having "nice," "pleasant," "cheerful," "lots of," "no," or "little" personality. We talk about entertainers having "personality" if they are vivacious, active, likeable and attractive. We say that someone whom we find dull and boring has "no personality." The term, as it is used in everyday language, refers to the degree of attraction that we experience towards someone. The implication is that one can have either a "good" or a "bad" personality.

The first thing that must be done before we continue further with a discussion of individual behavior is to clarify the term *personality*. There is no single generally accepted definition. There are probably 25 or more current theories, each with its own definition. Allport listed more than 50 definitions of personality in 1937 and the last 40 years or so has multiplied that a couple of times. Most definitions, however, emphasize two common things:

- its basic consistency;
- its responsiveness to situational influences.

For our purposes, personality can be defined as: *"those relatively stable and enduring aspects of the individual which distinguish him from other people and, at the same time, form the basis of our predictions concerning his future behavior."* (Wright et.al., 1970).

It has been maintained for many years that personality becomes virtually fixed at about age five. Current research indicates that we are more flexible than that, but changing one's attitudes, values, beliefs and aspirations—the substance of personality—is difficult. As our definition strongly implies, we tend more to stability than to flexibility in our basic values and behavior.

Personality does *not* mean social skills (the ability to elicit positive statements and actions from others). When we refer to an individual's personality we are attempting to describe him or her in some fashion without any normative connotations. There is no "good" or "bad" connected with the concept of personality. We may apply various labels such as "dominant," "ascendant," "friendly," "submissive," "responsive," "emotional," but none of these characteristics is *in itself* good or bad. They are simply descriptions of attitudes and behaviors.

We are not going to get into a discussion of the various theories of personality. We cannot expect to become experts, in the psychoanalytic sense. There is far too much disagreement about what goes on inside the "black box" of the individual. Freud maintains that men are basically beasts and that our behavior is based on sexual drives. Others have linked personality characteristics to physique—almost a "fat-people-are-jolly" type of theory. Still others have looked at certain traits and have developed "profiles" of personality. Where does that leave us? If we are studying organizational behavior, we must have some understanding of what makes individuals tick. The device, or concept, we will use to examine *individual* behavior is the *self*.

Carl Rogers (1951) maintains that,

> "The best vantage point for understanding behavior is from the internal frame of reference of the individual himself."

When we talk about individual behavior, we must talk about three things: *personality, perception,* and *motivation*. The three are inextricably intertwined. Rogers (1951) says that "behavior is basically the goal-directed attempt of the organism to satisfy its needs as experienced, in the field as perceived." In other words, we all have goals or *needs* which direct our behavior (which "motivate" it), and these goals are influenced by how we *perceive* ourselves and the world around us.

THE DEVELOPMENT AND MAINTENANCE OF THE "SELF"

Rather than use the term personality, we shall talk about the *self*. What we show to others (our self) is essentially a product of what we see ourselves as, or would like to be seen as. Let's look at how we develop this concept of "self." How do we become what we are? Rogers says we develop our concept of self through our interactions with, and perceptions of, the environment.

> As a result of interaction with the environment, and particularly as a result of evaluational interaction with others, the structure of self is formed—an organized, fluid, but consistent pattern of perceptions of characteristics and relationships of the "I" or the "me," together with values attached to these concepts.
>
> The values attached to experiences, and the values which are part of the self structure, in some instances are values experienced directly by the organism, and in some instances are values introjected or taken over from others, but perceived in distorted fashion, as if they had been experienced directly.
>
> (Rogers, 1951)

As the infant experiences and interacts with his environment, he begins to build up a set of beliefs or perceptions about himself. He begins to experience pleasure in certain actions and situations, discomfort in others. He is successful in obtaining gratification by some actions, but not by others. He begins to develop a feeling of "me," an identity as something. He feels, although he cannot express it verbally, an "I'ness"—"*I* can clap my hands." As he continues to grow and develop, he begins to run into *other* people, all of whom are larger, and more powerful. These people are able to "say" to the infant "that's good" (usually accompanied by a reward of some kind) or "that's bad" (usually accompanied either by no reward, or more often, some form of punishment). The infant begins to learn what behavior is acceptable. He also learns more about his own physical capabilities and the environment surrounding him. He learns that stoves are hot, stairs can be painful, dogs will try to take your food.

It is through this process of *perception* of the environment that the individual builds up a concept of himself. In simplified terms, if he experiences success in most of his adventures, if he is given love, support and affection, is praised for achieving things, is able to explore the environment in a relatively safe fashion without experiencing severely jolting setbacks, he is likely to develop a perception of himself as a competent individual, able and eager to meet the challenges of the world with a better than even chance of succeeding. If, on the other hand, he experiences more failures than successes (or at least *perceives* more failures) he is likely to develop a self image as a person who is not successful, who is likely to fail, who is not popular, etc.

Robert White (1959) talks about the concept of competence. He maintains that there is a "competence motive"; people who experience success seek success. They feel competent, confident and able to take on the challenges of the world. And, perhaps partly due to a self-fulfilling prophecy, they *are* successful.

In popular terms, Norman Vincent Peale talked about the "Power of Positive Thinking." The idea is that if you *believe* you can do something, you are more likely to be able to do it. In his heyday, Arnold Palmer was famous for the "charge." Behind, and coming into the last round of a golf tournament Palmer would begin a "charge," attacking the course and picking up birdies one after another. He adopted a different stance and style of walk when he was charging, hitching up his trousers after a shot, walking rapidly, bent forward, tugging at his glove. Anyone who saw Palmer knew when he was charging, and it was clear that he was determined to win and did not countenance failing. On the other hand, Rod Funseth, a recent runner-up in the Masters, admits that he is not a "positive thinker"; he does not *know* he is going to win when he steps on the course (and incidentally, while he is a first class golfer, and a high finisher, he rarely does win).

A MODEL OF THE SELF

The *self* is a product of the individual's

- Beliefs;
- Values;
- Goals;
- Feeling of competence/inadequacy;
- Perceptions of the outcomes of his/her behavior.

Figure 4-1 illustrates the relationship.

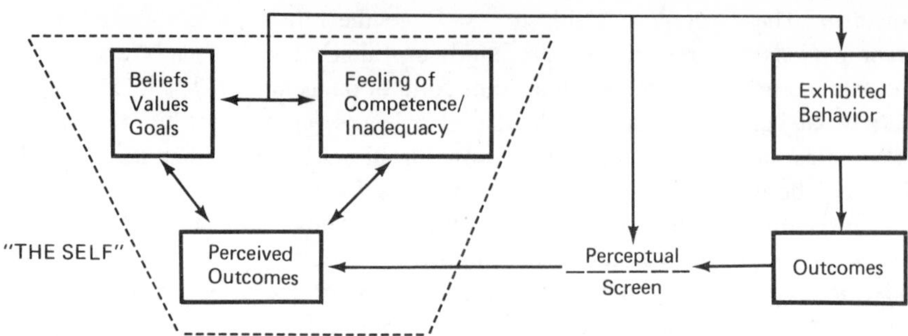

FIGURE 4-1: THE MAINTENANCE AND DEVELOPMENT OF "SELF."

Beliefs and Values

It is difficult to differentiate between an individual's *beliefs* and *values*. Both reflect an *idea of how the world operates*. We separate this "world idea" into two categories because some ideas are more easily changed than others. We define beliefs as being ideas which are at least *available* for change while basic values are ideas which are deeply imbedded and tend to remain constant. Perhaps this is an artificial separation, but the fact remains that people can change religious *beliefs* while maintaining their basic *values* concerning deity and the nature of man. Beliefs are more tentative. We are more willing to discuss them. Values are the basic foundations we have laid for our lives. One may see honesty as a value—a basic tenet of behavior. In this instance, there is no *real* argument over whether one should or should not be honest. A value is not situational. A belief may be. A value is a digested and internalized belief.

Goals

Goals are those outcomes which we strive to attain in order to satisfy certain needs. Our goals are a reflection of our needs. The answer to the question, "What would you like as the epitaph on your tombstone?" can be most revealing. The question is asking what you would like to have people remember about you most—your main achievement in life.

On a more immediate level, having a goal to get an "A" in a course may reflect a number of needs: a need to confirm your own brilliance, a need for others to see proof of your brilliance and thereby give you *recognition* for it, or a need to confirm your parent's faith in you (or disconfirm their skepticism).

We rank order our goals, whether consciously or subconsciously. Sometimes we encounter conflict within ourselves when two of our goals run counter to one another. For instance, getting an "A" may make you feel good for one reason, in that it confirms a good job, but it may mean that you have to spend a lot of time working and away from the company of friends and family. Individuals often experience a great deal of discomfort sorting out these conflicting goals.

Rogers emphasizes the centrality of goals to life: ''one of the most basic characteristics of organic life is its tendency toward total, organized, goal-directed responses.'' (1951) Our goals represent a map for our behavior. If you had a clear idea of an individual's goals you would be able to predict a great deal of his behavior.

Looking at Figure 4-1, we can see the relationship between beliefs, values, goals, the feeling of competence/inadequacy, and perceptions of the environment, as they interact to form the ''self.''

The individual behaves in some manner (*exhibited behavior*), and this behavior results in some sort of *outcome*. (A diver executes a dive, which turns out to be well done, or not so well done). Others perceive the result of the behavior and convey this to the individual, in the form of some sort of assessment (the dive is rated ''7.5''). The individual perceives the outcome, and maybe the reactions and assessments of others to that outcome, and feeds that data into the bank which makes up the self. But the individual may not relay the *same* data to his self as others perceive; he screens the data and only transmits perceptions which are consistent with his beliefs, values and goals, and his feeling of his own competence/inadequacy. This perceived outcome is fed into the system and becomes part of the self-concept. As various perceptions are introduced into the self system, they affect the individual's feelings of competence/inadequacy, his goals, and his beliefs and values. The self then acts to change the perceptual screen, either allowing more data in or screening it out. We will discuss why more or less data is admitted to the self system later, but first we must have a look at how the screening, or filtering, process takes place—the concept of perception.

Perceptual Screening

The perceptual process is the screen through which all data from the real world must pass before it is processed to become part of the self. Each individual screens data differently, but the role of this screening is critical, because it must do two things:

1. *Protect* the individual from data which is potentially damaging to his self, and yet
2. Give him *sufficient* data on which to base his beliefs, values and goals and align his concept self with reality (at least as it is perceived). There can, of course, be no ''reality'' *per se*; for the individual, the perceptual field *is* reality.

Perception

Perception is truly situational. How we perceive things depends on a host of factors, such as our beliefs, values and goals, our needs at the time, our knowledge and feelings, our past experience, and even our physical characteristics. Little children, for instance, perceive things as being bigger than do full grown adults. Weren't you surprised at the size of some things you hadn't seen since you were a small child? Because of the personal, situational nature of perception, we really cannot be truly objective about anything. In order to get as true a picture as possible, the best we can do is become aware of our biases.

Perception involves the sensory system. We experience *sensations*—"The noise is deafening"; "the pain is sharp"; "he is a pleasant person"; "she is very bright"; "it is dark." All these statements are reports of sensations which we have experienced. They are put into words by a transformation process which expresses our *perceptions*, or how we have *organized* and *categorized* them.

Perception is the process whereby sensory data are organized and dealt with.

We mentioned earlier that a function of organization was to achieve some level of consistency and predictability. The perceptual process performs this function by organizing what we see, hear, feel, or smell into some form that is meaningful to us. In order to perform this organizing process, the perceptual mechanism performs the function of *selection*. We *select* which data we will accept, and the form in which we will accept it.

We are constantly bombarded with sensory data. There is noise from the radio, TV, traffic, household appliances, people talking, machines running. There are visual cues from everything around us. There is a mixture of smells in the air. We experience changes in temperature, feel clothing on our bodies, are touched by wind, rain, and snow. But we only register *some* of this data consciously. Do you know, for instance, how many stairs there are on the staircases you travel daily, how many utility poles are on your block, which advertisements were in the last magazine you thumbed through, how many people you have talked with this week? Unless these data are important to you for some reason, the chances are that you cannot answer these questions. We collect data through the senses and register it subconsciously, but there is too much for us to remember, or even to notice. So what we do is notice the important things—important to us.

How is this selection process determined? First of all, we perceive things from a certain *frame of reference*. For example, what do you see in Figures 4-2, 4-3, and 4-4? How many blocks are there in Figure 4-2? Six, or seven? What do you see in Figure 4-3? Two faces or one goblet? What is Figure 4-4 a picture of? A young girl or an old hag? The same stimuli, or sensations, are presented to everyone, but we perceive them differently, depending on the frame of reference we take. This frame of reference is the product of our past experience. That experience determines what we recognize, how we categorize, what we see as threatening or supporting, and

Perception is concerned with selection, organization and interpretation of sensory data. What are some of the "rules" of the selection process? What do we *know* about it?

The first statement we can make about the selection process is that *we perceive those things which help satisfy our needs*—i.e., what we want to perceive. Leavitt (1964) comments on this process:

FIGURE 4-2: HOW MANY BLOCKS?

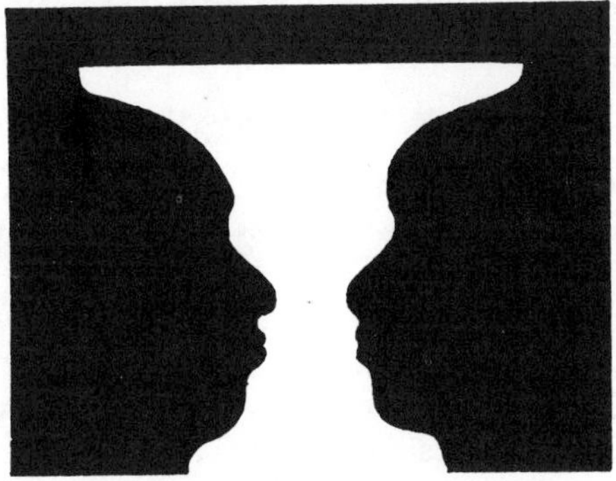

FIGURE 4-3 TWO FACES OR ONE GOBLET?

People's perceptions are determined by their needs. Like the mirrors at amusement parks, we distort the world in relation to our own tensions. Children from poorer homes, when asked to draw a quarter, draw a bigger than actual one. Industrial employees, when asked to describe the people they work with, talk more about their bosses (the people more important to their needs) than about their peers or subordinates, and so on.

This does not mean that we don't perceive unpleasant things, because, of course, we do. But we tend to forget the unpleasant more easily than the satisfying. When you revisit some place that you enjoyed in the past and are disappointed, it is

FIGURE 4-4: YOUNG GIRL OR OLD HAG?

not necessarily that things have changed, but that, over time you have forgotten (the psychologists use the word *repressed*) the less pleasant parts and have retained your memories of the good aspects.

We tend to ignore things that are mildly unpleasant or disturbing. Experiments demonstrate that subjects who see a series of words flashed rapidly on a screen tend to remember more of those with pleasant connotations than those with unpleasant or threatening connotations. Smokers ignore the clear data that what they are doing is dangerous. We tend not to think that we will be involved in a serious automobile accident. Many areas of the country have had to legislate compulsory wearing of seatbelts (and there are still many violators) because people are reluctant to admit the danger to themselves—it is always the other guy who gets hurt, never us.

But when the threatening data persists and increases, it reaches a point where it is able to intrude into our perceptions. Residents of New York City are far more aware of violent crime than are the residents of Joe Batts Arm, Newfoundland. *When the threat is imminent and intense, we tend to focus a lot of our attention on it*. The more imminent and intense, the more attention it receives, to a point. In cases of *extreme* threat, we sometimes repress everything; that is, we refuse to face it. Individuals who have undergone severely traumatic experiences often cannot remember much of them. Combat soldiers in the midst of battle tend to block out the terrible things that are happening around them; they carry on as normal people in the face of highly abnormal events.

PERCEPTION AND THE SELF

How does the perceptual process affect the development and maintenance of the "self"—our personality? Most ways of behaving adopted by the individual are those which are *consistent* with one's perception of self (Rogers, 1951). Experiences which are *in*consistent with one's concept of self may be perceived as threatening, and the more "threats" there are, the more rigidly the self-concept is structured to maintain its *status quo*.

We develop our self-concept—our personality—through experiences with the environment that we perceive in one way or another. As a result of these experiences we begin to form an idea of what we are, what type of person we are. Once this self-concept is constructed, we can see how difficult it is to change it, since we tend to perceive things that are consistent with our ideas of ourselves and to ignore things that are inconsistent. But even though the process of personal change is difficult, it is not impossible. We know that people do change and that they do, on occasion, take critical comment to heart. Rogers says that we accept inconsistent data quite easily when it is not threatening, and that we are able to assimilate this data to reform our image of self. The easiest way to get people to change, then, is to present them with data about themselves that is not threatening. That is not always easy to do. Some people are more easily threatened than others.

The degree to which an individual feels threatened by something is directly related to the strength of his need for whatever he potentially may lose. People who value life highly are fearful when faced with the threat of losing it. In cultures where life is seen as a transient phenomenon, there is less fear of death. An individual who keenly feels the need to be esteemed by his peers is deeply threatened by anything that may affect this esteem. People are often very conscious, for instance, of the status of their work. When asked to describe what they do for a living, garbage men may refer to themselves as "sanitary engineers," salesmen as "account executives," or university teachers as "professors," or "doctors." A salesman who insists on being called something else is telling you something about his perceptions of his job, himself, and his relationships with others.

A major implication of the proposition that threat to the self-concept is directly related to strength of needs is that, if we are interested in getting people to change their behavior, or to change our own behavior, it will be much easier if the "selves" involved are not burdened with highly superordinate needs. People with strong, intrusive needs are less sensitive to others, and less open to change themselves.

CONSISTENCY OF THE SELF

As our discussion so far has implied, there are various perceptions of the self with which we must deal. To begin with, we have our own perceptions of our self (self-by-self). Then there are the perceptions of ourselves held by others (self-by-others). And finally, we have a concept of what we would *like* to be (an ideal self).

A great deal of behavior is based on the efforts of the individual to bring these three concepts of self into alignment with one another.

The phrase ''getting it all together'' gives the flavor of what we attempt to do in managing the self-concept. The organism tends to move towards consistency and stability. We find it difficult to cope with wide inconsistencies. If there is a major difference in how we think of ourselves and how others think of us, we attempt to lessen that difference in some way or other. We either try to think of ourselves more as others see us, or else we try to get the others to change their opinions of us. It is difficult to live in a situation where these two perceptions are widely different.

Figure 4-5 illustrates varying degrees of consistency between the three concepts of self. The closer the three circles, which represent the different aspects of the self concept, the more the individual ''has it all together,'' and the more consistent his behavior is likely to be. Those individuals who see themselves as one thing, would *like* to be seen as something quite different, and *are* seen as something else again experience tremendous emotional strain. They *don't* have it all together.

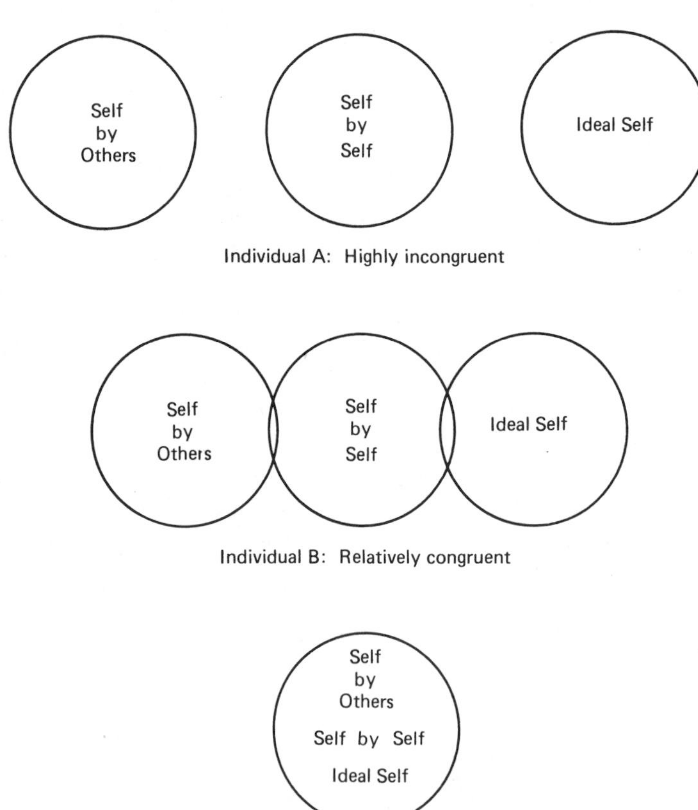

FIGURE 4-5: DEGREES OF CONGRUITY BETWEEN THE VARIOUS CONCEPTS OF SELF.

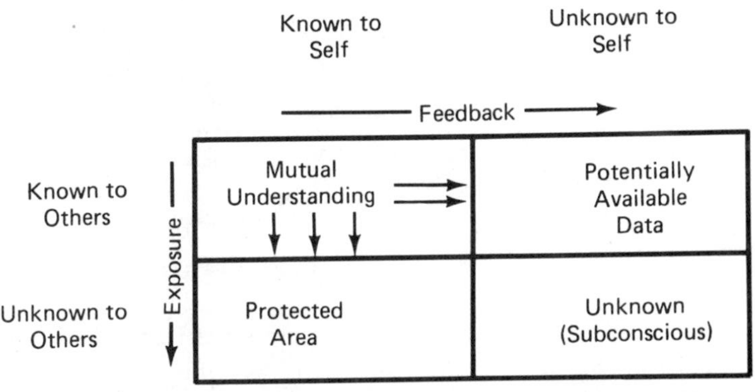

FIGURE 4-6: A MODIFIED REPRESENTATION OF THE JOHARI WINDOW.

There are a number of points which should be made about the congruity or incongruity between the three aspects of the self-concept. To begin with, looking at self-by-self and self-by-others, we can put forward some behavioral propositions.

In the instance illustrated by Individual A in Figure 4-5, where his concept of self is widely different from the self seen by others, the person has four basic alternatives:

1 He can alter his perception of himself and begin to see himself more as others see him;
2 He can attempt to get others to change their perceptions and opinions about him, presumably by acting differently and projecting a more consistent image of his concept of himself;
3 He can do a little of both (1) and (2) and move towards a middle ground;
4 He can ignore the conflicting data that he receives from others and thereby avoid the conflict.

Harry Ingham and Joe Luft have developed a model they call the "Johari Window" (Luft, 1969) which illustrates how an individual can acquire more data about himself. Their hypothesis is that the more data mutually held between ourselves and others with whom we have to interact, the more productive and effective our relationships with these people will be and the more likely we will be to function effectively, and to grow and develop. An adaptation of the Johari Window is shown in Figure 4-6.

Essentially what the Johari Window illustrates is that there are means available for obtaining more data concerning how other people see us, and that we can also benefit from sharing more data with others about ourselves. The larger the area of Mutual Understanding in the model, the more effective and productive we tend to be in our relationships with others, and the more at peace we tend to be with ourselves.

Given the alternatives for increasing the area for Mutual Understanding illustrated by the Johari Window, the mechanics of exercising options (1), (2) and (3)

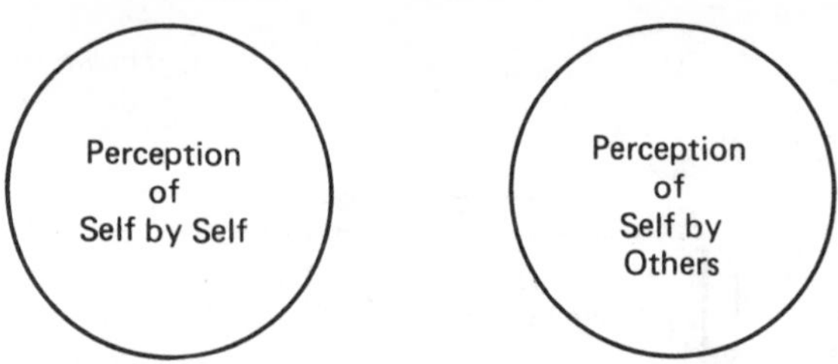

FIGURE 4-7: CONFLICTING DATA ABOUT THE SELF.

are clear. We simply get more feedback about ourselves from others, and share some of our perceptions of ourselves with them, hopefully assimilating the data from these exchanges into an altered perceptual set. But what about option (4), the denial that any perception other than the one we currently hold of ourselves is correct? Given a wide difference between perception of self-by-others and perception of self-by-self, as in Figure 4-7, we often erect *defenses* which screen out the conflicting data and protect us from feedback which is inconsistent with our views of ourselves.

The reason for defensive behavior, of course, is that we feel threatened. There is some data about ourselves that we don't want to know because it poses too much of a threat to our self-esteem, our love and respect for ourselves. It threatens to strip us of our present self-concept and leave us naked and in need of fundamental change to acquire a new "covering." On the other hand, if we shut ourselves off from too much data, we become a closed system and suffer the entropic fate of all such systems. We have to have a certain amount of feedback to function effectively, but we don't want so much that it hurts. That is the dilemma.

Defense of the Self

There are a number of *defense mechanisms* which we employ to avoid receiving data which we feel is inconsistent with our self-concept.

Rationalization. Rationalization refers to giving reasons or excuses for one's behavior that are less ego-threatening, or perhaps more socially acceptable, than the real reasons. For instance we rationalize failing a course by saying, "I was sick," or "The book was bad," or something else, rather than admitting to ourselves that we didn't work hard, or the material was too much for us to cope with. There is an old saying that "It is a poor workman who blames his tools"—i.e., who rationalizes his poor performance.

Reaction formation. Reaction formation is a variant of rationalization that aims at avoiding unpleasant situations by behaving in exactly the opposite way than one would like to. For instance, we may wish to really hurt someone, but, being afraid of the consequences of this action, go out of our way to be super-nice to him. Our behavior attempts to conceal, both to him *and to ourselves*, our real feelings, about which we feel guilty.

Projection. Projection simply means attributing one's own feelings to somebody else. It is also associated with guilt about the way one feels oneself. If we possess some trait which we do not like in ourselves, one way to "get rid of it" is to ascribe it to someone else. In labor relations situations both sides tend to attribute feelings of malice and dishonesty to each other, but never admit to such feelings themselves.

Regression. In the face of frustration and pressure, individuals sometimes revert to more childish forms of behavior. We call this regression. It may take the form of horseplay and joking and is often helpful in breaking tension.

Repression. We have already referred to repression in passing. It simply means denying something to the conscious mind. Forgetting. We often "forget" to do things that we don't want to do.

Aggression. The saying "the best defense is a good offense" is often taken quite literally in situations where we feel threatened. Just as an animal will attack when cornered and severely threatened, we "attack" when our self-concept is jarred. Winston Churchill is said to have remarked that he knew he had an opponent beaten in a debate in the House when the opponent began to shout; he had moved to the defensive as demonstrated by his aggressive behavior.

Avoidance. A form of repression, avoidance behavior refers to the individual's conscious effort to evade those things which he finds threatening or unpleasant. We all avoid confronting people we are afraid of, or doing things that we dislike doing. Procrastination is a most common form of avoidance behavior. ("I have been meaning to set up a National Association of Procrastinators, but I just haven't had the time.")

Just as incongruity between perception of self-by-others and self-by-self may lead to defensive behavior such as rationalization, projection or repression, so incongruity between the perceived self and the *ideal* self may cause problems.

We all have goals which we set for ourselves in life, and we all have dreams about what we would like to be, or what we plan to be. Fantasizing is an important part of life. It helps us maintain a balance and a course and it provides an escape from the pressures of life. But, like anything else, one can indulge in too much of it. Fantasizing is a form of defensive behavior. Individuals who cannot cope with the real world move into a fantasy world where they can maintain control of "what goes

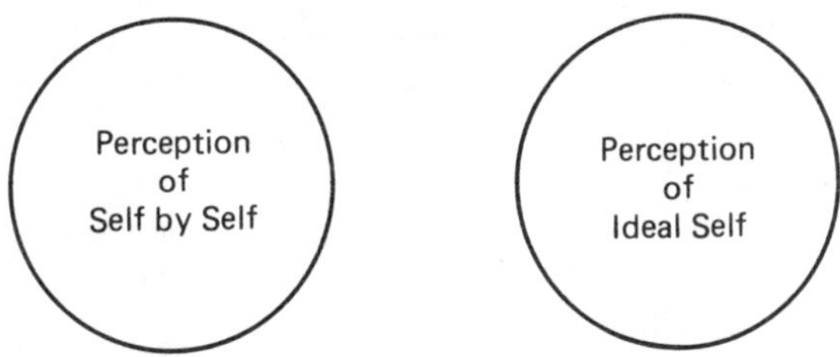

FIGURE 4-8: TO DREAM THE IMPOSSIBLE DREAM.

on." This escapism may be the result of the feeling that the ideal self cannot ever be attained. If the individual possesses a very strong concept of an ideal self that centers around being rich and powerful, but he is, in fact, neither of these things and is unable to become either, he will tend towards some form of escape from the dilemma. This may take the form of indulging in a fantasy life, like Walter Mitty, experiencing deep feelings of failure and worthlessness (increasing the gap between actual and ideal self even further), lashing out at the unfairness of it all (projecting the failure on some external object), or even suicide or severe psychological withdrawal.

Our personalities, our very *lives*, are concerned with building a concept of the self and then aligning that self-concept with how we are seen by others and how we would *like* to be and be seen. Consistency of the self-concept is a primary goal.

IN CONCLUSION

We have talked about the development of the self-concept and its maintenance, seen how intimately this is bound up with how we perceive things, noted how we tend to distort our perceptions, and seen how we twist and change our behavior to protect our images of ourselves. The discussion has been far from complete. There is much more to the concept of self than can be brought out here. The processes of perception and perceptual distortion are far more complex and detailed than we have described them. And the range of behavioral adaptation to various stimuli, either supportive or threatening, is wider than we have indicated. But this is not a textbook on psychology. Our objective here is to provide the reader with a basic framework of behavior, primarily in organizational situations, in order to increase his ability to understand what is going on around him and be able to react appropriately. We will discuss many of the concepts covered in this chapter in subsequent parts of the book. The behavior of individuals is central to our study; it can hardly be encapsulated in a chapter or two.

SOME THOUGHTS ON THE JIM WATSON INCIDENT

How Jim reacts to the events of "Jim Watson Day" depends to a large degree on various factors in the overall system. It would help to know a little bit more about the Western Manufacturing Company. For instance, is there a strong concern for people in the organization? Is there a sense of belonging and cohesiveness among the employees? Is this a good place to work? Are people here generally friendly and accepting?

It would also be useful to know how the rest of the company thought of, and acted towards, Jim normally. Is he close to his fellow employees? Do they joke with one another in a friendly fashion? Is he respected by them? Does management enjoy the same type of relationship?

It would be useful to know what the general educational level of employees in the company was, what the average age was, whether summer students were offered permanent jobs, and if so, at what level. It would also be useful to know whether Jim was typical of other men at his level, in terms of age, seniority, skill, knowledge and education.

Depending on the answers to these questions, Jim might react to the ribbing of "Jim Watson Day" in a variety of ways. What we are concerned with is essentially how he views himself (self-by-self), how he thinks others see him (self-by-others), and what he aspires to be (ideal self). We know that his self-concept will affect his perceptions of events, that he will either see them as flattering, inconsequential, or threatening, and that he will react to them either positively, neutrally, or defensively, depending on these perceptions.

What data do we have to work with?

To begin with, the students have known him for two summers, and they appeared to have a strong liking and respect for him. This is substantiated by the fact that they gave up their acting when Jim began to get annoyed. They wanted to kid him, but not hurt him. Imitation is said to be the purest form of flattery, and on that basis the students seemed to be demonstrating respect, liking, and admiration. The rest of the organization seemed to have perceived the kidding as being good-natured, and the remarks aimed at him during the day seemed to be lighthearted. But, bear in mind that they *seemed* lighthearted *to us*, and not necessarily to Jim. We are talking about *our* perceptions here, not his.

We know that Jim is "an old regular worker." He is to some extent a traditionalist, as exemplified by his dress—a flannel lumberjack shirt, ill-matched tie tucked into the third button, rows of pens and pencils in the pocket, and a notebook in hand. This is the stereotype of a foreman in cartoons of the '20's and '30's. It would seem unlikely that Jim is heavily into rock-and-roll.

We may assume that Jim relates well to people. We know he has supervised the students for two summers, and they appear to be fond of him. We do *not* know anything about how competent he is on the job. And we do not have any data as to how his career in the company has progressed to date. He does not appear to have advanced past the first level or so of supervision, and we don't know if that was by mutual consent between him and the company or whether he has differing perceptions concerning his abilities from those held by higher management.

Finally, we know that he appeared to take the kidding well at first, and then got quite upset (threatening to "take on" students who did not desist). It appears, then, that he found the incident threatening to his self-concept in some way.

Let's indulge in a "what if" or two. What if Jim saw himself as being worthwhile and competent and useful, but saw the organization's perception of him as being a bit old-fashioned, a bit over the hill, not with it? What if he felt that he had deserved a bit better than he had received over the years? What if he felt he did a good job, but he was unsure whether others saw things the same way? What if he felt that his age and seniority were deserving of respect and esteem and that he expected his colleagues to support him in this feeling? What if, because of a number of things, he was ambivalent as to his "real" (seen by others) competence/inadequacy as a supervisor (and man) in the company? What if his main goal, at this stage of his career, was to complete his tenure with dignity and the respect and gratitude of his colleagues and company?

If these assumptions are true, then we can predict that Jim would be deeply threatened and hurt by the events of the day. He would perceive the actions of his fellow workers and managers, because of their seeming support of the ribbing, as meaning that they don't respect him. Maybe they think he is an "old fool" rather than just an "old regular worker." Maybe they think he is no better than a student. Maybe they think his use of a memo pad and his general demeanor on the job are silly, old-fashioned, and ineffective. If this is how he perceived the situation, then he would react defensively. He could not afford to admit too much of this data into his self. He somehow would have to ignore it, avoid it, rationalize it, or change or deflect it. In order to main his self-concept as a worthwhile person, he would have to screen the data and defend himself from it.

If, however, all the "what ifs" we listed are incorrect, and in fact he sees things as just the opposite of what we have been assuming, then his reactions would be very different. If he perceived the kidding as being flattery, of confirming his competence and the respect and esteem in which he is held, he would react positively. He might come to work some day soon dressed as a "student" and turn the joke around. He would tend to recount stories about the day and laugh about the incidents. He would tell the stories with pride, as proof that he was well liked, well respected, well known, and valued as a person as well as a supervisor.

The point to be made about the Jim Watson case is that his subsequent behavior depends largely on his *perception* of the events, which in turn depends heavily on his *self-concept*. If he has a strong self-concept as a useful, competent, respected, likable person, his perceptions reinforce that concept. If he conceives of himself as not so competent, not so useful, not being so well respected or liked, then he more likely would perceive the events as confirmation of his worst fears.

Our predictions are based on our *assumptions* about Jim Watson's concept of himself. It is important to recognize that fact. We are not Jim. We are not inside him, and we don't know how he feels. We can only make some assumptions, and we do that generally by trying to put ourselves in his shoes. But it is *us* we put in his shoes, and that is *never* the same as *him* in his shoes. It's a warning we should all heed.

Chapter Summary

1 Individual behavior can be understood only in the context of the overall system in which it takes place.

2 We can describe, understand and predict the behavior of individuals on the basis of their personality, those characteristics

a which they exhibit more or less consistently over time,

b which serve to distinguish them from other people, and

c which form the basis of our predictions concerning their future behavior.

3 We use the concept of "self" as a means of understanding personality. The self is composed of a set of beliefs, values, goals, feelings of competence or inadequacy, and perceptions of the environment and one's interactions with it.

4 Our behavior is basically goal-oriented. Goals are a map for behavior. They are a reflection of our needs.

5 We see the world around us through a set of perceptual screens that allow us to filter out what we do not want to see, and to accept what we *do* want.

6 Perception is situational. How we perceive things depends on such factors as beliefs, values, goals, needs, knowledge and feelings, and past experience.

7 Perception performs the function of organizing and categorizing the wide variety of sensations with which we are continuously bombarded.

8 The perceptual process is interrelated with our goals and needs and our perception of self—selective perception allows us to "see" more of what is *congruent* with our goals, needs and self, and less of what is contradictory to them.

9 A major force underlying individual behavior is the move towards consistency of the self—towards a consistency between the concepts of self-by-self, self-by-others, and ideal self. Individuals react to this need for consistency either by altering one or more of the elements of the self-concept or by erecting defense mechanisms which screen out the conflicting data and protect them from threatening feedback.

JIM WATSON (B)

Jim Watson did not report for work on Friday, July 22nd. The students and the regular workers speculated about the reasons for his absence. Some of the regular workers thought that the students had shamed him; others felt that he was "broken by this incident." Few said, "He seems to be sick in the head." Some of the students remarked that in the past Jim had been "not a bad egg" and that it was too bad that they had hurt him.

On Monday morning, the men wondered why Jim Watson did not appear in the shed at the usual time. Around nine o'clock, one of the more senior workers, George Watts, returned from the medical department and related to some of the men that Dr. Hill had received several calls from Mrs. Watson through the weekend because Jim had been unable to sleep or eat.

5

Motivation

OBJECTIVES

When you have completed this chapter you should

- see the relationship between motivation and the self-concept;
- be aware of the basic motivational factors that affect the performance of individuals in a work setting;
- be able to differentiate between first level task goals and second level goals and rewards—the Vroom model;
- appreciate the complexity of money as a motivator;
- recognize the situational nature of motivation: matching the motivational needs of the individual with the motivational characteristics of the job.

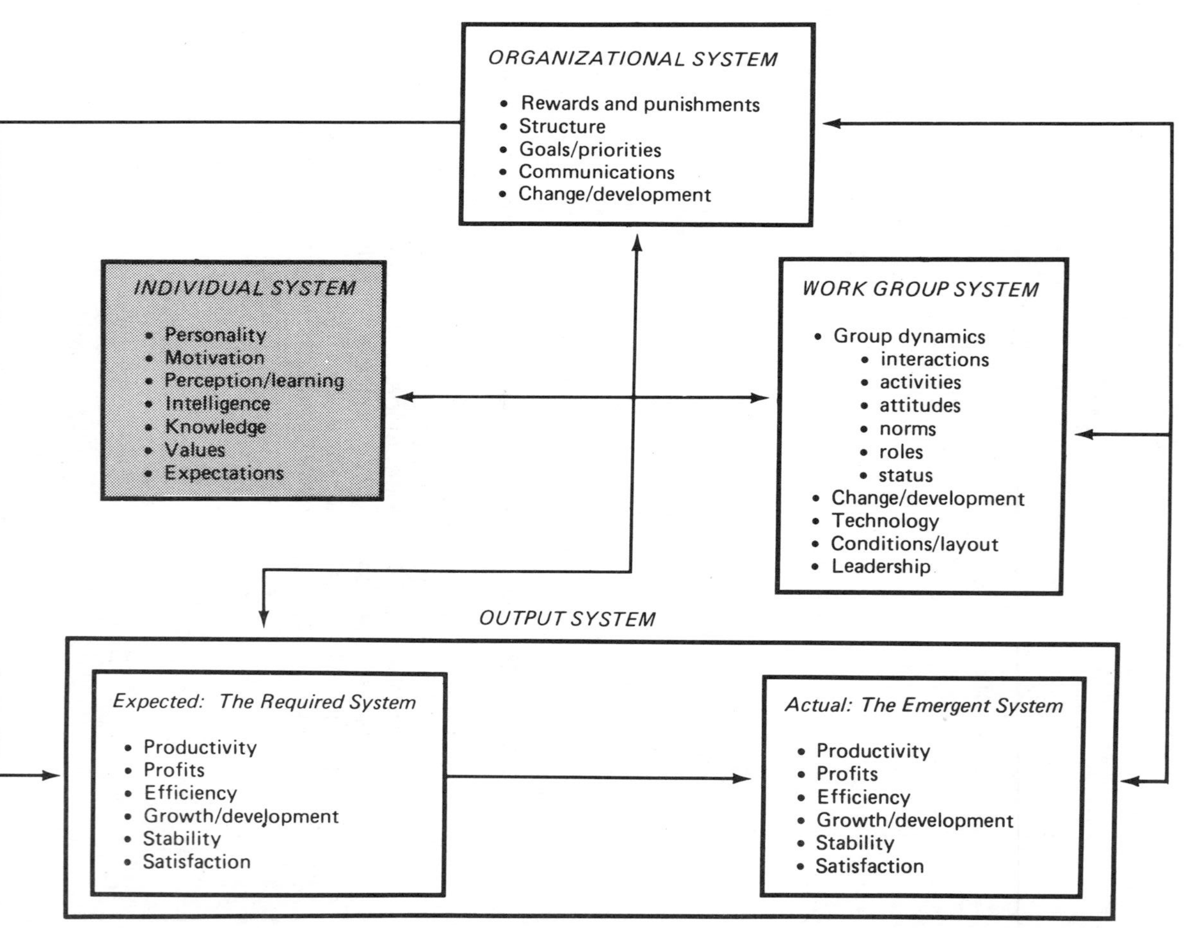

ORGANIZATIONAL SYSTEM
• Rewards and punishments
• Structure
• Goals/priorities
• Communications
• Change/development
INDIVIDUAL SYSTEM
• Personality
• Motivation
• Perception/learning
• Intelligence
• Knowledge
• Values
• Expectations
WORK GROUP SYSTEM
• Group dynamics
• interactions
• activities
• attitudes
• norms
• roles
• status
• Change/development
• Technology
• Conditions/layout
• Leadership
OUTPUT SYSTEM
Expected: The Required System
• Productivity
• Profits
• Efficiency
• Growth/development
• Stability
• Satisfaction
Actual: The Emergent System
• Productivity
• Profits
• Efficiency
• Growth/development
• Stability
• Satisfaction

Earlier on in the book we gave you an opportunity to look at the situation in the Hovey and Beard Company and to predict the reaction of the girls to the change in the method of painting wooden toys. Here is Part 2 of the case, describing what in fact did happen after two months of operations under the new system.

Take a moment to read over Part 2 of the case and to check back with your predictions at the end of Chapters 1, 2, and 3. If you can, discuss your predictions, and the actual outcome, with one or more of your colleagues or friends, and look to see where you were on target or off. Discuss *why* you were either accurate or not in your predictions.

HOVEY AND BEARD COMPANY PART 2

By the second month of the training period trouble had developed. The girls learned more slowly than had been anticipated, and it began to look as though their production would stabilize far below what was planned for. Many of the hooks were going by empty. The girls complained that they were going by too fast, and that the time study man had set the rates wrong. A few girls quit and had to be replaced with new girls, which further aggravated the learning problem. The team spirit that the management had expected to develop automatically through the group bonus was not in evidence except as an expression of what the engineers called "resistance." One girl whom the group regarded as its leader (and the management regarded as the ringleader) was outspoken in making the various complaints of the group to the foreman: the job was a messy one, the hooks moved too fast, the incentive pay was not being correctly calculated, and it was too hot working so close to the drying oven.

Before you begin to read Chapter 5, take a few minutes to decide what you, as foreman of the paint room, would do now. Is there a way to get the girls' productivity up to the predicted rate? What about the messiness of the job, the speed of the hooks, the calculation of the incentive pay, and the heat from the ovens? What should you do about them?

Write down what you would do to resolve the problems in the paint room at this juncture. We will be returning to the case at the end of the chapter.

In the last chapter we talked about the individual's goals being an important part of his self-concept. However, we did not go into the matter of *how* these goals are set, and how the individual decides what he wants to do, how he wants to do it, how often, with what intensity, and to what end. An underlying assumption of the self-concept model is that behavior is goal-oriented; that is, all behavior is directed towards the attainment of some goal or the satisfaction of some needs. Joe Kelly (1974) presents a simple model that illustrates the process of motivation:

cause — generate — to reach — lead to

NEEDS ---→ DRIVES ---→ BEHAVIOR ---→ GOALS ---→ REDUCTION OR RELEASE OF TENSION

FIGURE 5-1: THE MOTIVATION SEQUENCE.

MOTIVATION AND THE SELF-CONCEPT

This model is not unlike the one we used in the last chapter to describe the development and maintenance of the self-concept. Once again we are talking about goals, behavior and outcomes. When we talked about the self, we said that it was made up of a set of beliefs, values, and goals, interacting with a sense of competence/inadequacy, all of which were built and maintained by a flow of perceptions of the environment. If we made the model slightly more complex and added the concept of *needs* to it, we could see the relationship between the *self* (personality) and *motivation*.

Behavior is both directed to, and results from, unsatisfied needs. The word "unsatisfied" is most important. Maslow (1943) says,

> If we are interested in what *actually* motivates us and not in what has, will, or might motivate us, then a satisfied need is not a motivator.

Goals and Needs

Our model of personality/motivation presents a sort of chicken-egg dilemma: Which comes first, the goal or the need? When we talk about behavior being goal-oriented, we mean that individuals feel a need, want, desire, or drive to do

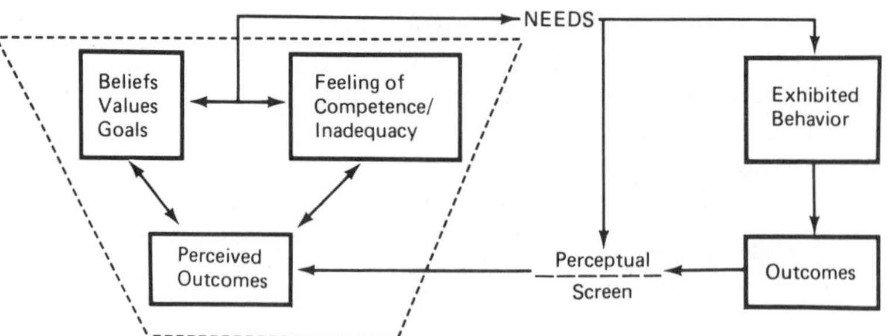

FIGURE 5-2: MOTIVATION AND PERSONALITY: THE RELATIONSHIP BETWEEN NEEDS AND THE OPERATION OF THE SELF.

something that leads to the achievement of a goal. But is the goal, as part of the self, already there, and is it the factor that stimulates the need? Are goals and needs the same thing?

It is useful to separate the two concepts. In the last chapter we defined a goal as "that outcome which we strive to attain in order to satisfy certain needs." The goal is the end result, the need the driving force that spurs us towards that result. As we mentioned before, an individual might have a goal to get an "A" in a course, but this goal may reflect a number of quite different needs. He may feel a need to confirm his competence; his friends may all be getting "A's" and he may feel a need to get one in order to remain a member of the group; he may wish to have the esteem of others; he may simply want to do his best; he may have to have the "A" in order to keep his scholarship. It is difficult to infer needs from goals.

When we talk about money as a motivator, this point will be raised again. Money represents so many different things to different people that saying that individuals "work for money" is meaningless. What we have to know is what *needs* the money is satisfying. Is it survival, status, belonging, achievement, a convenient scorecard for performance? Remember, *behavior is both directed to, and results from, unsatisfied needs*.

Every individual has a number of needs which vie for satisfaction. How do we choose between these competing forces? Do we try to satisfy them all? Much like a small child in a candy store, faced with the dilemma of spending his allowance, we are forced to decide what we want most; that is, we satisfy the strongest needs first.

Although there is general agreement among psychologists that man experiences a variety of needs, there is considerable disagreement as to what these needs are, and what their relative importance is. There have been a number of attempts to present models of motivation which list a specific number of motivating needs, with the implication that these lists are all-inclusive and represent the total picture of man's needs. Unfortunately, each of these models has weaknesses and gaps, and we are as yet without a general theory of motivation.

MASLOW'S HIERARCHY OF NEEDS

One model of motivation that has gained a great deal of attention, but not complete acceptance, has been put forward by Abraham Maslow (1954). Maslow's theory argues that individuals are motivated to satisfy a number of different kinds of needs, some of which are more powerful than others (or, to use the psychological jargon, are more *prepotent* than others). The term prepotency refers to the idea that some needs are felt as being more pressing than others. Maslow argues that until these most pressing needs are satisfied, other needs have little effect on an individual's behavior. In other words, we satisfy the most prepotent needs first, and then progress to less pressing ones. As one need becomes satisfied, and therefore less important to us, other needs loom up and become motivators of our behavior.

Maslow represents this prepotency of needs as a *hierarchy*, shown in Figure 5-3. The most prepotent needs are shown at the bottom of the ladder, with prepotency decreasing as one progresses upwards.

SELF-ACTUALIZATION
Reaching your maximum potential
Doing your thing best

ESTEEM
Respect from others.
Self-respect. Recognition.

BELONGING
Affiliation, acceptance,
being a part of something

SAFETY
Physical safety, psychological
security

PHYSIOLOGICAL
Hunger, thirst, sex, rest

FIGURE 5-3: MASLOW'S HIERARCHY OF MOTIVATIONAL NEEDS. PREPOTENCY OF NEEDS DECREASES AS ONE PROGRESSES UP THE LADDER.

The first needs that man must satisfy are *physiological*. They are concerned with such things as hunger, thirst, sex, rest. As Maslow says (1954):

> Undoubtedly these physiological needs are the most prepotent of all needs. What this means specifically is that in the human being who is missing everything in life in an extreme fashion, it is most likely that the major motivation would be the physiological needs rather than any others. A person who is lacking food, safety, love, and esteem would probably hunger for food more strongly than for anything else.

Once the first level physiological needs are largely satisfied, Maslow maintains, the next level of needs emerges. Individuals become concerned with the need for *safety and security*—protection from physical harm, disaster, illness, and security of income, life-style and relationships.

Similarly, once these safety needs have become largely satisfied, individuals become concerned with *belonging*—a sense of membership in some group or groups, a need for affiliation, and a feeling of acceptance by others.

When there is a feeling that the individual ''belongs'' somewhere, he is next motivated by a desire to be held in *esteem*, both by others, and by himself. He needs to be thought of as a worthwhile person by others, to be recognized as a person with some value. Just as individuals experience a need to be held in esteem by others, however, they also have a strong need to see *themselves* as worthwhile people. As we intimated in the last chapter, it is important that individuals see themselves as having some worth. Without this type of self-concept, one sees oneself as drifting, cut off, pointless. Much of the dissatisfaction with certain types of jobs centers around the fact that they are perceived, by the people performing them, as demeaning, and therefore damaging to their self-concept.

Finally, Maslow says, when all these needs have been satisfied, at least to some extent, people are motivated by a desire to *self-actualize*, to achieve whatever they define as their maximum potential, to do their thing to the best of their ability. Maslow describes self-actualization as follows:

> A musician must make music, an artist must pain, a poet must write, if he is to be ultimately happy. What a man *can* do, he *must* do. This need we may call self-actualization . . . It refers to the desire for self-fulfillment, namely, to the tendency for one to become actualized in what one is potentially. This tendency might be phrased as the desire to become more and more what one is, to become everything that one is capable of becoming.
>
> The specific form these needs take will of course vary greatly from person to person. In one individual it may be expressed maternally, as the desire to be an ideal mother, in another athletically, in still another aesthetically, in the painting of pictures, and in another inventively in the creation of new contrivances. It is not necessarily a creative urge although in people who have any capabilities for creation it will take this form.

Several points must be made concerning Maslow's model of motivation. First, it should be made clear that he does *not* mean that individuals experience only one type of need at a time. In fact, we probably experience all levels of needs all the time, only to varying degrees. While it could be said that hunger is not a problem for most people in North America, we have all experienced the phenomenon of not being able to concentrate on a job or game because of a growling stomach. Productivity drops just prior to lunch as people transfer their thoughts from their jobs to the upcoming meal. After lunch, food is not uppermost in most people's minds, but perhaps rest is, as a sense of drowsiness sets in. Similarly, in almost all organizational settings, individuals juggle their needs for security ("Can I keep this job?") with needs for esteem ("If I do what is demanded by the job, how will my peers see me, and how will I see myself?"). Given a situation where management is demanding a certain level of performance, but where the group norms are to produce below these levels, all these issues are experienced. If the individual does not produce to the level demanded by management he may lose his job (security). But if he conforms to management's norms rather than to those of his group, it may ostracize him (belonging) and regard him as a turncoat (esteem), while he may see himself as having let the side down (self-esteem). We do not progress simply from one level in the hierarchy to another in a straightforward, orderly manner; there is a constant, but ever-changing pull from all levels and types of needs.

A second point that must be made about Maslow's hierarchy is that the order in which he has set up the needs does not necessarily reflect their prepotence for every individual. Some people may have such a high need for esteem that they are able to subordinate their needs for safety, or their physiological or belonging needs to these. The "war hero" immediately springs to mind. There is little concern for safety or physical comfort as the seeker of glory rushes forward into the muzzle of destruction.

A third, and very important point to be made about Maslow's hierarchical model is the assertion that *once a need is satisfied it is no longer a motivator*—until it re-emerges. Food is a poor motivator after an individual has just finished a large meal. The point in this is clear for management. Unfortunately, many organizations and individuals still fail to get the message. Most incentive systems are based on needs that have already been largely satisfied. If management placed emphasis on needs that have *not* been satisfied, rather than those which have been relatively well taken care of, employees would be more likely to be motivated towards achieving the goals of the organization. Human behavior is primarily directed towards *unsatisfied* needs.

Finally, an important aspect of Maslow's model is that it provides for constant growth of the individual. There is no point at which everything has been achieved. One is always striving to do things to the best of one's ability, having satisfied all lower level needs, and "best" is almost always defined as being slightly better than before. This is an attractive feature of the model, but not necessarily how motivation actually works. There has been a great deal of debate over Maslow's hierarchical concept of motivation. It has a basic attraction to most people because it seems to be logical, to make sense.

As a rather unfortunate postscript to this discussion of Maslow's theory, we have data that indicates that man may also move *down* the hierarchy under certain circumstances. The chronicle of the Donner expedition which became marooned in the Sierra Nevada in the early 1800's (Croy, 1955), and the more recent account of the downed aircraft passengers in the Andes (Read, 1974) detail how man, in the face of overwhelming physiological needs, can succumb to cannibalism. This is not an argument that *all* men react that way, but simply that the pull is strong.

HERZBERG'S DUAL-FACTOR THEORY

A second theory which has attracted a great deal of attention is Herzberg's dual-factor theory. Frederick Herzberg and his associates began their research into motivation during the 1950's, examining the models and assumptions of Maslow and others. The result of this work was the formulation of what Herzberg termed the Motivation-Hygiene Theory (M-H). The basic hypotheses of this theory are that:

1. There are two *types* of motivators, one type which results in *satisfaction* with the job, and the other which merely *prevents dissatisfaction*.
   These two types of factors are quite separate and distinct from one another.

Herzberg called the factors which resulted in job satisfaction *motivators*, and those that simply prevented dissatisfaction *hygienes*.

2 The factors that lead to job satisfaction (the *motivators*) are:

- achievement
- recognition
- work itself
- responsibility
- advancement

3 The factors which may prevent dissatisfaction (the *hygienes*) are:

- company policy and administration
- working conditions
- supervision
- interpersonal relations
- money
- status
- security

Hygienes, if applied effectively, can, at best, prevent dissatisfaction: if applied poorly, they can result in negative feelings about the job.

Motivators are those things that allow for psychological growth and development on the job. They are closely related to the concept of self-actualization, involving a challenge, an opportunity to extend oneself to the fullest, to taste the pleasure of accomplishment, and to be recognized as having done something worthwhile.

Hygienes are simply factors that describe the *conditions* of work rather than the work itself.

Herzberg's point is that if you want to motivate people you have to be concerned with the *job itself*, and not simply with the surroundings.

As in a medical situation, growth, healing and development occur as natural internal processes. They are the result of proper diet, exercise, sleep, etc. Hygienic procedures simply prevent disease from occurring; they do not promote growth, *per se*. Herzberg says that we should focus our attention on the individual in the job, not on the things we surround him with. He maintains that we tend to think that growth and development will occur if we provide good working conditions, status, security, and administration, whereas in fact what stimulates growth (and motivation to grow and develop) are opportunities for achievement, recognition, responsibility and advancement.

Once again, this theory has a basic attraction. As Joe Kelly (1974) puts it, however,

> It is always as well to bear in mind that academics, who place considerable value on autonomy and inner direction, have an obsession about

making work meaningful. The notion that it is possible to realize man's true nature through creative work which is its own reward is an exceedingly attractive proposition to the learned don which is rarely fully shared by his wife.

Herzberg goes further than Maslow, cutting the hierarchy off near the top and maintaining that motivation only results from some elements of esteem needs and self-actualization (Figure 5-4).

There are two other current theories of motivation which are related to the concept of self-actualization, but which are more specific in their definition. These are Robert White's *competence motive* (1959) and David McClelland's *need for achievement* (1961).

We talked about the competence motive in the last chapter and saw that a feeling of competence is an integral part of the self-concept. We also saw that it is this feeling of competence/inadequacy, that, interacting with beliefs, values, and goals, has a major effect on the needs that an individual experiences. The need to feel *some* sense of competence is strong. We have been referring to the concept so far as competence/inadequacy because, quite clearly, we all feel competent about *some* things and inadequate about some others. Individuals who have *no* sense of competence at all, or stated in reverse form, feel totally inadequate, suffer severe psychological disorder.

THE COMPETENCE MOTIVE

Apart from satisfying basic physiological, safety and social needs, Robert White maintains that people also want to understand and manipulate their environment. They like to "make things happen," to control what goes on around them. He

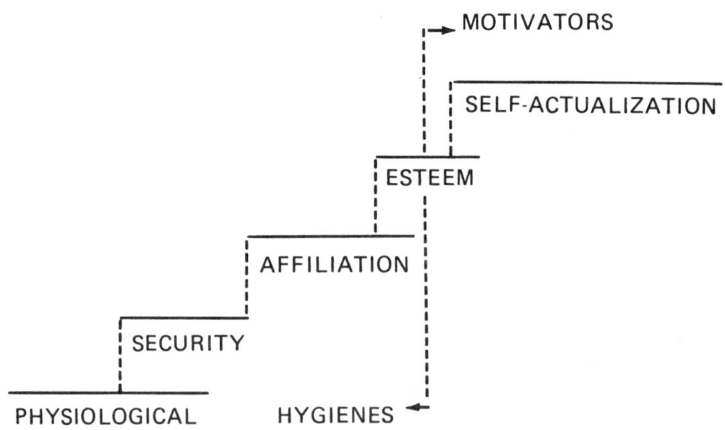

FIGURE 5-4: HERZBERG'S DUAL-FACTOR THEORY RELATED TO MASLOW'S HIERARCHY OF NEEDS. (FROM: *MANAGEMENT OF ORGANIZATIONAL BEHAVIOR*, HERSEY & BLANCHARD, PRENTICE-HALL, 1969, p. 48.)

argues that this need for mastery over the environment is present even in small babies and can be observed as they fondle objects and explore their surroundings. Subsequently, they begin taking things apart and reassembling them, looking at things closely, experimenting with their feel, smell and function. This, says White, is how young children acquire the confidence that they can handle themselves satisfactorily in life. They gain a sense of "competence."

The degree to which an individual feels this sense of competence is a result of his life experiences to date. If his experiences have been largely successful, he will view life optimistically, with little fear and trepidation. If, however, his experiences of failure have outweighed his successes, he is far more likely to see his efforts as being futile and be prepared to await whatever circumstance has declared for him. He is less likely to be adventuresome, aggressive and dynamic.

White maintains that since everyone is faced with a daily series of interactions with the environment, the balance of success and failure can be altered over time so that an individual can become more successful, and therefore more motivated towards striving for success, after he has experienced a string of positive transactions. However, White is unsure about the degree to which this change can actually take place in individuals because of the phenomenon of the "self-fulfilling prophecy." That is, one tends to achieve what one *thinks* one can achieve; the confident, successful individual achieves continued success by pushing aside any obstacles that are placed in his path, while the more timid person sets lower goals for himself and accepts blockages as inevitable and often insurmountable.

In organizational settings the competence motive is manifested by a desire for mastery over the job, growth and development. To some extent this is rather similar to Maslow's self-actualization. But while self-actualization may be hard to measure, the competence motive is less difficult. Individuals who exhibit a high sense of competence, in White's terms, are usually successful in jobs which require initiative, drive, innovation, and decision-making. Therefore, if organizations wish to get the most out of individuals who measure high on competence, they should steer them into appropriate jobs.

NEED FOR ACHIEVEMENT

The one *single* motivating factor which has received the most attention, in terms of research, is the need for achievement *(n-ach)*. As a result, we know more about *n-ach* than any other motivational factor. Much of this knowledge is due to the work of David McClelland of Harvard. To illustrate what he means by the need for achievement, McClelland (1966) cites the following example:

> Several years ago a careful study was made of 450 workers who had been thrown out of work by a plant shutdown in Erie, Pennsylvania. Most of the unemployed workers stayed home for a while and then checked with the U.S. Employment Service to see if their old jobs or similar ones were available. But a small minority among them behaved differently; the day they were laid off, they started job hunting. They

> checked both the U.S. and Pennsylvania Employment Office; they studied the "Help Wanted" sections of the papers; they checked through their union, their church, and various fraternal organizations; they looked into training courses to learn a new skill; they even left town to look for work, while the majority when questioned said they would not under any circumstances move away from Erie to obtain a job. Obviously the members of the active minority were differently motivated.

The individual with a high *n-ach* has a number of distinctive characteristics which separate him from his peers. First of all, he likes situations where he can take *personal responsibility* for finding the solution to problems. This allows him to gain personal satisfaction from his achievements. He does not like situations where success or failure results from chance. The important thing is that the outcome be the result of his own skill and effort.

A second characteristic of the high *n-ach* individual is that he likes to *set moderately high goals* for himself. These goals are neither so low that they can be ahieved with little challenge, nor so high that they are impossible. The high *n-ach* individual prefers goals that require all-out effort and the exercise of all his abilities. Once again, the achievement of this type of objective results in greater personal satisfaction. This phenomenon can even be observed in very young children. A child may be given a game of ring toss, told that he scores whenever he succeeds in throwing a ring over the peg, and then left alone to play the game. McClelland (1962) comments,

> Obviously, if he stands next to the peg, he can score a ringer every time; but if he stands a long distance away, he will hardly ever get a ringer. The curious fact is that the children with high concern for achievement quite consistently stand at moderate distances from the peg where they are most apt to get achievement satisfaction . . . The ones with low n-Achievement, on the other hand, distribute their choices of where to stand quite randomly over the entire distance. In other words, people with high n-Achievement prefer a situation where there is a challenge, where there is some real risk of not succeeding, but not so great a risk that they might not overcome it by their own efforts.

A third distinctive characteristic of the high achiever is that he wants *concrete feedback* on his performance. Only certain types of jobs provide this kind of feedback, however, and so some kinds of jobs are unattractive to the high achiever. For instance, teachers receive only imprecise, hazy feedback as to the effectiveness of their efforts, while production managers have a daily output chart to look at with either joy or disappointment.

There are some additional minor characteristics possessed by high achievers. They tend to enjoy travel, are willing to give up a bird in the hand for two in the bush, and prefer experts to friends as working partners. The image is clear; the high achiever is a personality type suited admirably to certain jobs and not others. It would be wrong to treat all individuals as high achievers and attempt to motivate them by offering them challenging jobs, rapid and objective feedback on performance, and personal responsibility for success or failure. Many people would find this sort of situation too demanding.

NEED FOR AFFILIATION AND NEED FOR POWER

Building on research done in the 1930's, McClelland has also identified two other types of needs, the need for affiliation (*n-affil*), and the need for power (*n-pow*). His testing procedure is concerned with the application of what is known as the Thematic Apperception Test (TAT), a series of pictures which are presented to a subject, one at a time. The individual is asked to tell a story about each picture. The underlying assumption of the TAT procedure is that it will reveal the dominant thoughts and attitudes of subjects. For instance, an individual with a high *n-ach* will formulate stories that are concerned with getting things done, challenging situations, feelings of satisfaction at having done a good job, and so on. The individual with a high need for affiliation (*n-affil*) will reflect a sensitivity to the feelings of others, a desire for friendly relationships, and a reference to situations which involve human interactions. High *n-power* subjects will relate stories reflecting the process of influencing, controlling and manipulating others.

NEED FOR AFFILIATION

The need for affiliation is very similar to Maslow's need to belong. It can be a dominant motivating force affecting behavior, and may manifest itself in many different ways. The novelist John O'Hara was supposedly obsessed with the fact that, not having a college degree, he was excluded from membership in certain clubs and societies. At the other end of the spectrum, James Coyne, a former Governor of the Bank of Canada, was described as the most "unclubbable" man in the country, as he held an aversion to joining groups. In its most straightforward form, a need for affiliation manifests itself in a desire to be liked by others, to be part of a group, to enter into warm, personal relationships with others. The high *n-affil* individual values relationships over accomplishments, and friendship over power ("The most important thing in this organization is the people, not the money, the status, or the authority.")

NEED FOR POWER

In studying the motivational profiles of North American managers, McClelland has noticed that many of those who reach the top of their organizations and are rated as highly effective in these positions demonstrate a concern for influencing people. This is, in McClelland's terms, a need for power. The need for power is not simply seen as the raw desire to control others, or to simply exert authority. McClelland (1976) makes the point that,

> . . . this need must be disciplined and controlled so that it is directed toward the benefit of the institution as a whole and not toward the manager's personal aggrandizement. Moreover, the top manager's need for power ought to be greater than his need for being liked by people.

Power motivation refers not to autocratic, tyrannical behavior, but to a need to have some impact, to be influential and effective in achieving organizational goals.

McClelland examined the motivational needs of a large group of managers whose units demonstrated varying degrees of morale. The most important factor in predicting whether a manager's subordinates would exhibit high morale or not turned out to be how their need for power related to their need for affiliation. The most effective managers (at least in terms of high morale among their subordinates) were those whose power motivation exceeded their desire to be liked. Why is this? McClelland (1976) puts forward the following explanation:

> Sociologists have long argued that, for a bureaucracy to function effectively, those who manage it must be universalistic in applying rules. That is, if they make exceptions for the particular needs of individuals, the whole system will break down. The manager with a high need for being liked is precisely the one who wants to stay on good terms with everybody, and, therefore, is the one most likely to make exceptions in terms of particular needs. . . . Sociological theory and our data both argue . . . that the person whose need for affiliation is high does not make a good manager.

The power-motivated manager, like his counterparts the achiever and the affiliator, demonstrates distinct characteristics.

1. He is highly organization-minded. He feels responsible for building organizations to which he belongs. He also believes strongly in centralized authority.
2. He likes to work. This is different from the high achiever who likes to minimize work by becoming more efficient. While the high achiever minimizes effort and maximizes output, the power-motivated manager enjoys work for its own sake.
3. He is willing to sacrifice some of his own self-interest for the good of the organization.
4. He has a strong sense of justice, feeling that hard work and sacrifice should be rewarded.

The picture of McClelland's power-motivated manager is reminiscent of the "organization man" caricatured by William Whyte (1956). The message seems to be that if one is dedicated to the institution, committed to the work ethic, and unflagging in energy and devotion, success will follow. However, the increasing popularity of switching jobs as a method for rapid advancement somewhat contradicts this type of thinking.

VROOM'S EXPECTANCY THEORY OF MOTIVATION

The final motivational model we will look at is more complex and difficult to grasp than the others, but it raises some of the key issues in motivational theory and fills some of the glaring gaps in other approaches to the subject. Victor Vroom, of Carnegie-Mellon in Pittsburgh, has challenged the assertion of the human relationists that job satisfaction leads to increased productivity (this theory has been called the "contented cow" approach to management). The assumption is that if management keeps employees happy, presumably by satisfying their needs for safety, belonging, esteem, and so on, they will respond by increasing productivity. Herzberg, in a delightful little film on motivation, highlights the fallacy of this assumption with an interview between a manager and his secretary. The secretary is complaining about the job, and the manager lists all the things he has done for her—increased salary, new typewriter, better hours, status and so on—at the end of which she looks straight at him and asks, "So what have you done for me lately?" The point may be made that satisfied needs do not motivate people, or that hygienes simply keep employees quiet for a time. However, this anecdote also points to a fundamental aspect of motivation that has been largely overlooked. For an individual to be motivated to perform a certain task he must expect that *completion of the task will lead to the achievement of his goals*; i.e., the task is not necessarily the goal itself, but is often the *means* of goal attainment.

Vroom (1964) defines motivation as:

> A process governing choices, made by persons or lower organisms, among alternative forms of voluntary behavior.

In organizational terms this concept of motivation pictures an individual, occupying a role, faced with a set of alternative voluntary behaviors, all of which have some associated outcomes attached to them. If he chooses behavior 1, outcome A results, if behavior 2, outcome B, and so on. This situation is represented in Figure 5-5.

Knowing that individuals choose behaviors in order to obtain certain outcomes is nothing new. The question is why they choose one outcome over another. The answer provided by the motivational theories examined so far is that the choice reflects the strength of the individual's desire or need for a *specific outcome* at a certain time.

However, Vroom makes the point that *task goals* (productivity, quality standards, or similar goals attached to jobs) are often the *means* to an end, rather than the end itself. There is a *second* level of outcomes which reflect the "real" goals of individuals, and these may be attained, in varying degrees, through task behavior.

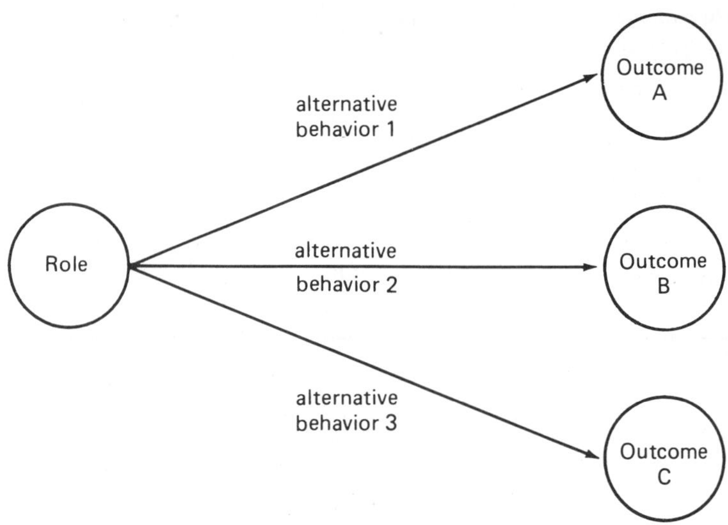

FIGURE 5-5: ALTERNATIVE VOLUNTARY BEHAVIORS RESULT IN SPECIFIC ASSOCIATED OUTCOMES.

We have a situation, then, where an individual is motivated to behave in a certain manner because (a) he has a strong desire for a certain task outcome and a reasonable expectation of achieving that outcome; and (b) because he also expects that achievement of the task outcome will reward him in terms of pay, promotion, job security, or satisfaction of individual needs—physiological, safety, esteem, and so on. Figure 5-6 illustrates this process.

Let us take a look at how the model works. For example, a university professor might have as a *task goal* "receiving good ratings as a teacher." The choice of this goal reflects three things:

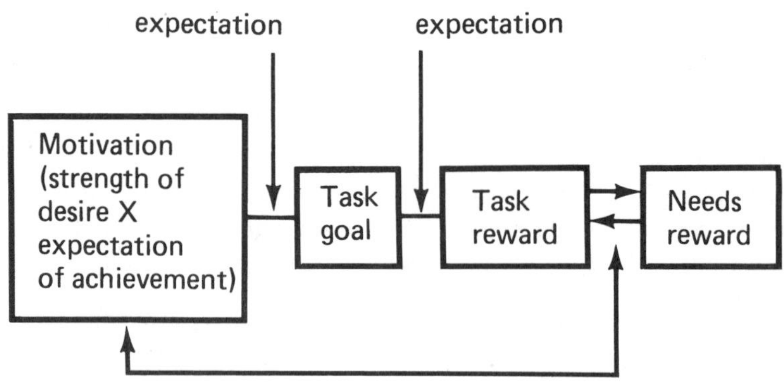

FIGURE 5-6: VROOM'S MODEL OF MOTIVATION.

1 The strength of the need for good ratings versus some other goal;
2 The expectation that this goal can be achieved;
3 The expectation that the achievement of this task goal will lead to certain desired rewards—maybe a *task reward* of "being given tenure," and, in turn, a *needs reward* of "feeling secure in the job."

Vroom would maintain that we do things in our jobs in order to achieve *second level* rewards:

> If a worker sees high productivity as a path leading to the attainment of one or more of his personal goals, he will tend to be a high producer. Conversely, if he sees low productivity as a path to the achievement of his goals, he will tend to be a low producer. (Georgopoulous, et. al., 1957)

Certainly, Vroom has hit on an important aspect of motivation. We do not attempt simply to satisfy a need, or even a set of needs, in a straightforward "If I do this, then I will achieve that" manner. We work with a *chain* of goals and rewards, where goals in one area are only means of achieving goals in another area. Vroom has described his model in mathematical terms and in much greater detail than it is described here. It is a first step towards quantifying motivation. He has defined a number of variables that now await suitable means of measurement.

MONEY AS A MOTIVATOR

The old joke line goes, "Money isn't everything, but it's way ahead of whatever is in second place." Why, then, has it not been mentioned in any of the motivational theories so far? The common argument is that money is simply a means to an end, and that the end is satisfaction of some psychological need. The only problem with this explanation is that it does not state which needs money satisfies, when it satisfies them (or fails to), or how or why?

Money is used as a motivator for several reasons. First, it is easy to manipulate. It is far easier to design pay packages and monetary incentive systems than it is to decipher motivational patterns in the workforce. Second, many managers have a high need for achievement, and they perceive money as a convenient way of "keeping score." (For example, the high *n-ach* individual likes concrete feedback: the better you do, the more you receive.) Third, based on the assumption that money can be used to satisfy psychological needs in one way or another (it may make one more secure; it can be used for esteem and status; it may allow one to belong to certain groups; it is a measure of achievement) it seems far easier to pay people than to try to deal with each of these needs separately.

We mentioned earlier that motivation depends on how the individual perceives his environment. While we have been talking about needs, expectations, rewards, etc., we have failed to make note of the fact that what we are talking about is the *perceptions* of these things by the individuals involved. Money is confusing as a motivator because we (as the dispensers of the money) may perceive it as satisfying certain needs for the recipients, while they perceive it as performing quite a different function.

To use money as the main incentive in an organization is also to overlook, or ignore, the *situational* aspects of motivation. What should have become clear as we looked at each of the motivational models in this chapter is that different folks have different strokes. It should also be noted that certain jobs can only be done certain ways and that they contain specific motivational aspects, which are largely unchangeable. If a job requires affiliative behavior (where there must be a great deal of interaction between people in order to make decisions, avoid confusion, and coordinate activity) it makes little sense to motivate the people involved with individually oriented achievement rewards. All this does is encourage some individuals to violate group norms, and often group pressure is too powerful to allow this. The incentives, therefore, are useless. The question is not whether money is a useful motivator in this type of situation, but whether it is being used in such a way as to facilitate the *match between job motivational content and individuals' motivational needs*.

There has been a great deal written and said about money as a motivator. It seems to work for some people in some situations and not in others. While money may be used to satisfy various needs, Vroom's model points to a major difficulty. Simply because an individual would like to make more money to satisfy certain needs does *not* mean that his means of acquiring this money will coincide with achievement of organizational goals. McClelland (1967) illustrates this dilemma:

> People with relatively low achievement motivation . . . will work harder for increased financial rewards. It is not the task itself that interests them, however, nor does the money they get by doing it interest them primarily as a measure of accomplishment. Rather it has other values for them.
>
> Two consequences flow from this simple fact. First, if there is any way to get the reward without doing the work, they will naturally tend to look for it. This means that managers who rely primarily on money to activate people who are low in achievement motivation will have a much harder job of policing the work situation than they would if the work satisfied certain other motivational needs.

A discussion as to the motivational power of money tends to obscure the real issues. Money is a symbol, and as such can convey a myriad of meanings. Gellerman (1963) comments,

> . . . money derives its compelling power to motivate most people some of the time, and some people all of the time, from the fact that *it has no intrinsic meaning of its own*. It can therefore absorb whatever meaning people want to find in their lives.

So let us ignore money for the moment and concentrate on discovering what basic drives motivate individuals, and how they feel they can satisfy these drives through their jobs. Once we know this, we can attempt to design their jobs in such a manner that both the individual's goals and the organization's goals will be achieved through specific likely behavior. Match the job to the individual and the individual to the job. Increased productivity should result.

MOTIVATION AND PERFORMANCE: A LAST WORD

The musical *Damn Yankees* told us that to win, "You've gotta have heart. All you really need is heart." It is a pleasant thought, and much of the writing on motivation would tend to give the same impression. If you have highly motivated employees, high productivity will naturally follow. Unfortunately there is one other aspect of high performance: *ability*. You can have all the heart in the world, but if you have no ability to go with it, you are not going to win. It is one thing to want to be another Joe DiMaggio, Louis Armstrong, or John Steinbeck, but quite another to become one.

There is an interrelationship between motivation and ability. Clearly, wanting to do something very much will tend to increase the chances of being able to do it. The world is full of stories of people whose will and determination allowed them to overcome incredible obstacles on their path to fame or stardom. The Baltimore Colts' Raymond Berry was an example of someone who overcame some physical limitations to become a star receiver; Calvin Murphy puts the lie to the idea that only big men can be good basketball players; José Feliciano proves the same sort of thing. But lack of ability does put severe limitations on achievement.

On the other side of the coin, ability affects motivation. People who succeed at something tend to be motivated to repeat the behavior, and improve on the skill.

As far as motivation in an organizational context is concerned, however, the clear inference for management is that it is of little use trying to motivate employees to perform well if they have not got the necessary abilities or training. Motivational effort and motivational dollars should be carefully placed where they are likely to produce the highest results. Motivate the employees with ability. Train those who are lacking it.

SOME COMMENTS ON HOVEY AND BEARD (PART 2)

In Hovey and Beard, management expected that the installation of a group bonus would motivate the girls on the line to develop a "team spirit." The main motivational factor, in management's eyes, was monetary. If the girls produced to expectations, they would be rewarded with bonuses.

Is the problem here that the job has just been designed poorly? Are the girls' complaints valid? Is the job messy (or messier than before)? Is it too hot? Does the line go by too fast? If these things are adjusted, will the problem be solved, and will production rise accordingly? Or is this problem centered on motivational issues? It is important to know. If the girls *cannot* do the job, then there is no sense in adding motivational factors. But if they *can*, but *will not* do the job as expected, the messiness, heat, speed and bonus calculation may have little effect on performance.

What is the issue here: lousy job design, inadequate skills of the girls, or poor motivation? Whatever the problem, here is what management did. Read Part 3 and decide whether things will now change.

THE HOVEY AND BEARD COMPANY PART 3

A consultant who was brought into this picture worked entirely with and through the foreman. After many conversations with him, the foreman felt that the first step should be to get the girls together for a general discussion of the working conditions. He took this step with some hesitation, but he took it on his own volition.

The first meeting, held immediately after the shift was over at four o'clock in the afternoon, was attended by all eight girls. They voiced the same complaints again: the hooks went by too fast, the job was too dirty, the room was hot and poorly ventilated. For some reason, it was this last item that they complained of most. The foreman promised to discuss the problem of ventilation and temperature with the engineers, and he scheduled a second meeting to report back to the girls. In the next few days the foreman had several talks with the engineers. They and the superintendent felt that this was really a trumped-up complaint, and that the expense of any effective corrective measure would be prohibitively high.

The foreman came to the second meeting with some apprehensions. The girls, however, did not seem to be much put out, perhaps because they had a proposal of their own to make. They felt that if several large fans were set up so as to circulate the air around their feet, they would be much more comfortable. After some discussion, the foreman agreed that the idea might be tried out. The foreman and the consultant discussed the question of the fans with the superintendent, and three large propeller-type fans were purchased.

HOVEY AND BEARD—FURTHER PREDICTIONS

In the light of the above data, and what you now know about organizational behavior, make the following predictions (revise your earlier ones) and note your reasons as fully as possible:

1 Production

Will the rate of production

a exceed

b equal

c fall short of

the levels predicted by the engineers?

2 **Job satisfaction**
Will the girls be

a highly satisfied

b have no feelings either way

c dissatisfied

with their jobs now?

3 **Attitude toward supervisors**
Will the girls' attitudes toward their foreman (and management in general) be

a favorable?

b neutral?

c unfavorable?

4 **Interaction concerning the job**
Will the girls

a talk together a lot about the job and the change?

b not mention the job or the change much?

Chapter Summary

1 Behavior is both directed to, and results from, unsatisfied needs.

2 There are a number of models of motivation, but none, to date, are comprehensive in presenting a complete picture of man's motivating needs.

3 Maslow's hierarchy of needs emphasizes that the degree to which a need remains unsatisfied determines, in large part, its potency: once it is satisfied, it is no longer a motivator.

4 The Maslow model implies some order of prepotency of needs, although this does not necessarily hold in every case. It is also important to recognize that more than one motivator may be at work at the same time.

5 Herzberg's two-factor theory argues that the only motivating forces that affect people in a working situation are to be found in the job itself. It is the intrinsic nature of the work which provides motivation in the form of such things as achievement, recognition, responsibility, advancement and the opportunity to grow and learn.

6 Herzberg argues that the conditions which surround the job—company policy and administration, working conditions, supervision, money, status, security, and interpersonal relations—act only to *prevent dissatisfaction*. If you fail to provide the hygienes you get dissatisfaction, but if you *do* provide them, the best that results is that you prevent dissatisfaction from occurring.

7 White's competence motive relates strongly to the development of a self-concept which sees the world as controllable, interesting and rewarding. The degree to which an individual exhibits the competence motive is determined largely by his experiences in life. If he has generally been able to master his environment, he will continue to rise to the challenge; but if life has mastered him, he will be less likely to be adventuresome, aggressive and dynamic.

8 Individuals who exhibit a high degree of the competence motive tend to be successful in jobs which require initiative, drive, innovation, and decision-making.

9 A powerful motivator for some people is the need for achievement (*n-ach*). High achievers exhibit the following characteristics:

- They like to be personally responsible for the outcomes of their actions;
- They set moderately high goals for themselves;
- They like a challenge;
- They like rapid and concrete feedback on their performance.

10 McClelland has also identified a need for affiliation (*n-affil*), and a need for power (*n-pow*). *N-affil* individuals reflect a need to belong and to be liked, value relationships over accomplishments, and prefer friendship over power. *N-pow* people reflect a need to control the behavior of others and to be able to direct the actions of others towards organizational ends. They are organizationally-oriented, they like to work hard, they are willing to sacrifice some of their own self-interest for the organizational good, and they believe that this type of behavior will, and should, be rewarded.

11 Vroom introduces the concept of second level rewards and goals. He maintains that behavior in organizations is not primarily directed to task goals *per se*. The individual only attempts to achieve a task goal if he perceives that by achieving it he will achieve his "real goal."

The conclusion is that if we want to motivate people to work towards achieving specific *task* goals, we must make it clear to them that by doing so they will achieve their other, more basic goals. In other words, getting the job done must lead to the provision of something which satisfies the individual's basic needs, whatever they may be at the time.

12 Money is a complicated motivator, largely because it can stand for so many basic factors—achievement, esteem, status, recognition, secu-

rity, affiliation, power, and so on. In using money as a motivator, one should consider what needs it satisfies for the individuals concerned, and what needs it does *not* satisfy.

13 Motivation has a strong situational dimension. Jobs, if we are to agree with Herzberg, contain certain motivational factors. People have certain motivational needs. All people are different in their needs, and there are many types of jobs available. Motivation of employees results from matching their unsatisfied needs with the need-satisfiers of the job.

14 Individuals require certain skills, knowledge and abilities to perform various jobs. Unless they have the basic ability to perform their jobs, no amount of so-called motivation is going to improve their performance. Motivate the employees with ability and train those who lack it.

Part 3

The Work Group System

6

The Group: The Key Organizational Subsystem

OBJECTIVES

When you have completed this chapter you should:

- recognize that behavior in organizational settings is almost always a product of a group situation;
- understand the relationship between Interactions, Activities, and Sentiments in the understanding and explanation of behavior;
- know what a primary work group is, and what criteria define it;
- be aware of the basic characteristics of primary work groups;
- recognize the effects of factors outside the work environment, such as the surrounding culture and our basic biological inheritance, on the behavior of individuals in work group settings.

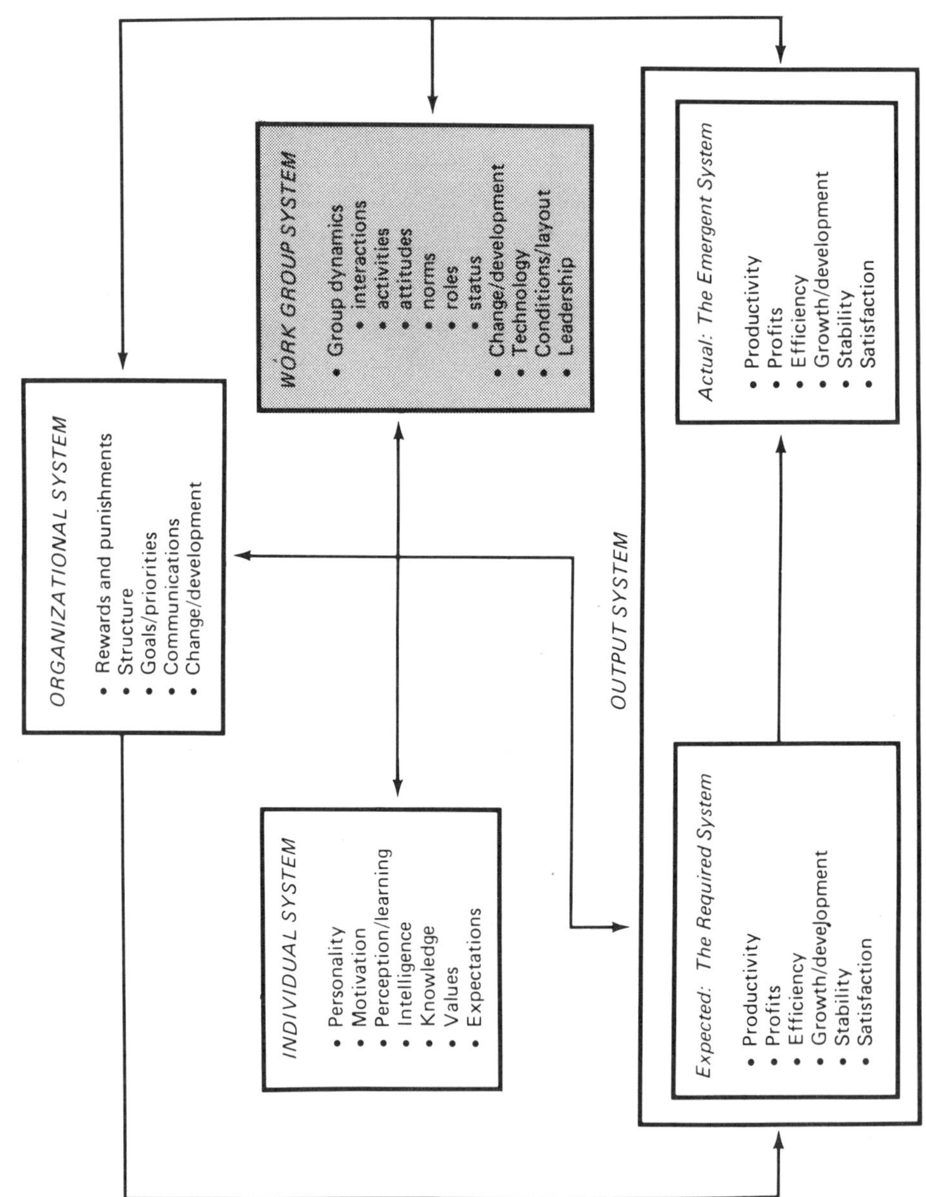
ORGANIZATIONAL SYSTEM
• Rewards and punishments
• Structure
• Goals/priorities
• Communications
• Change/development
WORK GROUP SYSTEM
• Group dynamics
• interactions
• activities
• attitudes
• norms
• roles
• status
• Change/development
• Technology
• Conditions/layout
• Leadership
INDIVIDUAL SYSTEM
• Personality
• Motivation
• Perception/learning
• Intelligence
• Knowledge
• Values
• Expectations
OUTPUT SYSTEM
Expected: The Required System
• Productivity
• Profits
• Efficiency
• Growth/development
• Stability
• Satisfaction
Actual: The Emergent System
• Productivity
• Profits
• Efficiency
• Growth/development
• Stability
• Satisfaction

"Every man is in certain respects
a. like all other men
b. like some other men
c. like no other man."

—Kluckhohn and Murray

BEFORE YOU BEGIN THIS CHAPTER

Before you begin this chapter, read Part 2 of the Daniels Computer Company case and check your earlier predictions as to the behavior of the individuals involved. As we can see from Part 2, the sections of the project group became competitive rather than cooperative, production began to fall behind schedule and enthusiasm for the project decreased. Could you have predicted these things if you had known more about motivation, or the self-concept, or perception?

As you read through this chapter, consider Daniels Computer Company and see if any of the concepts presented help to explain the behavior in the situation. Do they help in predicting the behavior of the people involved?

Keep Hovey and Beard in mind, too. On the basis of the information presented in this chapter on behavior in a group setting, and the characteristics of groups, would you change any of the predictions you made at the end of the last chapter? Do you think the installation of the fans made any difference? What happened?

DANIELS COMPUTER COMPANY PART 2

In late August, 1962, the project engineers of the four special groups met for the first time to explore the technical prerequisites each had discovered. The goal of the meeting was to establish parameters for each group's subsequent design effort. It quickly became apparent that each group had discovered concept limitations within its own area which were considered by that group to be controlling. Inevitably, the position of any one group required considerable extra work by one or more of the others. The meeting concluded without compromise of original positions.

In the ensuing weeks all four groups worked desperately to complete certain design segments before complementary segments were completed in other groups. Haste was believed necessary so that the tardy group would have to reformulate its designs, basing them upon that which was already completed. Development of the new memory proceeded in this fashion until the project engineer of the slowest group proved experimentally and theoretically that several designs completed by other groups imposed technologically impossible conditions upon his area of design. A number of personal frictions developed between the groups at this time, with aspersions cast concerning the competence of out-group members. Even department members not formally involved in the special project became involved, siding with their section mates. Enthusiasm for the project on the part of group members waned.

"EVERY MAN IS IN CERTAIN RESPECTS LIKE ALL OTHER MEN"

Desmond Morris (1967), in his book *The Naked Ape*, makes the unsettling point that man's biological heritage is very strong and that we have tended to ignore it (or repress it) in favor of a model of man as a sophisticated, flexible, intelligent being in full control of his destiny, behavior and direction. Morris maintains that,

> We are, despite all our great technological advances, still very much a simple biological phenomenon. Despite our grandiose ideas and our lofty self-conceits, we are still humble animals, subject to all the basic laws of animal behavior.

This is not a cry from the wilderness on the part of one isolated writer. The so-called New Biology hammers home the point strongly that we are very much creatures of our biological past. Konrad Lorenz (1963) asserts that all humans have an aggressive drive that must be discharged in some fashion or other. He makes the point that lower order animals possess inhibitory mechanisms which tend to prevent violence within species. It is rare for a lion or wolf to kill one of their kind; their "fights" tend to be concerned with territory, dominance in the pack, and possession, but usually end with one or the other acknowledging defeat and backing off. The defeated animal is not normally pursued and killed; the winner's behavior is governed by a set of inhibitory mechanisms which prevent further violence. Man, says Lorenz, because of a series of technological advances and because of such things as overcrowding, which increases the propensity to aggressive behavior, is far less affected by these mechanisms. The technology of violence is such that we are "separated" from the object of the aggression, either physically or psychologically, and therefore we fail to respond to the cues that would normally prevent harmful behavior. "The distance at which all shooting weapons take effect screens the killer against the stimulus situation which would otherwise activate his killing inhibitions" (Lorenz, 1963).

The point is that man has a very strong biological heritage; much of our behavior is based on genetic makeup and deeply rooted instinctual patterns. However, we have advanced so rapidly technologically, intellectually and culturally that most of these instincts have been covered over and ignored. The New Biologists would argue that man is indeed, "in certain respects, like all other men," but that we fail to recognize it (and that we will pay dearly for this failure).

This book cannot pursue the biological roots of behavior. To begin with, the debate in the field is hot and heavy. People like Lorenz, Morris, Tiger and Ardrey are accused of overstating the case, of making sweeping generalizations about human behavior from observations of animal behavior, and (although not often stated this way) of denigrating man's superior status among the order of animals. We are somewhat reluctant to be called "naked apes," and we do not want to be reminded of our humble past and our basic "animal" natures. While the author is not unwilling to admit to either of these things, the second, and major, reason for not pursuing the topic further is that the data in the field are unclear. We do not know the degree to which behavior is inherited or learned. We *do* know that it is both; it is the percentage of each that is up for grabs.

"EVERY MAN IS IN CERTAIN RESPECTS LIKE SOME OTHER MEN"

Of the three aspects of behavioral commonality pointed out by Kluckhohn and Murray, it is this second one that we will deal with in this and the following chapter. We have said that we are backing away from arguments centered around the statement that we are all alike in some respects, and we have just finished dealing with the concept of individuality (that man is like no other man) in the past few chapters.

But before we begin to examine the behavior of people as it is modified in groups, we should briefly look at a basic factor affecting our values, attitudes and beliefs: our culture. We could add another box to our systems model of organizational behavior. It might be labelled "The Cultural System." (Figure 6-1.)

Largely because of our ability to conceptualize and communicate, we transmit learned patterns of behavior to one another. That is, we pass on what we have experienced, what we believe, what we value, what we dislike, and what we wish to maintain or change. The cumulative effect of this transmission of learned behavior is *culture*. By culture we do not mean a liking for art, theater and classical music. Culture may be defined as "the integrated system of learned behavior patterns characteristic of the members of a society which are not the result of biological inheritance" (Hoebel, 1954). The way people behave is, to some extent, determined by the culture in which they have developed. Ross Webber (1969) describes culture this way:

> We are immersed in a sea. It is warm, comfortable, supportive, and protecting. Most of us float below the surface; some bob about, catching glimpses of land from time to time; a few emerge from the water entirely. The sea is our culture.

Travellers to foreign countries often experience what is termed "culture shock." That is, they are unable to accept the local customs as reasonable or rational. They

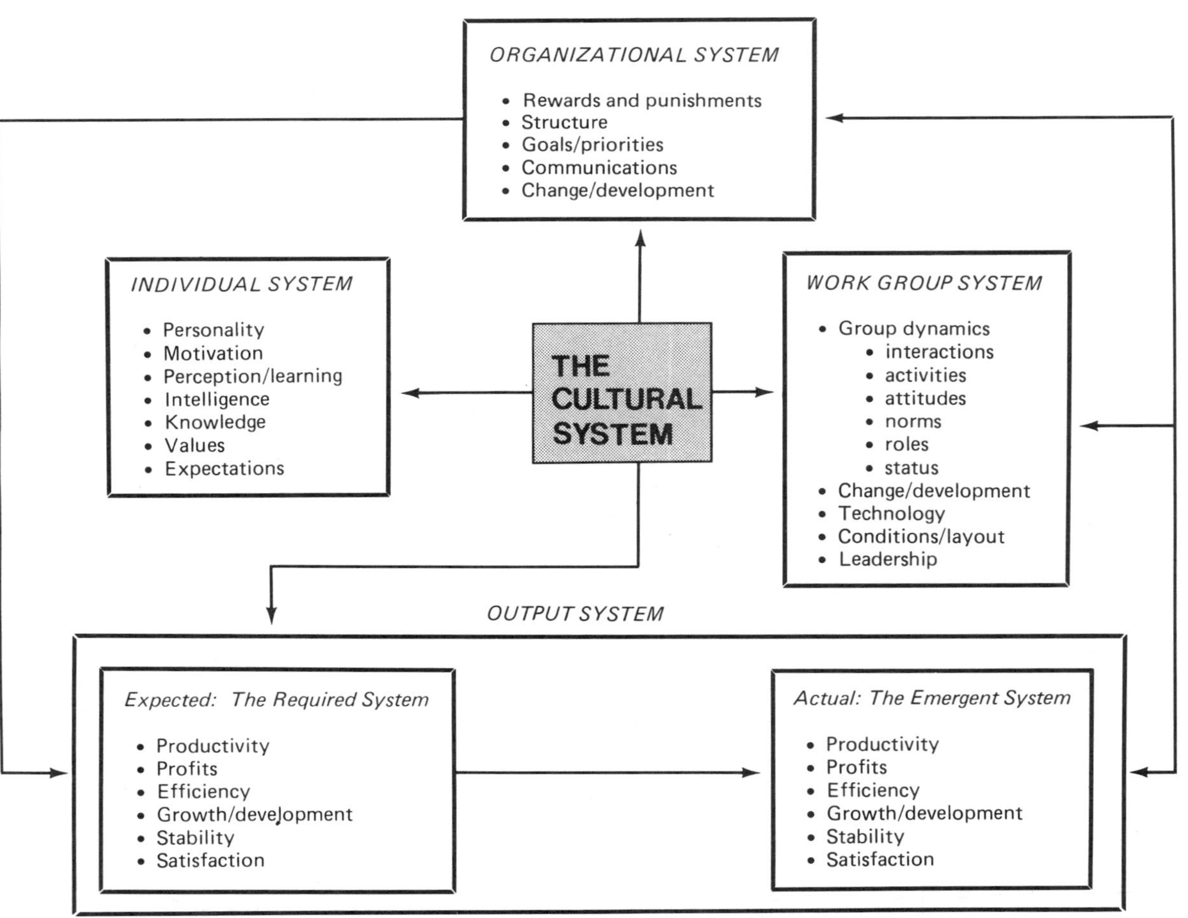

FIGURE 6-1: A SYSTEMS MODEL OF ORGANIZATIONAL BEHAVIOR.

think things are stupid, odd, unsanitary, barbaric, or whatever. These are the people who "float below the surface," in Webber's terms. They assume that what is done in their culture (having not experienced anything else) is "right" and that other means of behaving must therefore be in some fashion "wrong."

We are all products of our environments. We assimilate our values, attitudes and beliefs from people around us. If society values competitiveness, we are likely to value competitiveness. If our society abhors violence, we abhor violence. An anthropologist (American), living and travelling with a band of nomadic Eskimos in the high Arctic, once intervened when a trader "ripped off" the band. The anthropologist got very angry and shouted at the trader and threatened him. What she did not know was that the band abhorred violence or any display of anger. For weeks after that, each night they built her her own snow house, gave her food, *and left her completely alone*, never speaking to her once. She was only able to repair the damage of her actions some time later when a missionary interceded with the band on her behalf and explained that "she did not understand how to behave."

In specific behavioral terms, our culture influences what human needs are emphasized and what behavior is approved or disapproved. Culture influences our motivations, our basic attitudes and values, and our perceptions. Individuals from a culture therefore tend to act alike in many ways. The Japanese culture values the family unit and builds organizations on this basis. There is an emphasis on security and the maintenance of a "contract" between organization and individual for life.

There are cultural stereotypes for people of many different nationalities. Clearly these stereotypes do not apply to *all* members of the nation concerned, but they tend to reflect some of their basic values. For instance, Englishmen tend to value privacy (take a walk through any English town or village and see the fences erected around every backyard, as opposed to the more open gardens and lawns of North America); Egyptians like to express emotion (watch a political rally, a funeral, or even the trading in a market in Cairo to see the animated gestures, the strength of the facial gestures and the pitch of the voices); Irishmen tend to value social interaction (it is probably easier to engage in a conversation with the locals in an Irish country pub than anywhere in the world); German society reflects orderliness and precision (the German countryside demonstrates this admirably); the Swiss are generally neat and law-abiding (there is little or no litter in Switzerland, little or no pollution, and a very low crime rate. Switzerland is one of the few places in the world where people actually obey the "Do not walk on the grass" signs.)

While not all Englishmen, Egyptians, Irishmen, Germans or Swiss have the characteristics ascribed to them in their national stereotypes, these behaviors manifest themselves frequently enough in their cultures to illustrate the point that we should be aware of another box in our model which affects the behavior of people in organizations. The cultural dimension tends to be overlooked because we are usually "bobbing about under the sea," as Webber puts it.

But international organizations are very aware that managers and workers in different cultures behave differently.

Our culture is North America. While there are regional differences in North America, we essentially share the same cultural values. Despite the agonized cries of Canadians that they are "different," they are far more similar to, than different from, their American cousins. And within both Canada and the United States, differences between the values and beliefs of people in one geographical area are far smaller than their overwhelming similarities.

We are not going to go into the differences in behavior brought about by specific cultural differences. But you should be aware that people from different cultures perceive the world through different "screens." Therefore they are motivated differently and may behave differently when presented with certain situations. If you wish to understand the behavior of people in organizations, then you must be sensitive to these differences. They will tend to be reinforced when all members of a small work group come from the same culture.

THE WORK GROUP SYSTEM

Bearing in mind that a cultural system affects our entire model, let us focus on the work group. We made the remark earlier that *behavior in organizations rarely occurs in an isolated individualistic setting; it is almost always a product of a group situation*. That is, a person's behavior is usually a result of some interaction with another person or persons. In the final analysis, as we have seen, much of what we term "personality" is developed as a result of these interactions with others. The point was made by John Donne in the seventeenth century that "No man is an island, entire of itself." While there is really no such thing as "group behavior" (it is *individuals* in the group that do things), the group exerts considerable force on how each of its members acts. Individuals behave differently as a result of being a part of a group.

INTERACTION, ACTIVITY, SENTIMENT (I-A-S)

The behavior of individuals in groups can be thought of in terms of three aspects—interaction (I), activity (A), and sentiment (S). Much of the behavior in a group setting may be explained by examining the interrelationships of these three variables.

Interaction "refers to any interpersonal contact in which one individual can be observed acting, and one or more other individuals responding to his action. . . . Interaction can take place when no words are spoken, as, for example, one man makes a hand signal to another man . . . and that other man is observed to respond in some way."

Activities are "simply the things that man does at work and at play."

Sentiments "refer to the mental and emotional reactions we have to people and physical objects."

Sentiments have three elements:

1. An idea about something or somebody;
2. Emotional content;

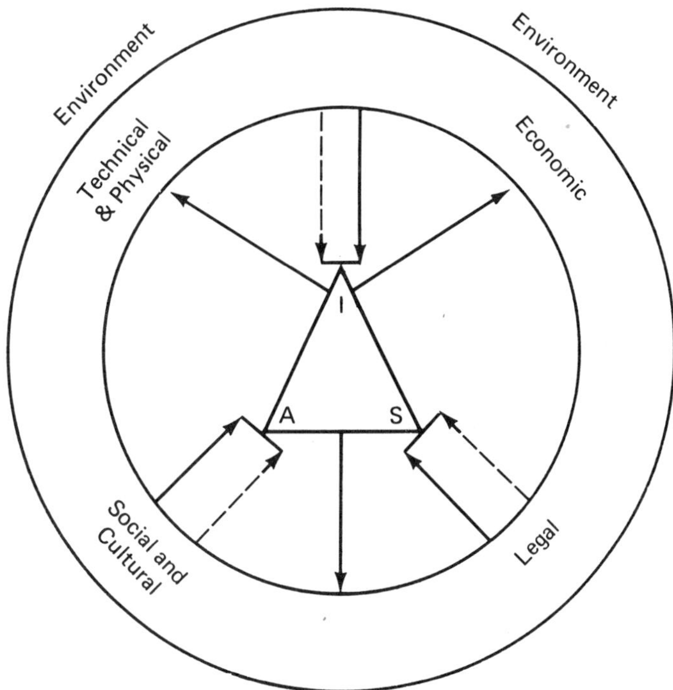

FIGURE 6-2: INTERACTIONS, ACTIVITIES, AND SENTIMENTS AND THEIR RELATIONSHIP WITH THE ENVIRONMENT. (*FROM:* W.H. WHYTE, "AN INTERACTION APPROACH TO THE THEORY OF ORGANIZATION," IN *MODERN ORGANIZATION THEORY*, MASON HAIRE (ED.). NEW YORK: WILEY, 1959.)

3 A tendency to recur when the individual is presented with the same symbols that have been associated with the particular sentiment in the past.

They manifest themselves through changes in:

- Self-concept (How do I see myself?);
- Evaluation of activities (Are they good or bad?);
- Personal identification (Who are my friends, and who are my enemies—i.e., Whom do I identify with?)
- Ranking (How do I rank the relative prestige of everyone around me, including myself?)

Interactions, activities and sentiments are *interdependent*. That is, a change in any one brings about a change in the other two, which in turn brings about a change in the first variable. This system is represented in Figure 6-3. The two-way arrows indicate that each of the variables affects the other variables, and is affected *by* them.

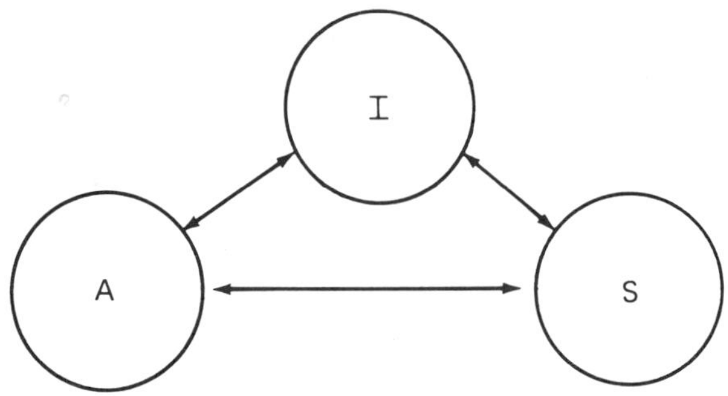

FIGURE 6-3: INTERACTIONS, SENTIMENTS AND ACTIVITIES ARE MUTUALLY INTERDEPENDENT.

To illustrate this relationship, let's look at an example. A nurse in a hospital has, as one of her activities, to administer medication to various patients as prescribed by the doctors. The nurse reads the prescription on the patient's chart and then administers the drug. If she happens to notice that a patient who has regularly been receiving a particular medication has no note of this on his chart for the day, she may get in touch with the doctor to check whether this is an oversight, or whether he intended to stop giving the drug to the patient. The interaction with the doctor may be a positive one, that is, he thanks the nurse for having brought this to his attention, and either assures her that it was his intention to omit the drug or, perhaps, that it was indeed an oversight, and would she remedy it. In such an interaction, her sentiments will be affected in one direction. If, on the other hand, the doctor makes some kind of remark as, "Just do what the chart says and don't bother me with stupid questions," the nurse is likely to have quite different sentiments.

In this latter case, for instance, where the sentiments are negative, the *activity* pattern of the nurse may be seen to change. Next time she may not call to check what she suspects is a mistake, for fear of being "told off." Her *interaction* pattern with the doctor may also change. She may not pass on observations to him or say things to him that might elicit the type of response she received earlier. If the interactions between the nurse and doctor continue to take the form of his speaking to her harshly for what she sees as no good reason, she may request a transfer from the ward (activity), or see the Head Nurse (activity) about things, or tell the doctor where to get off (activity and interaction).

A change in interactions, in activities, or in sentiments brings about a series of changes in the system. Therefore, if we can note some change in *one* of these variables, we may be able to predict changes elsewhere.

In the nurse example, the first change took place in an *activity*; she called the doctor to find out whether there had been a mistake. As a result, some interaction took place, and sentiments were affected. This in turn affected subsequent activities, interactions and sentiments.

Let's take a look at how an initial change in *interaction patterns* may affect behavior. The following incident illustrates the process.

Manager "A" spent a fairly large proportion of his time talking with his subordinates, either in groups or individually. Observation of these conversations showed that the subordinates did most of the talking. Much of the time they told Manager "A" about problems they were experiencing, made suggestions as to how these problems might be solved, and discussed the various alternatives with him. The subordinates, in fact, initiated many of the conversations.

When Manager "A" was moved to another job, he was succeeded by Manager "B." Manager "B" liked to make decisions himself. His interactions with his subordinates took the form of asking them what problems they were experiencing, and then telling them how they could handle them. He also made it a point to identify problems and point them out to the subordinates, once again suggesting means for their resolution. Observation of the interactions with Manager "B" showed that he initiated most of the conversations and did most of the talking; the subordinates mainly responded to his questions and orders.

Under Manager "A," subordinates felt they made a contribution to the running of the departments. They saw themselves as being important (self-concept); they felt their decisions were generally good as a result of their discussions with their superior (evaluation of activities); they felt warmly towards their manager (identification); and they felt themselves to be valuable members of the group (ranking).

Under Manager "B," subordinates saw themselves as being of little value in running the department (ranking/self-concept), saw their activities as being less effective than before (evaluation), and disliked the manager (identification). In other words, their pattern of *sentiments* changed dramatically as a result of the changed interaction patterns of the two managers. This change in sentiment showed up also in a change in activities. The subordinates no longer brought problems to the attention of the manager; rather, they attempted to conceal them. There was a conscious attempt to "avoid the boss, if you can." They tried to "keep their noses clean" and to keep to themselves, and they performed their duties "by the book" so that they could not be faulted as easily. Creativity disappeared from the department. Relationships became more formalized, and productivity declined. We can see from this example that by looking at interactions, activities and sentiments in a group, we may be able to explain and predict behavior to some degree.

WHAT IS A GROUP?

In the study of organizational behavior, we are concerned with what sociologists term a "primary" group, that is, a group which is made up of people in face-to-face relationships. "Secondary" groups, such as trade unions, professional societies, social clubs, and so on, have a wider membership which does not enter into overall face-to-face relationships. It is quite likely that a member of a golf club does not even know the *names* of 75 percent of the membership.

A group, as the word is used here, may be defined as *"a plurality of persons who interact with one another in a given context more than they interact with anyone else*'' (Sprott, 1958). Thus, in an organization, those people who either interact with one another more than anyone else because they *have* to, or because they *want* to in order to do their jobs, may be termed *work groups*.

An example of a work group is the crew of a fishing trawler. They work together to set and gather the trawls, and to clean and store the fish. These jobs can only be performed by groups of men working as a team. Unlike the individual fisherman working in his own dory, the technology of modern fishing is so complex that it requires specialized skills and a number of individuals, each doing their own part, to make the job successful. The behavior of a fishing crew on a modern trawler is likely to be quite different from that of a series of individual fishermen working by themselves. This is due to a number of reasons, among which is the fact that the crew gets paid a *group* bonus, depending on the catch, and if one man does not do his share of the work, others suffer in some way, either by having to do more work themselves, or receive less bonus. As a result, there are pressures which develop in the group, defining acceptable behavior for the members.

CHARACTERISTICS OF GROUPS

Primary (work) groups have a number of characteristics:

- interaction;
- common goals/purposes;
- norms (standards) of behavior;
- awareness of membership;
- limited size.

All primary groups possess these characteristics to some degree. As we shall see later, the differentiation between a primary or secondary group can be made only with reference to these criteria.

Interaction

Without any interaction between its members, a group could not exist. This interaction does not always have to be verbal. It can consist of non-verbal communications, pre-arranged behaviors, etc. A football team can operate successfully with little verbal communication, as can a fishing crew. Each member of the work team has an assigned role. Variations in the roles may be planned ahead of time (''if such and such happens, then do . . .'') or may be discussed within the group (''Fred, instead of doing . . ., try doing . . . and maybe we can be more effective'').

Sooner or later, however, a group must have a chance to get together and talk with one another. Without such an opportunity it will simply be a collection of individuals working on their own.

Common Goals

If a group is to last for any length of time, it must have a goal or purpose of some kind. In a working situation, a group may have as its purpose to earn a certain amount of bonus pay; to limit the amount of work that each of the members has to do; to solve some problem or set of problems; to accomplish a certain task; or simply, to survive. By definition, a group must have some purpose or else there would be no attraction for its members. This is not to say that the objectives of the individual members are identical to the objectives of the group, but, to some extent, each member must be in agreement with the overall group goals. Within a group, some individuals may have a desire to lead, to initiate actions and make suggestions, while others may wish simply to have the security that group membership brings. But though each individual has his own particular motives for remaining a member of a group, he must also conform to some of the standards, beliefs and behaviors of the group.

Norms

All groups develop some standards of behavior for their members. These are termed *norms*. Every member of the group must conform to certain norms, as part of his membership "payment." A little girls' "club" had the following rules: "Do not talk to boys; Always share your candy with others; Do not tell outsiders club secrets." Any member of the club found violating one of these rules was to be expelled. Is there a great deal of difference between this children's group and a group of workers on an assembly line who have an unwritten agreement to do the work of any of their members who wish to visit the bathroom briefly, to cover for anyone coming to work late, to work at a certain pace each day, or to keep improved methods of doing their work to themselves rather than talking about them to management?

Norms are simply the group members' accepted consensus of which behavior is appropriate and acceptable in certain situations. Group norms may include sharing lunch with the rest of the members, always taking the side of the underdog, drinking lots of beer, wearing a shirt and tie, and so on. Such things do not have to take the form of written "rules," but they may be enforced just as rigidly. In the famous Bank Wiring Room study at Hawthorne (see Appendix A), it was discovered that the workers limited their production to a certain level, that individual workers did not exceed this level, and that the financial incentives offered by the company to increase production had no effect. This group had set some norms for production. They decided on what they felt represented a fair day's work for a fair day's pay (for whatever reasons) and they maintained that level regardless of company efforts to get them to change.

In industrial settings, a common group norm is one that affects the level of production. The group decides to produce at a certain rate, and resists attempts by outside parties to influence that decision. Workers may limit production because they fear that if they work harder and produce more, management will revise their quotas upwards and demand more of them for the same amount of pay. They may set limits so as to enable various members to work less at times when they may not feel well, or may be tired. They may set limits in order to achieve some level of pay for all of the members. There are clearly many different reasons for a group to decide on acceptable levels of output.

Of course, not all people in a work situation are prepared to accept the norms of a group. There may, for instance, be an individual who feels that he or she needs extra money for certain reasons, and who is therefore prepared to produce at a higher level than that tacitly agreed to by the rest of the group. By violating the group's norms, of course, he places it in jeopardy, and therefore the members will attempt to get him to conform. The *deviant* individual may be approached by members of the group who try to reason with him. If this fails, he may be subject to threats or even violence. If he continues to ignore the group's norms he will be ostracized. In other words, the group will try to make his life on the job as uncomfortable as they know how, and one of the most uncomfortable situations for many people is to have affection and esteem withdrawn. Those individuals who are not affected by this sort of treatment may continue to operate on thir own, outside of the group. They are termed *isolates*, in sociological jargon.

Awareness of Membership

Members of a primary group are conscious of their membership. They are aware that they belong to the group, and they are also aware of who the other members are. This latter characteristic, of course, does not hold for the larger, secondary group, where a member is unlikely to know who else belongs, beyond his immediate circle of acquaintances. There is therefore less feeling of "belonging" to an organization as a whole than there is to a particular group within the organization. A sense of belonging is often signalled by the feeling of "we" in a group: "We try to maintain quality standards"; "We think that . . .;" and so on.

Membership awareness is indicated, and often supported, by the development and use of special language, dress, habits and customs. A clear sign of group cohesion is the development of some sort of unique vocabulary. The group begins to use terms which have special meanings for it. An example of this type of language is provided by a group of security traders in a large investment firm we know of. The group is composed of ten young men, all between the ages of 24 and 30. They work together in one large room and socialize with one another off the job. Their incomes vary widely, and their job specialties are marked. Each one, however, considers himself, and is considered by his fellow group members, to be an expert in his own particular area. They speak to one another in a jargon of their own, quite unfamiliar to outsiders. For example, one might say, "I've got a size deal here. Arnold has been taking a bath and I'm taking him out. That's firm." In translation, that means, "I have just completed a large transaction. Arnold (a nickname for another firm) has been suffering a large loss, and I am buying all his holding of X securities. The deal has been confirmed by both parties."

Modes of dress also signify membership in a group. That, in part, explains why some large organizations such as the armed forces have a uniform for their members. It also explains why social groups adopt certain types of dress. Street corner gangs wear the gang jacket; fraternities wear rings. Both indicate membership in the group. It has been argued that not requiring nuns to wear the habit will make it harder for them to maintain their roles as nuns in an open society. Formerly, the "Uniform," bolstered by the company of other nuns, made it easier for women in the Orders to maintain their roles. They felt a clearer sense of membership in the Order as a result of these reinforcing devices.

Certain customs also develop in groups. These may take the form of traditions, or may simply be types of behavior that operate less formally. Norms of sharing, mutual protection, respect for privacy, horseplay, etc., are all of this type. Each of these things indicates that individuals within the group are aware of their own membership and the membership of others. In a group where horseplay between members is an accepted form of behavior, outsiders are rarely involved; everyone knows who to "get" and who to leave alone.

Size

How many people make up a group? Do two people constitute a group? How about three, or twenty? There is clearly no hard and fast size for a group. However, for purposes of working together and combining activities to meet commonly agreed upon goals, ten members appears to be about the limit. Problem-solving groups, that is groups involved with the completion of some specific set of tasks, or the resolution of certain problems, tend to operate best with between five and nine members. If the group begins with more than that number, it tends to split up into smaller groups after a while. This may be largely a function of communications. Twenty people cannot interact well with one another; it simply takes too long for everyone to have his say, and the task of getting consensus to decisions is very difficult. Seven people discussing a problem however, can all make inputs, can all listen to one another, and can come to some sort of agreement among themselves much more easily.

While it is difficult to make clear statements concerning the *ideal* size of a problem-solving group, there are a number of research studies which shed light on the issue. Gibb (1951) compared groups of different sizes up to a membership of 96, each discussing a problem for half an hour, and found that the larger the group, the more inhibited individual members tend to feel. Also productivity decreases as group size increases. It appears that as the size of a problem-solving group increases, more people are forced into silence. Since other research on problem-solving groups shows that when the matters discussed are concerned with actual facts, rather than just opinions, the more potential contributors and critics the better, we can see the negative effects of size on groups. The size of the group may keep people with good contributions quiet, but the bore, by definition, is rarely discouraged from babbling on.

DANIELS COMPUTER COMPANY RECONSIDERED

To begin with, the project group set up to handle the design of the new memory was subdivided into four subgroups, one from each section. We know that the sections, prior to the new project, were used to working essentially by themselves and then passing their finished product on to the next section for further work. No friction that we know of occurred under this system. When the new project began, however, instead of reinforcing the idea of one project group that was department-wide, the memory department manager left the subsections alone to work on their own segments of the new design. They did this for a period in excess of a month.

There do not seem to be any strong pressures for these people to get together to form a unified group. We know, for instance, that it is difficult to keep groups above nine or so people together as a single unit. We also know that groups are defined by membership which interact face-to-face with some degree of consistency. If the sections remain within their old geographic confines (Part 1), then the likelihood of this sort of interaction is lessened. We might, therefore, suspect that they will *not* coalesce as one unit.

We know that primary work groups have a common goal or purpose. While the project group as a whole has the common goal of designing the new memory, each *sectional* group has a goal of completing its portion only. The factor which will decide cohesiveness or competitiveness between sections is which of these goals is seen as more important. In this case the sections chose their own goals as being more important (not an unusual phenomenon—we tend to look out for ourselves first).

The interaction between groups was probably limited by the geographic separation and the goal definition of each group. As the interaction was limited, positive sentiments had less chance to form (if you do not interact much with someone, you tend not to form strong opinions or feelings about them one way or another). This was reinforced by the activity pattern. Activity took place primarily *within* sections, therefore, there was less interaction, and a lower degree of positive sentiment.

When the groups finally got together in late August and things were seen not to be working out as hoped, they indulged in defensive behavior in order to protect themselves from the negative feedback concerning their performance. They each rationalized themselves as right, and the others as at fault.

They then went back to work separately *for another month*. From what we know about what had gone on before and about groups in general, we could predict that they would dig in even more, and become even more competitive. Now the goal became "beat the others before they beat us." When finally the slowest group managed to show that they had been given an impossible job technologically, the cat was among the pigeons, because it was fairly clear that *everyone* was at fault. In order to screen out that data, sections closed ranks even more, became more defensive, and indulged in further defense mechanisms such as aggression (casting aspersions on people from other sections) and avoidance (just staying clear of "outsiders''). So what are we to do now? We still have to get the new memory designed by a certain time, but the sectional subgroups will not get together and cooperate. Instead they have tightened their boundaries, and the negative sentiments, interactions and activities between them have driven them even further apart than before they started the project.

Does what we know about primary work groups help us with a solution? Do we know what we *want* to change, or *have* to change, in order to get these people working together? *How* we do it is a question we will address later in the book. For now it is sufficient to see *what* has to be changed. What are the critical entry points into this system? What variables have to be altered? What processes have to be changed?

Take a moment to go over the case, and these comments, and make a list of the things that will have to be changed in order to make the system work as it is supposed to. You might want to consider Hovey and Beard in the light of this chapter as well. We will not comment on it now, but will get back to it in the next chapter.

Chapter Summary

1 We have a biological heritage that evidences itself in certain inherited behavior. It is not clear the extent to which behavior is learned or inherited, but it would appear to be a combination of both.

2 Behavior of individuals, as we observe it in a work situation, is also influenced by the culture of the people involved. We are all, to some extent, products of our environment.

3 The major influence on behavior in the workplace is the small work group. An individual's behavior is usually a result of some interaction with another person or persons.

4 One method of looking at the behavior of people in groups is to examine the interrelationships between their Interactions, Activities and Sentiments (I-A-S). Patterns in each of these variables affect the manifested behavior in the other two. They operate as a *system*.

5 When we talk about a "group" we are referring to a primary work group, that is, a group made up of people who interact on the basis of face-to-face relationships.

6 Primary work groups have a number of common characteristics:

   a There is interaction among all the members, on a face-to-face basis (this may not necessarily be verbal).

   b They have a goal or purpose that is generally shared by all the members.

c They develop norms of behavior—rules (which are generally unwritten) to which the members are expected to conform. Norms are the group members' accepted consensus of which behavior is appropriate and acceptable in certain situations. Members who violate the norms are termed *deviates*, and those members who consistently refuse to conform, and who are subsequently expelled from the group, are termed *isolates*.

d Members are all aware of who "belongs" and who does not. Membership is often reinforced by dress, habits or symbols.

e The size of a primary work group lies somewhere between three and a dozen or so people. Highly interactive groups, which require input from all members to solve problems, tend to work best with from five to nine members. Larger groups tend to split into subgroups after a time.

7

Basic Forces That Shape Group Behavior

OBJECTIVES

When you have completed this chapter you should:

- understand the basic forces that promote group cohesiveness and conformity to group norms;
- recognize those forces that foster non-conformity among group members;
- have a better understanding of how the I-A-S model can be applied to explain behavior in work groups;
- understand the concept of behavioral exchange;
- understand the concepts of social comparison and control and how they affect the behavior of individuals in an organizational setting.

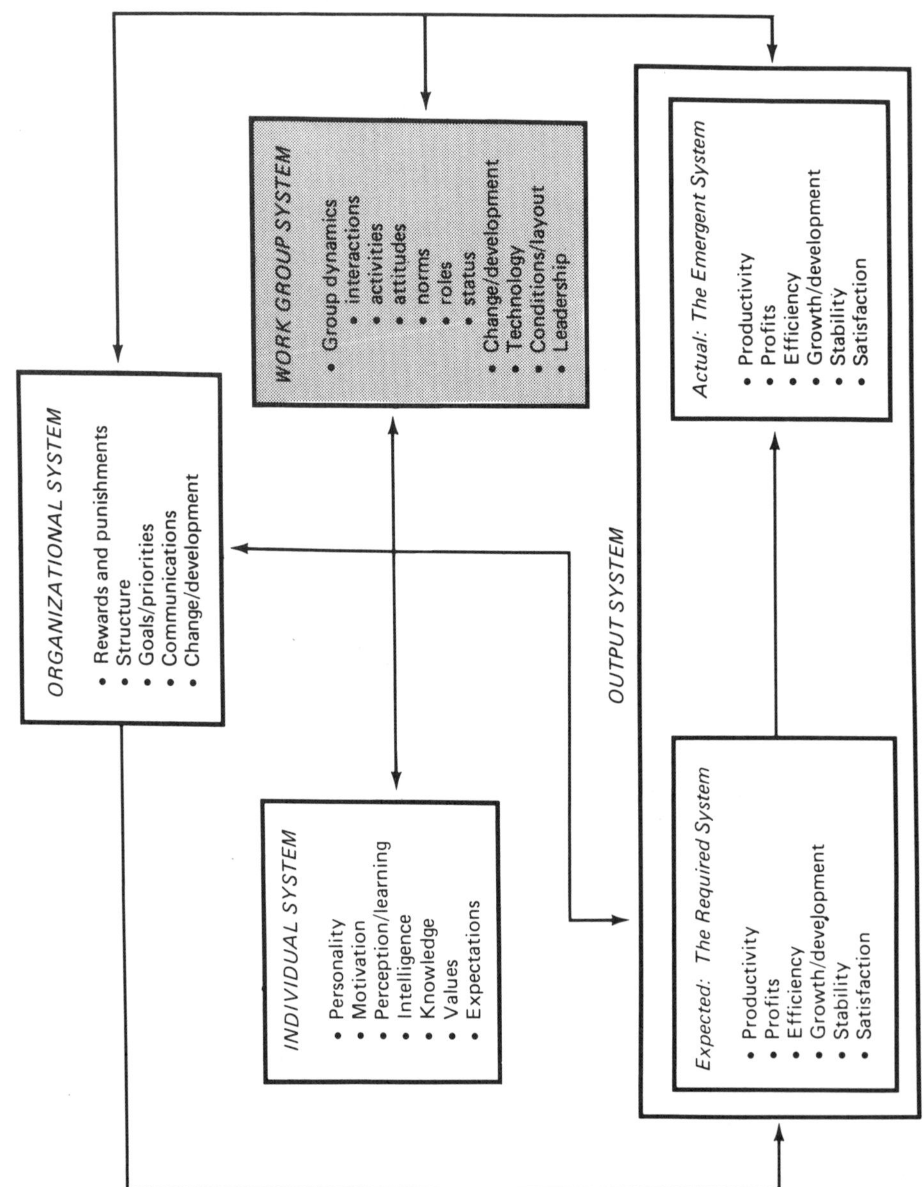
ORGANIZATIONAL SYSTEM
• Rewards and punishments
• Structure
• Goals/priorities
• Communications
• Change/development
WORK GROUP SYSTEM
• Group dynamics
• interactions
• activities
• attitudes
• norms
• roles
• status
• Change/development
• Technology
• Conditions/layout
• Leadership
INDIVIDUAL SYSTEM
• Personality
• Motivation
• Perception/learning
• Intelligence
• Knowledge
• Values
• Expectations
OUTPUT SYSTEM
Expected: The Required System
• Productivity
• Profits
• Efficiency
• Growth/development
• Stability
• Satisfaction
Actual: The Emergent System
• Productivity
• Profits
• Efficiency
• Growth/development
• Stability
• Satisfaction

In the last chapter we looked at some of the characteristics of groups. We also had a brief glimpse at some of the behavior that takes place in groups, such as the setting of norms. It is now time that we looked at *why* individuals in groups behave as they do, and what sort of behavior we may expect from work groups. There are a number of forces at work in group settings which bring about certain behavior. These are internal to the group itself, and concern such things as the interrelationships between the members, the roles they play, their relative status, the type of leadership available, and communication patterns.

A group may be thought of as a network of relationships. Each individual in the group feels some pressure from the other members to behave in a certain manner, and at the same time, he exerts various pressures on his fellow members' behavior. This interplay results in each member taking a specific role and determines the degree to which members either support or attack the values and goals of the group.

Figure 7-1 shows a group composed of four members, A, B, C, and D. The lines between each of the members, and the lines extending beyond the encompassing circle, represent one dimension of the relationships between these four people and other people and groups: *attraction* and *repulsion*. The large circle represents

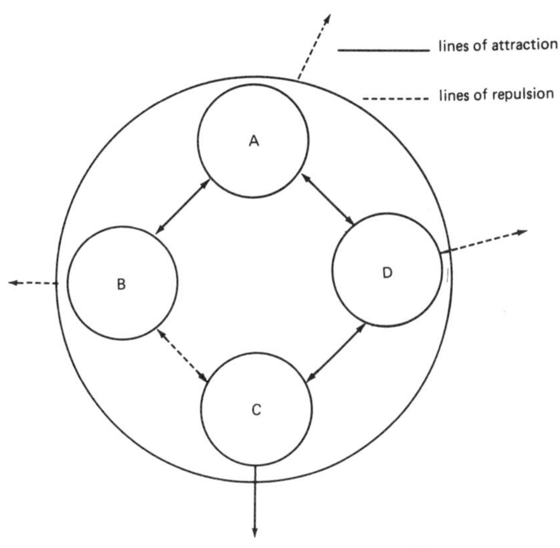

FIGURE 7-1: LINES OF FORCE IN A GROUP. (FROM: JOE KELLY, *ORGANIZATIONAL BEHAVIOR, REV. ED.*, HOMEWOOD, ILLINOIS, 1974.)

the *boundary* of the group, as it is perceived by the members. Remember that members of a small group have a clear perception of who belongs and who doesn't, and that they have a feeling of group identity (the "we" feeling). These feelings define some sort of boundary for the group. Those within the boundary are "in," and others are outsiders. As Kelly's diagram illustrates, this boundary is largely a result of the attraction of individuals for one another and the lack of attraction for "outsiders"; people wish to belong to some groups and not to belong to others.

Members A, B and D all show negative feelings towards other groups around them. Member C is attracted by some outside group, and at the same time, he and B show negative feelings for one another. On the basis of these sorts of relationships we might be able to predict that member C will eventually leave the group and that A, B and D will be drawn closer together to form a more *cohesive* group.

However, Kelly's diagram does not explain *why* each of these individuals feels either attracted or repelled by other individuals or groups. It is helpful to know that these relationships exist, but it would be even more useful if we could explain why they arose in the first place and how to predict their occurrence. One means at our disposal for such an analysis is the Interaction-Activity-Sentiment (I-A-S) model we saw in Chapter 6.

INTERACTION ANALYSIS

Relationships between individuals and groups can be described and explained by an analysis of interactions, activities and sentiments. For instance, if the same four group members, A, B, C and D, worked on a moving assembly line in the following order,

C ———→ B ———→ A ———→ D

and we noticed the following activities, we might be better able to predict the relationships and behavior of the group:

1 *C is the initial man on the line. He takes components from a set of bins near his position, assembles them in a specific order and then passes them down the line to B for subsequent additions. C works very quickly and sends assembled units to B faster than the latter can handle them. As a result, B has an increasing stack of units waiting for him. When his stack gets to a certain level, C stops work for ten or fifteen minutes and smokes a cigarette while B catches up. As soon as it appears that B is about to get to the end of the stack, C begins work again. Thus B does not get the opportunity to have a cigarette break as C has done.*

2 *From time to time the foreman comes around and exhorts B to work faster. Between these visits, when B is getting quite far behind, A will move up the line to help him reduce the backlog.*

3 *D works at the end of the line, packaging finished units. He is a fast worker and rarely has a backlog of work at his position. Whenever, C, B, or A want to visit the washroom or make a telephone call, D will fill in for them on the line.*

4 *B and A usually have lunch together and drive back and forth to work in one car. They are occasionally joined by D for a drink after work. C, on the other hand, is a keen card player and spends his lunch time playing euchre with three men from an adjoining department. He and D are members of the plant bowling team.*

Having observed this set of activities we might be able to predict the interaction patterns between the four group members, their sentiments regarding one another, and therefore, their "lines of attraction and repulsion" as indicated in Figure 7-1. Even more important, we would have an idea of how to change things so that C can become better integrated into the group.

TRANSACTIONAL EXCHANGE

One additional concept is useful in describing and explaining the relationships in this four-man group. It is the idea of *exchange* (Homans, 1961). Interactions and activities can be evaluated in terms of the rewards and costs inherent for each party. In any interaction, each party experiences some "costs." These may be in the form of such things as time or energy expended, anxiety or frustration experienced, loss of status or power, and so on. At the same time, each party may also experience some rewards. Rewards include anything that satisfies the needs of the individual involved, such as a need for affiliation, power, achievement, order, or safety.

At the conclusion of an interaction, rewards and costs are added up and balanced, and the outcome of the transaction is evaluated as being either positive or negative (a sort of "net balance"). Therefore, the three basic types of exchange which can take place between two people are:

1 Positive-Positive: both parties benefit from the exchange;
2 Positive-Negative: one party gains at the expense of the other;
3 Negative-Negative: both parties lose.

If the first outcome takes place, we would expect the two individuals to continue to interact with one another, and to become "closer" to one another (that is, to experience increasingly positive sentiments towards one another). Their activities might be described as typifying teamwork.

If the exchange takes the form of *positive-negative*, we can expect a different interaction, activity and sentiment pattern. The "loser" may attempt to reverse the positions or may decrease his contacts with the "winner." He is likely to experience more negative sentiments towards the winner and to act differently towards him as a result.

If the exchange is *negative-negative* (both sides ''lose'') we can expect the relationship to be terminated. (It has been suggested that this type of relationship can continue if the two parties are both masochists, but in that event, ''losing'' satisfies a need, and is in fact ''winning.'')

One further refinement should be added to the theory of exchange. While two parties may both benefit from an exchange, they are still likely to evaluate their *relative* gains and losses. That is, if A perceives that B has gained *more* from him than he has gained from B, the transaction will be evaluated as less satisfactory by A than if the two had gained equally. Homans calls this concept *distributive justice*. An individual attempts to arrange that nobody with whom he interacts receives more net profit (rewards minus costs) than he does (''I do not want to end up with the short end of the stick.'')

So, for ''lines of attraction'' to exist, the pattern of interactions, actions, and sentiments between two individuals (or groups) must result in both parties perceiving that they have received equal *net* rewards. The totals of net rewards may be in imbalance for short periods of time (''I owe him a couple of favors''), but if they persist, the attraction between the parties will diminish.

Figure 7-2 presents a more detailed representation of the relationships between individuals in a group. Each individual's behavior may be analyzed in terms of his I-A-S patterns, and the ''lines of attraction or repulsion'' can be replaced with lines of *exchange*.

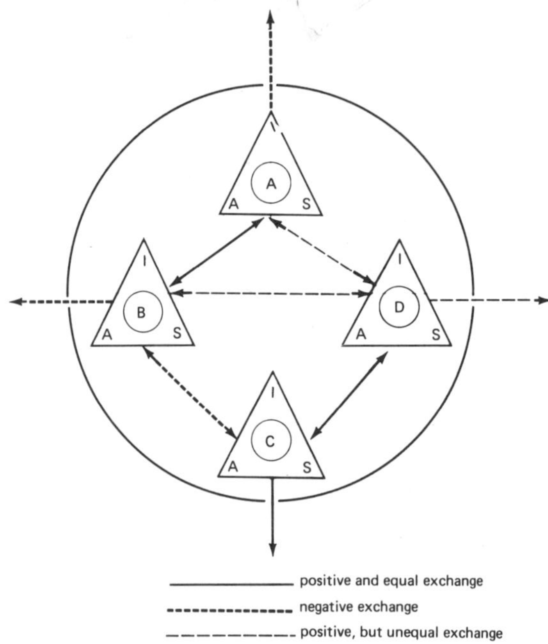

FIGURE 7-2: EXCHANGE RELATIONSHIPS IN A GROUP.

For instance, B and C perceive their relationship as negative-negative (both lose), while A and D perceive their relationship as positive, but unequal; D may perceive that A benefits more from the relationship than D does.

This type of analysis explains group behavior better than the simple concept of lines of attraction or repulsion, and it also tends to increase the accuracy with which we can predict the behavior of the group. It now seems that not only is C likely to leave the group, but that D is a marginal member who feels that, in relationships with A and B, he contributes more than he receives in return.

GROUP COHESIVENESS

The degree to which a group is attractive to its members—the importance they attach to membership in the group—is termed *cohesiveness*. When we talk about a group being highly *cohesive*, we mean that they "stick together," support one another and stand fast in favor of the goals, values and beliefs of the group. Stated another way, the greater the cohesiveness of a group, the higher the degree of conformity its members will exhibit. Industrial studies show that the higher the cohesiveness in work groups, the smaller the variation in productivity among members. In the Bank Wiring Room (Appendix A) the productivity was highly uniform; group members adhered to group production norms very closely.

What are the factors that determine group cohesiveness? We have just been discussing the degree of attraction and/or repulsion individuals may have for one another. Clearly that dictates the "togetherness" of a group. Dorwin Carwright (1968) lists a number of additional factors affecting group cohesiveness. He maintains that the individual's attraction to the group is determined by four basic factors:

1. His basic motivational set—the degree to which the organization is able to satisfy his needs for such things as security, achievement, affiliation, recognition, and so on.
2. The incentive properties of the group—its ability to provide some of the things that relate to his motivational set. The group's prestige, the type of membership, its goals, or its activities may provide the necessary incentive for the individual to want to be a member.
3. His expectancy that membership will be beneficial to him—expectancy here can be thought of in the same manner as it was used when we discussed Vroom's motivational model; the individual has some expectation that membership in the group will satisfy his motivational needs, and this will lead to some expected benefit.
4. His comparison level—his perception of what *sort* of benefits group membership will provide. The term "comparison level" is used because it is not the *actual* benefit that the group can bestow on a member that matters, but his *perception* of how great that benefit is. Some of us might feel that the status of belonging to a particular group is minor, while others might think it was the greatest thing since sliced bread.

Groups, of course, manipulate their "incentive properties." They try to make themselves more enticing. For instance group cohesion is increased by such things as:

- The perception of a common enemy—the group provides security;
- The importance of the task—the group provides achievement, recognition, and so on;
- The prestige of the group—the group provides status;
- The interpersonal attraction of the members—the group provides friendship and belonging;
- Success in achieving goals—the group provides self-esteem.

Group cohesiveness is an important concept in organizational behavior because groups that exhibit a high degree of cohesiveness tend to operate with, or tolerate, less external supervision of their activities. If the norms and goals of a tightly knit work group happen to coincide with those of the organization, then great, but if they run counter to the organization's goals, problems occur. The very terms "cohesive," "tightly-knit," and "close" describe the strong boundaries these types of groups set up. Penetrating these boundaries to introduce changes in their behavior is far from easy.

THE NONCONFORMING MEMBER

Despite the pressure towards cohesiveness and conformity in work groups, some degree of nonconformity is tolerated from certain members. To some extent, the nonconformist represents the conscience of the group. Much like the Fool in Shakespearian plays, the Court Jester whose role allowed him to say outlandish things to the King without getting his head chopped off, the nonconformist is allowed to say and do things which would not be tolerated from other quarters. The group, like the medieval King, needs someone who can challenge accepted ideas and authority, but not pose a threat at the same time. The eccentric, or nonconformist must almost, by definition, have low power needs. His role is to provide comic relief, to act as a target for scapegoating, and to raise issues which challenge the accepted goals, values, opinions and expectations of the group, thereby providing a vehicle for change alternatives. Effective groups tolerate some nonconformists. Total conformity means that interaction with the world outside the group's boundaries is cut off, and, as we know from our discussion of systems, that leads to entropy—a decay of the system.

At the other end of the scale, no group can tolerate a high proportion of nonconformists. In order to survive, it must have commonly accepted goals, norms of behavior and means of membership identification. If too many "members" challenge the goals, disregard the norms, and do not identify closely with the group, the whole thing disintegrates. There is no group.

Even the few nonconforming group members who exist must play their roles carefully. Too much nonconformist behavior will get them expelled. The effective nonconformist must show a real degree of loyalty, or have a strong record of achievement, in order to gain sufficient acceptance to allow for his deviant behavior. The exchange mechanism we looked at earlier works at the group level too. If the group receives enough support, it will allow some challenge to its goals and norms, but the bottom line has to come out positively in terms of support. If the nonconformist challenges more than he accepts, then he gets to be too much of an annoyance. It is a difficult role to play.

REFERENCE GROUPS

Henry David Thoreau remarked that, "If a man does not keep pace with his companions, perhaps it is because he hears a different drummer. Let him step to the music which he hears, however measured or far away." The nonconformist may simply be marching to the beat of a different drummer, that drummer being what we term in psychological jargon his *reference group*.

Shibutani (1961) defines a reference group as *that group, real or imaginary, whose standpoint is being used as the frame of reference by the actor*. As he says, "every man acts for some kind of *audience*, and it is important to know what this audience is and what kinds of expectations are imputed to it."

The reference group is the audience that *counts* to the individual. It may be imaginary, but it is important to him. It represents the values, ideals, goals and beliefs that he *identifies* with: that he emulates or aspires to. The individual does not have to "know" any of the members of his reference group; he identifies with their attitudes and values more so than with them personally.

An individual uses his reference group as something against which to evaluate himself and his performance. Having a knowledge of an individual's reference group allows us to predict his behavior more accurately. We can expect the individual to act in a manner which is congruent with this group, real or imaginary. In England, where social class is a dominant factor in the society, people have a greater tendency to act in terms of their definitions of their own actual or aspired social standing. Elizabeth Bott (1954) found that even though Englishmen did not have a clear concept of what constituted various class strata, they tended to project their expectations onto a certain "class" which they defined for themselves, and which served as a reference group for their behavior.

Sociologists and political scientists use an interesting categorization of reference groups to explain certain behavior. They differentiate between individuals they term as *cosmopolitans* and *locals*. These types of individuals are interesting for our purposes because the major differences between their reference groups is that one exists largely *outside* the boundaries of the organization in which they work, while the other is largely *within* the organization. The cosmopolitan is an expert who sees his reference group as fellow experts. Professionals such as lawyers, engineers and accountants tend to be cosmopolitans. Their reference group is their profession.

Their loyalties tend to lie with their profession (engineers wear iron rings, accountants pay their membership dues to their professional society, lawyers are concerned with the procedures and practices of their calling) rather than with their organizations. Locals, on the other hand are organizational men. Their loyalties lie within the work group, and they have few ties to other work-related associations or groups.

Cosmopolitans tend to be more mobile. Because of their outward focus, they see other opportunities in other organizations. Locals tend to be the ones who keep the organization going, performing the administrative and line management functions that make up the day-to-day business. No organization can really do without some of each type of manager. The locals provide the stability and the cosmopolitans the impetus for change. The cosmopolitan is, in our earlier discussion, the nonconformist, the eccentric, the agent of change and friction.

CONFORMITY

In our efforts to understand group behavior we have taken several steps so far. We have seen that groups are really a system of relationships; that members feel either attracted or repulsed by one another; that these feelings can be explained by a pattern of interactions, activities and sentiments that emerge; that individuals perceive these relationships as a type of exchange, with costs and benefits attached; and that, over time, individuals feel that these relationships should balance out, with each party receiving about the same amount of *net* gain. Let us take one step further. What is it that determines the patterns of interaction, activity and sentiment which form the basis for our analysis of behavior? (The earlier explanation was that any one of these two factors could be explained in terms of the other two, but this is a bit of a chicken-and-egg situation. What starts the *initial* interaction, activity or sentiment?)

Our systems model of organizational behavior (Figure 7-3) shows the *individual system* interacting with the *work group system*, the *organizational system* and its *required behavior* patterns to produce actual behavior in the workplace. Somehow the work group system embodies forces that mold individual personality, motivation, perception, and so on, into a form acceptable to the group as a whole. The group exerts a force on its members; it influences their behavior. We call this process *social influence*.

THE INFLUENCE PROCESS IN GROUPS

There are two basic processes of social influence: *Social comparison* and *control* (Smith, 1973). *Social comparison* occurs in any situation where an individual uses another person as a reference point in determining his own actions. *Control* is the process whereby the behavior of an individual is influenced by the demands of another person to act in a particular way. The process of *social comparison* is active when you are uncertain of yourself and you test to see how you are

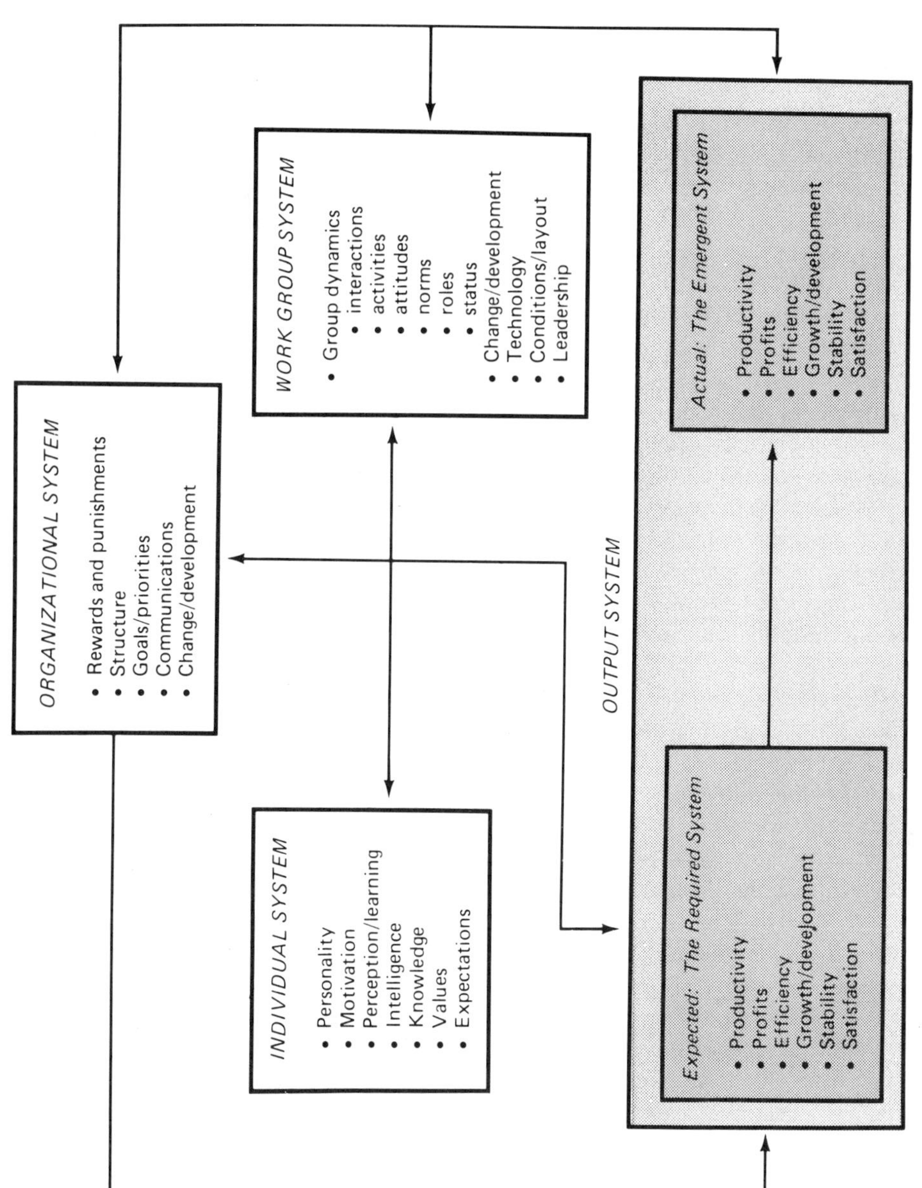

FIGURE 7-3: A SYSTEMS MODEL OF ORGANIZATIONAL BEHAVIOR.

''going over,'' or when you decide to adjust your behavior either to conform with group norms or to counter them. The process of *control* is being exercised when you are told to do something, and your behavior alters accordingly.

SOCIAL COMPARISON

An interesting illustration of the concept of social comparison is provided by the experiments of Asch (1965). Asch set out to study ''the social and personal conditions that induce individuals to resist or to yield to group pressures when the latter are perceived to be *contrary to fact*.'' He gathered eight individuals in a room and showed them three lines of unequal length. He then showed them a fourth line and asked them to say which of the previous three it matched in length. Each individual announced his judgment publicly, in front of the whole group. The experiment contained a series of these judgments. In fact, seven of the eight judges were stooges; they had met with Asch prior to the experiment and had been instructed to make incorrect comparisons at certain points. Therefore, at various points during the ''judging'' the seven confederates would make a clearly incorrect decision (the errors were sizable; the differences varied from 1/2″ to 1 3/4″). Asch was interested in seeing how the subject of the experiment reacted to this contradictory judgment. Because of the significant differences in the lengths of the lines, the subject had to reconcile what he ''saw'' with his eyes as a ''correct'' decision with the unanimous decision of seven of his peers. He then had to decide whether to conform to their opinion or stick to his own.

One third of the estimates made by the subjects *agreed* with the majority view when the latter were *wrong*. Obversely, 68 percent of the estimates made by subjects, in the situation where the majority chose the wrong solution, were *correct*—that is, they refused to be swayed by the group. Asch also found that conformity varied with individuals. Some of the subjects remained independent *all* the time, and some were swayed by the majority decision almost all the time. Twenty-five percent of the subjects remained completely independent, and a third of the subjects agreed with the incorrect majority decision at least 50 percent of the time.

Asch then introduced some variations into the experiment. He noticed that as the size of the majority making the incorrect decision decreased, independence tended to increase. That is, as subjects found others who were able to agree with them, their independence from the majority tended to increase. Asch also noted that as the discrepancies between the comparison lines grew greater, independence increased. If the difference was 1/2″, subjects were more likely to go with the majority than if it was 3″. However, even when the difference between lines was as much as 6″, some subjects continued to agree with the majority.

This is the process of social comparison at work. An individual is asked to make a judgment in the face of contradictory opinion from a group of peers. As can be seen by the profiles of both an *independent* and a *yielding* subject in Box 7-1, *all* individuals compared their judgments with those of the group. For various reasons, some chose to maintain their own opinions while others succumbed to the pressure of the group.

BOX 7-1:

PROFILES OF INDIVIDUALS WHO YIELD TO, OR REMAIN INDEPENDENT OF, GROUP PRESSURE. (ASCH, 1965)

In an experiment to discover the power of group pressure in getting an individual to change his opinion, Asch found that certain personality types reacted differently. Some were swayed by group opinion a large percentage of the time, while others remained independent and expressed their own judgments in the face of opposition from seven other group members. Personality is an important factor in determining the degree to which an individual will be influenced by group pressure.

INDEPENDENT SUBJECT PROFILE

After a few trials he appeared puzzled, hesitant. He announced all disagreeing answers in the form of "Three, sir; two, sir"; not so with the unanimous answers on the neutral trials. At Trial 4 he answered immediately after the first member of the group, shook his head, blinked, and whispered to his neighbor: "Can't help it, that's one." His later answers came in a whispered voice, accompanied by a deprecating smile. At one point he grinned embarassedly and whispered explosively to his neighbor: "I always disagree—darn it!" During the questioning, this subject's constant refrain was: "I called them as I saw them, sir." He insisted that his estimates were right without, however, committing himself as to whether the others were wrong, remarking, "That's the way I see them and that's the way they see them." If he had to make a practical decision under similar circumstances, he declared, "I would follow my own view, though part of my reason would tell me that I might be wrong." Immediately following the experiment the majority engaged this subject in a brief discussion. When they pressed him to say whether the entire group was wrong and he alone right, he turned upon them defiantly, exclaiming: "You're probably right, but you may be wrong!" To the disclosure of the experiment this subject reacted with the statement that he felt "exultant and relieved," adding, "I do not deny that at times I had the feeling: 'to heck with it, I'll go along with the rest.' "

YIELDING SUBJECT PROFILE

"This subject went with the majority in 11 out of 12 trials. He appeared nervous and somewhat confused, but he did not attempt to evade discussion; on the contrary, he was helpful and tried to answer to the best of his ability. He opened the discussion with the statement: "If I'd been first I probably would have responded differently"; this was his way of stating that he had adopted the majority estimates. The primary factor in his case was loss of confidence. He perceived the majority as a decided group, acting without hesitation: "If they had been doubtful I probably would have changed, but they answered with such confidence." Certain of his errors, he explained, were due to the doubtful nature of the comparisons; in such instances he went with the majority. When the object of the experiment was explained, the subject volunteered; "I suspected about the middle—but tried to push it out of my mind." It is of interest that his suspicion did not restore his confidence or diminish the power of the majority. Equally striking is his report that he assumed the experiment to involve an "illusion" to which the others, but not he, were subject. This assumption, too, did not help to free him; on the contrary, he acted as if his divergence from the majority was a sign of defect. The principal impression this subject produced was of one so caught up by immediate difficulties that he lost clear reasons for his actions, and could make no reasonable decisions."

This experiment raises some issues. When do people engage in social comparison? With whom do they compare themselves? What are the consequences of social comparison?

Leon Festinger (1954) maintains that everybody has a basic need to evaluate his opinions and abilities. He says that we all prefer to get *objective* evaluations (to evaluate if you can run fast, you can time yourself over a measured distance), but that where these are unavailable we seek *social* means of evaluation (to evaluate if you are amusing, you might tell some stories to a group and see if they laugh). Festinger goes further, maintaining that the people one chooses as the means of comparison or evaluation are *similar* to oneself.

There seems little doubt that everyone enters into the process of social comparison in some fashion or other. That is basically how we learn all our behavior; we try something out and see what the reaction is from others, or we observe others, and then copy their behavior to some degree, once again testing to see if our performance is acceptable. The degree to which one can gauge one's behavior objectively, rather than by social means, appears to be a function of the tasks in which one is engaged. For instance, an assembly line worker can gauge his performance by counting the number of units he produces within a specific time period, while a personnel manager has fewer objective criteria available and must look to other managers for evaluation. (Festinger's assertion that everyone prefers objective evaluation is supported by the widespread trend in business and government towards management by objectives.)

A second of Festinger's arguments appears to be less valid, however. He states that one tends to choose people who are *similar* as comparison objects. Experimental data does not confirm this hypothesis. It appears that when people are concerned with *improving* their performance they choose others who are *better* than they are to compare themselves with; when they feel *threatened* by unpleasant feedback on their performance they tend to choose people who are *worse* than they are; and when they are *uncertain*, anxious and afraid, they tend to compare themselves with people *similar* to themselves. Therefore, the choice of a comparison subject depends on the desired outcome.

This brings us to our third question, "what are the consequences of social comparison?" There appear to be three basic consequences of, or reasons for, social comparison. They are: *anxiety reduction, confirmation* and *disconfirmation* (Smith, 1973).

In situations where one is uncertain or anxious, comparison with others may serve to *reduce* the uncertainty—a paratroop trainee, jumping for the first time, may feel less anxious and uncertain when he sees that there are other people who are undergoing the same experience, and that they seem able to cope with it. Having others in the same boat helps reduce anxiety.

One may also use social comparison to *confirm* one's concept of self, or to confirm perceptions and feelings. The paratroop trainee confirms that it is "O.K." to feel nervous when he sees that his fellows are just as jittery as he is. It confirms his belief that he is not cowardly, and that perhaps the decision to jump in the first place was reasonable.

Or the process of social comparison may be used to *contradict* one's feelings, opinions or perceptions. The paratroop trainee attempts to put on a cool and brave front, but notices that his hands tremble and his face is drawn, and that the others see this and perhaps comment on it. His perception of himself as brave and cool may be called into question. His similarity to, or difference from, the rest of the trainees is noted in the comparisons he makes. Contradictions to his self-image must of course be dealt with in some way or another, as we have seen earlier.

Does the concept of social comparison help us predict how individuals will behave? Unfortunately, as the Asch findings illustrate, that depends on a number of other factors such as the individual's personality, the degree to which he sees the comparison subjects as "good," and his motivational needs.

SOCIAL CONTROL

There is, however, another process that may aid in our understanding of conformity: *control*. What is it that makes people carry out orders, even when the task is objectionable? The classic study into the process of control and obedience was conducted by Milgram (1967).

Milgram originally set up his experimental situation in a building on the Yale campus. Subjects were told they were taking part in a study on the effects of punishment on learning. Each of the subjects was assigned to the role of "teacher" in the experiment, while a second individual (secretly a confederate of Milgram's) was assigned the role of "learner" (Milgram even went to the trouble of setting up a process whereby the assignment of the roles appeared to be by chance so that the subject suspected no collusion).

The "teacher" (the subject) was seated at the console of an "electric shock generator.'' The panel of the console was marked with a series of volt levels from 15 to 450. Labels were also attached to the panel indicating the degree of shock of various voltage levels, ranging from ''Slight Shock'' to ''Danger: Severe Shock.'' To demonstrate how the apparatus worked, the subject was given a sample shock of 45 volts (in fact this shock was produced by a battery hooked up to the apparatus specifically for the purpose. At no time did the ''shock generator'' ever administer a shock to the ''learners''). The ''learner'' was then strapped into a chair, and electrodes were fastened to him. The subject was instructed to feed questions to the ''learner'' and to administer an *increasing level* of shock to him each time he made an error (the ''learner'' was programmed to introduce errors with relatively high frequency, so that the shock level increased rapidly). If the ''teacher'' balked at administering shocks at the higher voltage levels, the experimenter simply said something such as, ''The experiment requires that you continue.''

To begin with, Milgram concealed the ''learner'' from the ''teacher's'' view. However, the ''teacher'' could hear noises from behind the partition as he administered the various shocks. For instance, at about 75 volts, the ''learner'' grunted and moaned, at about 150 volts he demanded to be let out, at about 200 volts he screamed and pounded the wall, and at higher voltages he fell silent.

Milgram expected his subjects to stop administering shocks rather quickly, and you and I would have expected the same. However, *65 percent* of the subjects continued to administer shocks to the *maximum point of the scale!* How, in the face of the feedback coming from behind the partition (screams, pounding and yelling to be let out, and finally *nothing at all*), could anyone continue to increase the severity of the shocks? In an attempt to explain this blind obedience, Milgram introduced a number of variations into the experiment.

First, he transferred the site of the experiment to a seedy building away from Yale: only 48 percent of the subjects were now totally obedient. Next, he removed the experimenter from the scene, and had him communicate with the subject by telephone: obedience dropped to 23 percent. Then he varied the contact the subject had with the ''learner.'' When he could neither be seen nor heard, obedience was 65 percent; when he could be *heard* but not seen this dropped to 62 percent; when the ''learner'' was seated in plain view, next to the subject, obedience dropped to 40 percent; and when the subject actually had to place the ''learner's'' hand on the shock, 30 percent were obedient.

A conclusion that can be drawn from this series of experiments is that obedience may be a function of several situational factors: prestige of the source of orders (Yale, in this case), proximity of the control figure (the experimenter), and contact with the recipient of the punishment.

One might ask if there is any connection between the phenomenon of *control* and social *comparison*. Milgram (1964) in an attempt to answer that question, replicated his basic experiment, but used a group of three subjects, two of whom were his confederates. When they refused to carry out the experimenter's instructions, obedience fell to only 10 percent. We can thus see the interacting effects of social comparison and control. When social comparison points in the same way as the control figure, conformity is high. However, when social comparison acts counter to the control figure, it can severely limit his power.

IN CONCLUSION

This chapter has been concerned with those forces that bring about cohesion or fragmentation in work groups. Essentially we have focused on the issues of conformity and deviation from the norm. We can see that individuals are either attracted to one another or repulsed in some way. Whether they are attracted or not is dependent on the type of interaction between them, and their resultant sentiments and activities. An exchange takes place between interacting parties, with each side evaluating the positive and negative aspects of the transaction. Durability of relationships rests on both parties perceiving a positive benefit, or at least perceiving no net loss.

Cohesive groups are those in which the basic motivational needs of the members are satisfied, in which there are sufficient incentives to want to belong, where the expectation is that group membership will lead to need satisfaction, and where the exchange between individual and group is perceived by the individual as being positive. Groups work at being attractive to their members. If they fail to establish this attractiveness, they have no members.

How do the mechanisms of social comparison and control relate to group cohesion or fragmentation? We have seen that factors such as credibility, attractiveness, status and power affect the way in which individuals respond to influence. Kellman (1958) provides a summary of the different types of responses that each of these approaches to influencing others' behavior elicits. He argues that the way in which the subject perceives he is being influenced affects how he will respond.

If he sees himself being coerced in some way (as with the authority figure in Milgram's experiment), his response will be *compliance*, but, Kellman maintains, this compliance will only last as long as the subject is closely watched. From an organizational point of view, what this implies is that close, coercive supervision only works as long as it is kept up. Once the supervisor turns his back, compliance falls off.

If the subject perceives the influencing individual or group as being attractive, he will tend to *identify* with the individual or group. However, this identification will continue only as long as the factors that make for the "attractiveness" remain. In other words, as long as the individual or group is able to satisfy the subject's basic needs, he will perceive it as worthy of conforming to.

Finally, says Kellman, if the individual or group bases its influence on expertise and credibility, the subject is likely to internalize the values, attitudes and goals espoused. This internalization will continue to affect the subject's values and behavior even when he is not under observation. In other words, they become *part of him*, and he needs no external force to prop them up. In an organizational sense, if employees internalize the organization's values, goals and behavioral norms, management is home free, since little or no supervision is needed to enforce compliance.

APPLYING THE THEORY

At the end of Chapter 5, you read Hovey and Beard (Part 3) and made predictions concerning the production rate, job satisfaction of the girls, their attitudes toward their supervisors and their interactions concerning the job. We subsequently asked you to review these predictions in the light of what you learned in Chapter 6.

Flip back to your predictions at the end of Chapters 5 and 6, and reread Part 3 of the case now, to refresh your memory. It is on page 100, at the end of Chapter 5. Also take a moment or two now to review your predictions on productivity, and so on, and write down any changes you would make in the light of what we have looked at in this chapter. Note your reasons for changing.

HOVEY AND BEARD (PART 3): AN INCREMENTAL ANALYSIS

In Part 3 of the case we observed a high level of interaction among the girls. They had been talking about the issues concerning the new production process, and they had a spokesman (Part 2). They also had some suggestions to make to resolve the problems. These interactions seem to have resulted in positive sentiments among the girls (all eight appeared at the meeting immediately after work, and their behavior was supportive of each other). Their activities indicated that they had formed a cohesive group.

There are a number of factors in the situation that facilitated the formation of a cohesive group. They had a common enemy (management); the task they were engaged in was important (as seen by the interest expressed in it by management); their group had some prestige attached to it (otherwise why all the fuss, and why would management meet with them?); and they had achieved some degree of success (they have had three fans purchased for installation). Remember what we said about highly cohesive groups, however. They tend to operate with, or tolerate, less external supervision of their activities. The trick is to get them to adopt norms and goals that are congruent with those of the organization.

There was some hope that this process might occur. If we look at the I-A-S pattern between the girls and their foreman, we see an increasing level of interaction, positive actions on both parts (i.e., actions designed to solve the problem with some degree of mutual satisfaction), and increasingly positive sentiments between the parties (the girls *and* the foreman were willing to have a second meeting, and to discuss the matter without rancor). In Kellman's terms, we see the influencing party becoming more *attractive* to the girls, and we see the possibility of some *identification* on their part with his ideas and problems.

Going back to the chapters on motivation and the self-concept, we also see that the girls were receiving some positive strokes from management. They were being listened to. They were perceived as important. They were permitted to make suggestions. And these suggestions were acted on. They were regaining some of the control over their jobs that they lost when the automated process was first introduced. Some of the uncertainties were being removed from the job in that they were able to influence certain aspects of it, and they were being given attention that satisfied some of their esteem needs.

The picture is becoming quite positive. It would appear logical to predict some rise in productivity and in job satisfaction, plus an improvement in their attitudes towards management, and a high level of interest in developments that would likely manifest itself in high levels of interaction among them concerning the job.

Here is Part 4 of the case. After you have read it, would you please predict what happened to productivity, job satisfaction, attitudes toward supervision, and interaction patterns among the girls, as you have done previously. Write down your predictions and your reasons for making them. Do not forget what has been covered in earlier chapters. Incorporate all the theory you think is applicable to help you make an accurate set of predictions.

HOVEY AND BEARD COMPANY PART 4

The fans were brought in. The girls were jubilant. For several days the fans were moved about in various positions until they were placed to the satisfaction of the group. The girls seemed completely satisfied with the results, and relations between them and the foreman improved visibly.

The foreman, after this encouraging episode, decided that further meetings might also be profitable. He asked the girls if they would like to meet and discuss other aspects of the work situation. The girls were eager to do this. The meeting was held, and the discussion quickly centered on the speed of the hooks. The girls maintained that the time study men had set them at an unreasonably fast speed and they would never be able to reach the goal of filling enough of them to make a bonus.

The turning point of the discussion came when the group's leader frankly explained that the point was not that they couldn't work fast enough to keep up with the hooks, but that they could not work at that pace all day long. The foreman explored the point. The girls were unanimous in their opinion that they could keep up with the belt for short periods if they wanted to. But they did not want to because if they showed they could do this for short periods they would be expected to do it all day long. The meeting ended with an unprecedented request: "Let us adjust the speed of the belt faster or slower depending on how we feel." The foreman agreed to discuss this with the superintendent and the engineers.

The reaction of the engineers to the suggestion was negative. However, after several meetings it was granted that there was some latitude within which variations in the speed of the hooks would not affect the finished product. After a considerable argument with the engineers, it was agreed to try out the girls' idea.

With misgivings, the foreman had a control with a dial marked "low, medium, fast" installed at the booth of the group leader; she could now adjust the speed of the belt anywhere between the lower and upper limits that the engineers had set.

Chapter Summary

1. A group can be thought of as a network of relationships between members who are either attracted to one another, or to outsiders, or are repulsed by them.
2. Group cohesiveness or disruption can be analyzed through the use of the interaction-activities-sentiments model. Patterns of behavior which emerge from this analysis can give us a clue as to the degree of attraction or repulsion between parties.
3. Interactions form the basis for an exchange between individuals and groups, and are evaluated by the parties involved on the degree to which they "gain" or "lose" from the process. In interactional situations where one or both of the parties perceive themselves as losing, the frequency of interactions decreases and finally terminates. Those associations which tend to endure over time are ones in which both parties enjoy positive rewards.
4. Individuals are attracted to groups if the latter are able to satisfy basic motivational needs, if they offer certain incentives to membership such as prestige, if it is perceived that membership will lead to the satisfaction of basic needs and goals, and if the group is seen to offer a positive exchange.
5. Some factors that make groups more attractive to their members, and therefore make them more cohesive are:

    - The perception of a common enemy;
    - The importance of the task;
    - The prestige of the group;
    - The interpersonal attraction of the members;
    - The group's success in achieving its goals.

6. Highly cohesive groups tend to operate with, and tolerate, less external supervision of their activities.
7. Most groups have nonconforming members. These people are expelled from the group if they do not display any sense of loyalty, or achievement on the group's behalf. But, given a basic loyalty to the goals and

norms of the group, one or two nonconformists may be tolerated. Their role is to advance change suggestions, to provide an evaluative feedback link on the group's performance, values and aims, and to act as comic or scapegoat from time to time.

8 One of the bases for nonconformity is the association of the individual with a different reference group. This reference group may be real or imaginary, but it represents the values, attitudes, beliefs and goals with which the individual identifies.

9 We can think of organizational members as being of two types—cosmopolitans and locals. Cosmopolitans are mobile, expert, outward-looking individuals whose reference group lies *outside* the organization. Locals are the "organization men" whose loyalties and attentions are directed *within* the organization. They represent a force for stability and the status quo, while the cosmopolitans represent a force for change and the acceptance of new ideas.

10 Two basic influence processes are social comparison and control. Social comparison takes place when an individual compares himself with others in similar situations and decides whether to emulate them or to deviate from their attitudes or behavior. Control is the process of influencing the activities of others directly in one direction or another. It implies some degree of coercion, but may take its force from the status of the authority figure, his proximity to the subject, and the lack of support which the subject can muster for his own position.

11 It has been suggested that when individuals are coerced, their reaction is compliance, and this compliance only lasts as long as they are closely controlled. When they are "sold" by an attractive influence source, they react by identifying with the source, and their compliance with the influencing party will remain only as long as the issues on which the sales pitch are based remain important. When individuals are influenced by a source that reflects high credibility and expertise, they tend to internalize the values, attitudes and actions espoused by the influencing party, and they remain committed to these even if they are not subjected to external supervision or observation.

8

The Dynamics of Effective Operating Groups

OBJECTIVES

When you have completed this chapter you should:

- understand the concept of role and its importance in understanding and analyzing organizational behavior;
- recognize how roles and status are acquired;
- understand how status rankings are arrived at;
- be aware of the type of criteria that can be used to analyze and evaluate group process;
- recognize that there is no best method of group operation, but rather that effectiveness depends on a number of situational factors.

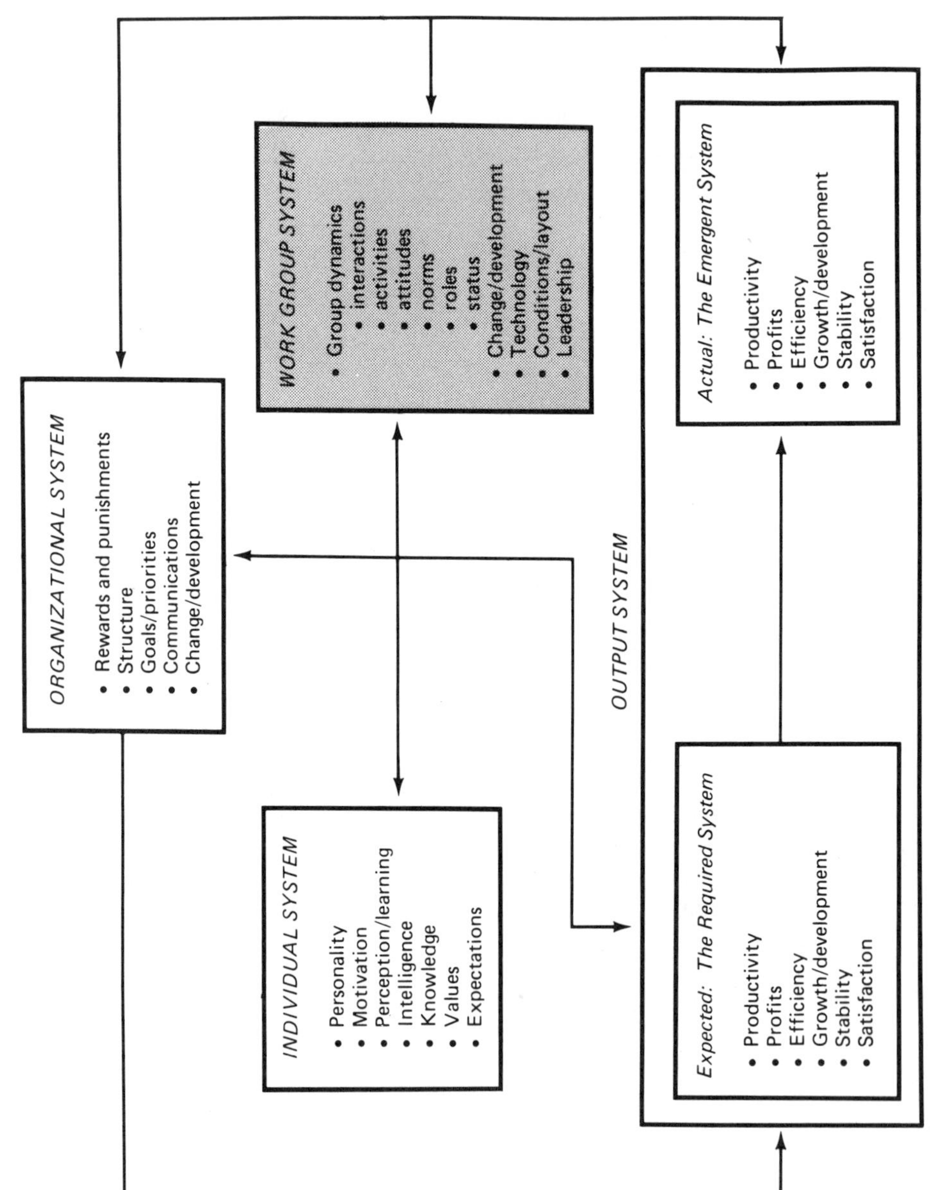
ORGANIZATIONAL SYSTEM
• Rewards and punishments
• Structure
• Goals/priorities
• Communications
• Change/development
WORK GROUP SYSTEM
• Group dynamics
• interactions
• activities
• attitudes
• norms
• roles
• status
• Change/development
• Technology
• Conditions/layout
• Leadership
INDIVIDUAL SYSTEM
• Personality
• Motivation
• Perception/learning
• Intelligence
• Knowledge
• Values
• Expectations
OUTPUT SYSTEM
Expected: The Required System
• Productivity
• Profits
• Efficiency
• Growth/development
• Stability
• Satisfaction
Actual: The Emergent System
• Productivity
• Profits
• Efficiency
• Growth/development
• Stability
• Satisfaction

When we talk about work groups we are really only talking about collections of individuals. The basic building block of the group *is* the individual. But while each individual brings his distinctive personality, motivation, perception, intelligence, knowledge, values and expectations to the group, these are molded and formed to fit the group's structure. The individual does not merely work in the group as a person, he *fits* into a specific *role*. That role is prescribed by his position in the group. *A role may be defined as a set of behaviors that attaches itself to a particular position in an organization, no matter who occupies that position.*

A role is made up of a set of expectations about how an individual should act in a certain position. The role of President of the United States is circumscribed by a wide set of expectations. President Nixon, in failing to live up to many of these expectations, was seen as violating the role demands of the position. The manager of a bank has a certain role to play; we expect him to act in a certain fashion. By the same token, mothers are expected in our society to perform certain functions and act in certain ways. The remark, "She is not much of a mother to her children," means that the individual in question is not fulfilling the speaker's expectations of what a mother should do.

The concept of role is important to the study of organizational behavior because individuals tend to exhibit a great deal of consistency in their behavior when they occupy specific positions in an organization. The feeling of "doing my duty," or "doing my job" explains a great deal of behavior; we can expect someone to act in a certain way *as a result of his job*. For instance, policemen, doctors, and priests all have specific roles to fulfill; we expect them to act in a certain way, and we are rarely disappointed.

ROLE

An individual may be a member of a number of different groups. He may belong to a *work* group, a *social* group such as a bridge club or bowling team, a *family* group, or a *task* group outside regular work such as a volunteer fire department. His position in each of these groups may be very different. He may be the father at home, the junior member of the fire-fighting unit, the captain of his bowling team, and a novice bridge player. It is interesting to note, however, that his behavior *in* each of these groups tends to be fairly consistent. That is not to say that he behaves in the same way *across* groups, but that *in each specific group of which he is a member*, he tends to act in a specific manner. His *role* prescribes his behavior.

ROLE LINKAGE

Organizations are basically composed of a large set of interlocking roles. Every individual fills a role in some group, and these groups are, in turn, connected with one another through members who belong to more than one group. Likert (1961) has called this function the "linking pin." Figure 8-1 shows the linking pin role with a two-headed arrow. A member of one work group also belongs to a second one. He may be a subordinate in the first group and the boss of the second group. In this manner he is able to transmit the policies, goals and objectives agreed upon by the higher level group down to his own work team.

At each successive level down the organization, these policies, goals and objectives become more specific, and jobs (roles) are described in greater detail.

If one were to observe the behavior of one of the linking pin managers, without any knowledge of his role, one might see that he acted quite differently in various situations throughout his working day. In one interaction he might initiate all the conversation, ask a lot of questions, and issue a series of orders. In another he might say little, signify agreement a great deal, answer direct questions and rarely initiate any comments. In a third he might initiate approximately an equal amount with his interacting partner, laugh and joke a little, and listen as much as he talked. Why would one individual act so differently in three seemingly similar situations in one day? If we knew the *role* he was playing in each of these situations, we would have a better chance of explaining his behavior. In the first interactions, if we knew he was talking with a subordinate, we could understand his domination of the conversation; in the second interaction, if we knew he was talking with his superior,

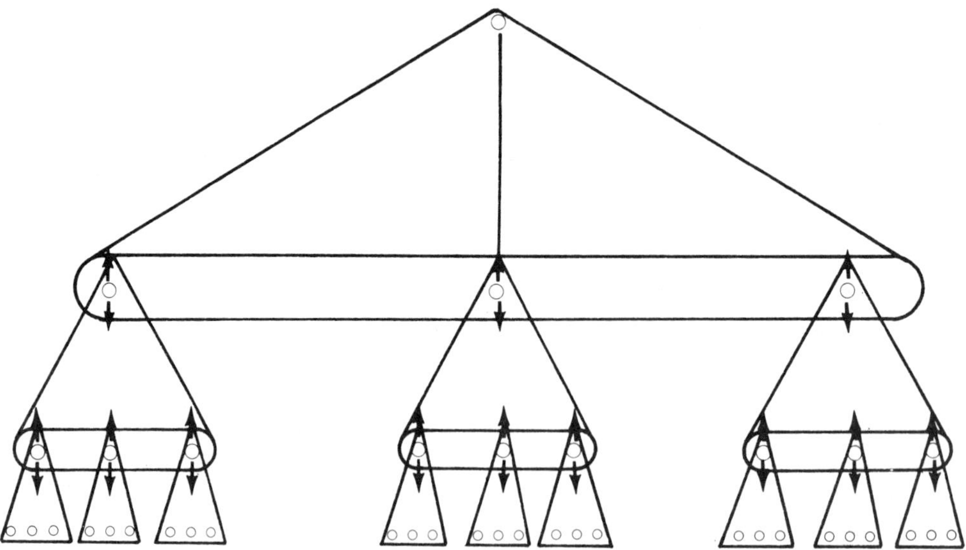

FIGURE 8-1: INDIVIDUAL ROLES ACT AS LINKS BETWEEN WORK GROUPS IN AN ORGANIZATION. (LIKERT, 1961)

we could understand why suddenly he became so attentive; and in the third situation, if we knew that he was meeting with a co-worker, his feeling of being at ease, the joviality and the seemingly equal give-and-take of the conversation would be more understandable. (These three situations are caricatures, illustrating extremes of behavior. We cannot always expect people to be obsequious to superiors, dominating to subordinates, and friendly with co-workers, but the roles expected in these three relationships often result in this type of behavior.)

ROLE PLAYING

Erving Goffman (1959), a Canadian sociologist, has studied the behavior of individuals in varying roles and looked at the demands these roles make. Because of the diversity of roles that we must all play, and the fact that we must play them in front of other group members, we try to determine the most effective manner of acting, congruent with the view that we want to project of ourselves. We then attempt to act appropriately in each particular situation. Goffman suggests that we do, in fact, perform like actors, ''presenting'' roles to our audiences. A woman may have an idea of how a mother should act, how an executive should act and how a tennis partner should act. She then attempts to project the correct image of herself in each of these roles. Goffman calls this the ''presentation of self in everyday life.''

ROLE DEMANDS

Recalling what was said in Chapter 4, we can see that the ''acting out'' of perceived role demands is deeply involved with the management of the self-concept. The concept of *role demands*—those behaviors that are expected from an incumbent in a certain position—helps to explain some of the conflicts that we saw occurring in Chapter 4 between an individual's *actual* self-concept (what he sees himself as), his *ideal* self-concept (what he would *like* to be) and his *projected* self-concept (what he would like others to see him as). Role demands may pressure an individual into projecting an image of himself that he knows is at variance with his idea of who and what he is. When this variance is detected by others, we say that the individual is simply ''playing the role.'' We recognize his behavior as phony and ungenuine. He cannot fill the role demands adequately.

One of the functions of effective role playing is what Sprott (1958) calls managing the framework of expectations in a group. Both he and Goffman point out that individuals expect certain behavior from others, and, in turn, certain behavior is expected of them. We tend to use our behavior as a *manipulative device* in order to elicit certain behavior in return. The degree to which we can alter our behavior and call on a range of different presentations, however, is limited by the expectations of the rest of the group. They have some idea of what behavior is normal or acceptable, and will react in somewhat regular fashion to behavior in this range. When an individual presents himself in some manner outside the range of the expected, however, he is less likely to be able to predict the reactions this will elicit from his fellow group members. Too much bizarre behavior will eventually cause him to be rejected by the group. He is violating his role expectations too greatly.

The point was made in Chapter 2 that the two main reasons for organization were to reduce uncertainty and to provide some sense of continuity and stability. This is clearly the function of role prescription in groups. The significance of a framework of expectations is illustrated by remarks like, "I can't get on with him, you never know how to take him," or "You never know what he will do next."

ROLE TRAP

In our society, role demands often become a trap. We become forced into a pattern of behavior that is against our nature or desires. Executives talk about being caught in the "rat race," and housewives rail against being trapped in the "female role." Often these role demands are so severe that one cannot cope adequately. The results of this inability to cope are such things as ulcers, heart attacks, high blood pressure, nervous diseases or even suicide. Unfortunately, we have not developed a mechanism whereby we can throw off the constraints of these heavy roles and still live amicably in society. We tend to institutionalize those who refuse to bow to the demands of various societal roles. Other societies however, have developed processes to deal with this problem. (Box 8-1)

BOX 8-1

WILD MAN BEHAVIOR (OR HOW TO SHAKE OFF THE BONDS OF A SUFFOCATING SOCIETY AND MAINTAIN YOUR COOL). FROM: NEWMAN (1964)

Phillip Newman has described a rather distinctive type of behavior that takes place among a small tribe in New Guinea. Within this tribe, an individual at times feels that the pressures of the society and its requirements to perform various duties and enter into various obligations, are too much for him. At this juncture he adopts what is termed "Wild Man" behavior. That is, he forcibly takes the property of others and violently confronts them. He remains impervious to any attempts to dissuade him from behaving in this manner and ignores any sanctions placed on him for not honoring his various tribal obligations.

Newman interprets this behavior as a cry for release from the pressures of tribal life. The man's peers sit down and evaluate his behavior and judge whether it is genuine or simply an attempt to get out of doing a number of things around the village. If they decide that he is genuine, the "wild man" is released from all obligations, and is allowed to continue to live in the village under a revised set of rules. Less is expected of him in the future. There are no recriminations against him. He is not expected to pay off debts fully or promptly, to fulfill various obligations completely, or be subjected to strong commitments concerning the amount of food he will contribute to the community fund. In short, his obligations are erased. As Newman says, "The outcome of wild man behavior is a reduction of demands made without loss of social support. The wild man does not become an outcast or deviant in the eyes of others; he becomes a man now known to be incapable of, or unwilling to participate in, certain affairs with the same degree of intensity as others, but still a man who can participate to some degree."

It appears that as we have advanced from the primitive, we have lost some of the sensitivity that less developed societies still maintain for their members' problems. We tend to treat our "wild men" like McMurphy in *One Flew Over the Cuckoo's Nest*.

ROLE AND PERSONALITY

Every individual interprets the role demands placed on him in terms of his own personality. If the linking pin manager described previously had a different personality, he might be less submissive to his boss, and more equalitarian towards his subordinates. The same role can be played by different personalities and result in very different actions. The ways in which Eisenhower, Kennedy, Johnson and Nixon acted as Presidents of the U.S. were quite different although the expectations surrounding the President's office (role demands) remained basically the same.

To a large extent, the way in which a person chooses to play a role is determined by the sort of relationship he wishes to establish with others. Recalling Goffman's idea of presentation of self, what we tend to do is estimate the amount of "psyching out" that is necessary to any relationship. Mohammed Ali feels that this process is very important, and much of his efforts, both before and during fights, are designed to make his opponent feel inferior. Any player of games is well aware of the "psyching" process. Steven Potter (1947), in a brilliantly amusing book, has termed the process "Gamesmanship," which he defines as "the art of winning games without actually cheating."

The role of a commander in war time is also to win. He is *expected* to win, to lead his troops to victory (or at least to save them from defeat). Individual commanders interpret their roles very differently. The personalities of Alexander, Montgomery, Eisenhower and Patton strongly influenced the manner in which they handled their commands. Their approaches were very different, yet each was highly successful.

What these examples illustrate is that while a role is made up of the expectations of others as to how the incumbent is to act, strong personalities are able to *change these expectations*, and hence alter their roles. One of the strengths required of a manager taking over a new job is his ability to approach the task differently and *get others to accept his approach as valid*. In many ways the new incumbent is expected to change things, but there are also very strong pressures from those within the organization for maintenance of the status quo. New Chief Executive Officers are often brought into office with the expectation that they will ''turn things around,'' or ''bring fresh approaches to corporate problems.'' In other words, they are expected to redefine their own roles and those of other positions in the organizations.

ROLE CONFLICT

In an organization when two individuals clash, the situation is usually described as a ''personality conflict.'' However, the conflict is rarely one of straight personality; it more often is a fight over *role* (''Whose job is this?'').

Kelly (1974) separates role conflict into two types: *inter-role conflict* and *intra-role conflict*. *Inter-role* conflict occurs when an individual occupies more than one role. In an actual example, one individual in a government agency was head of two departments simultaneously. Conflicts developed over his allotment of time and resources to each of the departments, and subordinates found it difficult to pin him down since they could never be sure which role he was acting in.

Intra-role conflict refers to the conflict of expectations from different sources. For instance, a sales manager may experience the following different (and conflicting) demands:

- His salesmen may expect him to increase total sales volume;
- The controller may want him to decrease the amount of credit loss;
- The production manager may want him to align sales more closely with production schedules;
- The research and development group may want him to get his salesforce to test new product ideas.

It may be impossible for the sales manager to meet all these expectations simultaneously. He is placed in a position where he must choose some actions over others (and then defend his choice to those he cannot satisfy).

While personality certainly affects how an individual interprets his role, much of the conflict in organizations is based on how jobs are shared. An oil company in Europe operates a number of gasoline stations, next to which are located company motels and restaurants. The gasoline stations are the responsibility of one vice-president, and the motels and restaurants the responsibility of another vice-president. These two men have a running battle, which becomes rather bitter at times. The problem is that the gasoline stations, in an attempt to increase profitability, have taken to selling a range of prepared food and drinks which the motorist may buy and then consume in a roadside park. The motel managers argue that this stops people from eating in their dining rooms and coffee shops. However, each division is independent, and each is concerned with its own profits. The clash between the vice-presidents is not due to their personalities. It is due to the fight over jurisdiction.

ROLE AND STATUS

The concept of role is closely tied in with the idea of status. Inevitably in any group, individuals go through a process of ranking. Some are given higher rankings than others. We often term this the ''pecking order'' because of the phenomenon, observed amongst chickens, whereby the flock orders itself into a hierarchy. Any chicken may peck any other chicken *below* it in the hierarchy and not be pecked back, but it cannot get away with this behavior if it attempts to peck one *higher* on the scale. Similar behavior is found among many types of animal societies, and, not surprisingly, among humans.

Konrad Lorenz (1966) explains that the function of status ordering is to limit fighting between members of a society. We are reluctant to challenge those of much higher status than ourselves. Like a ''ladder'' in tennis, a player can only challenge another player who is a few rungs ahead of him. The assumption is that the fiftieth ranked player on the ladder would have little chance against the first ranked player, and that, in order to earn the privilege of challenging the top player, he must first beat all the other people in between. This fits Lorenz's theory, since it cuts down the number of challenges (fights) that the champion must fend off.

Status refers to the rank an individual occupies in a group. This rank is accorded to him *by* the group. That is, *it* decides on the individual's status; he does not decide it himself. The Queen of England is accorded very high status by many of her subjects, but anti-monarchists see her as having little or no status. King Constantine of Greece suffered a marked fall in status in his own country when a popular vote decided to end the monarchy. He fell from being a King (by definition, one who is supreme) to being an ordinary man.

Status is acquired when the individual meets certain criteria within the group. The highest status member in a gun club might be the best shot. This same individual might rank very low in a group of pacifists who were against the use or ownership of weapons. *A group defines its needs, values and goals and ascribes the highest status to those of its members who best meet these needs, values and goals.*

Organizations have different needs, values and goals. They may value productivity, creativity, conformity, loyalty, energy, aggressiveness, etc. Depending on which of these sorts of attributes are most highly regarded, different individuals will acquire varying degrees of status or ''rank.''

Vance Packard (1959) lists six factors which contribute to the status ranking of an occupation. They are:

- Importance of the task performed;
- Authority and responsibility inherent in the job;
- Knowledge required;
- Brains required;
- Dignity of the job, and
- Financial rewards.

STATUS SYMBOLS

One of the problems with the status system in an organization, however, is that in order for it to perform its function of regulating behavior (making sure people realize where others are in the pecking order and treating them accordingly) it must be *visible*. It is important, therefore, to be able to judge where a person stands in the hierarchy before you begin to interact with him. Hence the preoccupation with *status symbols*—the trappings of power, rank, and prestige. Many organizations go to great lengths to differentiate between managers by subtle, but observable status symbols (Box 8-2).

BOX 8-2

THE USE OF STATUS SYMBOLS FROM: PACKARD (1959)

A stranger walking into a large organization often needs to know where the power lies and who's who. Without having a formal organization chart to look at, he may be able to discern the relative importance of various managers just by observing their "trappings of office." Vance Packard cites some examples:

"First, there is the physical problem of assigning office space. This is often done by rule. Crown Zellerbach Corporation, in planning its move to a new twenty-story building, has arranged walls so that offices for executives of equal rank can all be built to within a square inch of one another in size. In a typical corporation, the head of the hierarchy assigned to a floor gets the corner office with the nicest view, and the offices of his subordinates branch out from his corner in descending order of rank. Physical closeness to the center of power is considered evidence of status; and nobody wants to be put out in left field.

"Desks, too, typically are categorized by rank. Mahogany, of course, outranks walnut, and walnut outranks oak. The man who is entitled to wall-to-wall carpeting is likely to have a water carafe, which has replaced the brass spittoon as a symbol of flag rank, and also probably has a red leather couch. An executive with a two-pen set on his desk clearly outranks a man with a one-pen set. The private washroom, in many companies, is reserved for vice-presidents and up. Some have gold faucets. At a Midwestern oil firm, however, a fine line is drawn. The vice-presidents, like the president, have a private washroom; but it is literally that. Their washroom has no toilet, as the president's has.

"The circumstances under which an employee arrives for work also are highly indicative of status. Does the employee have to punch a time clock or not? Does he or she come through the plant gate or the office door? At what time does he or she arrive in relation to others? Bosses typically make it a practice to arrive either earlier or later than their flock. In England, a government proposal to ease the rush-hour traffic by persuading some business firms to start their day a half hour earlier encountered a snob barrier. White-collar workers of one large company that was considering opening a half hour earlier (at 8:30) vehemently objected. When questioned they reluctantly made the point that factory employees commonly started their work at 8:30, so that for them to do so would involve a loss of social prestige.

"Perhaps the most precise assigning of status symbols—certainly the most visible to the general public—is seen in the way many corporations assign company cars. A large oil company divides its management people into five levels for the purpose of distributing all sorts of special "perks," including the company cars. A Class I person (division managers, etc) is assigned a Cadillac or comparable limousine. A Class V person (salesman, etc.) is confined in his choice to certain specific models of Chevrolet, Ford and Plymouth.

"The hierarchy of a company can often be noted visually by inspecting the name posted before each parking space in the parking lot reserved for management. At an Ohio rubber company's office, the president's space is nearest the door (in case it rains), and the ranking vice-president's is next in line, and so on down the hierarchy."

ACQUIRING ROLE AND STATUS IN PRACTICE

Every group engages in a process of sorting out its members. This process of differentiation between group members is comfortable and easy to discuss in the *general* case. We can talk about how the status and background that individuals bring with them into a group help determine their ranking and role. We can talk about relative adherence to norms, differing skills, fitting the expertise of various individuals to certain tasks that the group must tackle, etc. But when a group of peers is confronted with the question of whether they are different, whether some are more skillful in certain areas than others, who should lead the group, who are its most valuable members, and so on, they tend to shy away from admitting any differences. Newly formed student groups are almost always reluctant to admit that there are any significant differences between their members. Stranger groups of managers exhibit the same tendency. Unless there are differences in hierarchical rank among the individuals in a group, they tend to say that all members operate similarly and contribute the same amount to the group's goals. The fact is, this is rarely true. Observers can spot the individual differences in behavior after a very short period of group discussion and activity. There are some people who tend to do most of the talking. There are some who answer questions rather than ask them. Some initiate interactions; some only respond; some are left out most of the time; some focus on task; some are mainly interested in the feelings of the other members of the group.

Perhaps one of the reasons that we are reluctant to admit to any differences when we are surrounded with a group of our peers is that our culture maintains the value that we are all equal. North Americans do not feel a strong sense of class difference. The feeling is still that "anyone can be President." Clearly that is not true, but it is not a myth that we wish to destroy. We value individuals for what they are more than who they are, for what they have done rather than what their ancestors have done.

Whether or not we value equality, however, we still engage in an assessment process of our fellow working members in a group. The criteria we adopt may not always be the best ones, but we all have some means of inferring value from behavior. Alex Bavelas and several of his colleagues (1965) conducted an interesting experiment to determine whether the amount of talking done by a group member significantly influenced his peers' ratings of his effectiveness, and if this "verbal output" could be affected by any outside reinforcement. Based on the observation that people tend to be fairly consistent in the amount of talking they do in a group, the experimenters were interested to see if they could change these patterns and thereby change the relative positions of group members.

Groups of four individuals (strangers) were seated around a table and presented with a problem to discuss. The experimenter retired from the room and (what else?) observed them through a one-way mirror, recording the amount of talking each person did. After ten minutes, the discussion was stopped by the experimenter and the four individuals were asked to fill out questionnaires ranking their fellow members on such scales as the amount of talking they had done, the quality of their ideas, and the amount of leadership they had exhibited. The data generated by these questionnaires showed that there was very high agreement by individuals on all three scales. These rankings also agreed with the experimenter's rankings of *who had talked the most*. It appears, therefore, that one of the initial criteria used for assessing an individual's value to a group is the amount of talking he does. Fortunately, that is not the only criterion we use.

DETERMINANTS OF STATUS RANKING AND INFLUENCE

Even before individuals have a chance to open their mouths and really contribute to a group's operation, the process of status ranking begins. People bring what might be termed *external status* with them when they join a group. The factors that may influence their peers' assessment of them include such things as age, sex, race, religion, education, experience, skills, or the formal role they occupy "outside" the group. For instance, in a group formed to solve a complex engineering problem, a group member with an engineering degree, experience in similar problem areas, and an "outside" job as president of an engineering company would likely be accorded high status and rank. His peers would expect him to be a valuable member of the group, helping them to achieve their task objectives.

Depending on the values, attitudes, beliefs and goals of the group members, different "external" factors will be seen as important. In some groups, age may be important; if all the members are over 50, perhaps they will look down on someone who is 26 as being "young and inexperienced." In certain groups, formal education might set a member in a high status position, but where all members have Ph.D.'s, the *lack* of this qualification affects status ranking. Some groups are formed on religious or racial lines; some require certain types of experience from their members; some require specific performance criteria to be met before an individual is admitted to membership (e.g., sports teams). Every working group has an idea of what criteria define valuable and effective team members, and individuals who meet these criteria are accorded higher status; those who do not meet them are placed lower on the list.

Something you might look for next time you become involved in a new working group is the manner in which people introduce themselves. Individuals often attempt to manipulate their initial status rankings by mentioning things about themselves that they feel will accord them high status. For instance, when an individual introduces himself with the phrase "I have a great deal of experience in . . .," or, "I am the vice-president of . . .," or some other heavy line, we all know what is going on. Sometimes the behavior is far more subtle than that. The individual who takes it on himself to introduce everyone, to begin to organize the group's activities, or to assign himself the position of chairman or secretary ("only until we get things rolling, of course") is also influencing the perception of his peers towards a high status ranking.

Ultimately, the whole process of initial status ranking can be summed up by the analogy with hiring someone for a job. The hirer (the group) has a list of criteria which are assumed to predict success in the job; applicants are reviewed in the light of the degree to which they match these criteria, and those who have the best "fit" go to the top of the pile. The only thing you have to know to predict initial status rankings in a group is what its members' criteria are—their goals, values and beliefs.

ANALYSIS OF GROUP PROCESS

Leaving aside for a moment the sort of subjective criteria that individuals immersed in the process of group operation use, how can an "outsider" identify role differentiation? We have maintained that a trained observer can make inferences from the behavior of group members that reflect their roles and relative status. This "behavior" is simply the interaction pattern that is evidenced in the group. Remember that when we talked about the I-A-S model, we defined interaction as "any interpersonal contact in which one individual can be observed acting, and one or more individuals responding to his action." (Whyte, 1969). Most of the "acting" that is observed tends to be verbal. We are as interested in what people say as what they do.

Robert Bales (1950) has developed a set of categories which he maintains includes all types of interactions in a working group. All interaction, says Bales, is either concerned with the group's *task accomplishment*, or with the maintenance of *social-emotional* factors.

The *task-oriented* interactions are concerned with:

- Asking for or providing *information*;
- Asking for or giving *evaluative comment*;
- Asking for or giving *direction*.

The *social-emotional* interactions are concerned with:

- Agreeing or disagreeing with *decisions*;
- Releasing or building *tension*;
- Helping and rewarding others, or attacking and deflating them—affecting the *integration* of the group.

A trained observer, watching a group in a problem-solving session is able to note not only the *type* of interactions engaged in by each member, but the *frequency* with which he speaks (or acts), the *direction* of the interaction (to whom he speaks), and whether the interaction was *initiated* or was in *response* to a request for something. On the basis of these data, it becomes clear who the leaders of the group are (they tend to be the ones who initiate more task-oriented interactions than their peers), who the isolates are (they neither say much nor have much said to them), who make up various subgroups (they are the people who tend to interact with one another more than the rest of the group), who performs the important function of maintaining a pleasant atmosphere and keeping conflict at an acceptable level (the individual(s) who tend to make the highest number of positive social-emotional comments), and so on.

Another means of analyzing the structure of a group is to construct what sociologists call a *sociogram*. A sociogram is simply a diagram which indicates the preferences people in a group have for their fellow members. Figure 8-2 is a simple sociogram, showing "lines of attraction." The sociometric procedure simply asks each member of a group to specify, privately, which of the other members he enjoys working with, or socializing with, and which members he would like to stay clear of. The resulting data allows the researcher to build up a diagram which shows the patterns of mutual attraction, dislike, or indifference among group members. This data, like the information from Bales' categories, presents a picture of the makeup of subgroups, leaders, isolates, popular members, or members valued for their task contributions.

One of the things that the Bales interaction process analysis and sociometric studies of groups show is that individuals are seen as valuable to the group for *different reasons*. Some are seen as being valuable for their attempts to get the task achieved, while others are valued for their social skills which make the work atmosphere more pleasant. Effective groups usually have members of both types. When task-oriented individuals are applying pressure on the group to get a job done and tension is mounting, the people-oriented members calm things down with a joke or with some action designed to relieve the emotional pressure for a moment.

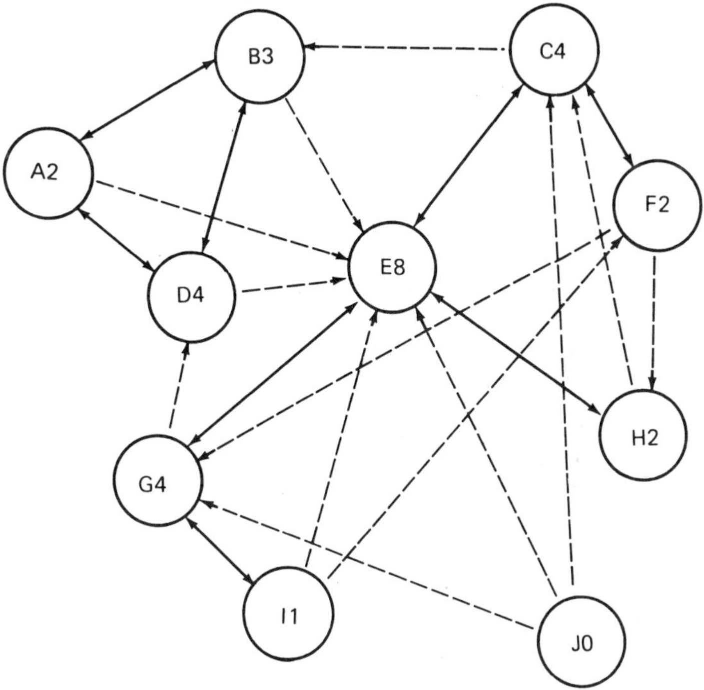

FIGURE 8-2: SOCIOGRAM OF A GROUP OF 10 EMPLOYEES SHOWING LINES OF ATTRACTION. EACH EMPLOYEE WAS ASKED TO VOTE FOR THE THREE PERSONS HE MOST DESIRED AS WORKING COMPANIONS. THE NUMERALS IN THE CIRCLES SHOW THE NUMBER OF VOTES EACH RECEIVED. (FROM: NORMAN R.F. MAIER, *PSYCHOLOGY IN INDUSTRIAL ORGANIZATIONS*, 5TH ED. BOSTON: HOUGHTON MIFFLIN, 1973.)

Groups which are composed of either entirely task-oriented or people-oriented types of individuals tend not be to effective. Either they are all task, and cannot "get together," or else they are all happiness, and can't get down to business.

EFFECTIVE OPERATING GROUPS

Managers spend a great deal of time working in groups. A study conducted in 1950 (Kriesberg) found that executives spent an average of 10 hours per week in formal committee meetings. More and more decisions are made by group process. Antony Jay (1976) remarks that "meetings fulfill a deep human need. Man is a social species. . . . If there are no meetings in the places where they work, people's attachment to the organizations they work for will be small." But on the other side of the coin, many meetings are unproductive or unpleasant. What are the essential dynamics of group meetings, and how can we manipulate them so as to make working with a group a pleasant and productive experience? In other words, how can we make group work effective?

There are a number of basic issues which are common to all working groups, from a group of workers in a fish filleting plant, to students working on a class project, to a group of engineers working on a bridge design, to a team of managers involved in the solution of a business problem. The effectiveness of each of these groups is a function of two things: (a) how they deal with these basic issues, and (b) the situational factors surrounding them.

The "basic issues" that groups face in working together center around what is termed in the jargon as *process*: They are the processes that the group must go through in order to decide on the way in which it will operate. The result of these process decisions affects the emergent behavior of the group and, depending on the situation in which they are working, helps determine their effectiveness.

These basic process issues include:

1 *Underlying goals*. What are the real goals of the group? These may center on getting the task done, or they may involve such things as *avoiding* the task, maintaining a friendly atmosphere in the group or adhering to procedure and precedent. Work groups do not always do what they are set up to do, as we know.

2 *Member contributions*. Who makes contributions to the group's discussions? Of what kind? How often? To whom?

3 *Listening*. The other side of the coin to contributing to a discussion is listening to what others say. How well does the group listen to one another? What sort of things do they pay attention to? Does everyone get a fair audience for his ideas and contributions?

4 *Conflict resolution*. In any group's discussions there must be disagreement at some point or other. How is this disagreement handled? Is conflict avoided at all costs? Is disagreement stifled by overpowering any weak members who dare to differ? Are differences openly explored in the quest for achieving the best possible group decision?

5 *Decision making*. How are decisions finally made? Does the "chairman" make them? Are they the result of a full consensus of all group members? Do the more powerful members "railroad" decisions?

6 *Leadership*. How is the question of leadership handled in the group? Is there a formal leader? Is there a veiled struggle for supremacy? Does nobody want to assume a leadership role? Does leadership vary within the group from task to task?

7 *Self-evaluation*. Does the group look at the way in which it operates and evaluate its own effectiveness? Is there a conscious attempt to modify behavior in order to become more effective? Does the group never really pay any heed to the way in which it works, simply operating in the same fashion time after time?

8 *Division of labor*. Who is to do what? Who is responsible for what? Who decides on the various assignments and responsibilities?

In an attempt to discover what makes some groups more effective than others, Douglas McGregor (1960) looked at these types of process issues and listed the characteristics of some of the highly effective teams he had observed and some of the less effective teams he had observed.

CHARACTERISTICS OF EFFECTIVE TEAMS	CHARACTERISTICS OF INEFFECTIVE TEAMS
UNDERLYING GOALS	
1 The task or objective of the group is well understood and accepted by the members.	From the things which are said, it is difficult to understand what the group task is or what its objectives are.
MEMBER CONTRIBUTIONS	
2 There is a lot of discussion in which virtually everyone participates, but it remains pertinent to the task of the group.	A few people tend to dominate the discussion. Often their contributions are way off the point.
LISTENING	
3 The members listen to each other. Every idea is given a hearing.	People do not really listen to each other. Ideas are ignored and overridden.
CONFLICT RESOLUTION	
4 There is disagreement. The group is comfortable with this and shows no signs of having to avoid conflict or to keep everything on a plane of sweetness and light.	Disagreements are generally not dealt with effectively by the group. They may be completely suppressed by a leader who fears conflict, result in open warfare between subgroups, or be "resolved" by a vote in which the minority is barely smaller than the majority.
DECISION-MAKING	
5 Most decisions are reached by a kind of consensus in which it is clear that everybody is in general agreement and willing to go along.	Actions are often taken prematurely before the real issues are either examined or resolved.
LEADERSHIP	
6 The chairman of the group does not dominate it, nor, on the contrary, does the group defer unduly to him.	The leadership remains clearly with the committee chairman. He may be weak or strong, but he sits always "at the head of the table."

	CHARACTERISTICS OF EFFECTIVE TEAMS	CHARACTERISTICS OF INEFFECTIVE TEAMS
	SELF-EVALUATION	
7	The group is conscious about its own operations. Frequently it will stop to examine how well it is doing or what may be interfering with its operation.	The group tends to avoid any discussion of its own "maintenance."
	DIVISION OF LABOR	
8	When action is taken, clear assignments are made and accepted.	Action decisions tend to be unclear—no one really knows who is going to do what.

These lists, drawn from McGregor's book *The Human Side of Enterprise*, picture group behavior as tending towards two poles—effective behavior being associated with openness, participation and democracy, and ineffective behavior being associated with mistrust, direction and autocracy. This dichotomy can be represented on a continuum, as in Figure 8-3.

A rather different approach to group effectiveness is taken by Reddin (1967) and others, who, building on Bales' findings that group interactions either focus on "task" issues or "relationships" issues, see some other options to the two proposed by McGregor. Figure 8-4 shows the Bales dimensions of group behavior as being independent of one another. That is, the degree to which a group, or an individual in a group, indulges in either *task oriented* behavior is not affected by, and does not determine, the degree to which they behave in a *relationships-oriented* manner.

Using the Bales findings, we come up with four basic modes of group operation, which we have labelled for convenience of reference. Before we begin to assess the effectivenes of these different types of groups, let's examine how each of them handles the process issues we mentioned earlier. This should give us a capsule description of how each of them operates.

A *systematic* group shows low concern for either achieving specific task goals or for building and maintaining warm, friendly relationships among its members. Its major goal centers on administering a set of rules or procedures. Contrib-

Effective Group Behavior	Ineffective Group Behavior
• Participative	• Directive
• Equalitarian	• Large Power Differences
• Open	• Veiled
• Trusting	• Suspicious
• Democratic	• Autocratic

FIGURE 8-3: A MODEL OF GROUP EFFECTIVENESS BASED ON A CONTINUUM FROM PARTICIPATIVE TO AUTOCRATIC OPERATION. A SUMMARY OF THE MCGREGOR VIEW.

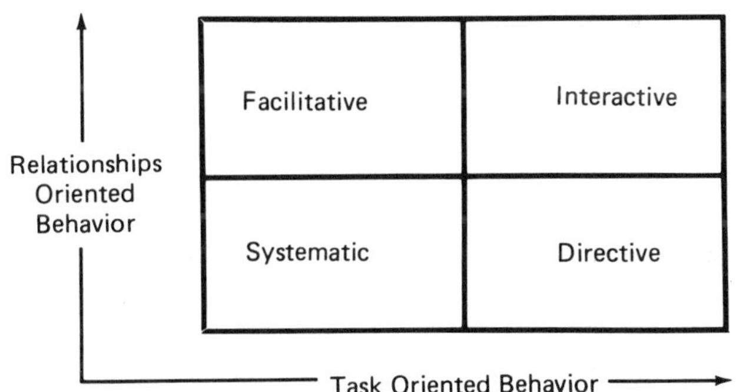

FIGURE 8-4: FOUR BASIC MODES OF GROUP OPERATION.

utions are formal, the group has a chairman, and discussion tends to be regulated according to some accepted rules of debate. Decisions are made by voting and conflicts are handled in the same manner. Responsibility is formally assigned to various individuals or sub-groups. There is a low degree of "listening," in the full sense of the word, and little or no self-evaluation on the part of the group to assess its effectiveness. This type of behavior is often seen among formal legislative groups—city councils, legislative assemblies, school boards, etc.

A *facilitative* group shows low concern for achieving specific task goals, but high concern for building and maintaining warm, friendly relationships among its members. In fact, its major goal is to have a happy, friendly group. Contributions are informal; there is no official chairman; equality is the order of the day; everyone has a say; the discussion often ranges far off topic, but nobody seems to mind very much; conflict is avoided; decisions are made largely on the basis of being able to please everybody concerned; there is a high degree of commitment to the group because it is pleasant to work in; tasks are equally shared; listening is good; the motto might be "let every flower grow." This type of group is often found in student organizations or creative or artistic parts of organizations.

A *directive group* shows low concern for building and maintaining warm friendly relationships among its members, but is deeply concerned with achieving certain task goals. This is clearly a work group. There is little room for personal relationships. Its major goal is to accomplish some task. Its actions tend to be directed by a strong leader who pushes the group towards the task; decisions are often pushed through the group by its more powerful members; conflict is suppressed; there is a lot of talking, but not much real listening to the points of view of others; the strongest arguer tends to win discussions; and the group does not reflect on its method of operation to see whether it is utilizing its resources most effectively. This type of group is often found where there is heavy pressure for getting things done quickly, or in organizations with distinct hierarchical levels of power and authority.

An *interactive* group is one that shows a high concern for *both* task achievement and the building and maintenance of warm, friendly relationships among its members. It not only gets things done, but its members enjoy working together. Its characteristics match many of those of McGregor's effective teams. Goals are clear and accepted by all involved; decisions are made on a consensus basis; discussion flows openly and involves everyone; leadership tends to move to the individual with the most relevant expertise for the task involved; the group spends time examining its behavior and seeking ways of increasing its effectiveness; conflict is openly confronted and sorted out. This type of group may be found in situations where complex problems are being confronted, decisions are difficult to make, and without precedent. This is what Reddin calls the "problem-solving" group.

So now we have capsule descriptions of *four* types of groups rather than two. So what? The question still remains, what is the most effective way for a group to operate? If McGregor's two types did not fill the bill, which of these four we have just looked at is best? The answer is, as you might now expect, "it depends on the situation."

GROUP EFFECTIVENESS—A SITUATIONAL VIEW

Clearly, these four group "styles" are caricatures. The world is not so simple that it can be neatly separated into four little boxes. There are very few working groups that would be described *completely* by one of these capsule descriptions alone; most would have the attributes of more than one pure type. However, these four boxes illustrate the *dominant* characteristics of most working groups. And we can identify some situational factors that determine, to a degree, the effectiveness of each of these four types of groups.

None of these group styles is "best." *What makes one or the other effective is the situation in which it operates*. For instance, *directive* groups are most effective when there are very tight time pressures. When the size of the group becomes very large, a *systematic* style works best. *Facilitative* groups are most appropriate where a high degree of creativity and commitment are required. *Interactive* groups are required for the solution of complex, one-of-a kind problems that utilize the resources of people from varied backgrounds and with differing areas of expertise.

Some of the major situational determinants of group effectiveness are listed in Figure 8-5. As the model indicates, each one of our four group "styles" is more effective under certain conditions than others.

If there are two main underlying dimensions to the behavior of people in groups, their orientation to task or their orientation to relationships, and if we can relate these types of behavior to effectiveness in certain situations, we're off and running. What the model in Figure 8-5 does is give us some guidelines as to how to act in order to make our groups function well. If you find yourself in a situation where a few members of your group have a good deal of expertise, there is a tight time deadline for completion of the group task, and quick decisions must be made in the face of rapidly changing conditions, you should probably encourage a directive style of operation. Cries for equality of contribution, decisions by full consensus, and rotating leadership should be recognized as more likely to *reduce* group effectiveness than increase it. The issue in working groups is not democracy vs. autoc-

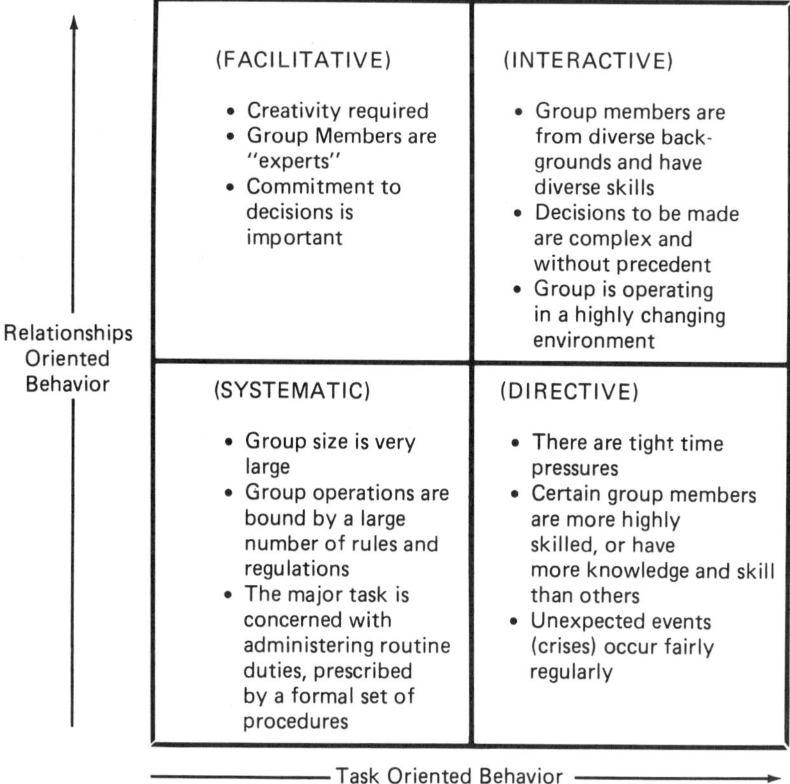

FIGURE 8-5: SITUATIONAL FACTORS THAT AFFECT GROUP PERFORMANCE.

racy; it is effectiveness vs. ineffectiveness. While we are strongly attracted to a model of behavior that emphasizes a high degree of relationships orientation, there are times when we have to swallow these notions a bit and let some decisions be made more directly. As the poet Tennyson put it,

> "Ah God, for a man with heart, head, hand,
> Like some of the simple great ones gone
> For ever and ever by
> One still strong man in a blatant land
> Whatever they call him, what care I,
> Aristocrat, democrat, autocrat—one
> Who can rule and are not lie."

DANIELS COMPUTER COMPANY REVIEWED

In Chapter 6 we presented you with Part II of Daniels Computer Company. At the end of that segment of the case, we saw that the project group had fragmented into four subgroups, based on the sections of the Memory Engineering Department.

These subgroups were competitive with one another rather than operating cooperatively, personal frictions began to develop between members of the different groups, the sections closed ranks around their members, and enthusiasm for the project as a whole waned. Not an ideal situation!

Take a moment now to read over Part II of the case, to review the predictions you made, and the changes you listed as being necessary at the end of Chapter 6 (and that you perhaps revised at the end of Chapter 7). Does what you now know about role theory, about status ranking, and about group process affect your thinking on the situation at all? What should be done now in Daniels Computer to rectify this situation? (We shall assume that the development of the new memory is an important job for the firm, and that it still wishes to complete it on time.)

Make a detailed action plan of what you propose be done to get the project back on track. Explain the reasons for your decisions. Please complete this task prior to reading the comments on the case that follows.

Some Applications to Daniels Computer Company

In Chapter 7 we saw the factors that either encourage group cohesiveness or discourage it. In this case we are talking about two levels of groups. One is the overall project group, and the other is the set of four subgroups comprised of people from the four sections in the department. If we look at each of these two levels of groups in turn and consider the forces that act either to encourage or discourage cohesion within them, we see that while the overall project may be perceived as important at higher levels of the organization, the independence and prestige of the various subgroups is overpowering at operating levels. The subgroups have never had to work together before. They see problems through the screen of their own technology and expect the other subgroups to adapt their work to it. The common enemy here is the three other groups.

There is already a strongly developed system of interpersonal attraction among the members of the subgroups, and the only success experience they have had in the past has been related to their *own* efforts, and not the efforts of others. They have little reason to begin cooperating with outsiders. The boundaries of their subgroups are too tight.

In some sense, the engineers and technicians of the subgroups are locals. Their focus is within the organization. They are used to their separate technologies, to working within their own physical confines, and to the status quo in general. What may be needed here is a "cosmopolitan" overview which can adapt outside approaches and technologies to the solution of the problem.

Looking at Kellman's model of influencing behavior, is there a specific strategy which should be adopted to get the individuals and subgroups to alter their behavior and get behind the project as a total group?

If we consider the issue of role and status for a minute, we can see that roles have become relatively rigid. Individuals are expected to exhibit subgroup loyalty first, departmental loyalty second and presumably organizational loyalty last. Expectations have been, and remain, that individuals in a particular section will apply only the technology of that section. There is no expectation either of having to take directions from outside the section or to work *with* other sections or technologies. Since each group has operated independently in the past, they may view having to work with others as a decrease in status. Their independence is at stake. The importance of their particular part of the technology may be in question.

Finally, if we were to look at the situational model of group process, presented at the end of this chapter, we might get some insight into the *direction* which the groups should ideally take in order to become more effective. The next question is how to get them there.

Chapter Summary

1 Organizations are composed of a set of roles. Each position in an organization has a set of role demands which it places on the incumbent.

2 A role may be defined as a set of behaviors that attaches itself to a particular position in an organization no matter who occupies that position.

3 Individuals may occupy a number of different roles, both in their organizations and outside. Each of these roles may demand different behaviors.

4 The demands of certain roles can be too much for the individual to cope with. Violation of role demands is disruptive of interaction patterns and may cause either the individual, or those people around him, to alter their behavior.

5 Individuals modify their roles through their personality. Roles are interpreted and played in a manner which is basically congruent with the individual's self-concept.

6 The role system in organizations often induces role conflict—a situation where either an individual is forced to occupy two roles simultaneously, or is bombarded with conflicting expectations concerning his role from different sources.

7 Groups of people living or working together impose a status ordering on themselves. Animal behaviorists explain the function of this ordering as a means of limiting fighting and challenges between members of a society—a "pecking order."

8 The term status refers to the rank an individual occupies in a group. It is accorded by the group, not the individual, and is based on criteria developed by the group.

9 In organizations, Packard suggests six factors which are used in determining status rankings:

- Importance of the task performed;
- Authority and responsibility inherent in the job;
- Knowledge required;
- Brains required;
- Dignity of the job;
- Financial rewards.

10 Status symbols are visible badges of status ranking, for example, office size, make of company car, and so on.

11 The manner in which groups operate (their "process") can be analyzed and evaluated in a number of ways. Bales has developed a technique of categorizing and evaluating interactions. Sociometric techniques look at the interaction patterns in groups, patterns of affiliation, power relationships, and so on.

12 Bales classifies all interactions in groups as being either task-oriented or social-emotionally-oriented. A simpler terminology is task-orientation and relationships-orientation.

13 There are a number of criteria on which group operation can be assessed. They include such things as the group's underlying goals, how it handles the question of member contributions, and so on. Each of these issues can be assessed on the degree to which it represents a participative, equalitarian approach to operation, or a directive, authoritarian approach.

14 Basing group analysis on the Bales dimensions of task-orientation and relationships-orientation, Reddin, Blake and others view group process as having two dimensions rather than simply functioning on a participative-authoritarian continuum. We have taken this approach and developed a model of four "types" of groups, each utilizing a different combination of task- and relationships-oriented behavior.

15 There is no ideal method of group operation. Group effectiveness is situationally based. We have developed a simple situational model which indicates when each of the four "types" of group process is most effective.

Part 4

Achieving the Outputs of the Required System

In this final section of the book we will begin to focus more on *action* issues. We understand something about why people behave as they do, first of all from an individual base, and then as a result of group pressures. We will still have to look at the types of forces that are exerted by the organization as a whole, but, given what we now know, perhaps the question should be raised, "What are we, as managers, supposed to *do*?" This section focuses on the answer to that question. It looks at how you, as a member of an organization, can "manage" others (or "lead" them), and get them to change their behavior appropriately as situations change.

Bear in mind as you read this section that the overall goal of management is *effectiveness*. We are concerned with achieving the goals of the organization, first and foremost. The achievement of results is what we're after: this section tells, "how to do it."

9

Making It Work: Leadership

OBJECTIVES

When you have completed this chapter you should:

- have a working knowledge of the concept of management style;
- be able to recognize the basic management styles used by managers in organizations;
- recognize that there is no one "best" management style; the effectiveness of any particular management style depends on the situation in which it is used;
- be able to diagnose organizational situations to determine which style a manager should use to handle them most effectively.

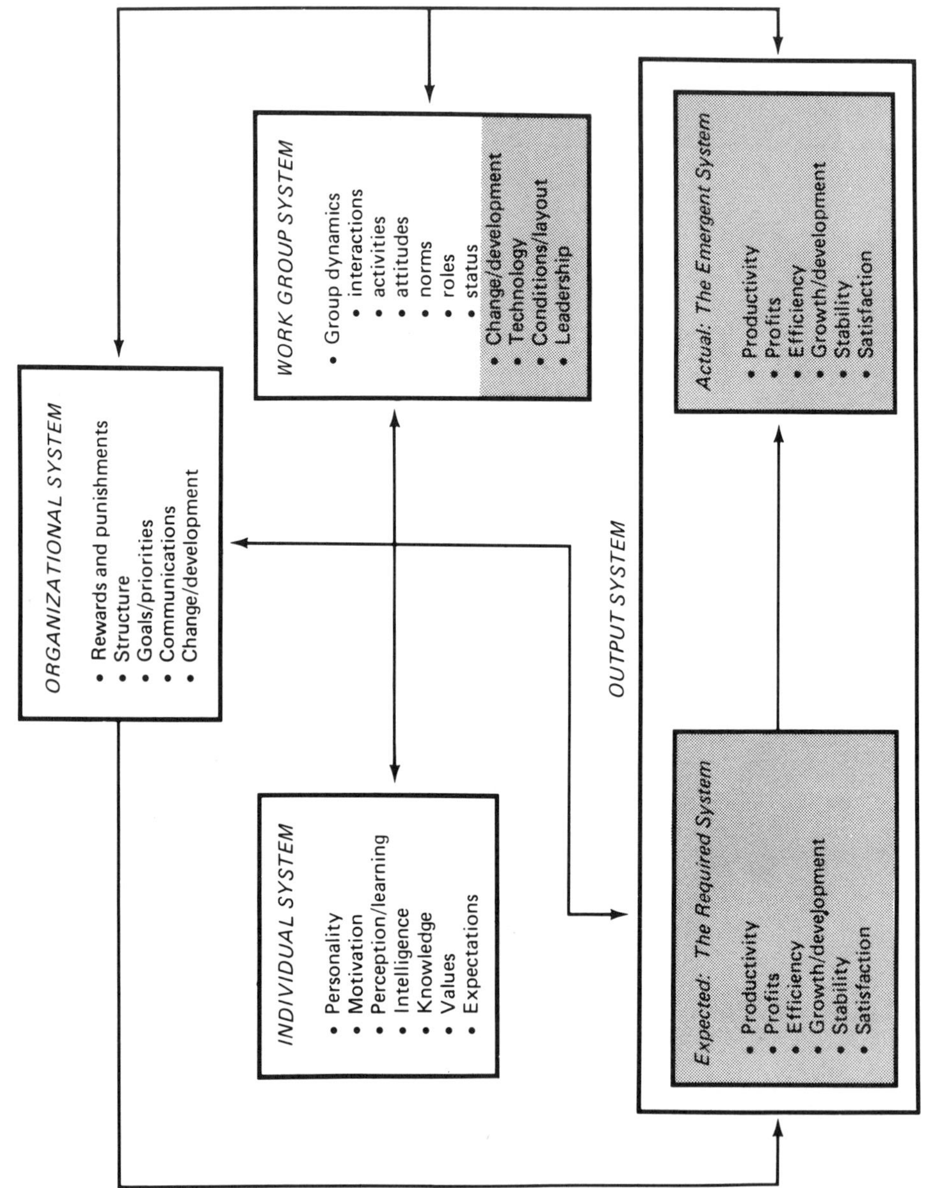

ORGANIZATIONAL SYSTEM
• Rewards and punishments
• Structure
• Goals/priorities
• Communications
• Change/development
INDIVIDUAL SYSTEM
• Personality
• Motivation
• Perception/learning
• Intelligence
• Knowledge
• Values
• Expectations
WORK GROUP SYSTEM
• Group dynamics
• interactions
• activities
• attitudes
• norms
• roles
• status
• Change/development
• Technology
• Conditions/layout
• Leadership
OUTPUT SYSTEM
Expected: The Required System
• Productivity
• Profits
• Efficiency
• Growth/development
• Stability
• Satisfaction
Actual: The Emergent System
• Productivity
• Profits
• Efficiency
• Growth/development
• Stability
• Satisfaction

A LETTER FROM DOUGLAS MCGREGOR*

"It will require time to think back over the many events that have been crowded into these few years and to draw a proper meaning from them. However, two related convictions have developed slowly but steadily out of this experience.

The first is a conviction which has been derived from my personal struggle with the role of college president. Before coming to Antioch I had observed and worked with top executives as an advisor in a number of organizations. I thought I knew how they felt about their responsibilities and what led them to behave as they did. I even thought that I could create a role for myself which would enable me to avoid some of the difficulties they encountered.

I was wrong! It took the direct experience of becoming a line executive and meeting personally the problems involved to teach me what no amount of observation of other people could have taught.

I believed, for example, that a leader could operate successfully as a kind of advisor to his organization. I thought I could avoid being a "boss." Unconsciously, I suspect, I hoped to duck the unpleasant necessity of making difficult decisions, of taking the responsibility for one course of action among many uncertain alternatives, of making mistakes and taking the consequences. I thought that maybe I could operate so that everyone would like me—that "good human relations" would eliminate all discord and disagreement.

I couldn't have been more wrong. It took a couple of years, but I finally began to realize that a leader cannot avoid the exercise of authority any more than he can avoid responsibility for what happens to his organization. In fact, it is a major function of the top executive to take on his own shoulders the responsibility of resolving the uncertainties that are always involved in important decisions. Moreover, since no important decision ever pleases everyone in the organization, he must also absorb the displeasure, and sometimes severe hostility, of those who would have taken a different course.

A colleague recently summed up what my experience has taught me in these words: "A good leader must be tough enough to win a fight, but not tough enough to kick a man when he is down." This notion is not in the least inconsistent with humane, democratic leadership. Good human relations develop out of strength, not of weakness.

I'm still trying to understand and practice what is implied in my colleague's statement."

*From B. von Haller Gilmer's *Industrial Psychology* (2nd ed.), McGraw-Hill, 1966. Reprinted with permission.

''Desire for leadership is like an infectious virus: once it seizes a victim, it rarely relinquishes him. The wish demands attention; the impulse its gratification, even at the sacrifice of pleasures others take for granted. The man who aspires to leadership soars on the fantasies of expectation. He will build, he will mold, he will shape destiny.''

—Levinson, 1968

''There is an almost universal assumption that even a small subpart of an organization can operate successfully only if some person has been formally designated as leader.''

—Katz and Kahn, 1966

Everyone is interested in leadership. It is a topic that fascinates man. We tend to believe that every group of people should have a leader, and we either praise or blame that leader for the group's performance. In wartime, when things are going badly, the first action taken is to change the commander. In the sports world, when things are going badly, the coach gets fired. In business organizations we fire the senior executives when performance is poor, and in politics we vote people out of power. The question that might be asked is whether changing the individuals at the top of an organization really changes the basic organization itself.

While the organization *itself* might not change, the *direction* in which it is headed often does. Organizations tend to reflect the values of their leaders. The leader's role is key to the success or failure of the unit.

But leadership is one of those concepts that, like personality, everybody talks about, but defines differently. Stogdill (1974) remarks that, ''there are almost as many different definitions of leadership as there are persons who have attempted to define the concept.'' The problem is that leadership is closely tied up with a number of other things, such as authority, power, communication, influence, personality, persuasion, etc.

We can think of leadership as being composed of two main elements:

1 What the leader does, (the *process* of leadership);

2 What the followers do, (the *results* of leadership).

There can be no leaders without followers. By the same token, we cannot really judge leadership effectiveness by what the leader *does*, but rather by what he *achieves*. Effective leaders may vary tremendously in their methods. For instance, Patton and Montgomery used very different approaches to their commands in World War II, but both were successful. Compare the two styles of management of Harold Geneen, retired Chief Executive Officer of International Telephone and Telegraph Corp., and Joachim Zahn of Daimler-Benz AG (makers of Mercedes-Benz)—see Box 9-1.

Leadership is concerned with getting people to do things. That may imply persuasion, coordination, initiative or whatever. But a leader, in any position, is expected to get something done. In many organizational settings, people behave in a certain way because of the manner in which the system is set up. The *job* requires certain behavior; i.e., getting in at 8 a.m., filling out certain forms, making certain decisions, performing certain duties. Once the individual in the job knows what he has to do, there is not much "leadership" that has to be applied; he is simply left to do it. Many supervisory jobs require little leadership capability. All they require is that the supervisor make sure there are enough materials for the job, that everyone is present, and that they are working. While there is *some* leadership in this sort of situation, it is largely the systems and procedures of the jobs that determine behavior. As Katz and Kahn (1964) remark, we should focus our attention on the kinds of individual behavior that go *beyond* required performance. They define leadership, therefore, as *"the influential increment over and above mechanical compliance with the routine directives of the organization."* Leadership is present when people are influenced to behave in a manner above and beyond the call of the routine aspects of the job alone. That is what we are concerned with: getting people to *move* and to *change*.

BOX 9-1

Managers vary quite widely in the way they run their companies. Some exert a great deal of personal pressure through the forcefulness of their personalities, literally driving their subordinates to high performance. Others seem far more prepared to delegate responsibility and to rely on subtler forms of persuasion. Harold Geneen of ITT and Joachim Zahn of Daimler-Benz are both highly successful men who have led their companies most effectively. The style is different, but the end result is similar.

Geneen's management style was described in an article in *Businessweek* (May 15, 1978) in the following terms:

> "(He ran) ITT's marathon general management meetings, legendary sessions in which he once dazzled some 150 managers at a time with his detailed knowledge of ITT's far-flung operations and established a reputation among his senior managers as something of a tyrant. He thought nothing of humiliating managers in front of their colleagues, or of keeping them in their meeting rooms for 15 hours or more at a stretch . . . He rarely minced words."

Zahn is described by *Fortune* (December 1977) as being somewhat different:

> "Zahn's relationship to his colleagues on the *Vorstand*, or management board, might be compared to that of Frederick the Great to his generals: one of mutual trust and informality . . . Most of the time . . . Zahn adopts a . . . conciliatory stance. He says, 'When I want to put forward an opinion in a meeting of the *Vorstand*, I am wise enough to do it in the form of a question.' "

IN SEARCH OF AN EFFECTIVE LEADERSHIP STYLE

Discussions of which style of management is most effective have been carried on since antiquity. Confucious, in about 500 B.C., travelled about China through the various small feudal kingdoms, attempting to persuade each of the rulers that he had a formula for effective leadership. Confucious believed that, to be effective, a ruler should be benevolent, humane, just and moderate. In the light of the behavior of rulers of the time, which was more accurately characterized by such adjectives as brutal, greedy, cruel and tyrannical, he was certainly putting forward a radical formula.

The first Emperor of China, Ch'in Shih Huang Ti, expressed his distaste with the idea 200 or so years later by having 460 Confucian monks either buried alive or buried to their necks and decapitated. A poor start for the Human Relations movement!

THE TRAIT APPROACH

Early twentieth century approaches to the problem of ascertaining the determinants of effective leadership style were based on what has been termed the "Great Man Theory." The assumption was that if we studied the lives of "great men"—leaders of proven excellence—we should be able to identify those qualities that differentiated them from more ordinary people. It was suggested that there were certain qualities, such as energy, intelligence, friendliness or aggressiveness that were essential for effective leadership. It was assumed that these traits were inherent in the good leader, that he was born rather than made, and that he could apply them in varying situations and always be effective. This approach resulted in the development of a vast number of lists of personal characteristics, each of which purported to describe the effective leader.

The trait approach was dealt a knockout blow in the late '40's, however, when an extensive survey of more than a hundred leadership trait studies (Stogdill, 1948) came up with the basic conclusion that "the qualities, characteristics, and skills required in a leader are determined to a large extent by the demands of the situation in which he is to function as a leader." This research made it clear that it was not enough simply to examine the behavior of leaders, but that one had to take into account the situations in which they operated. Leaders who were effective in one situation were not necessarily effective in another.

QUESTIONING THE BASIC ASSUMPTIONS

The situational banner was taken up by Douglas McGregor in his book, *The Human Side of Enterprise*, to which we referred in the last chapter. McGregor has been widely misinterpreted as saying that a participative, open, democratic style of leadership is more effective than an autocratic, directive, authority-based one. In fact, McGregor simply raised the issue of *alternative* behavior patterns which might lead to effective management.

Building on the motivational theories of Maslow, McGregor argued that the traditional assumptions about the nature of man held by most managers were largely inadequate. As McGregor remarked, "Behind every managerial decision or action are assumptions about human nature and human behavior." We all have a "theory" of human behavior. As we discussed in Chapter 1, these theories, or assumptions, to use McGregor's term, help us in dealing with what would otherwise be an unpredictable and uncertain phenomenon: people. Just as this book will hopefully challenge some of the assumptions you might presently hold about human behavior, McGregor sought to challenge some of the widely held assumptions of managers about the nature of man and his relationship to work and authority.

McGregor listed what he saw as common assumptions reflected in managerial thinking and writing, terming them "Theory X." The assumptions of an individual who subscribes to Theory X are such things as: (McGregor, 1960)

1 The average human being has an inherent dislike of work and will avoid it if he can.
2 Because of this human characteristic of dislike of work, most people must be coerced, controlled, directed, threatened with punishment to get them to put forth adequate effort toward the achievement of organizational objectives.
3 The average human being prefers to be directed, wishes to avoid responsibility, has relatively little ambition, wants security above all.

These assumptions, claimed McGregor, formed the basis for the highly widespread belief in a directive, autocratic style of management (leadership) as being most effective. *But*, said McGregor, the findings of the motivational theorists suggest that man is not like that at all; that in fact there is a completely different set of assumptions which we could make about human behavior, and maybe we should give them some consideration in deciding on the best type of approach to use in the supervision of people. McGregor (1960) termed these assumptions "Theory Y." They are:

1 The expenditure of physical and mental effort in work is as natural as play or rest. The average human being does *not* inherently dislike work.
2 External control and the threat of punishment are not the only means for bringing about effort toward organizational objectives. Man will exercise self-direction and self-control in the service of objectives to which he is committed.
3 The motivation to work results from such higher level needs as self-actualization, achievement, self-esteem, etc., as well as from needs for security and physiological wants.
4 The average human being learns, under proper conditions, not only to accept but to seek responsibility.

5 The capacity to exercise a relatively high degree of imagination, ingenuity, and creativity in the solution of organizational problems is widely, not narrowly, distributed in the population.
6 Under the conditions of modern industrial life, the intellectual potentialities of the average human being are only partially utilized.

As you can see, the Theory Y assumptions reflect the same sort of assumptions about human behavior that Maslow's theory does. McGregor did *not* say that Theory Y assumptions reflected the "truth" about the nature of man, but only that they represented another view that deserved some attention, and that they appeared to be supported by current research in motivation. But clearly, the leadership style of a manager with Theory X assumptions would tend to be quite different from that of one with Theory Y assumptions.

There you have it. Two quite opposite theories of human behavior. Theory "X," based on one set of assumptions, but the more widely held ones. "X" thinkers dominated organizations. Their assumptions seemed to have worked well to date (Frederick Taylor was very successful using them. See Appendix.).

Theory "Y" was based on quite different assumptions of human behavior. These assumptions were not widely held; they had not been tested a great deal; they were the product of non-industrial thinkers—academics and philosophers. If you were a manager, which would you choose to accept?

McGregor appealed for a situational approach to leadership and management:

> "There are at least four major variables now known to be involved in leadership: (1) the characteristics of the leader; (2) the attitudes, needs, and other personal characteristics of the followers; (3) characteristics of the organization, such as its purpose, its structure, the nature of the tasks to be performed; and (4) the social, economic, and political milieu. The personal characteristics required for effective performance as a leader vary, depending on the other factors." (McGregor, 1960)

However, we have always been in search of the Holy Grail in some form or other, so a lot of effort was expended in the investigation of which style of management was "best."

THE MICHIGAN STUDIES

Beginning in 1947, the Institute for Social Research at the University of Michigan instituted a large-scale program of research on the human problems of administration, part of which was concerned with discovering "the organizational structure and the principles and methods of leadership and management which result in the best performance." (Likert, 1961). Studies were conducted in a wide variety of organizations, including automotive, electronics, food, insurance, paper, and railroad companies. The basic design of most studies was to look at the type of leadership and other variables in the best units in an organization as compared to the worst units. ''Best'' was measured on the basis of such criteria as productivity, job satisfaction, employee turnover, absenteeism, wastage, motivation, etc.

In terms of leadership styles, the studies identified two basic orientations of managers and supervisors: *job-centered*, or *employee-centered*. The job-centered manager operates on a ''scientific management'' basis: break down the job, find the best way to do it, hire the right person for it, train him properly, supervise him closely, and reward him with money on the basis of a piece rate if possible. The employee-centered manager focuses his attention on the human aspects of the job, builds working teams, gets close to his subordinates, and participates in the setting of goals with them. These two styles are represented on a *continuum* (Figure 9-1).

Job-centered leadership ←---------→ Employee-centered leadership

FIGURE 9-1: THE MICHIGAN STYLE CONTINUUM. EMPLOYEE-CENTERED LEADERSHIP IS SEEN AS MORE EFFECTIVE THAN JOB-CENTERED LEADERSHIP.

The general conclusion drawn from these studies was that employee-centered managers were more effective than job-centered managers. Tannenbaum and Schmidt (1958) elaborated on the Michigan continuum and produced a model that provided ''stages'' of job-centered (boss-centered) or employee-centered (subordinate-centered) behavior. The implication was still, however, that the further one moved toward the employee-centered end of the continuum, the more effective one was likely to become. (Figure 9-2)

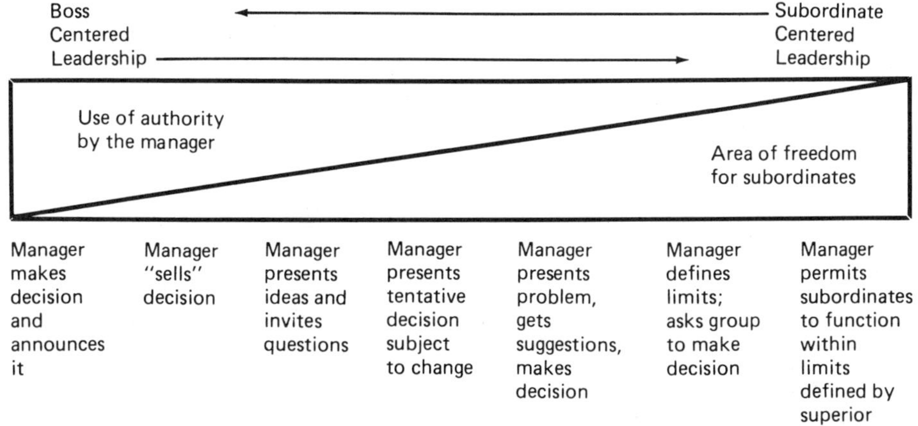

FIGURE 9-2: TANNENBAUM AND SCHMIDT'S CONTINUUM OF LEADERSHIP BEHAVIOR. (FROM: R. TANNENBAUM AND W.H. SCHMIDT, ''HOW TO CHOOSE A LEADERSHIP PATTERN.'' *THE HARVARD BUSINESS REVIEW*, MARCH-APRIL, 1958, P. 96)

THE OHIO STATE STUDIES

At about the same time that the Michigan studies were taking place, Carroll Shartle was initiating the Ohio State Leadership Studies (Shartle, 1956). Their focus was on the *behavior* that individuals exhibited while they were in a leadership role. While their results are far more complicated than we present here, the central finding of the Ohio State research was that leadership behavior is basically concerned with two independent factors called *initiating structure* and *consideration*.

- *Initiating structure* concerns such behavior as organizing and defining group activities, and defining roles within the work group. It has to do with planning, organizing, controlling and directing.
- *Consideration* involves such things as developing trust, respect and warmth between a manager and his subordinates.

One of the most important findings of the Ohio State Research was that initiating structure and consideration were basically *independent* of one another. That is, that the amount of 'structure' that a manager exhibited in his behavior in no way predicted the amount of 'consideration' he might exhibit, and vice-versa.

This is an extremely important finding in that it means that a manager may exhibit a number of combinations of these two basic behaviors and that the use of one does not necessarily exclude the other. Being independent of one another, the two basic factors can be represented (Figure 9-3) as being at *right angles*, rather than being on a continuum. A leader can exhibit *both* a high degree of "consideration" (employee-centeredness) *and* a high degree of "structure" (job-centeredness) at the same time. Or, on the other hand, he can exhibit a *low* degree of both, or a high degree of one and a low degree of the other.

If the two scales of structure and consideration were each to be divided into a "high" and "low" category, the model would look like Figure 9-4, and we would have *four* basic leadership styles, as represented by the four possible combinations of high and low degrees of structure and consideration.

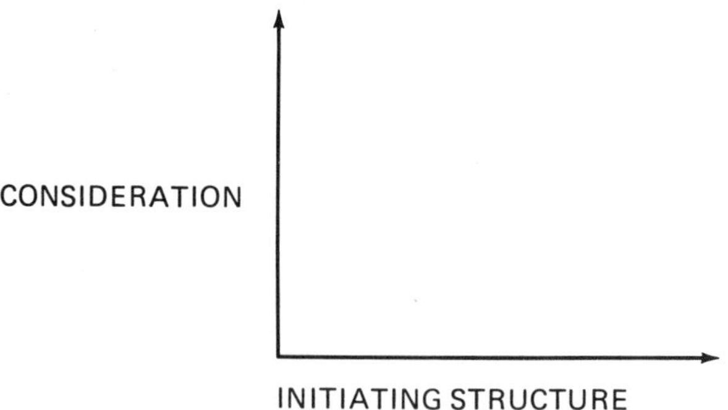

FIGURE 9-3: THE OHIO STATE LEADERSHIP FACTORS.

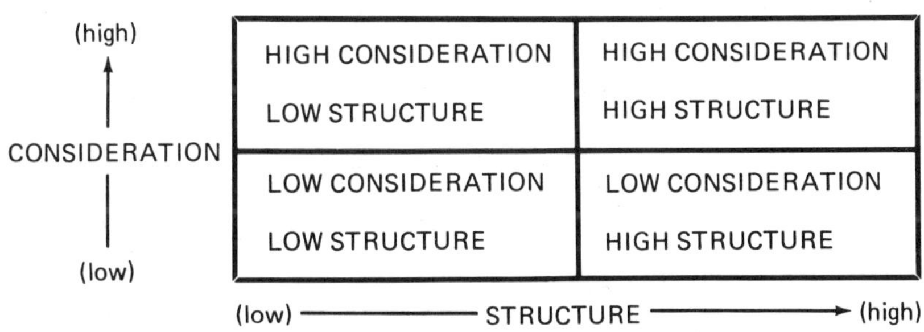

FIGURE 9-4: FOUR BASIC STYLES OF MANAGEMENT, COMPOSED OF VARIOUS COMBINATIONS OF STRUCTURE AND CONSIDERATION.

CHOOSING A LEADERSHIP MODEL

The Michigan and Ohio State models are quite different from one another. The former says that if you want to become more employee-centered, you have to become less job-centered, and vice-versa. The latter says you can be both simultaneously. Which do you prefer? Is it a question of two styles versus four? What difference does it make? Are they both saying the same thing?

The Michigan model has undergone some changes and the two variables are now seen as being more independent of one another than previously represented (Kahn, 1960), but the basic model is still behind much of the writing in leadership (Likert and Likert, 1976). The major reservation which must be expressed about it, however, is that it fails to predict effectiveness in *all* cases. If we are talking about a "best" style of management, then it might be assumed that the style would *always* give the best results. Likert (1961) summarized the findings from one study which looked at the productivity of sections in a company under job-centered and employee-centered management. These data are presented in Figure 9-5.

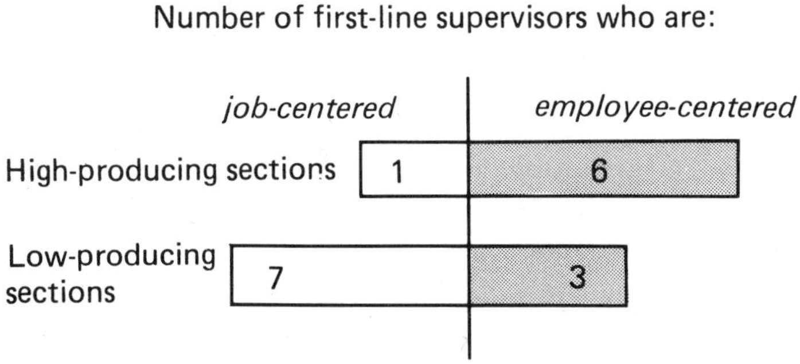

Number of first-line supervisors who are:

	job-centered	*employee-centered*
High-producing sections	1	6
Low-producing sections	7	3

FIGURE 9-5: LIKERT'S DATA ON PRODUCTIVITY OF SECTIONS SUPERVISED BY EMPLOYEE-CENTERED AND JOB-CENTERED SUPERVISORS. (LIKERT, 1961.)

While 6 out of the 7 high-producing sections were managed in an employee-centered manner, one of them was run by a *job*-centered supervisor. And when we look at the low-producing sections, we see that 7 out of 10 were managed in a job-centered manner—but why weren't *all* the job-centered supervisors' sections low-producing? What about the three *employee*-centered sections that failed to be productive?

All that this sort of data indicates is that *it is highly unlikely that there is one ideal style of leadership, a style that is always "best."*

What we should be looking for (and you should be getting used to this by now) is a *situational* model. The real question is not which leadership style is best, but which leadership style is best in which situation?

Reddin (1970), building on the Ohio State findings, has argued that the four basic styles of leadership which result from the various combinations of high and low degrees of consideration and structure are all effective if used in the appropriate situation. He states his case this way:

> "Some managers have learned that to be effective they must sometimes create an atmosphere which will induce self-motivation among their subordinates and sometimes act in ways that appear either hard or soft. At other times, they must quietly efface themselves for a while and appear to do nothing. It would seem more accurate to say, then, that any basic style may be used more or less effectively, depending on the situation."

In Chapter 9 we developed a situational model of group behavior, labelling four group "styles." In that model, we used the term *relationships-oriented* behavior and *task-oriented* behavior rather than "consideration" and "structure," to describe the two main style variables. We can use the same terms to talk about leadership style. Our model is shown in Figure 9-6.*

Task-oriented behavior (TOB) is that behavior which is centered around planning, controlling, scheduling, designing and directing the activity of subordinates.

Relationships-oriented behavior (ROB) is that behavior that is centered around establishing and maintaining warm, friendly, personal relationships with subordinates. It is manifested in such activities as building close working teams, developing the potential of subordinates, and building an atmosphere of trust and encouragement.

We have labelled the four basic styles of management (we will use the terms management and leadership interchangeably, since we define a manager as an individual who is responsible for the performance of one or more subordinates) *systematic, directive, facilitative,* and *interactive* simply for ease of reference. You

*There is nothing particularly new and original about this model. Blake and Mouton (1964) have developed a managerial grid based on the same variables, and Reddin's 3-D Theory of Managerial Effectiveness (1970) also talks about four basic styles of leadership. Our situational model is largely based on Reddin's and most of the following discussion is drawn from his work (Reddin, 1970, 1972; Reddin and Stuart-Kotze, 1976).

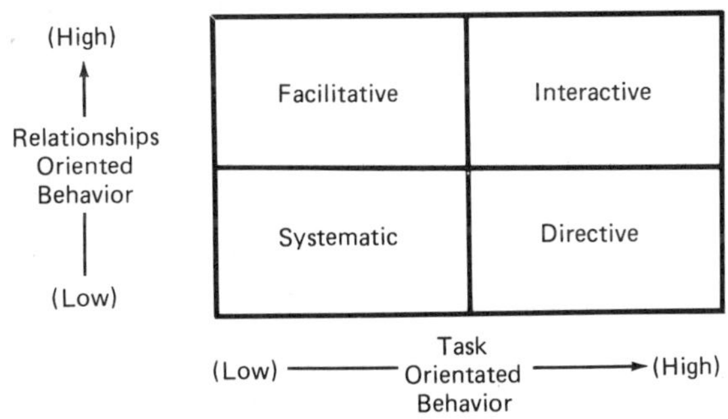

FIGURE 9-6: FOUR BASIC LEADERSHIP STYLES.

could call them whatever you like. The following are capsule descriptions of the four styles:

The systematic manager exhibits a low degree of both task-oriented behavior (TOB) and relationships-oriented behavior (ROB). His activities center around the administration of a system of rules and procedures. He does not take the initiative to personally plan, direct or design the activities of his subordinates, nor does he involve himself in developing the skills and abilities of subordinates, or in building close working teams among them. His behavior is involved with doing again what was done before; he works on the basis of precedent and "the way we always do things." He tends to be formal in his communication, preferring to write memos, reports, and letters rather than communicate verbally. He handles meetings formally, structuring them with a chairman and secretary, and often using rules of debate. He works from as detailed a job description as possible and administers to his subordinates on the basis of their job descriptions. He arbitrates conflicts according to the rules. His behavior is dominated by a concern for procedures, rules, systems and codes of behavior. He is conservative.

The directive manager exhibits a high degree of task-oriented behavior (TOB) and a low degree of relationships-oriented behavior (ROB). His activities center around planning, controlling, scheduling, designing and directing the activities of his subordinates. He does not attempt to establish warm personal relationships with them, nor does he concern himself particularly with developing them and helping them realize some level of potential. He gives them jobs, tells them what to do, when to do it, and watches to make sure they *do* do it. He likes things done his way, and as quickly as possible. His time frame is "now." He is energetic and dominant. In communication with subordinates, he does most of the talking. He doesn't like open and free-wheeling discussions; he dominates meetings and keeps the conversation on track. He tells subordinates only what they need to know to do their own jobs, and when conflict arises, he suppresses it. His behavior is dominated by a concern for getting the job done—his way. He is assertive.

The facilitative manager exhibits a low degree of task-oriented behavior (TOB) and a high degree of relationships-oriented behavior (ROB). His activities center around establishing and maintaining warm, friendly, personal relationships with his subordinates, building close working teams, and helping subordinates grow and develop in their jobs. He delegates jobs to subordinates and places himself in an advisory, helping role, offering assistance if they need it. He tends to build supportive work groups in which the members aid one another in accomplishing their tasks. He does not closely supervise or control the work of his subordinates; he sees subordinates largely as equals and friends. He tends to let people do their own thing. He is more concerned with the future than the present and generally fails to see any sense of urgency in things. He offers little direction, lets meetings and discussions get off track easily, and prefers verbal to written communications. He avoids conflict. His behavior is dominated by a concern to be liked. He is sentimental.

The interactive manager exhibits a high degree of both task-oriented behavior (TOB) and relationships-oriented behavior (ROB). His activities center around guiding and coordinating the activities of subordinates. He involves himself in planning, controlling, scheduling, designing and directing the activities of his group, by making himself a part of the group and involving all of the members in these decisions. He is deeply concerned with getting the job done, and done well, but sees himself as only a part of the team that must accomplish the task. He builds working teams where there is maximum contribution from all members, and he emphasizes the setting of challenging but achievable goals. He would prefer to work in an atmosphere of harmony but realizes that conflicts are inevitable and often highly constructive. His approach to conflict is to face it openly, uncover its roots, and try to reach a consensus solution to it. He has a low concern for power differentials and sees himself as largely working with a team of colleagues. He gets the work group to set performance objectives and monitors and evaluates their achievement. In meetings he listens as much as he talks, but he tends to keep the discussion on track. He is more concerned with results than activities. His behavior is dominated by a concern for teamwork. He is professional.

These capsule descriptions are intended to give you a feel for the *type* of behavior that a manager exhibiting each of these styles would use. They are not intended as comprehensive descriptions, nor do they represent a checklist which must be completed for a style analysis to be made. You should, however, be able to recognize the basic differences between the four styles. The question now is, which of them is effective?

MATCHING STYLE AND SITUATION

The interesting thing about this model is that each of the four basic managerial styles can be effective, if it is used in the appropriate situation. We are not caught in the dilemma of choosing between job-centered and employee-centered approaches to management, with the assumption that one is better and more effective than the other. Our problem is a different one. What we have to do is recognize *when* a certain style is best. In other words we have to be able to analyze the situation.

A manager's situation can be thought of as being made up of two sets of

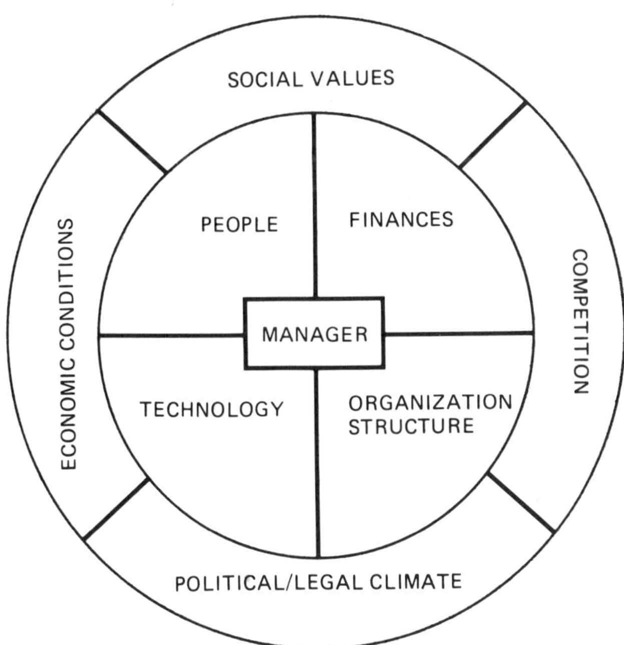

FIGURE: 9-7: THE MAJOR ELEMENTS AFFECTING A MANAGERIAL SITUATION.

factors. The *internal* elements of the situation include the *technology* he must manage, the *people* above, below and around him, the *organization structure* within which he must work, and the *financial* limitations on his actions. These factors all exist within the boundaries of the organization itself, but in turn may be influenced by factors outside the organization's control. These *external*, environmental, factors include general *economic conditions*, the *competitive situation* in the industry, the *political climate* of the country or region, and the set of basic *social values* that govern the behavior and expectations of the work population (Figure 9-7).

The manager finds himself at the center of this system. It is his job to diagnose the demands each of these factors is placing on him and to handle them most effectively.

Having a picture of the elements which go to make up a managerial situation is a step in the right direction, but, in order to be able to manage in an effective manner, one must be able to recognize *different types* of situations which require different methods of handling. In other words, the manager must know when the *specific* technology he is managing requires that he act in a certain fashion, or when the *particular* people with whom he has to work will react most positively to one type of action rather than another. What is required is some way of classifying situations.

One method of classifying situations is by the kind of management style which will be most effective in each type of situation. One can think of *situations* as being systematic, directive, facilitative, or interactive.

The management style of fishing captains has not changed for hundreds of years. The most effective captains operate in a directive manner. They retain almost sole control over the planning and operation of their voyages. They give precise, direct orders and expect them to be carried out exactly. They keep a distance from the crew and do not enter into personal relationships with them. They identify with the ship's owners and with the technical aspects of fishing. They judge their subordinates on the degree to which they carry out their functions efficiently and as directed. They have a great deal of power over the ship and its crew. Their bond with the crew is productivity; the captain depends on the crew to do its job well and the crew depend on the captain to give the right orders and take the ship to the right place. If the catch is good, all parties benefit. If the catch is poor, barring some accident over which the captain had no control, he is held personally responsible, and a captain who has several bad catches in a row finds it extremely difficult to get a crew together.

Clearly, the managerial situation facing a fishing captain is a directive one. It requires a directive style of management and all good fishing captains know it.

The captain's management style is largely determined by the *technology* he has to manage. But the *organization structure, financial arrangements* and *people* also affect the way in which he operates.

The *technology* of modern ground-fishing is characterized by a combination of sophisticated machinery and individual know-how and experience. The captain, because of his experience and his grasp of all the elements of fishing, has far more knowledge about how to carry out the task than anyone else on board ship. The technology of fishing entails a large number of unexpected, unscheduled events, things like changes in weather, movements of fish, etc. And performance is easily measured at the quayside at the end of the voyage. This type of technology calls for a directive style from the manager.

The *organization structure* places the captain in sole command, with almost unlimited power, and with ultimate and complete responsibility for the success of the voyage. It makes him at once the servant of the owners, and the servant of the crew; both depend on him for their success. It centralizes all decisions with him and cuts him off in large part from being able to delegate either upwards or downwards.

The *financial aspects* of commercial fishing also place the captain in a position which requires him to use a directive style of management. He is entrusted with a capital sum in the form of a ship, equipment and crews. The return on this capital investment to the owners, and the return on the crew's investment of time and effort are dependent on the captain's effectiveness in finding and catching fish. He cannot afford failure in the eyes of either party. He is under tight time and money constraints from both sides.

And, of course, the demands placed on him by the crew—the *people* element of this managerial situation—are for output, not input. The crew wants fish and lots of them. They do not particularly care if the captain sleeps all the time or drinks constantly, as long as they continue to catch lots of fish quickly and get home safely. They are not concerned with how hard he works or what he has to do, as long as he produces. Nor does it matter particularly if they like him, as long as he does a good job for them and does not make their lives and jobs unbearable. They want neither sophistication, friendship nor participation; they want performance—the right decisions and orders at the right time.

DETERMINING THE STYLE DEMANDS OF THE SITUATION

If we accept the idea of classifying situations in terms of the management styles they "require" to be handled effectively, how do we actually make these classifications? Are there a number of questions one can ask of each element of the situation that will point to the most effective style to use in managing it? Can the various types of situations be described in terms of each of the separate elements that go to make up the whole situation?

STYLE DEMANDS OF TECHNOLOGY

All we mean by technology is *"how the job is done."* For instance, some jobs are done by following rules and procedures that have been set down, others require a good deal of individual creativity; some are repetitive and simple, others are unique and complex; in some, time is of the essence, in others there is no great rush; some are performed in isolation, others require a good deal of interaction. The way the job has to be done exerts demands on the manager to behave in certain ways. In other words, the way the work is done determines, to some extent, the appropriateness of a managerial style.

Box 9-2 contains a set of technology "indicators." These are about *"how the job is done."* They are grouped into sets of five statements.

In assessing what style, or behavior, an individual should use in managing a particular *job*, go through the technology style indicators for each basic style and ask this question of each, *"Does this statement describe the way the job is done?"* If, for a particular set, you get five yesses, it's a pretty clear indication that the manager should use that basic style in order to manage effectively. If you answer affirmatively only once or twice in any set of five statements, then the job does not strongly require this style from the manager.

A job can be described by the type of managerial style it requires to be performed most effectively. Some jobs are best supervised by managers using one particular style, and some require the blending of two or more styles.

STYLE DEMANDS OF ORGANIZATION STRUCTURE

Organization structure refers to *the way in which the work is organized*, or, more cynically, "who does what, and to whom." Organization structure concerns such things as status differentials between levels, the number of levels in the

BOX 9-2

TECHNOLOGY INDICATORS

Relationships-Oriented Behavior ↑

FACILITATIVE	INTERACTIVE
• subordinates are experts and know more about their own jobs than the manager; • few time constraints • no defined "best methods" of doing the job; • subordinates find the work intself intrinsically attractive; • a major requirement of the job is creativity.	• the subordinates and the manager have different and varying skills, expertise and knowledge; • the time frame for decisions is medium to longterm; • subordinates must interact with one another in order to get the job done; • decisions are of wide-reaching significance to the organization; • the major output of the job is a complex, one-of-a-kind decision or product.
SYSTEMATIC	**DIRECTIVE**
• the job requires close adherence to rules, procedures, and precedents; • decisions can only be made within certain limits; • communications are generally formal; • there is an emphasis on the maintenance of records and files; • a major requirement of the job is consistency.	• the manager has greater expertise or knowledge than the subordinates; • subordinates' jobs tend to be narrow and skill-oriented, and performance is easily measurable; • the work is governed by tight time pressures; • rapid and unexpected changes are introduced into the job from time to time; • major requirements of the job are speed and flexibility.

Task-Oriented Behavior →

organization, the nature of authority, control, and responsibility in the system, the communications network, and so on. The way in which a manager behaves is influenced by these sorts of factors, and once again, as we did with the technology indicators, we should ask the question ''Does this statement describe the situation in the job under consideration?'' (Box 9-3) Affirmative answers indicate the style demands of the *organization structure*.

STYLE DEMANDS OF PEOPLE

Another critical situational element with which a manager must deal is the *people* in his organization, his subordinates, coworkers and superiors. They often exert strong pressures on him to manage in a certain way and in many situations are the dominant element in determining which management style he must use to be effective.

Individuals respond to certain management styles better than others. The style demands which individuals in an organization place on a manager are a combination of their *expectations* as to how they should be managed and their *preferences* or likings for one style over another. Individuals enter jobs with a preference as to how they would like to be managed and modify this in the light of their expectations of the actual style which will be used. If expectations and preferences are too far out of line, the individual will not take the job. If they become out of line while he is incumbent, it will cause demotivation and dissatisfaction. Of course, some individuals misread situations initially and find themselves put into jobs where preferences and expectations *are* out of line. Skill in reading the situation can overcome this problem.

The Core Job Issues

People's style demands on their managers center around five core issues. These are essentially qualities of the job and reflect the ''culture'' or ''climate'' of the work unit. They are ''*the way people operate*.'' They come under the following general headings:

- Decision making and conflict resolution;
- Job measurement and design;
- Job communications;
- Change introduction;
- Basis for rewards.

To measure the style demands of people in a job situation the manager must ask himself the question, ''*Does this reflect the way in which my subordinates/coworkers/superiors expect and prefer this issue to be handled*?'' Affirmative answers indicate the style demands of the *people* in the situation (Box 9-4).

BOX 9-3

ORGANIZATION STRUCTURE STYLE INDICATORS

FACILITATIVE • There is little status difference between levels in the organization; • There are few levels and wide spans of control; • Jobs are loosely described; • Reporting relationships are blurred; • Informal groups form the work base.	INTERACTIVE • Project teams, made up of staff and line managers from different functions and levels, are widely used; • Information is openly and easily accessible; • Jobs are linked closely with one another through clear objectives and output requirements; • Responsibility is clearly assigned and agreed to; • Teams form the work base.
SYSTEMATIC • Position in the organization is based largely on formal qualifications and length of tenure; • Jobs are described in detail; • Career paths are formally designated and planned; • The chain of command is clear and inflexible; • There are distinct status differences between levels.	DIRECTIVE • There are many levels and a narrow span of controls; • There are major power differences between levels in the organization; • Performance is measured against regularly set targets; • Communication generally flows from the top down; • The individual forms the work base.

Vertical axis: Relationships-Oriented Behavior

Horizontal axis: Task-Oriented Behavior

BOX 9-4

PEOPLE INDICATORS

FACILITATIVE	INTERACTIVE
• Subordinates make their own decisions; • Subordinates set their own objectives; • Job communication is largely upward, from subordinates to superiors, and horizontal, among coworkers; • Change centers around people first and production second. Those affected by the change are consulted and made part of the decision-making process; • Creativity, effort, and interest in the job are the bases for rewards.	• Decisions are made by the team as a whole, on a consensus basis; • The team agrees on its outputs, and the outputs of each of its members; • Job communications flow in all directions. All channels are open; • Change is introduced by involving people at all levels. The objective of change is effectiveness for the organization as a whole; • Rewards are based on the extent to which teams and individuals meet their agreed objectives.
SYSTEMATIC	**DIRECTIVE**
• Decisions are made "by the book"; • Jobs are defined in terms of inputs, or activities; • Most job communication originates as interpretation of procedures and is referred to superiors for ratification; • Change is "legislated" by changing rules and procedures at the top of the organization; • Formal qualifications, job experience, and length of tenure are the bases for rewards.	• Decisions are made by the superior; • Objectives are decided on by the superior, and he prescribes suitable action plans; • Job communication is largely downward, from superior to subordinates; • Change is planned and implemented from above, and subordinates are "sold" on it; • Rewards are based on the superior's assessment of individual performance.

Relationships-Oriented Behavior (vertical axis) — Task-Oriented Behavior (horizontal axis)

STYLE DEMANDS OF FINANCES

Finances put a clear limit on certain actions and permit others. Every manager has to live with his budget. The general manager lives with a budget made up of cash flow and capital funding. The production manager lives with a budget representing that part of the overall firm's budget allocated to his function. Depending on the profitability of the organization's operations or the amount allocated to a department, or unit, certain managerial strategies and actions are possible and others aren't.

On the basis of financial considerations, managers may be forced to use a specific style of management in the running of their units, but financial constraints usually make themselves felt first in the structure and technology of the organization, rather than simply in management styles. For instance, when firms were reduced to working a three-day week in Britain in 1973-74 because of a power shortage, many firms experienced a cash flow problem due to shortened production. This cash shortage affected the structure of the organizations as they laid off personnel and restructured their remaining people. And the structural changes in turn affected the technology of many jobs. Work was not only organized differently, but had to be done by different *methods*. This, of course, implied a change in management style in a number of cases.

It is impossible to ignore the interrelationships between the various elements which go to make up managerial situations. Each element acts on all the others and is, in turn, affected by all the others. Changes in one element bring about changes in the others, and a change in the overall situation.

Unlike the other internal elements making up a managerial situation, however, financial factors do not necessarily create situations that are managed more appropriately one way than another. There do not seem to be any firm lists of questions which would indicate that, because of certain financial considerations, one management style would be more effective than another. There are, however, certain questions which must be asked of the financial side of a manger's situation. The answers to these questions can raise a number of *alternatives* for action to increase effectiveness, though not necessarily in the form of a specific management style.

Some Basic Questions Concerning Financial Constraints

Operating managers should ask the following five questions of their financial allocations:

1 How available is money? In what amounts?

2 What are the alternative, competing uses to which allocated money can be put?

3 What is the actual cost of allocated money to the firm? Does the return warrant the use of the funds?

4 How stable is the flow of allocated funds? Will the budget remain at least at a certain level, no matter what, or is it subject to unexpected changes?

5 What predictions can be made as to the changes in cost of money, availability, alternative uses?

Clearly, financial constraints affect decisions concerning such things as new product development, manpower resources, and the whole range of managerial decisions. The first question is often, "Can we pay for it?" or "Will it cover its costs and make us a profit?"

Finances, however, have a basic effect on the degree of change which an organization may undergo. While it is argued that the opposite should in fact hold true, generally those organizations which are financially profitable spend money on increasing effectiveness; the marginal firms, which perhaps need to increase their effectiveness more, are usually too busy clinging to what they have, to think about undergoing any major changes. While pain is certainly a motivator for organizations to consider change, severe pain seems to make them particularly resistant to it.

APPRAISING SITUATIONAL STYLE DEMANDS

Three of the four internal situational elements affecting managers can be appraised in terms of the basic styles of management they demand. A manager must ask himself the twenty questions concerning each of the situational elements to get an idea of the demands it is placing on him to manage in a certain fashion. Once he does so, he will get a picture of the situation and how to manage it. Effectiveness results from using the appropriate style of management in a particular situation.

The basic questions concerning the financial situation of an organization, department or unit serve to highlight some of the *additional* constraints in the situation. But they generally affect either the alternative technologies available or the structure of the organization, rather than having a direct bearing on the appropriateness of a particular management style. One of the dangers of financial constraints is that they are often used as excuses for *not* doing things that need to be done. Uses of money should be viewed as alternatives. Organizations which say they cannot afford to do certain things simply mean that they prefer to use their money to do *other* things. It is these priorities which deserve examination and review in the light of other data on the situation.

APPLYING THE MODEL

The model we have presented here for analyzing a situation has a lot of lists and questions and seemingly bewildering things attached to it. In essence it is very simple and easy to apply to organizational situations. What it attempts to tell you is the management style, or "leadership" style, that should be used in a given situation in order to manage it most effectively. It focuses on the *behavior* a manager should exhibit in order to achieve the best results in his job.

The best way to see how it works is to apply it to an actual situation. Daniels Computer Company provides an opportunity to do just that.

Read over Daniels Computer Company, Parts I and II. They are reproduced here for your convenience.

DANIELS COMPUTER COMPANY PART I

Daniels Computer Company's Memory Engineering Department was composed of four sections: magnetic, electronic, mechanical, and electrochemical. The customary development work undertaken by the department involved well-known principles of memory design. Each section carried on its phase of development in logical sequence, using the results of the previous section as a starting point. The members of each section were expert in their own fields. The sections were close-knit socially. The manager of the department left technical direction to section supervisors, reserving for his own responsibility the securing of essential services and maintenance of the development schedule. The department rarely failed to meet its schedule or technical requisites.

In July 1962, the Memory Department was assigned the development of a memory incorporating several new design concepts which had never been experimentally evaluated. The functioning of the special computer which was to incorporate the new memory depended upon the most advanced memory device possible within the limits of the new concepts. Development time was one-half the length of more routine developments.

The Memory Department manager selected the four most competent project engineers from the four sections to work on the special project. Each project engineer was directed to select five engineers and five technicians to work with him on the project. Because of time limitations and the unknown aspects of the new memory concepts, the four groups were to work on their own aspects of design simultaneously. Each team, remaining in the geographic confines of its home section, but independent of its former supervision, commenced immediately to test design schemes and components relevant to its own division of the technology. The project group members quickly became enthusiastic about their new assignment. The department manager left technical supervision to the project engineers of each group.

PART II

In late August 1962, the project engineers of the four special groups met for the first time to explore the technical prerequisites each had discovered. The goal of the meeting was to establish parameters for each group's subsequent design effort. It quickly became apparent that each group had discovered concept limitations within its own area which were considered by that group to be controlling. Inevitably, the position of any one group required considerable extra work by one or more of the others. The meeting concluded without compromise of original positions.

In the ensuing weeks all four groups worked desperately to complete certain design segments before complementary segments were completed in other groups. Haste was believed necessary so that the tardy group would have to reformulate its designs, basing them upon that which was already completed. Development of the new memory proceeded in this fashion until the project engineer of the slowest group proved experimentally and theoretically that several designs completed by other groups imposed technologically impossible conditions upon his area of design. A number of personal frictions developed between the groups at this time with aspersions cast concerning the competence of out-group members. Even department members not formally involved in the special project became involved, siding with their section mates. Enthusiasm for the project on the part of group members waned.

Things aren't going well in the Daniels Computer Company. The question we have to answer is "What should be done now to get the project back on track?" In other words, we are concerned with the *behavior* of the project manager. What managerial style should he use?

Our model tells us that effective management style is determined by the demands of the *job*, the *organizational structure*, and the *people*. So let's examine each of these factors individuallly to see if we have enough information on which to base a situational diagnosis.

Let's start with the *job*. The technology indicators look at *the way the job is done*. Consider each of the twenty statements in the technology list on the next page and ask if it describes:

a the way the job *was* done in Daniels Computer *before the project group was set up*. If so, place a check mark next to the statement.

b the way the job *should be* done if the project team were working properly. If so, place an "x" next to the statement.

A Diagnosis of the Job

You may not agree with our diagnosis of the job demands, but we see them as shown on the technology indicators list on page 201.

Principally, the job *prior* to the change was *facilitative*. The engineers were expert; there were no tight time constraints that we are aware of; presumably there were, or are, alternative methods of achieving the same objective, since the field of memory design, while based on "well-known principles," is presumably still a matter of coming up with new applications; the engineers found the work interesting and creativity played some part in the job, although perhaps not a major part.

Subsequent to the change some of these factors changed. There were still no best methods for doing the work that the engineers were aware of, and creativity became more important as they ventured into new areas not previously tested. In addition, time pressures were introduced, and (perhaps due to the competitive approach of the subgroups, trying to outdo one another and force the other sub-

TECHNOLOGY INDICATORS

FACILITATIVE	INTERACTIVE
• subordinates are experts and know more about their own jobs than the manager; • few time constraints • no defined "best methods" of doing the job; • subordinates find the work intself intrinsically attractive; • a major requirement of the job is creativity.	• the subordinates and the manager have different and varying skills, expertise and knowledge; • the time frame for decisions is medium to longterm; • subordinates must interact with one another in order to get the job done; • decisions are of wide-reaching significance to the organization; • the major output of the job is a complex, one-of-a-kind decision or product.
SYSTEMATIC	**DIRECTIVE**
• the job requires close adherence to rules, procedures, and precedents; • decisions can only be made within certain limits; • communications are generally formal; • there is an emphasis on the maintenance of records and files; • a major requirement of the job is consistency.	• the manager has greater expertise or knowledge than the subordinates; • subordinates' jobs tend to be narrow and skill-oriented, and performance is easily measurable; • the work is governed by tight time pressures; • rapid and unexpected changes are introduced into the job from time to time; • major requirements of the job are speed and flexibility.

Relationships-Oriented Behavior (vertical axis) ↑

Task-Oriented Behavior (horizontal axis) →

Our diagnosis:

TECHNOLOGY INDICATORS

FACILITATIVE	INTERACTIVE
√ • subordinates are experts and know more about their own jobs than the manager; √ • few time constraints X √ • no defined "best methods" of doing the job; √ • subordinates find the work intself intrinsically attractive; X √ • a major requirement of the job is creativity.	• the subordinates and the manager have different and varying skills, expertise and knowledge; • the time frame for decisions is medium to longterm; X • subordinates must interact with one another in order to get the job done; X • decisions are of wide-reaching significance to the organization; X • the major output of the job is a complex, one-of-a-kind decision or product.
SYSTEMATIC	**DIRECTIVE**
• the job requires close adherence to rules, procedures, and precedents; • decisions can only be made within certain limits; • communications are generally formal; • there is an emphasis on the maintenance of records and files; • a major requirement of the job is consistency.	• the manager has greater expertise or knowledge than the subordinates; • subordinates' jobs tend to be narrow and skill-oriented, and performance is easily measurable; X • the work is governed by tight time pressures; X • rapid and unexpected changes are introduced into the job from time to time; • major requirements of the job are speed and flexibility.

Relationships-Oriented Behavior →

Task-Oriented Behavior →

groups to refocus their work) rapid and unexpected changes became the order of the day. The project team also now required engineers to interact with one another as a team. The decisions reached were of great significance to the success of the project (and, we assume to the organization); and this is certainly a one-of-a-kind job, as opposed to a routine, repetitive one.

What about the managerial style of the project manager?

What we see is that while the style demanded *before* the change was highly relationships oriented, *after* the change to the project team structure, the job began to require more task-oriented behavior.

In fact, before the change, the department manager (who is also the project manager) *did* manage facilitatively. He left the sections alone, providing "essential services and maintenance of the development schedule" only. He deferred to their expertise and let them get on with the job by themselves, giving help when it was needed, and making sure that things went along according to some sort of schedule. The trouble started after the project team was set up. Now the job requires the manager to be more directive and more actively concerned with the planning and controlling of the work sections, but he hasn't changed his style.

People Demands

In order to illustrate the diagnostic process a little bit more, let's take a look at the effect that the *people* in this situation have on the managerial style of the department head.

Consider each of the 20 statements on the *people indicators* list on the next page and decide which of them reflect *the way in which the engineers expect and prefer to be managed.* Place a check mark opposite the appropriate statements. Please complete this analysis before you read further.

The way we see it, the engineers and technicians expect and prefer a *facilitative* managerial style from the department head. (And, as we know, he behaves in just that way.)

It is not quite clear as to whether the individuals set their own objectives and output goals, or whether these are set by the sections as a team. We don't have enough data on this point, so we have included the possibility of either one.

The results are clear. The subordinates want a facilitative style of management, and they are getting it. The only problem is that it isn't working! The basic *job* has changed, as we have just seen, and more task-oriented behavior seems to be required from the project manager.

We won't go through the process of checking off the appropriate statement concerning *organizational structure* demands. One of the reasons for foregoing that step is that we really have very little information about the structural variables in this organization. The point that a style change is needed has been made anyway.

At this juncture, take a minute or two to go over the action plan you outlined for Daniels Computer at the end of Chapter 8.

Then take a look at Part III of the case.

PEOPLE INDICATORS

Relationships-Oriented Behavior ↑

FACILITATIVE • Subordinates make their own decisions; • Subordinates set their own objectives; • Job communication is largely upward, from subordinates to superiors, and horizontal, among coworkers; • Change centers around people first and production second. Those affected by the change are consulted and made part of the decision-making process; • Creativity, effort, and interest in the job are the bases for rewards.	INTERACTIVE • Decisions are made by the team as a whole, on a consensus basis; • The team agrees on its outputs, and the outputs of each of its members; • Job communications flow in all directions. All channels are open; • Change is introduced by involving people at all levels. The objective of change is effectiveness for the organization as a whole; • Rewards are based on the extent to which teams and individuals meet their agreed objectives.
SYSTEMATIC • Decisions are made "by the book"; • Jobs are defined in terms of inputs, or activities; • Most job communication originates as interpretation of procedures and is referred to superiors for ratification; • Change is "legislated" by changing rules and procedures at the top of the organization; • Formal qualifications, job experience, and length of tenure are the bases for rewards.	DIRECTIVE • Decisions are made by the superior; • Objectives are decided on by the superior, and he prescribes suitable action plans; • Job communication is largely downward, from superior to subordinates; • Change is planned and implemented from above, and subordinates are "sold" on it; • Rewards are based on the superior's assessment of individual performance.

Task-Oriented Behavior →

PEOPLE INDICATORS

Relationships-Oriented Behavior ↑

FACILITATIVE

- Subordinates make their own decisions;
- Subordinates set their own objectives;
- Job communication is largely upward, from subordinates to superiors, and horizontal, among coworkers;
- Change centers around people first and production second. Those affected by the change are consulted and made part of the decision-making process;
- Creativity, effort, and interest in the job are the bases for rewards.

INTERACTIVE

- Decisions are made by the team as a whole, on a consensus basis;
- The team agrees on its outputs, and the outputs of each of its members;
- Job communications flow in all directions. All channels are open;
- Change is introduced by involving people at all levels. The objective of change is effectiveness for the organization as a whole;
- Rewards are based on the extent to which teams and individuals meet their agreed objectives.

SYSTEMATIC

- Decisions are made "by the book";
- Jobs are defined in terms of inputs, or activities;
- Most job communication originates as interpretation of procedures and is referred to superiors for ratification;
- Change is "legislated" by changing rules and procedures at the top of the organization;
- Formal qualifications, job experience, and length of tenure are the bases for rewards.

DIRECTIVE

- Decisions are made by the superior;
- Objectives are decided on by the superior, and he prescribes suitable action plans;
- Job communication is largely downward, from superior to subordinates;
- Change is planned and implemented from above, and subordinates are "sold" on it;
- Rewards are based on the superior's assessment of individual performance.

Task-Oriented Behavior →

DANIELS COMPUTER COMPANY
PART III

On November 1, 1962, an engineer with considerable memory design experience was hired from outside the Daniels Company to become chief engineer for the special project. The four project engineers were directed to report to the new man. After examining the work of each group, the chief engineer indicated the basic approach to be taken in designing the new memory. Outstanding technical conflicts between groups were summarily dismissed by reference to the new approach. Each group was given a clear set of design instructions within the overall design plan. Firm design time schedules, based on project group interdependence, were set. Frequent progress reports were required of each project engineer.

As we see, the problem of a style change was recognized by the department head. But rather than change his own style, he hired someone with a more task-oriented approach. The new chief engineer's style is *directive*. He appears to have defined the job demands as being more directive than we did—he is claiming more knowledge than the subordinates; he is implying that their jobs are narrower than they would like to believe, and more easily measurable; and he is responding to the demands of added speed and flexibility as the project is now well behind schedule. He seems to agree with *all* the *directive technology* statements. Do you? Is his diagnosis right? Will the new directive approach work?

Take some time now to consider this change. Compare it with your own action plan. Do you think the chief engineer will succeed in getting the project back on track? Write down what you now think will happen. Don't worry, we shall reveal all in the end. We will let you know how it all turned out, and even make a few comments about it.

Chapter Summary

1 Leadership can be thought of as being composed of two main elements: what the leader does (the *process*), and what the followers do (the *results*). Managerial effectiveness is concerned not so much with what the leader (manager) *does*, but with what results he *achieves.*

2 Management style is based, to a degree, on the basic assumptions held by the individual about human behavior. McGregor argues that Theory X assumptions lead to an autocratic, directive style of management, while Theory Y assumptions tend to lead to a more participative, democratic style.

3 Leadership style can be thought of in several different ways. One of these is represented by the *Michigan continuum*. It represents leader-

ship style as being either *job-centered*, or *employee-centered*. These dimensions are not independent of one another. A manager can only become more employee-centered by becoming *less* job-centered. The model is similar to the Theory X, Theory Y dichotomy.

4 A second major school of thought on management style is the Ohio State model, which sees the two dimensions of *initiating structure* and *consideration* as largely independent of one another. This leads to a model which allows a manager to exhibit varying degrees of *both* of these behaviors simultaneously. The result is a four-style model of leadership behavior.

5 Building on the Ohio State research findings, we have presented a model which consists of four basic management styles, each of which represents a different basic combination of relationships-oriented behavior (ROB) and task-oriented behavior (TOB). The four styles are given labels for convenience, and "profiles" are developed of each of the four "types" of management styles.

6 In determining which management style is best, the situation must be taken into account. The major factors affecting the appropriateness of a management style are the *job* (how the work is done), the *organizational structure* (how the work is organized), and the *people* (what type of behavior they expert and prefer).

7 Situations can be analyzed in terms of the degree of task-oriented behavior (TOB) or relationships-oriented behavior (ROB) that a manager should use in order to achieve the best results. Each of the major situational factors—*job, organizational structure* and *people*—can be examined to determine appropriate style.

10

Interpersonal Communication and Change

OBJECTIVES

When you have completed this chapter you should:

- have a clearer concept of what is meant by the term "communication";
- recognize the importance of the communication process in organizational operations;
- recognize that "communication" is not just a means of transmitting data, but a method of influencing and changing behavior;
- understand the major barriers to effective communication;
- understand the effects of structure on communication processes, job satisfaction, organizational power, and motivation;
- be aware of the phenomenon of non-verbal communication and some of its functions;
- understand the basis of transactional analysis;
- recognize the connection between communication, motivation, and behavior change, with specific reference to the technique of behavior modification.

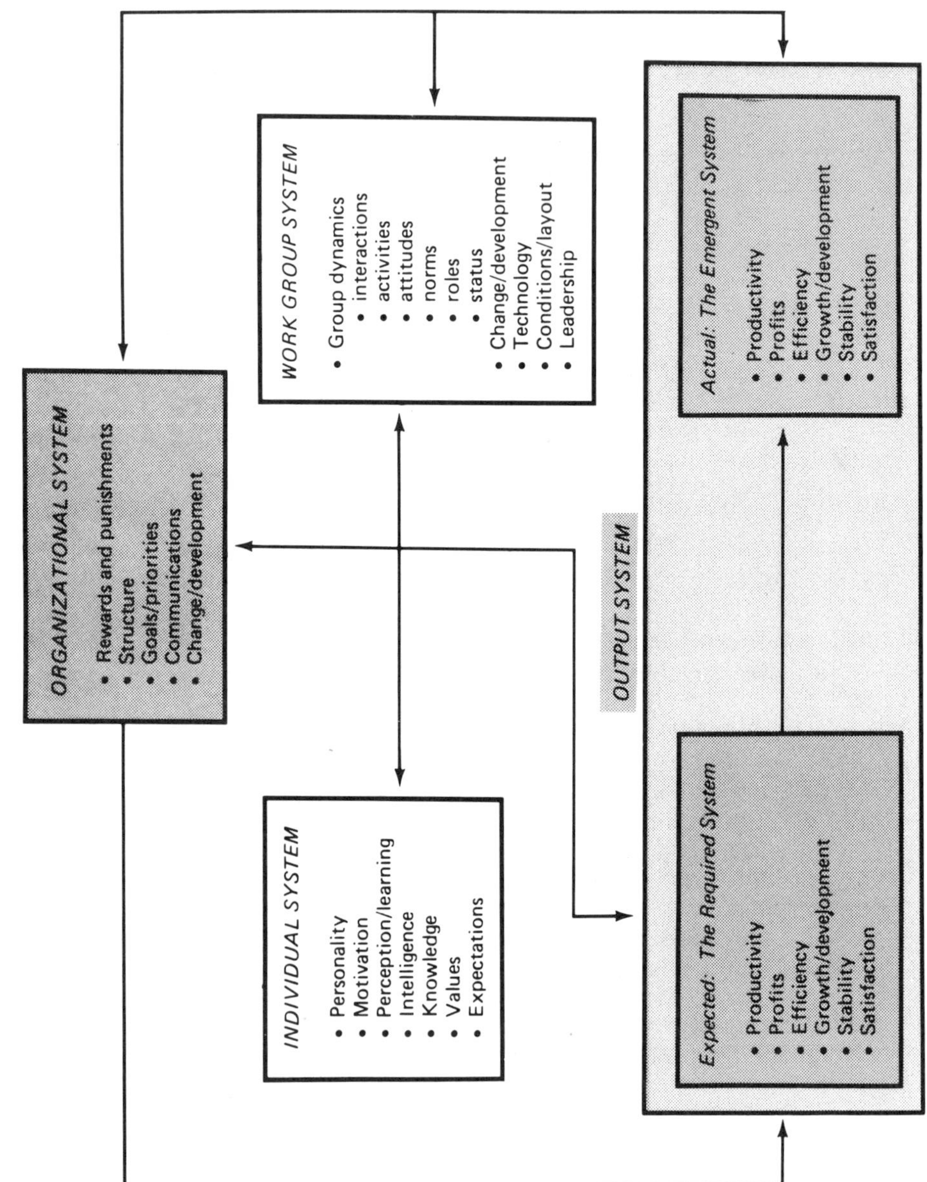

ORGANIZATIONAL SYSTEM
• Rewards and punishments
• Structure
• Goals/priorities
• Communications
• Change/development
WORK GROUP SYSTEM
• Group dynamics
• interactions
• activities
• attitudes
• norms
• roles
• status
• Change/development
• Technology
• Conditions/layout
• Leadership
INDIVIDUAL SYSTEM
• Personality
• Motivation
• Perception/learning
• Intelligence
• Knowledge
• Values
• Expectations
OUTPUT SYSTEM
Expected: The Required System
• Productivity
• Profits
• Efficiency
• Growth/development
• Stability
• Satisfaction
Actual: The Emergent System
• Productivity
• Profits
• Efficiency
• Growth/development
• Stability
• Satisfaction

''People begin, modify, and end relationships by communicating with one another. Communication is their channel of influence, their mechanism of change.

—Leavitt, 1964

''How else, except through person-to-person interaction, does most of the world's work get done? How else, except through improving our understanding of this process, can we learn what we need to learn from each other?

—Turner and Lombard, 1969

INTERPERSONAL COMMUNICATION

The term communication is grossly overworked. All behavioral conflicts or problems are explained away as being communication problems. Everything from billboards, to encyclopedias, to television, to holding hands is communication. Perhaps the term interaction might be better for our uses here. We have defined an interaction as *an interpersonal contact in which one individual can be observed acting (which includes speaking or writing) and one or more other individuals responding to this action*. That is the sort of ''communication'' we are concerned with: largely face-to-face interaction.

If we are to get the ''world's work'' done, to use Turner and Lombard's phrase, we must communicate with one another. The manager's job is concerned with directing and coordinating the activities of people, and the only way that can be done is by communicating with them. In order to do a good job, moreover, communications need to be clear and understandable. Rosen (1970) studied foremen who had received conflicting or unclear communications concerning organizational policies and found that they exhibited low morale. It makes sense that when job-related communications are unclear and confusing, performance suffers.

Studies indicate that managers spend 75 percent or more of their time communicating with others, either transmitting data or receiving it. About half of this time is spent talking with people, while the rest is split between preparing and writing reports, memos, letters, and so on, and reading them. Wickesberg (1968) has classified the purposes of communication in organizations into the following categories: *information* transmitted or received; *instructions* transmitted or received; *problem-solving* communications; *approval* transmitted or received; and *non-business related* communications. The percentages of communication time taken by both managers and non-managers for each of these functions are summarized in Table 10-1. The only major difference between the two groups is in the amount of

TABLE 10-1 FREQUENCY AND PURPOSE OF COMMUNICATIONS BY MANAGERS AND NONMANAGERS.

Purpose	*Position*	*Percentage of Total Communications*
Information	Manager	53.5
	Nonmanager	54.2
Instruction	Manager	22.4
	Nonmanager	21.3
Problem Solving	Manager	11.1
	Nonmanager	12.5
Non-business related	Manager	6.6
	Nonmanager	8.2
Approval	Manager	6.2
	Nonmanager	3.8

From: Wickesberg, A. K., "Communications Networks in the Business Organization Structure," *Academy of Management Journal, 11* (1968), 253–262.

time they devote to giving and receiving approval. Since managers must both receive approval from their superiors *and* pass it on to their subordinates, while non-managers only receive it, this difference is easily understandable.

In any interaction between two individuals there is an exchange of *content*, and of *feeling*. A conversation is about something—a book, a ball game, politics, sex, and so on. What it is about, at least on the surface, is what we term its content. The content deals with facts or opinions and is what the words convey without any overtones of feeling. But certainly the line, "Get out of here," can convey quite different meanings if the feelings of the speaker are taken into account. It can mean literally what it says if the speaker is annoyed, or it can mean "Stop kidding me" if the speaker is amused. Even "Hello" conveys a myriad of meanings depending on the tone of voice used, the volume, and the accompanying facial expressions or body postures.

Language is symbolic, just as gestures are symbolic. We attempt to convey something through the use of symbols which we hope are common to those we interact with. But we can never be sure that the same symbol means the same thing to someone else. It is very difficult to know if your feelings have been accurately represented by your communication. That is why we enter into such elaborate rituals when we interact with others. All the "cues" have to be aligned correctly in order to convey the complex message we are trying to transmit.

As Leavitt remarks, communication is our channel of influence and mechanism of change. To be understood fully, any communication must be taken in its full context. One very important contextual variable is the self-concept of the individuals involved in the interaction. Goffman (1959) puts it this way: "When an individual appears before others, he unknowingly and unwittingly projects a definition of the situation, of which a conception of himself is an important part."

The self-concept acts as a screen through which we both transmit and receive

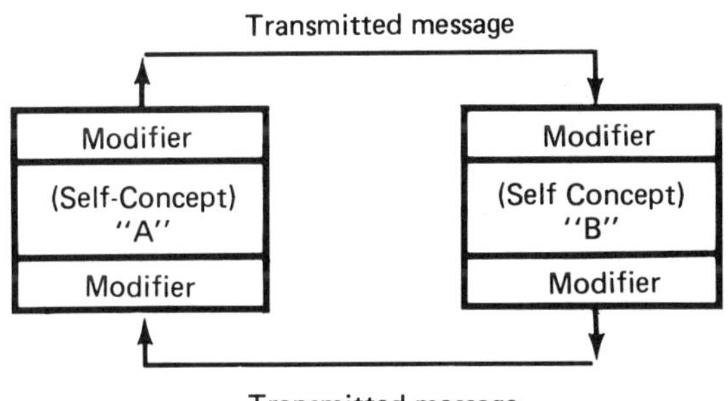

FIGURE 10-1 THE MODIFYING EFFECTS OF THE SELF-CONCEPT ON COMMUNICATIONS.

communications. We talked about the process of perception in Chapter 4, and saw how it was an integral part of the self-concept, allowing only relatively congruent data to enter the system. At the same time we saw that the behavior that an individual exhibits is modified by his concept of self.

Figure 10-1 illustrates the process of modification of communication between two people. The self-concept of each individual "modifies" messages both going out and coming in. We cannot separate personality and communication.

The modifications we make to our *transmission* of messages are intended to *change the other parties* to the interaction: those modifications that we make to the *incoming* messages are intended to *protect ourselves* from the changes being put forward to us. What we say isn't necessarily what we mean, and what we hear isn't necessarily what we were intended to hear. Is it any wonder that we talk about a "failure to communicate"?

In Chapter 4 we raised the issue of communication and change. Essentially we talked about how we, as individuals, resist change, and how, by opening ourselves more to others, we can achieve more effective relationships with them. The Johari Window in Figure 4-6 demonstrated this argument. At this juncture in the book we are interested in how we can change the behavior of *others*. Clearly, how we do this will involve communication, but as we see from Figure 10-1, there are some obstacles to the process that we will have to try to clear out of the way in order to do it well.

Rogers and Farson say that one way to bring about changes in people is to use a communications technique they call "active listening."

> "Active listening is an important way to bring about changes in people. Despite the popular notion that listening is a passive approach, clinical and research evidence clearly shows that sensitive listening is a most effective agent for individual personality change and group development."

Active listening means trying to understand both the content and feelings of what one hears, and attempting to reflect, to the speaker, the essence of what he is saying, thereby letting him know the degree to which you are "on his wavelength."

Rogers maintains that when people are listened to sensitively they tend to listen to *themselves* more carefully. It is exactly this sort of process that we see as being necessary when we look at the model of communication in Figure 10-1. We need to overcome the modifiers, or barriers, that exist both in the *receiver* and in the *sender* of a message. Sensitive listening also brings about changes in the listener since he experiences deeper relationships with others, thereby receiving more information concerning himself.

BARRIERS TO COMMUNICATION

The Self-Concept

The major barrier to communication is the self-concept. We know that whatever concept an individual has of himself, he clings to, shutting out data that are not congruent with it. A young girl who sees herself as being unattractive, when asked out on a date is more likely to rationalize the behavior of the boy involved as being motivated out of pity, or as a joke against her, or something of that nature, than to admit any data to her self-concept that says she is *not* unattractive. Her behavior is likely to be defensive: she can't trust the boy's behavior because it doesn't fit with what she "knows" to be the truth. Data does not have to be uncomplimentary to be threatening; it simply has to be incongruent with the idea of the self.

Attempts to get people to change on the basis of transmitting data to them runs into all these types of problems. Active listening, on the other hand, presents no threat to the individual. He is not being "told" anything. *He* is the one doing all the talking (and, by the way, the thinking). As Rogers and Farson put it:

> The active-listening approach . . . does not present a threat to the individual's self-picture. He does not have to defend it. He is able to explore it, see it for what it is, and make his own decision about how realistic it is. And then he is in a position to change.

Role Relationships (status)

A second barrier to clear, undistorted communications results from the role relationships, or status differences, of individuals involved in interpersonal communication. We know that a "pecking order" exists in any organization, from small informal groups to large formal ones, and those higher up in the order expect (and usually get) deference from those lower down. In a superior-subordinate interaction, the tendency is for the boss to control the conversation, to do most of the talking, to initiate discussion, and generally to transmit more data than he receives. Clearly not *all* superior-subordinate interactions are like that, but most tend to be based on these assumptions.

Status usually connotes power in an organization. Therefore, subordinates may be reluctant to be perfectly open and candid in their communications with their bosses. There is the fear that if they tell the boss something he doesn't like he will in some way punish them. They tend to tell the boss what they think he wants to hear, or at least what he will find acceptable. Upward communications are often distorted for this reason.

By the same token, managers may not relay the same instructions to their subordinates that they receive from their own bosses, on the assumptions that they must pass something more palatable downward. The subordinate then attempts to interpret the "real" meaning of the communication from the boss so that he can act appropriately and keep everybody happy. All kinds of distortions result from assumptions made about the true values and goals of people at different levels in the organization.

Credibility

Credibility of the source affects communication. Generally speaking, individuals of high status are accorded greater credibility. We tend to believe people who we define as "experts." Milgram's experiments on social control, which we discussed in Chapter 7, are a good example of the credibility given to a person of high status. If you recall, the subjects in the electric shock experiments were far more obedient when they thought that the experimenter was a professor from Yale.

Credibility may result from a number of different factors. The individual involved may have impressive credentials, may have been seen to demonstrate expertise, or may simply act in such a way as to inspire confidence. Confidence tricksters ("con men") are expert at this latter form of behavior.

Credibility of the communication source is simply another way of talking about congruence. We tend to accept certain data from certain sources when the data and the source appear congruent with one another. We would not be as likely to accept an explanation of the current economic ills of our society from a bus driver as we would from a professor of economics serving on the Presidential Advisory Committee. Orson Welles' famous radio broadcast of *The War of the Worlds* had thousands of people in a complete panic over what they believed to be a genuine invasion of earth by creatures from outer space. The source was a major radio network, and since the program was presented in the form of a news broadcast, those who had missed the start of the program, which stated that this was a dramatization of a novel and not the real thing, found it highly credible.

Emotion

Of course, no communication is free from emotion, either on the part of the sender or the receiver. We are all subject to some emotional state—anxiety, confidence, happiness, hate, trust, acquisitiveness, magnanimity, frustration, and so on. As we discussed earlier, these emotions form part of the "modifer" system that screens transmissions and inputs. A great deal of research has been done on the effects of various emotional states on communication. We know that when emotions are "positive"—people trust one another and interact in an atmosphere of openness and candor—organizations tend to operate more effectively. As Fritz Steele (1975) puts it,

> Regular disclosure is essential if members of a system are to be able to improve their own process, to develop new images of who they are and what they are trying to do, and to learn from the experiences which they share. Unless the data from those experiences are shared, no patterns can be seen, and therefore no generalizations of any real complexity can be developed.

Repetition

An old standby method of teaching is to repeat material a number of times. The assumption here is that repetition allows information to "soak in." However, it is difficult to know just how detailed to be in explaining something, or how many times to go over it, since different individuals comprehend at different rates. Some catch on early and find the subsequent explanation boring; others find repetition and detailed explanation useful. The dilemma facing a teacher is to decide on the level of detail and explanation required to get a class of different individuals to learn the same material. It appears that you can satisfy some of the people some of the time, but not all of the people all of the time—unless you individualize your communications and tailor them to the specific individuals involved.

Managers often suffer from data overload. The new technology of computers and the phenomenon of photocopying have meant that reports are more frequent, more detailed, and often less relevant. If the machine can spit out any number of copies of something, it appears to be easier to send everyone a copy rather than to have to sit down and decide who really needs it, who needs only certain information, and who has no need for it at all. Many organizations suffer from information indigestion.

One-way Versus Two-way Communication

These are terms you are bound to run across in any discussion of communication. One-way communication simply refers to a transmission from A to B, with no feedback from B to A concerning its effectiveness, or even its receipt. A letter is an example of a one-way communication (until you get a reply and then we are into two-way communication). The two-way process includes a feedback loop where the recipient of the message provides some data as to his understanding. The processes are illustrated in Figure 10-2.

There is a constant debate over which form of communication is most effective. Of course, as we know, that depends on the situation. If you have very little time, if the message is straightforward and if you are not concerned with employees' (recipient) satisfaction, then one-way communication makes sense. You deliver the message quickly, clearly, and directly, in the belief that it will be acted on appropri-

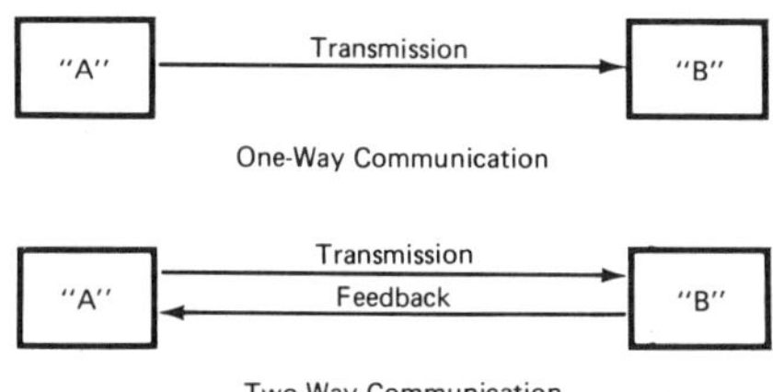

FIGURE 10-2 ONE-WAY AND TWO-WAY COMMUNICATION.

ately. However, if the message is complex, if you have time to make sure that it gets across properly, and if you are concerned with recipient satisfaction and commitment to acting in an appropriate manner, then two-way communication is best.

Sometimes messages are complex enough that they are difficult to explain or convey clearly at a single stroke. In order for full understanding to take place, the recipients must have a chance to ask questions and to discuss them. Given what we know about leadership style and motivation, we would also expect that where commitment to action is required of the recipients they should be given an opportunity to participate in the decision in order to get a sense of "ownership" of it. Two-way communication (discussion) does that. One-way, top-down communication ("I tell you what to do and you don't answer back") may be satisfying for the transmitter, but it is generally unsatisfying for the receiver over any length of time. Communications in a football huddle tend to be more one-way than two-way because of the limited time dimension, and because of the "simplicity" of the communications (the plays have all been rehearsed and everyone understands what they are to do), but the quarterback who fails to listen to a player's input on weaknesses he has discovered in the other side is less likely to succeed in the long run. There are times to speak and times to listen; knowing when to do each is the skill of a good communicator.

THE EFFECTS OF STRUCTURE ON COMMUNICATION

We are talking about communication in an organizational setting, and organizations, as we know, *structure* the roles and relationships of their members to some degree. That is, they decree who is to do what and to whom, and who is to communicate what and to whom. We use the term "communication net" to describe the structure of relationships between a group of individuals who interact with one another. The way in which a communication net is structured affects the behavior of the individuals involved.

Let's take a look at the way in which communications within a group of five people can be structured. The following are some of the possible variations (Figure 10-3):

How does each of these communication structures perform? Are some more effective than others? The situational factors that affect performance in each of these networks are:

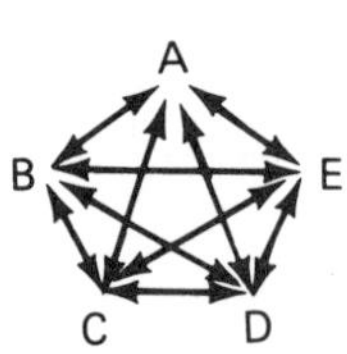

(1) "All-Channel Net"

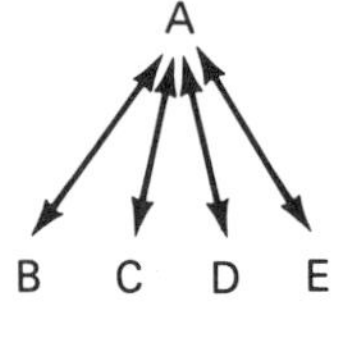

(2) "Star Net"

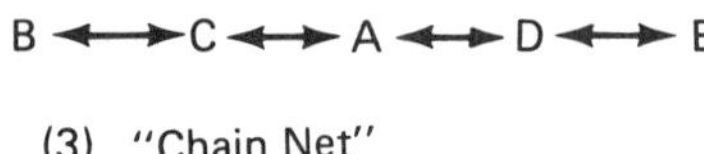

(3) "Chain Net"

FIGURE 10-3 SOME TYPES OF COMMUNICATION NETS.

- Task complexity;
- The superior's power requirements;
- Available time;
- The subordinates' satisfaction requirements.

Generally speaking, the more complex the task, the more an open flow of information is required: the simpler the task, the more directive and controlled communications can be.

We are all aware that information is power: if you know something that others don't, you have some power over them. The axiom applies in card games or business "games." Therefore, the more power a manager wants to maintain, the more he should attempt to control the flow of information, communicating only what he wants, to whom he wants. When information is freely available to everyone, nobody has a power edge.

Our discussion of leadership style indicated that when time demands are tight, a directive style is often most effective. In other words, the manager employs more of a one-way communication style, as in the "Star Net." When there is lots of time, one may consider the luxury of an open ("All-channel") discussion.

Since we also know that feelings of satisfaction, achievement, commitment and recognition are associated with perceiving oneself as being a useful and integral part of something, communication nets which allow this sort of participation—e.g., the "All-channel"—also result in the highest degree of subordinate satisfaction. The "Star Net" is highly satisfying for the manager (A), but provides little satisfaction for B, C, D, and E.

Given a communication net like the "Chain," we can therefore see that A will

TABLE 10-2 SITUATIONAL FACTORS AFFECTING THE PERFORMANCE OF COMMUNICATION STRUCTURES.

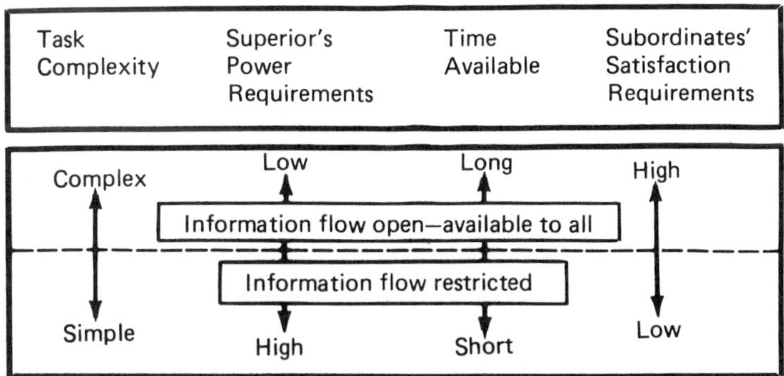

tend to become the most powerful member of the group since most of the information must pass through him, that he will also be the most satisfied with the arrangement, and that B and E will be least satisfied and lowest in power. Because of the cumbersome and uncertain nature of the flow of information in the "Chain," it is not likely to be an effective structure for coping with complex problems, or problems requiring rapid decisions.

The general relationships between task complexity, superior's power requirements, available time, and subordinates' satisfaction requirements are summarized in Table 10-2.

NON-VERBAL COMMUNICATION

Up to now, we have been discussing communication as if it were almost solely spoken or written, but we have noted that a spoken communication can be interpreted in a number of different ways depending on the way in which it is presented. One of the aspects of presentation is what is termed non-verbal communication (NVC). We define non-verbal communication as actions rather than speech. Clearly such things as print, memos, and so on, are non-verbal, but we are concerned with face-to-face behavior when we talk about NVC.

Albert Mehrabian (1972) argues that non-verbal communication is developed as a means of expressing certain feelings which may be "socially unacceptable."

> Both negative feelings (frustration, irritation, anger, hostility) and positive feelings (pleasure, liking, love) are part of social life, so if the expression of either is discouraged, it is conveyed less deliberately with implicit behaviors. Such means for expression, while more subtle, nonetheless assume similar significance for many. The de-emphasis of implicit communication in education helps to perpetuate a situation where "socially unacceptable" feelings must be expressed in behaviors other than speech and must not be recognized "officially" as part of a

person's communication: we learn to express a variety of feelings in these more subtle ways to avoid being accused of transgressing the social norms.

Face-to-face communication takes place at two levels. One is verbal and the other is non-verbal. Non-verbal communication is composed of such things as facial expressions, tone of voice, posture, gestures, changes in body coloring, direction of gaze and spatial arrangements. These "signs" are unintentional. They do not convey an intended message: they convey something that is quite *un*intended. A blush of embarrassment deepens when the individual blushing realizes it: the intention, if it could be carried out, would be to extinguish the blush.

The field of non-verbal communication is relatively well developed and there are a lot of easily readable books on the subject. It is far too detailed for us to go into here. Suffice it to say that we tend to use language to *disguise* what we feel more often than to communicate these feelings. Non-verbal communications represent a more "honest" display. We unconsciously convey messages through the way we gesture, look, move, and act. Desmond Morris (1977) in his marvellously presented book *Manwatching*, gives us this example of what he calls "Nonverbal Leakage"—that is, leaking our true feelings when we are actually trying to hide them (Box 10-1).

BOX 10-1

NON-VERBAL LEAKAGE: COMMUNICATING SOMETHING WE WOULD RATHER HIDE.

Actions do, indeed, speak louder than words. We often communicate our inner feelings more accurately by gesture and action than by speech. There are many occasions when we would like to hide our true feelings, but are unable to do so. Desmond Morris describes and explains a set of experiments which examined changes in behavior of a group of nurses forced into a situation where they were to tell lies:

"(The experimenters) . . . asked trainee nurses both to lie and to tell the truth about certain films they were shown. The young nurses were confronted with filmed scenes of gory operations such as limb amputation, and also with contrasting scenes of a harmless and pleasant nature. At a number of sessions, they were asked to describe what they saw, sometimes truthfully and at other times untruthfully. While they were doing this their every action and expression was recorded by concealed cameras. It was then possible to analyze in detail all the actions that accompanied truthful statements and all those accompanying deliberate lies, and to study the differences between them.

The nurses tried hard to conceal their lies because they were told that skill at deception was an important attribute for their future careers. This it is, for anxious patients require repeated reassurance that they are on the mend, or that risky operations are really quite safe, or that baffled doctors know exactly what their complaint is. What is more, they ask for this reassurance while at the same time being acutely tuned in for the slightest sign of any half-hidden pessimisms. To be a successful nurse one must learn to be a convincing liar. The experiment was therefore more than an academic exercise—and in fact it turned out that in later training the nurses who came top of their classes were also the ones who were the best body-liars in the film-report tests.

Even the best body-liars were not perfect, however, and the experimenters were able to assemble a set of key-differences in body actions between moments of truth-telling and moments of deception. They are as follows:

1. When lying, the nurses decreased the frequency of simple gesticulations they made with their hands. The hand actions they would normally use to emphasize verbal statements—to drive home a point, or to underline an important moment—were significantly reduced. The reason for this is that the hand actions, which act as 'illustrators' of spoken words, are not identified gestures. We know we 'wave our hands about' when we engage in excited conversation, but we have no idea exactly what our hands are doing. Our awareness that our hands do *something*, but our unawareness of precisely what it is, makes us suspicious of the possible transparency of these actions. Unconsciously we sense that perhaps they will give us away and we will fail to notice, so we suppress them. This is not easy to do. We can hide them, sit on them, stuff them deep into our pockets (where they may still let us down by finding some coins and jingling them), or, less drastically, we can clasp one firmly with the other and let them hold each other down. The experienced observer is not fooled by this—he knows that if those tiny hands are metaphorically frozen, there is something amiss.

2. When lying, the nurses increased the frequency of hand-to-face auto-contacts. We all touch our faces from time to time during conversations, but the number of times these simple actions are performed rises dramatically during moments of deception. Some hand-to-head actions are more popular than others, in this context, and the nature of the hand movement varies according to the part of the head involved. Deception favorites include: the Chin Stroke, the Lips Press, the Mouth Cover, the Nose Touch, the Cheek Rub, the Eyebrow Scratch, the Earlobe Pull and the Hair Groom. During deception attempts any of these may show a marked increase, but two in particular receive a special boost. These are the Nose Touch and the Mouth Cover.

3. When lying, the nurses showed an increase in the number of body-shifts they made as they spoke. A child who squirms in his chair is obviously dying to escape and any parent recognizes these symptoms of restlessness immediately. In adults they are reduced and suppressed—again because they are so obviously signs of unease—but they do not vanish. Watched closely, the adult liar can be seen to make tiny, vestigial body-shifts and to make them much more frequently than when telling the truth. They are no longer squirmings, instead they are only slight changes in the resting posture of the trunk as the speaker moves from one sitting posture to another.

These unobtrusive body-shifts are saying: 'I wish I were somewhere else,' the posture changes being intensely inhibited intention movements of escape.

4. When lying, the nurses made greater use of one particular hand action, namely the Hand Shrug. While other gesticulations decreased in frequency, this became more common. It is almost as if the hands were disclaiming any responsibility for the verbal statements being made.

5. When lying, the nurses displayed facial expressions that were almost indistinguishable from those given during truthful statements. Almost, but not quite, for there were, even in the most self-aware faces, tiny micro-expressions that leaked the truth. These micro-expressions are so small and so quick—a mere fraction of a second—that untrained observers were unable to detect them. However, after special training, using slow-motion films, they were able to spot them in normal-speed films of interviews. So, to a trained expert, even the fact cannot lie."

We said earlier that communications convey both content and feelings. While verbal communications (or even written ones) convey both these elements, non-verbal communications play solely on the emotional plane. We all respond to nonverbal cues, often quite unwittingly. Sometimes we are attracted to people for no seemingly good reason; they simply give off "good vibes." We seem to dislike or distrust other people almost immediately. What we may in fact be responding to are the non-verbal cues exhibited by the person in question. If their gestures, facial expressions and posture exhibit positive feelings—they smile, look directly at us, give a firm handshake, stand at a comfortable distance from us, appear relaxed, open and at ease, listen attentively to what we say, perhaps nod in agreement with us from time to time—we tend to feel positive "vibrations." We like them. If, on the other hand, their non-verbal behavior is negative—they look away from us when they shake hands, the handshake is limp and "disinterested," they turn their bodies slightly away from us, stand back from us, remain behind physical barriers of some kind such as a desk or table, and look at other people or objects when we talk to them—we quickly sense this transmission of negative feelings and put ourselves on guard.

Once again the concept of congruence is important. We are at ease when both verbal and non-verbal communications from an individual are congruent with one another. We feel a lot more comfortable when friendly words are accompanied by friendly actions and gestures. We are even more comfortable when hostile words are accompanied by hostile gestures; at least we know where we stand. The difficulty arises, when an individual is saying one thing verbally and something quite different by his actions, expressions and posture. We tend to sense this incongruence, and it makes us feel uncomfortable. An interesting point, however, is that when faced with this type of situation we tend to rely on the *non-verbal* cues for our interpretation of what is going on. We know that animals basically communicate nonverbally. There is some support for the idea that we have not outgrown our biological heritage and that, even if we don't recognize it, we still have the skills to interpret gesture, posture and expression.

Perhaps the major point to be made by our brief discussion of non-verbal communication is that for communication to be clear, it must be congruent. That is, what we say, and how we say it, must present the same message. We must be aware of our own feelings and attempt to communicate them openly. And at the same time we must try to understand the feelings of those with whom we are interacting, and realize the effect that these feelings have on what they say and do.

TRANSACTIONAL ANALYSIS (TA)

Transactional analysis (TA) is a method for recognizing incongruent communication and moving towards congruence. Developed by Eric Berne and popularized by him in his book *Games People Play* (1964) and by Thomas Harris in his equally successful book *I'm OK—You're OK* (1969), it presents a simple framework for understanding why we adopt the interaction patterns we do, why others respond in the ways they do, and how to improve on these interactions.

Whenever a manager sets policy, makes decisions, responds to questions, or requests information, he is acting from a certain frame of reference. TA maintains that we have three behavioral ''sets'' which we can draw on in deciding what type of behavior to use. Harris refers to these behavioral sets as ''states of being.'' He calls them the *Parent*, the *Child* and the *Adult*. Any behavior is a reflection of one of these three frames of reference or ''states of being.'' Each of these states represents a large data bank of experience, particular to the individual. We build these data banks for ourselves, recording events and feelings, recalling them, and reliving them.

Harris (1967) remarks that ''Continual observation has supported the assumption that these three states exist in all people . . . (they are) produced by the playback of recorded data of events in the past, involving real people, real times, real places, real decisions, and real feelings.''

The data bank which makes up the *Parent* is composed of observations of the behavior of authority figures from the individual's past—primarily the mother and father, or parent substitutes, such as bosses or leader figures. Harris maintains that the Parent data bank is fixed by about the age of five. It contains all the rules, laws, and norms that the individual has observed among the authority figures with whom he interacted closely. As Harris puts it, ''In this set of recordings are the thousands of 'no's' directed at the toddler, the repeated 'don'ts' that bombarded him, the looks of pain and horror in mother's face when his clumsiness brought shame on the family in the form of Aunt Ethel's broken antique vase.'' The Parent also contains all the notations of approval given by the authority figures.

The Parent records all this data *as if it were the ''truth''* :it does not interpret or evaluate any of it. Furthermore, this record is *permanent*: it cannot be altered subsequently. It is always available for recall. The admonition to ''never tell a lie'' or "always work hard" remains in the Parent data bank as a constant reminder. We can't erase it. If it was powerfully introduced, we may find it very difficult to get rid of at all.

The Parent represents a state where data is recorded under a condition of *dependency*. The little child is dependent on the authority figures surrounding it for just about everything. It is not free to question data; it simply accepts it and records it.

The Child data bank is composed of recordings of "internal" events—the feelings and emotions of the individual in response to what he observes. While the Parent is composed of *rules*, the Child is composed of *feelings*. The Child is the emotional side of the personality. When an individual's behavior is dominated by feelings, he is behaving from his *Child* frame of reference.

An important aspect of the *Child*, however, is that it is the source of creativity. Infants are curious and creative. We all have this potential, but in some people, the Parent has become so dominant, and the Child so defensive, that this creativity is severely dampened.

The *Adult* is a "data-processing computer" which makes decisions based on the data available both from the Parent and the Child and the information it gathers on its own. Its data bank is the result of exploring and testing for reality, as opposed to the "givens" of the Parent or Child data. An important function of the Adult is to examine the rules of the Parent to see if they still apply, and to examine the feeling responses of the Child to see if they are still valid. It continually attempts to *update* this data.

How does a concept of an individual's personality in terms of a *Parent, Child* and *Adult* help us understand or modify behavior in an organizational context? Is there an application for managers?

What transactional analysis says is that in every situation where interaction (transaction) takes place, the parties to the interaction reflect one or another of the three frames of the Parent, Child or Adult states. And furthermore, when one individual initiates an interaction, and another person responds "inappropriately," communication breaks down.

Harris states two "rules" of communication:

- When stimulus and response of the P-A-C transactional diagram make parallel lines, the transaction is complementary and can go on indefinitely.
- When stimulus and response cross on the P-A-C-transactional diagram, communication stops.

The examples in figure 10-4 illustrate these rules. Transaction (a) might be something like:

Worker "A" (Parent): All management ever cares about is getting more production. They don't give a damn about the workers.

Worker "B" (Parent): Stick it to them before they stick it to you.

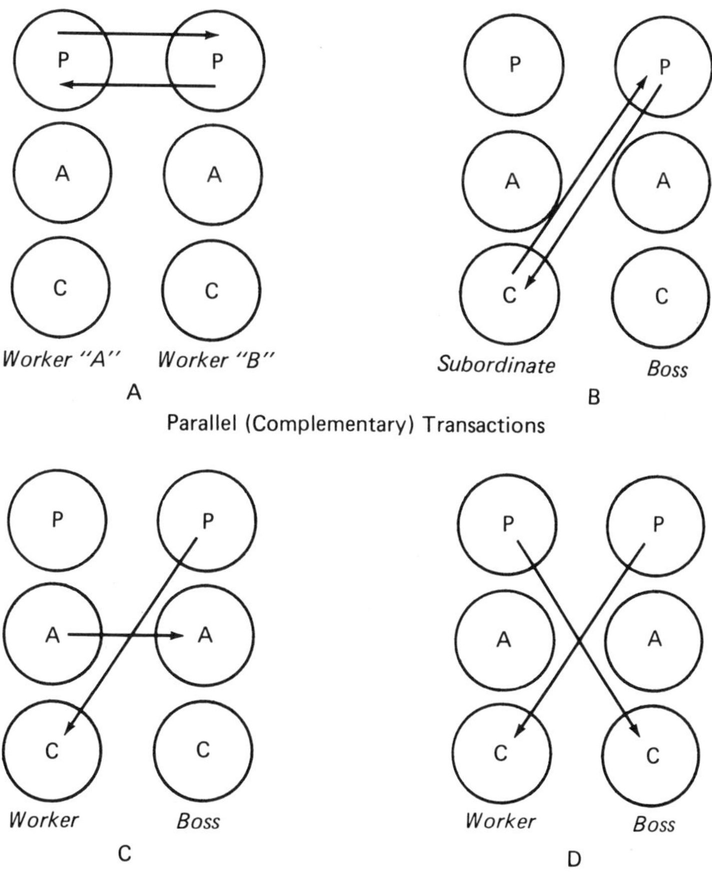

FIGURE 10-4: PARALLEL AND CROSSED TRANSACTIONS.

These two individuals could go on all day making this sort of Parent statement. They both have a "position" that may be completely independent of the situation. There is no conception of a management that is anything other than unfair and oppressive. This type of transaction is mutually satisfying because the two workers are able to blame management for the ills of the job and to rationalize their own behavior. As Harris says, "Finding someone to agree with you and play the game, produces a feeling well-nigh omnipotent."

The transaction in (b) might be:

Subordinate (Child): Is this report OK?
Boss (Parent): Keep up the good work.

Once again, the transactions are complementary. The subordinate (Child) is asking the boss (Parent) for approval, and the pat on the head is given in return.

Everybody is happy. The boss feels superior, having been asked for his approval, thereby having his position and power acknowledged, and the subordinate has received the "stroke" he wanted.

Looking at the sort of transaction in (c), we might see something like:

Worker (Adult): My machine broke down for an hour today so my production is below quota.
Boss (Parent): Why can't you take better care of your machine?

The Adult remark of the worker, reflecting the facts of the situation, is responded to by a Parental "zap." It is unlikely that this conversation will continue unless the worker responds emotionally (Child), or the boss can process the data rationally as an Adult.

Transaction (d) might be:

Boss (Parent): Fix that switch on your machine.
Worker (Parent): The union says that's electrician's work. Go find an electrician to fix it.

With both sides doing a power trip on the other, things can't continue for long.

A manager can benefit from an understanding of transactional analysis in two ways. First of all, he can understand where both he and others are "coming from" when they speak or act, and therefore he may be better able to adjust his communications to fit the situation. But secondly, and more important, he may adjust his transactions so that he is able to dispense "strokes" or rewards to the people around him. Transactional analysis is based on the premise that we all want to be "stroked." We get a stroke when we receive a parallel transaction—that is, when we get what we expect out of an interaction. When the Child addresses the Parent, he expects the Parent to respond accordingly. When the Adult addresses the Adult, he expects an Adult-Adult response. When an unexpected, or undesired response occurs (cross transactions), there is a "zap" rather than a stroke.

Not only can a manager dispense strokes by responding appropriately, but he can encourage the development of his subordinates by moving them towards an Adult-Adult exchange. An underlying goal of TA is to strengthen the Adult so that it can process data more effectively in its attempt to solve problems. A Parent-Child exchange can be mutually satisfying, but the Child does not "grow," and neither does the Parent. Only by dealing with data in an objective manner can an individual hope to change the pattern of his behavior.

As Harris (1967) says:

> When the Parent or the Child dominates, the outcome is predictable. This is one of the essential characteristics of games. There is a certain security in games. They may always turn out painfully, but it is a pain that the player has learned to handle. When the Adult is in charge of the transaction, the outcome is not always predictable. There is the possibility of failure, but there is also the possibility of success. Most important, there is the possibility of change.

CHANGING BEHAVIOR

The opening quotation to this chapter by Harold Leavitt emphasized the importance of communication to the process of change. But how, in real life, do you communicate with someone to get him to change his behavior? How do you get a worker to perform his job more carefully? How do you get someone to stop coming to work late? How do you get a friend to stop smoking? What form of communication is required? Should you attempt to persuade him, threaten him, charm him, reason with him, or plead with him? Granted, you need to communicate the desired change to him, but what makes him act on it?

We are talking here about getting an *individual* to change his behavior in some direction desired by a second party. We know from our systems model of organizational behavior that actual behavior—the emergent system—is influenced by forces within the individual himself (basically his self-concept), by forces within the work group, and by forces within the organization as a whole. Since these three systems interact with one another, we can't talk about changing the behavior of a person in an organization without taking all of them into account.

But the fact still remains that the final decision to change rests with the subject of the change—the *changee*. Everyone else is in the role of chang*er*, bringing various influences to bear. From what we know of the self-concept, though, we might expect that the stronger the pressure for change, the stronger the defenses erected around the self to preserve it. Schein (1960) describes the results of relatively sophisticated brainwashing procedures used by the Chinese on about 50 Western prisoners as being largely unsuccessful.

> Successful brainwashing, in the sense of the repatriate espousing Communist attitudes and reiterating his crimes following release from Communist China, was a rare outcome. Genuine attitude change could only occur if there were already a predisposition in the prisoner and if he encountered a highly effective prison regimen built around the use of the group cell.

These changes were designed to change the basic attitudes and values of the self. Prisoners were intended to see the error of their ways as Capitalists and espouse Communist doctrine and values. Given that they were held in custody for several *years* and were completely under the control of the Chinese (escape was virtually impossible), the fact that very few changed is a powerful testimonial to the resilience of the self under pressure.

We must realize that the self is constantly being bombarded with a wide array of data, all of which it must process in some way or other, ignoring some, modifying some, and accepting some. Our efforts to introduce a specific change into this system represent only a small fraction of the data input it receives. How do we get our data through the complex screen of defenses and modifiers that surround the self so that it can be accepted and acted upon?

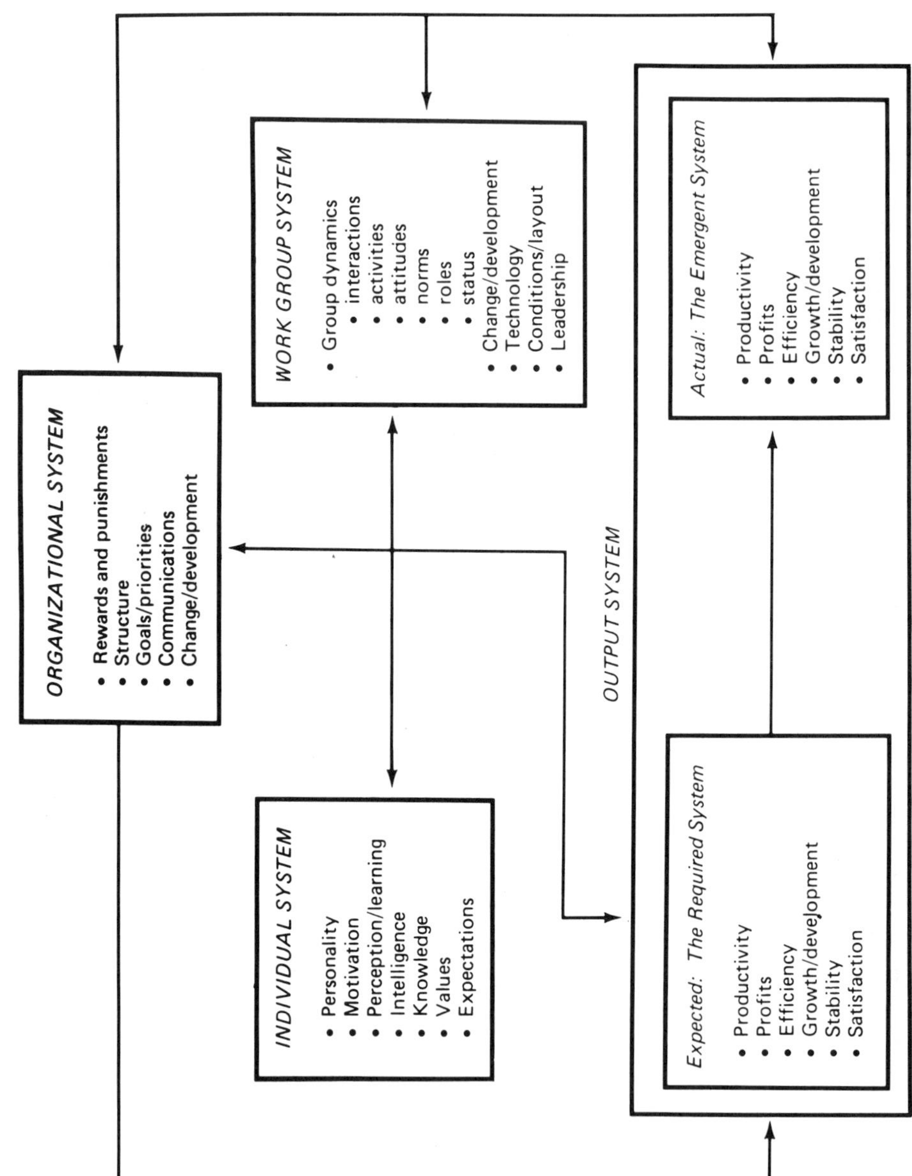

FIGURE 10-5. A SYSTEMS MODEL OF ORGANIZATIONAL BEHAVIOR.

We remarked earlier on in the chapter that the "modifiers" that surround the self to process *incoming* data are geared to *protect the self from change*. That is, their function is to ensure that the existing concept of self is not violated or threatened. Data that is *congruent* with the self-concept, however, is acceptable. It is not threatening; it tells the self what it wants to hear. It "massages" the self-concept rather than violating it. It provides strokes, not zaps. This is how communication affects change: it complements the self-concept and flatters it, it satisfies its needs.

We have looked at two communication techniques that do this: active listening and transactional analysis. They both massage the self and coax it to decide to change on its own, rather than attempting to force it. They let the individual decide on change based on his *own* experience and his *own* data-processing. They let him define his own "strokes" and let him discover which behavior results in stroking. Their focus is on the chang*ee*.

BEHAVIOR MODIFICATION

A specific approach to changing the behavior of others which branches out from the communication process is behavior modification. It is a motivational technique, and perhaps could have been discussed in our chapter on motivation. But it is more application-oriented than most of the theories we discussed there. It also relies more on the communication process than those theories, depending on being able to demonstrate approval for certain actions largely in a face-to-face interactive context.

Based on the theories of B.F. Skinner, behavior modification has become an increasingly widely used tool for changing the behavior of people in organizations. Its systematic application in industry was pioneered by Edward J. Feeney at Emery Air Freight Corp., where the term "positive reinforcement" was adopted rather than the more ominous sounding behavior modification. The underlying assumption of behavior modification is that all behavior can be affected by the application of positive rewards. These rewards may take the form of such things as recognition of a task well done, praise or promotion, or monetary rewards. The *form* of the reward is less important than its clear linkage to desired behavior and its timing and frequency of application.

The process of behavior modification is presented in highly simplified form in Figure 10-6 on page 230.

The whole process is based on Thorndike's Law of Effect which states that behavior which leads to (or appears to lead to) a positive outcome tends to be repeated while behavior that appears to lead to a negative outcome tends to be stopped. Therefore in our model in Figure 10-6, that behavior whose outcome leads to rewards tends to be repeated, while that behavior whose outcome leads to punishment (or lack of reward) tends to be stopped.

This is all highly reminiscent of Vroom's model of motivation which we discussed in Chapter 6. We are still talking about motivation here, since we are

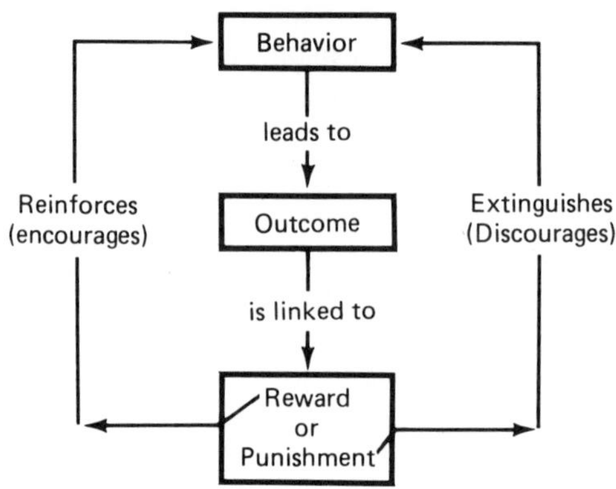

FIGURE 10-6: A SIMPLIFIED MODEL OF THE PROCESS OF BEHAVIOR MODIFICATION.

trying to get someone to do something, but our emphasis is rather more on communication and action at this point in the book. Be that as it may, Vroom said that initial outcomes (task goals) are often the *means* to an end rather than the end itself. There is a *second* level of "outcomes" which reflect the real goals of individuals. These second level outcomes, in behavior modification terms, are the *rewards* associated with the first level outcomes.

From the manager's point of view, there are two areas on which he must focus very carefully. First of all he must be able to define desired outcomes clearly, and secondly he must be able to associate the rewards (or punishments) he dispenses with the attainment of these outcomes (or the failure to attain them). The essence, then, of the manager's task is *identifying desirable behavior* and *reinforcing desirable behavior*.

How do we reinforce whatever we have decided is desired behavior? Are we really talking about a "piece rate" system of reward where the worker gets paid on the basis of the number of units he produces? Unfortunately piece rate systems don't always result in good performance. The principles of reinforcement are slightly more complex than "a nickel every time you finish a widget."

In essence, when we talk about reinforcement we are talking about manipulating the outcomes of behavior. We make the outcome of some behavior pleasant (positive reinforcement), the outcome of some alternative behavior decidedly *un*pleasant (punishment and avoidance behavior), and ignore the outcome of some other behavior (extinction).

Negative Reinforcement

In order to get an individual to exhibit desired behavior—what we *want* him to do—we can either reward him when he behaves "properly" (positive reinforcement) or we can punish him when he behaves *im*properly (negative reinforcement).

The former encourages desired behavior, while the latter does the same thing by encouraging the individual to *avoid im*proper behavior.

We attempt to get people to drive safely by imposing a whole set of punishments for driving *un*safely. The hope is that people will attempt to avoid the punishments, and thereby drive in the desired manner. One of the problems with systems based on *avoidance behavior* is that they often find it difficult to punish unsatisfactory behavior frequently enough: too many violations go unnoticed or unpunished. Then, unfortunately, the need for avoidance is no longer necessary. If it is highly unlikely that you will be punished for exceeding the speed limit, why bother to stay within it?

Negative reinforcement can also take the form of withholding rewards for behavior that previously was rewarded. This process (*extinction*) may be used when you wish to get people to stop doing what they have been doing even though the behavior was desirable in the past. Sometimes the rules change in life, just as they do in games, and we have to stop doing what we used to do. When a firm no longer wants its salesmen to emphasize a certain line of goods, it removes the incentive to sell the line by removing the commissions attached to it. Over time (and in this case, probably a relatively short time) the behavior ceases. Mothers often have the problem of their babies crying when they are put to bed. To begin with the mother is worried about the baby, so she picks it up and cuddles it, rocking it to sleep, and singing softly to it. Needless to say, the baby finds this rather pleasant, so when it is put down in its bed it cries, expecting to be rewarded for the crying by being picked up again. If, however, mother is able to control her worries enough to let the baby cry itself to sleep a few times, the behavior quickly disappears. The baby has learned that there are no rewards for crying when it is put to bed.

Finally, of course, negative reinforcement can be directed right at the behavior that is deemed undesirable. We have an elaborate system of *punishments* for what we define as crimes. These penalties are not designed to get people to act in a specific way, but rather to *stop* them from acting in certain other specific ways. There is a wide range of behavior that is not punishable by law.

Positive Reinforcement

Behavior modification, as it has been practiced in industry, focuses on positive reinforcement rather than negative reinforcement. The emphasis is on rewarding desired behavior, and *not* rewarding undesired behavior. Rather than applying sanctions, experience to date has been that by combining positive reinforcement with extinction, results have been excellent.

There are some clear steps to implementing behavior modification in an organization. They are:

1 *Define the desired behavior*. And do it in terms of the *results* you want if at all possible. That way, you can reinforce achievement rather than just activity.

2 *Get the agreement of the people involved as to what desirable behavior is*. It is no use defining some result as desirable when the people involved in its achievement feel it is quite the opposite. Agreement to the list of criteria of desirable behavior implies some sort of commitment to attempt to meet them.

3 *Decide on the rewards to be applied*. The experience of companies such as Emery Air Freight has been that praise for a job well done, expressed in quantitative terms, is the most effective reward. Edward Feeney gives an example of saying something *specifically* related to performance, like, "Joe, I liked the ingenuity you showed just now getting those crates into that container. You're running pretty consistently at 98 percent of standard. And after watching you, I can understand why." (*Organizational Dynamics*, Winter 1973).

4 *Design the task so that the desired outcomes occur—soon and often*. It makes no sense to set criteria of effective performance that can never be achieved. It does make sense to give the individuals involved a chance to feel good about doing well as quickly as possible.

5 *Monitor behavior (performance) closely*. Make sure you recognize when the desired behavior has occurred. And also, make sure that the employee knows it too. A useful technique is to have both the employee and the supervisor monitor performance and keep a record of results. Just having the opportunity to look at his own record of accomplishment can be a reinforcing experience for the employee.

6 *Apply rewards as quickly as possible after the desired outcome*. One of the problems of most reward systems is that they fail to make the clear connection between *specific* behavior and reward. The longer the wait between the behavior and its reinforcement, the greater the chance that the individual involved will not see the behavior as having positive consequence.

7 *Design rewards so that they are appropriate to the desired outcomes*. Gilbert and Sullivan urged that the punishment be made to fit the crime. By the same token, rewards should fit the behavior. Overrewarding behavior makes people feel guilty. Underrewarding them makes them feel resentful. There is a delicate balance where both parties feel the exchange has been fair.

8 *Don't reward every single instance of desired behavior*. The problem with continuous reinforcement is that while desired behavior increases rapidly, as soon as the reward is omitted, the desired behavior falls off just about as rapidly. Giving a child a candy every time it eats its meal leads to the expectation of a candy every time. If the candy is omitted, it appears to be a punishment. The warnings against feeding the bears in Yellowstone Park are not necessarily because the food is bad for the bears. It's because when your food runs out, the bear is unlikely to view the situation with the same understanding as you do.

Research indicates that partial reinforcement, where rewards are given only part of the time, results in slower behavior change, but far stronger commitment to the change. The best type of schedule for these rewards is what is termed a *variable interval schedule*, in which the rewards are given at unpredictable times, but with some overall average of frequency.

SUMMARY

In this chapter, we have gone from a discussion of general communication theory to the examination of some specific communication methods and applications. One thing should be very clear: communication is closely associated with motivation and leadership. A manager's job can be likened to a card game—he is taught the rules (provided with the theory), dealt a hand (given certain individual, work group and organizational systems), and expected to play the hand in order to achieve certain results (the output system). How he plays the hand is determined by how he communicates, motivates and leads. These are the three "action" dimensions of management. While we have, by necessity, talked about each of them separately, they cannot be isolated from one another. They are a closely intertwined "system"—the "action system."

DANIELS COMPUTER COMPANY, CONCLUDED

This chapter has looked at some of the processes of communication, influence and change that might be applied in a situation such as Daniels Computer. The new chief engineer in the company is faced with the problem of getting the project group members from the various subgroups to change their behavior patterns and cooperate with one another. As we saw in Part III, his tactic was to tell each of the groups what to do. He adopted a *directive* stance, in line with the demands of the situation which called for a greater degree of task-oriented behavior.

But much of the success or failure of this approach will depend on how the chief engineer manages communications. Currently, he is operating a "star net" where he is the apex of the star to whom, and through whom, all communication flows. As we know, in time that tends to be demotivating for the other members of the net. It is a short-term strategy which works when the boss has most or all of the data, where the task is complex and he wants to get it on track fast, when there are tight time constraints, and where the boss wants to establish his power clearly. Since these factors describe the situation at the moment in Daniels Computer, the chief engineer appears to be acting appropriately. But what happens when the project *does* start to get back on track, and when the chief engineer *has* established his authority clearly? What about the satisfaction of the subordinates? How can they be motivated to take the ball themselves? A change in the communication process is required at this stage.

What the chief engineer could, and should, do is:

a Begin to move the transactions with his sectional heads to an adult-adult level. He has been operating on a parent-child level, telling them what to do and getting them in line, but if he wants them to act independently, to be motivated to take responsibility themselves, and to grow and learn in the job, then he is going to have to move communication to a more rational, equal level.

b Apply some of the techniques of behavior modification. As the project engineers begin to do things right, he should visibly stroke them. When they do *not* behave appropriately, he should zap them or ignore them. Somehow he must establish that it is pleasant and rewarding to operate as a team member of the overall project group, and that it is *un*pleasant and *un*rewarding to maintain tight subgroup allegiances.

c Move the communication structure more towards an all-channel network. Bear in mind that the *job* requires some directive behavior on the manager's part, so we are not suggesting that he run things in a fully participative, equalitarian fashion. But he must move back from the totally *directive* towards the *interactive* style because of the complex, unique nature of the job, and the need for interaction between specialist subgroups to solve the design problems. Remember, there were a number of *interactive job* indicators that applied as well.

So much for what the theory tells us the chief engineer should do. Let's take a look at what he actually *did*. Here, as promised, is Part IV, the conclusion of Daniels Computer Company. When you have read it, and thought about it a bit, we highly recommend that you go back to the start of the book and follow the case through each of its parts, reviewing your thoughts on it at each stage. That will begin to give you a *systems* view of the case; you will see how all of the things about which we have been talking in the book hang together, and how it is difficult to separate them, and talk about them, or apply them, in isolation.

DANIELS COMPUTER COMPANY PART IV

For several weeks after the chief engineer set the direction of the project, the project engineers vied with one another to see who could catch the chief engineer in error. Considerable time was spent in experimentation designed to find a weakness in the new design plan. Few problems in the plan could be found. The chief engineer defended his theoretical positions vigorously and continued to demand that schedules be met.

Schedules were met and the four groups worked simultaneously on related design aspects. Communication with the chief engineer grew in frequency. Communication directly among groups at all levels became common. Design limits were quickly discovered before the effort of other groups was needlessly expended.

The cohesion within technical groups became less pronounced, particularly among lower status engineers and technicians. Several lunch groups comprising members of several technical groups began to appear. Enthusiasm for the project was again expressed by the team members.

Chapter Summary

1 The term "communication" is overused and fuzzy. We prefer to think of communication in the same manner in which we defined interaction—*an interpersonal contact in which one individual can be observed acting (which includes speaking or writing) and one or more individuals responding to this action.*

2 Communications have both "content" and "feeling." Because of the modifying effects of perceptual screens, both of these aspects of communication can be distorted. We translate content into feeling, and tend to respond more on a feeling level than we realize.

3 Communication is not just the process of transmitting data, but is a process for influencing and changing the behavior of others.

4 Barriers to communication center around the self-concept. As we know from our earlier discussions about the self-concept and the perceptual process, we "hear" communications that reinforce our self-concepts, and "screen" communications that are incongruent with it.

5 Role relationships affect communication. As we know, incumbents of certain roles are expected to act in a certain fashion, and we tend to perceive their communications, and to communicate with them, on the basis of these role expectations.

6 Communication, and its ability to influence behavior, is also a function of the credibility of the source—as we saw in the Milgram experiments.

7 Communications can either be one-way (no feedback) or two-way. Depending on the situation each of these methods of communication can be effective.

8 Organizational, or role, structure affects various aspects of the communication process. Structure affects such communication variables as the degree of feedback (one-way or two-way), the amount of information that is shared or given, and the degree of involvement required of people in the system. All of these things affect morale, job satisfaction, and task achievement.

9 We tend to use verbal or written communication more to disguise our intentions than to reveal them. At the non-verbal level, however, our real feelings are more often revealed.

10 Transactional analysis is a method for analyzing communications in terms of their emotional basis. Since communication involves at least two people, and it is a means of influencing the behavior of others, the way we communicate reflects our basic needs, values, and sense of relationship with others. Transactional analysis presents a framework which allows us to analyze and categorize underlying aspects of communication.

11 Building on Thorndike's Law of Effect, which states that behavior which leads to (or appears to lead to) a positive outcome tends to be repeated, while behavior that leads to (or appears to lead to) a negative outcome tends to be terminated, the technique of behavior modification builds an integrated system of communication and behavior which reinforces "good" performance, and undermines "bad" performance.
Behavior modification is a technique which is becoming more and more widely used in organizational settings, with positive results.

11

Managing the Organizational System: The Problems of Change

OBJECTIVES

When you have completed this chapter you should:

- be aware of some of the basic forces for change which exist in the environment;
- understand the dynamics of resistance to change;
- be aware of some of the basic underlying issues facing any organizational change effort;
- recognize that organizational change involves the entire system.

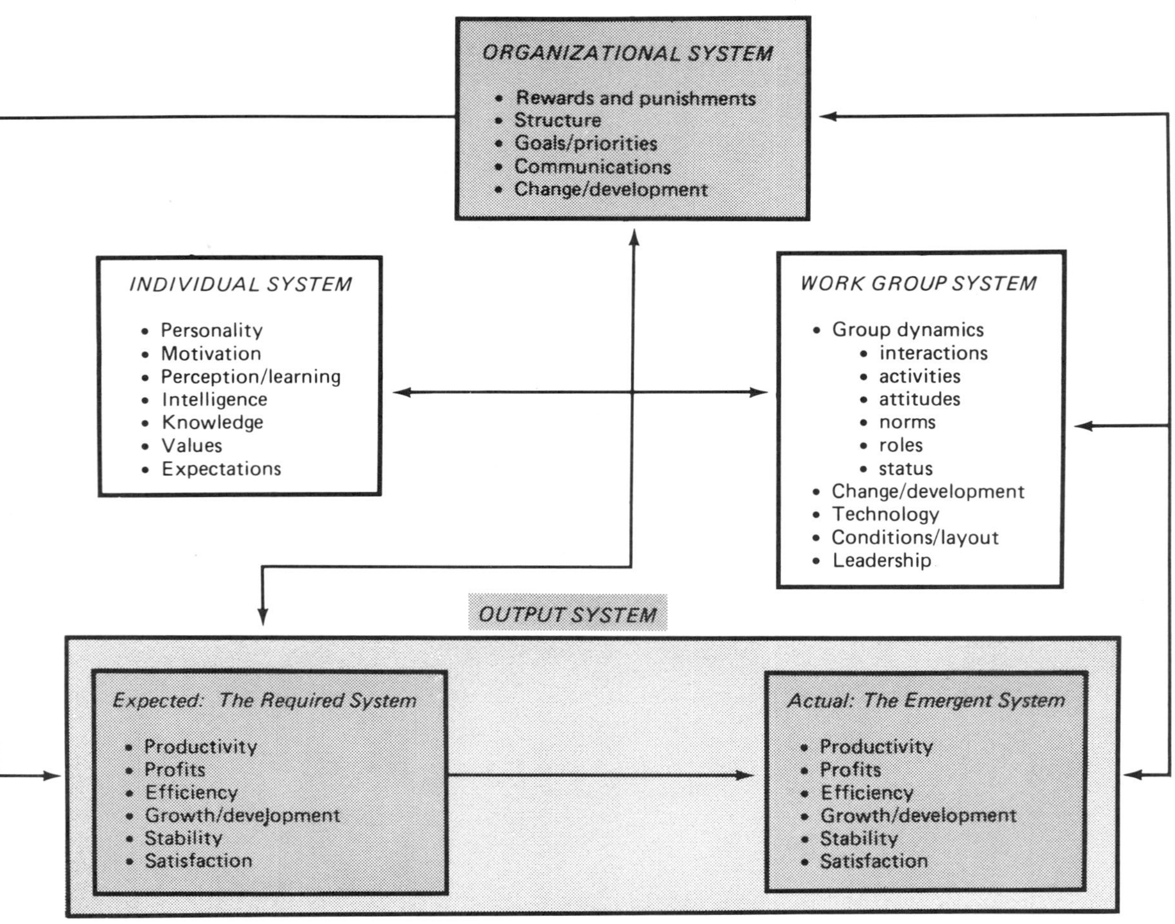
ORGANIZATIONAL SYSTEM
• Rewards and punishments
• Structure
• Goals/priorities
• Communications
• Change/development
INDIVIDUAL SYSTEM
• Personality
• Motivation
• Perception/learning
• Intelligence
• Knowledge
• Values
• Expectations
WORK GROUP SYSTEM
• Group dynamics
• interactions
• activities
• attitudes
• norms
• roles
• status
• Change/development
• Technology
• Conditions/layout
• Leadership
OUTPUT SYSTEM
Expected: The Required System
• Productivity
• Profits
• Efficiency
• Growth/development
• Stability
• Satisfaction
Actual: The Emergent System
• Productivity
• Profits
• Efficiency
• Growth/development
• Stability
• Satisfaction

"A state without the means of some change is without the means of its conservation."

—*Edmund Burke*

"Change is not made without inconvenience, even from worse to better."

—*Richard Hooker*

"The history of organizations (and of nations) is littered with the corpses of enterprises which failed to respond appropriately to the demands of the environment for change."

—*Katz and Kahn, 1966*

The job of a manager at the top of an organization is concerned with pulling all the various elements under him into one unified whole, ensuring that all members are working towards similar goals, and deciding just what those goals should be. The *organizational system* that we talk about is largely designed and determined by people at or very near the top. Their influence is highly pervasive. R.L. Hershey, a former vice-president of Dupont, comments that "The man at the head of the organization sets an example that is followed right down through the organization." (Morse and Warner, 1966) While managers lower down the ladder are concerned with the administration of the system, those at the top are concerned with its focus and direction.

The major dilemma facing the organization as a whole is the balance between maintenance of the status quo and change. In Chapter 2 we noted that the purpose of organization is to structure relationships between people, set goals for the unit, and coordinate the efforts of members towards the attainment of these goals. These things all contribute to giving the organization a sense of continuity without which it would have to start afresh with each "generation" of new members. By designing an overall system of operation it acquires stability. The more the members of the organization believe in the merits and importance of the system, the more stable it becomes. But the overall effect of reinforcing the values and goals of the system is to make its members conservative and protective of the status quo, while pressures from a rapidly changing environment demand that it be flexible and able to change.

Our model of the major elements affecting a managerial situation (Figure 11-1) illustrates some of the environmental factors that put pressure on an organization to change.

Changes in economic conditions, social values, competition, and government legislation all affect the way in which an organization operates, be it an industrial

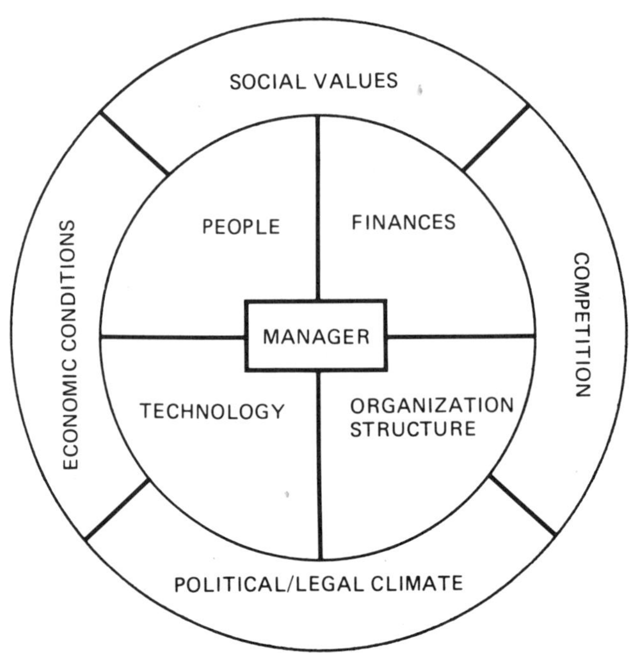

FIGURE 11-1: THE MAJOR ELEMENTS AFFECTING A MANAGERIAL SITUATION.

firm, a government agency, a health care institution, or a charitable organization. The March of Dimes was faced with a major change decision after the invention of Salk vaccine for polio. With polio effectively eradicated, the fund-raising mechanism had to be either disbanded or given another goal. As it turned out, the decision was made to maintain the structure of the March of Dimes, but redirect its efforts to the funding of research into respiratory diseases.

FORCES FOR ORGANIZATIONAL CHANGE

Economic Forces for Change

All organizations feel the effects of economic swings from growth to recession and back again. In boom times, new jobs are created, new projects are initiated, priorities altered (resources are available to do more things at once) and the structure of organizations changed. During an economic downswing, people begin to lose their jobs, organizations cut back on spending, projects are terminated and nonessentials are pared to make resources available for the ''bread and butter'' functions of the organization. The Arab oil embargo brought about drastic changes in many organizations; overnight, energy costs skyrocketed and it was not possible to pass these increased costs on. Goals had to be redefined and policies changed.

Cultural Forces for Change

Changes in social values have affected the operation of most organizations in North America markedly in the last fifteen or so years. The majority of Fortune 500 companies now report on social performance in areas such as minority employment, environmental controls and community involvement. Equal opportunity for women in the workforce has received a great deal of attention, and increasing numbers of females are finding their way into positions formerly the private domain of males.

Competition

Competition in such diverse areas as weapons production, religious movements, education, and the mail service have led to changes in government spending on defense budgets, changes in the emphasis of various religious groups to the maintenance and growth of their membership, shakeouts in the educational system, particularly at the university level, and the development of private agencies to compete with federal services. As anthropologists Arensberg and Neihoff (1971) note, ''Although the competition of national cultures is readily recognized as the main stimulus for widespread change, this tendency exists with any size of group or even with individuals.''

Political/Legal Forces

The government itself, often accused of being rigid and unchangeable, is a major force for change in society. While it moves ponderously, it certainly is able to put the cat among the pigeons as far as society as a whole is concerned. Legislation concerning gasoline consumption and pollution emission standards have caused huge changes in the automobile industry, while judgments such as the Bakke case affect organizations' hiring, training, and general manpower policies.

The reasons for change are many, but basically all change is the result of a need to adapt to environmental conditions. Some organizations simply seem better at it than others. Some are able to anticipate the need for change and move with consummate timing; some fail to see what appear to be obvious signs, and get caught. IBM has tended to be of the first kind, while American Motors may have been too often of the second kind.

THE ORGANIZATIONAL SYSTEM AS STEWARD OF CHANGE

In our opinion the most important function of a manager is the successful implementation of change. On the surface it appears that most of the organizational system remains constant while only a fraction of it undergoes change. However, almost every decision is concerned with a change of some kind. The question is, ''What shall we do now?'', and the decision must come down either as ''the usual,'' or as "something different" (change). Since decisions must be implemented by other people, the manager making them must consider how he can get them to behave appropriately, how he can motivate them to move in the right direction. That is where a great deal of a manager's skill is required. It is one thing to make a good decision; it is quite another to get other people committed to implementing it.

The crucial word in the last sentence is "committed." Commitment is the central issue in change. Change in organizations implies that *other* people behave differently. Certainly, the implementer of the change must also alter his behavior appropriately—he can't get away with "Do as I say, not as I do" for long—but the main emphasis is on the chang*ees*. *They* have to behave differently; *they* have to bear the brunt of uncertainty, anxiety and fear during the change; *they* have to put themselves on the line. Therefore they must be committed to the idea of the change, or else they won't make it work. It is irrelevant how committed top management is to implementing a change if it cannot secure the same sort of commitment from those lower down in the organization who are going to be involved in it.

THE PROCESS OF CHANGE

When we talk about change at the organizational system level, we mean change in the values, attitudes, goals and behavior of the people within the organization. Behavior changes are required whenever a new process or machine is introduced on the job, whenever a new boss who has different ideas about how to do things appears, or whenever the organization as a whole decides to alter its goals and priorities. Most of these behavioral changes require that the people involved also adjust their attitudes, values and goals. In order to act differently, one must be able to believe that it is "better" to do so. Therefore management is deeply involved in attitude change, whether it realizes it or not, and therein lies the nub of many of the problems that organizations face. It is not sufficient to decree that behavior will change—"From now on, we are going to do it this way"—without getting people to understand and accept *why*, without getting them to alter their value systems.

The process of change involves three basic stages: unfreezing, introduction of the change, and refreezing.

Unfreezing means demonstrating to the subjects of change that their present values, attitudes, goals and behavior are inappropriate. There is little incentive to alter beliefs or behavior if you feel that when you *now* believe and how you *now* act are perfectly OK. When you think that they are *not* OK, then you are more likely to cast about for some alternatives which will be more rewarding to you. In order to unfreeze attitudes, values, beliefs, goals, and the patterns of behavior which are manifested by them, the agent of change must be able to demonstrate that they are wrong—that they just don't work any more.

The Chinese brainwashing techniques which we referred to in Chapter 10 provide a vivid, if rather extreme, example of unfreezing. Captured Westerners were subjected to a treatment which punished them for values and behavior that did not conform to the Chinese Communist doctrine. In this way their captors attempted to demonstrate that their present behavior was inappropriate; nothing good would ever occur if they continued to believe and act as they did when first captured.

The same sort of process is applied in the basic training of Marines. The goal of the training is to convert the recruit to the ''Marine Corps way'' of behaving. The procedure is similar to the first stages of the Chinese indoctrination process. Four things are done: (1) the subject is removed from his usual physical and social environment; (2) he is denied any social support for his behavior (of the old type); (3) he is subjected to humiliation when he exhibits the old behavior; and (4) he is ''behavior modded''—rewarded when he acts appropriately and punished when he fails to do so.

An article in *Look Magazine* (August 12, 1969) described the process of Marine indoctrination. To begin with, the recruit is ''hermetically sealed in a hostile environment.'' He must ''drill for hours in the hot sun, eat meals in silence and stand at rigid attention the rest of the time; he has no television, no radio, no candy, no coke, no beer, no telephone.'' The drill instructor constantly harasses the recruit, to ''shock (him) out of the emotional stability of home, pool hall, street corner, girl friend or school.'' The recruit's self-concept is attacked. He is berated for not being able to behave properly—''For sixteen hours a day, for two weeks, (he) will do nothing right.''

Basically, the unfreezing process is concerned with removing the supports for present behavior, demonstrating that present values and actions are inappropriate. All institutions indulge in this type of process to some extent. When we enter them we are subjected to a series of ''don'ts.'' The assumption behind the unfreezing process is that eventually the subject will realize that what he is doing is not working, and he will cast about for more effective behavior patterns.

Introducing the Change

It is at this stage that the new values and behavior are presented to the subject of the change. Now that he realizes that what he has been doing is wrong, he is actively searching for some alternatives. In other words, he is in a highly aroused need state. When he is presented with a value or behavior set *which works* in the new environment, he is more likely to give it a try.

Refreezing

The trick, however, is to get people to *continue* in the new way. As we saw with the Chinese brainwashing experience, even after several *years* of intensive indoctrination, very few of the captives, when returned to Western society, failed to return to their old beliefs and behavior patterns.

Behavior, to be maintained, must be reinforced. We saw, in our discussion of behavior modification techniques, that an essential element in the process was a schedule of reinforcements, attached to the desired behavior. Without these reinforcements, behavior quickly lapses into the old patterns. Probably one of the major elements affecting the failure of the Chinese brainwashing attempts was the fact that the captives returned to an environment which no longer supported the values and behavior they had just "learned." They were no longer reinforced.

The Church, in its training of nuns, goes through the basic processes of unfreezing and change (and change from being a daughter of one's parents, to being a daughter of God is a profound one), but spends much more time on the refreezing stage. The converts remain in the convent for a long time, work in an environment where they can maintain a close attachment to a church, often travel in small groups, and are also reinforced by wearing a "uniform" which tells others how to act in their presence. (It will be interesting to see, over time, how the relaxation of rules concerning the wearing of the habit will affect the rate of renunciation of vows among nuns. The nun's "uniform" acted as a strong reinforcer of behavior because it reminded both the wearer and others of her role, so that appropriate behavior was encouraged.)

The examples discussed above are a bit out of the ordinary, but the principles of unfreezing, changing and refreezing that they illustrate hold true in most life situations. Whenever you enter a new school, new job, or new circle of acquaintances, you are subjected to some unfreezing. Behavior that is considered inappropriate is negatively reinforced. Change comes about if you wish to remain within the new environment, because you tend to adapt your behavior and values to fit it: you change. And, over time, your behavior becomes fixed in the new mold as it is consistently reinforced: you become refrozen. The socialization process we discussed as a group phenomenon in Chapter 7 reflects this. We constantly undergo some type of unfreezing, change and refreezing.

RESISTANCE TO CHANGE

We know, from our discussion of the self-concept, that resistance to change is a natural phenomenon in which we all indulge. Each time a force for change arises, a defense against the change appears as well. Kurt Lewin (1951) suggested that this situation could best be represented as a "force field," with forces pushing *for* acceptance of change and other forces pushing *against* its acceptance (Figure 11-2).

Looking at change from an organizational standpoint, the arrows on our change analysis diagram represent separate forces for or against alteration of the status quo. Whichever side is strongest will succeed in overcoming the other.

The only problem is that, like Newton's First Law of Dynamics, every force tends to be countered by an equal and opposite force. The greater the push for change, the stronger the resistance to it. How can we overcome that dilemma? We could either (a) increase the push for change so greatly that we simply overcome any resistance before it gets strong enough; or (b) we could seek some way of reducing the resistance forces; or (c) we could attempt to do both simultaneously.

If the bar representing the equilibrium state is thought of as a block of ice, and

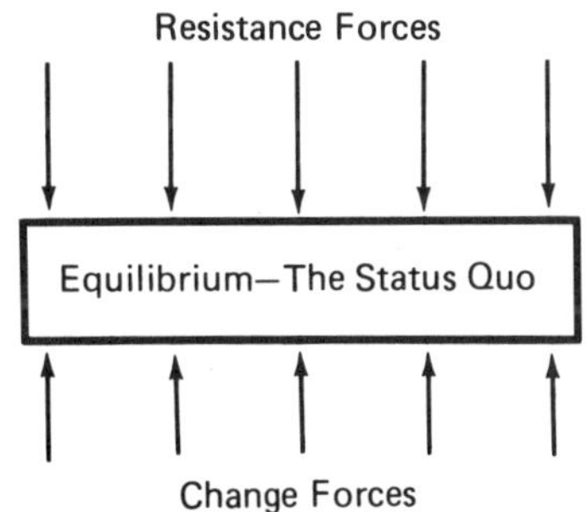

FIGURE 11-2: CHANGE ANALYSIS DIAGRAM. REASONS FOR CHANGE, AND REASONS AGAINST IT CAN BE THOUGHT OF AS WORKING EITHER TO ALTER THE STATUS QUO OR MAINTAIN IT.

we want to change its shape and position, the process becomes clear. If you push too hard on a block of ice, it cracks and breaks. Sometimes we push so hard to change the system that it breaks, and instead of a changed system we have rubble. Revolutions do that. Evolution does something else. It unfreezes the block of ice, places it in a new mold, and then refreezes it. In other words, it removes enough of the resisting forces to allow for the unfreezing, it uses the change forces to push the liquid into a new mold, and then it reinforces the system by refreezing it.

The use of a change analysis diagram can facilitate change implementation. The forces must be identified and placed on the diagram and their relative strengths must be estimated. Reddin (1970) provides an example of a manager faced with a change in his job. He enumerates the resistance forces and acceptance forces as he sees them and assigns them strengths (in this case, the more arrows, the greater the strength). His analysis is shown in Figure 11-3. The choices facing the manager are now clearer: he can ''work through'' his identified resistances and attempt to reduce their strength, and/or he can develop the strong points about the job change and build more of them into the new job, thereby making it more attractive to change.

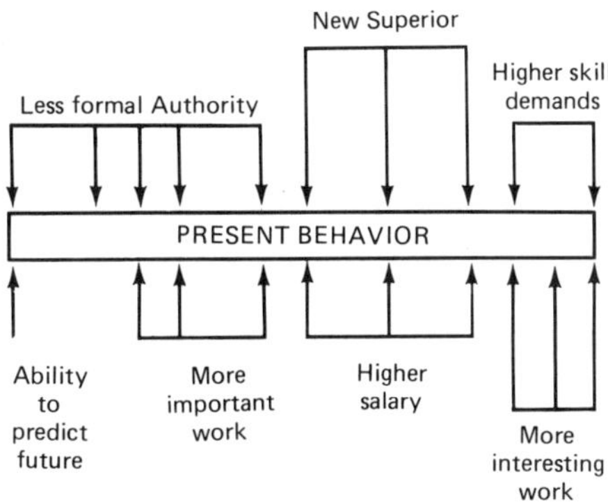

FIGURE 11-3: EXAMPLE OF A FORCE FIELD ANALYSIS. FROM: *MANAGERIAL EFFECTIVENESS*, W.J. REDDIN, NEW YORK: McGRAW-HILL, 1970.

ORGANIZATIONAL CHANGE/DEVELOPMENT

It is not fashionable to talk about organizational change. The current terminology is *organizational development (OD)*. The reason why the word ''development'' is used rather than ''change'' of course, is that the latter is too threatening. You may have experienced some negative feelings when we discussed the Chinese brainwashing process or the Marine boot camp procedures. We tend to feel manipulated and threatened when we see the sorts of things to which we are subjected in life. By the same token, talking to managers (or workers) about ''change'' doesn't tend to evoke open, welcoming, warm responses. People tend to get their guard up and ready. So the agents of change—consultants, managers, agencies, etc.—have found a softer word with more positive connotations. How can one resist ''development?'' It means growing, getting better, learning, adapting. But it also means *change*. There is no growing, getting better, learning, or adapting without change.

Organizational development (OD) is a separate field of academic research and practice. There is a vast literature on implementing change in organizations. OD is associated with such diverse activities as T-Group training, Management by Objectives (MBO), Team Building, and a whole host of technologies such as Grid, 3-D, and System 4, each of which is the product of a particular theorist and practitioner.

For our purposes, organizational development is any type of organization-wide change activity. It may involve rearranging the structure of the organization, getting managers to adopt a different approach to leadership, implementing a motivational system, or changing the focus of activities in an organization.

As Hersey and Blanchard (1977) point out, the focus for an OD effort can come out of almost any of the behavioral theories we have discussed. Change can be centered around identifying and satisfying basic needs of employees (Maslow); enriching jobs to provide a challenge, achievement, recognition and growth (Herzberg); improving the effectiveness of managers in leadership positions (Reddin); increasing productivity at the worker level (Behavior Modification); improving communications (Transactional Analysis; Active Listening); building work teams and linking them to organizational objectives (Likert); and so on. The theory of organizational behavior is the toolbox of organizational development.

CRITICAL ELEMENTS FOR SUCCESSFUL ORGANIZATIONAL CHANGE

There is no one ''best'' way of implementing change successfully. Like everything else in organizational behavior, it is situational. Sometimes one approach works better than another. A good grasp of the situation is essential before strategy is outlined. But there are a number of critical elements in the change process at the organization-wide level that must be considered. If they are handled correctly, commitment to the change will result and things will work smoothly. If they are bungled, or overlooked, resistance forces may gather enough strength to stifle the change or seriously impede it. The critical elements of organizational development, common to almost all change efforts are:

- Diagnosis
- Communication
- Objectives
- Top level support
- Benefits analysis
- Trust
- Consistency
- Unfreezing
- Early success
- Adaptation
- Reinforcement
- Resistance interpretation

Diagnosis

Any change effort is concerned with moving a situation from the actual to an ideal. Therefore two things have to be known: what is the actual situation *now* and what would we like it to become? The first step is to diagnose what the problems are which face the organization presently. Why is change seen as necessary?

Commitment to effective change and effective operation is the ultimate goal of an OD effort. So it is important that in the diagnostic phase, the organization which will be subjected to the change (which we shall refer to as the client-organization) identify its own problems as much as possible. Put in a personal framework, it is easier for you to diet to lose weight when *you* say you are overweight than when someone else says it. The client-organization must recognize its own problems before it can begin to engage in their resolution.

A second important point in diagnosis is to determine the frame of reference from which it is being made. Are you looking at the problem through the eyes of top management, of workers, of middle management, of a staff specialist, of one particular department head? We know that perceptions are distorted to fit one's own needs. Therefore, what one individual, or group of individuals, defines as a problem may not be seen that way at all in other segments of the organization. One of the points we will continue to emphasize is that organizational change is just that—organization-wide; it is dynamite to start changes which pit one segment of the organization against another.

Communication

Change, as we know, is often threatening, and that is particularly true when the change is initiated by an outside source over which we have little or no control. The less information about the change, the form it will take, whom it will affect, how long it will take, what adjustments will have to be made, and so on, the more nervous the changees become. We attempt to manage our lives in such a way as to reduce uncertainty as much as possible. Large additional doses of uncertainty do little to calm the nerves. One of the major causes of resistance build-up and failure of change programs is the lack of clear information about what is going on.

When we looked at communication nets, we saw that in the star net, the central figure, A, was the most powerful and the most satisfied with his job. All communication flowed through him and he was able to monitor information and give out, or hold back, what he wanted. The individuals at the points of the stars, however, operate largely in the dark. They get only the information that is provided them by A. But that is often not enough, so they resort to providing their own information. We call it the "grapevine." It is rumor, and may or may not be based on fact. But it is still information and it is acted on as if it were fact.

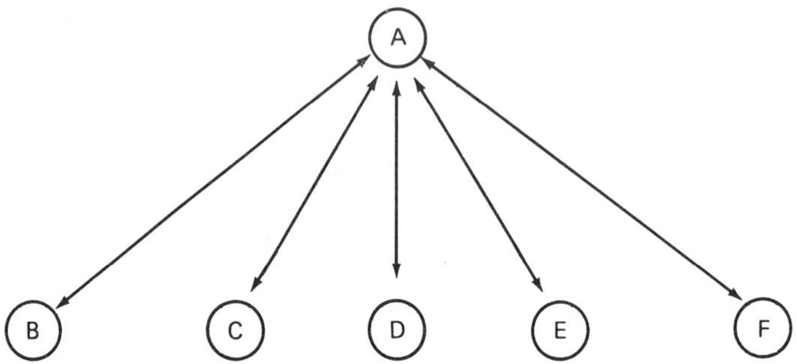

FIGURE 11-4: THE "STAR" COMMUNICATION NET. A CONTROLS ALL THE DATA.

The point is that if factual data is not provided about the change, non-factual data will be used by the client-population instead. Depending on the degree of trust in which the initiators of the change are held, the non-factually based data will be either positive or negative—largely positive if there is very high trust, and largely negative if there is low trust.

The type of information provided should include statements of the objectives of the change, its nature, its benefits, its possible drawbacks, and a description of the methods to be used. The more public the announcements, the better. We have all played the children's game of sitting in a circle and having one person whisper something into the next person's ear. The second person whispers the message to the third, and so on until the last person repeats the message out loud. There is little or no resemblance to the original message after eight or ten transmissions. By the same token, if data is provided to a select group to "filter" down to others, the potential for distortion is greatly increased.

One successful company has all its employees gather in the parking lot, or in a high school auditorium, one afternoon each six months, and the President addresses them, telling them how things are going (The "State of the Nation") and what plans are for the immediate future (change). Microphones are placed in the audience, and anyone who wishes to raise any questions or comments may do so. The President reserves the right not to answer immediately, but pledges to do so within one month, *in writing*, posted on all bulletin boards throughout the company. This type of open communication network (and this is only one part of the overall company's communications system) has resulted in high trust levels, an openness to change, and few rumors.

The importance of open, two-way communication about change cannot be overemphasised. Change is frightening. And the more secret it appears to be, the more threatening it is. Maximum information should be provided, and the subjects of the change should be given an opportunity to voice their doubts, fears, anxieties and questions.

Objectives

The objectives of a change effort—where the organization wants to end up—are often unclear. There is a feeling that "we are ill," and a desire to become "not ill," whatever that means. In the diagnostic phase, problems may be identified which require solutions, but the question is, what should the solutions achieve? Is the objective simply to remove the pain of the problem, or is it something deeper?

A simple trap to fall into is to treat symptoms rather than root causes of problems. We wake up each morning with a headache, and we take an aspirin. That treats the symptom, but the root cause may be what we have been eating and drinking. The aspirin takes the headache away today, but it comes back tomorrow. In the same manner, an organization may feel "pain" of some kind and want to get rid of it, but still not be sure of what it wants to achieve after the pain has gone. Maybe relief of the symptom is enough. The only problem is that it tends to keep recurring.

Because we are interested in commitment to making change effective, one essential aspect of the objective-setting process is to ensure that those who will be affected by the change—who will be involved in it—have a say in deciding on its goals. A great deal of resistance to change is based on either misunderstanding of its direction and consequences or recognition that it does against many of the things one wants to retain. If the changee has some control over the direction of the change, he also has a means of reducing its uncertainty. That means that he is likely to find it less threatening; he "owns" part of it.

The optimum situation is one where the subjects of the change set its objectives. When *they* agree to a goal, the likelihood of its achievement is much higher. It doesn't always work that way, but the research evidence suggests that participation in the objective-setting process tends to increase motivation and performance. There is more to the issue than simply allowing subordinates to participate in setting objectives. The organization is a system, and there are a large number of other factors which contribute to the success of change. Trust levels, status relationships, the reward system, and the entire list of factors being discussed here affect perceptions of change and reactions to it.

Top-level Support

Change that is initiated from the bottom of an organization, without the support or blessing of the top levels, is revolution. It can work, but it is often bloody. In the Navy it is called mutiny, and is punishable by death. The same thing applies in organizations. The unsuccessful leaders of organizational revolutions often get fired or otherwise emasculated.

To increase the chances of success, change should have the support of the top levels of the organization. To begin with, they have the power—they dispense the rewards and the punishments. This power can be used either to support or to block change. Why not enlist their support? They also have egos, like all of us, and it is just as flattering for individuals at the top of organizations to see themselves as the initiators of change as it is for individuals at the bottom. The basic, bare facts of the matter are that in most hierarchical organizations the top levels have a great deal of power, and change efforts initiated without their support have a low chance of success.

A final point to be made about top-level support is that organizational change has a higher likelihood of success if the top managers become actively involved in it and exhibit changed behavior themselves. Earlier on in the chapter we quoted R.L. Hershey, a former vice-president of Dupont, who remarked that "The man at the head of the organization sets an example that is followed right down through the organization." "Do as I do" is always more persuasive than "Do as I say."

Benefits Analysis

Whether the initiators of change wish it or not, those affected by it weigh its costs and benefits to them, as they perceive them, and make judgments based on these perceptions as to the degree to which they will support the change or not.

Often the initiators of change talk about its benefits exclusively and fail to mention any of the costs. As we know, every change has costs attached to it in a psychological sense. In order to change, there has to be a wrench in the self-concept somehow. There is always some anxiety and stress attached to change. We sometimes fail to recognize this aspect. Changing jobs, moving house, marriage, a death in the family, illness, and so on all create stress. Box 11-1 presents a stress scale which assigns points to various types of life-events. Accumulation of 200 points or more in a year results in a better than 50 percent chance of serious illness occurring in the following year. Measure yourself on the stress scale.

We are not suggesting that beneficial changes are not stressful. The scale of life-change units in Box 11-1 indicates that such things as "outstanding personal achievement" still have a stress rating. *All* change is stress inducing. But if the change can be beneficial, or, more accurately stated, can be *perceived* as beneficial by those affected by it, it will tend to produce less anxiety and stress. Christmas is stress inducing, but it is pleasant, expected, and familiar. Death of a spouse is none of these things and consequently has a much greater stress value.

BOX 11-1

LIFE-CHANGE STRESS SCALE.

One of the causes of stress is what Thomas T. Holmes calls "rate of life-change." His research at the University of Washington Medical School indicates that stress generated by rate of life-change is related to subsequent illness. The changes may be either favorable or unfavorable to the individual; in both situations they generate "waves" in the normal flow of life which have to be coped with. The relationship between stress and disease appears to involve the operation of the endocrine system which provides surplus energy to deal with new situations. When too many new situations occur, the system becomes overloaded and is unable to defend against attack by certain viruses.

Life-change stress scale

Life event	*Scale value*
Death of spouse	100
Divorce	73
Marital separation	65
Jail term	63
Death of a close family member	63
Major personal injury or illness	53
Marriage	50
Fired from work	47
Marital reconciliation	45
Retirement	45
Major change in health of family member	44
Pregnancy	40
Sex difficulties	39
Gain of a new family member	39
Business readjustment	39
Change in financial state	38
Death of a close friend	37
Change to a different line of work	36
Change in number of arguments with spouse	35
Mortgage over $10,000	31
Foreclosure of mortgage or loan	30
Change in responsibilities at work	29
Son or daughter leaving home	29
Trouble with in-laws	29
Outstanding personal achievement	28
Wife begins or stops work	26
Begin or end school	26
Change in living conditions	25
Revision of personal habits	24
Trouble with boss	23

Change in work hours or conditions	20
Change in residence	20
Change in schools	20
Change in recreation	19
Change in church activities	19
Change in social activities	18
Mortgage or loan less than $10,000	17
Change in sleeping habits	16
Change in number of family get-togethers	15
Change in eating habits	15
Vacation	13
Christmas	12
Minor violations of the law	11

From: L.O. Ruch and T.H. Holmes, "Scaling of Life Change: Comparison of Direct and Indirect Methods," *Journal of Psychosomatic Research*, 1971, 15, 224.

Open communication about change, the opportunity to discuss it, to explore its consequences and to weigh it, makes it much more palatable and digestible. The success of a change effort is greatly enhanced if it can be shown to be of benefit to all parties concerned.

Trust

Change is a venture into the unknown. It implies taking risks. In an organizational setting it also implies reliance on others to behave in certain ways; cooperation and coordination are required to achieve organizational objectives. Mounting a major change effort is rather like putting together a group highwire act: you have to be able to trust the others when they say they're going to catch you.

As soon as other people are involved in organizational change (and there cannot be any solo efforts, by definition) trust levels are critical. If the changees don't or can't trust the initiators of the change, resistance will be high. Memories are long, and sudden changes of behavior are highly suspicious. The management that claims to have the workers' interests truly at heart when they introduce a new change had better have proven that, because the lessons of the past are well learned.

It is interesting to note that certain areas of the country have consistently bad labor problems. Often these are areas where exploitation of workers by managers and owners was the rule a hundred or so years ago. The mining industry was a terrible example of such exploitation in many areas, and grandsons still remember the stories their grandfathers told them about how rotten the mine owners were. One thing they can count on is that management will stick it to them whenever they get the chance. It takes a long time to overcome these legacies of mistrust.

Organizations also teach inappropriate behavior. More specifically, they teach behavior that is appropriate at one time, but which becomes inappropriate as the

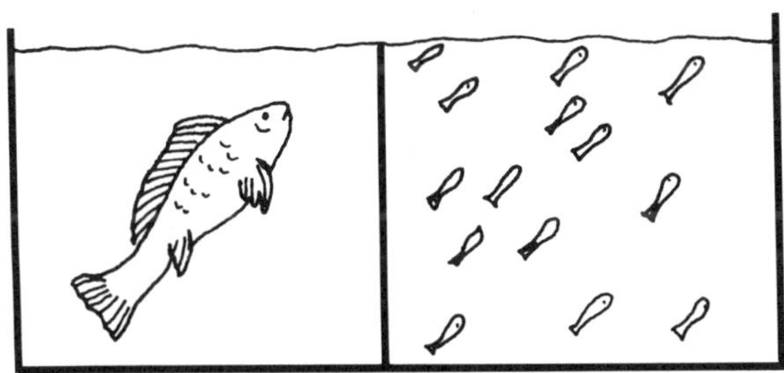

FIGURE 11-5: THE FISH EXPERIMENT. THE DIFFICULTY IN EXTINGUISHING LEARNED BEHAVIOR.

situation changes. The problem that they face is that not everyone recognizes the changes taking place in the environment, so when management changes the rules of behavior, the lessons of the past are still clear in the minds of the changees, and they can't believe that new behavior, which used to be punishable in the past, is now acceptable. This type of inappropriate learned behavior is demonstrated by an experiment conducted with a large fish in a tank. The tank is divided by a pane of glass, with the large fish on one side, and a group of small minnows on the other (Figure 11-5).

Since large fish generally eat minnows for a living, the big fish makes a lunge for one of them, bumping his nose on the glass. He repeats this behavior again and again, continuing to bump his nose on the glass. Eventually, in the dim recesses of the big fish's brain, the message comes through: "Every time I try to eat a minnow, someone comes out of nowhere and socks me right on the nose." Eventually, given enough tries, the big fish stops trying to eat the minnows. At this stage the glass partition is taken away and the minnows surround the fish, but he would sooner starve than eat one.

Top management puts the glass in the tank and takes it out, but the changees can't see the glass and they can't believe it's been removed when management tells them. Only Charlie Brown can continue to trust Lucy not to pull the football away when he goes to kick it. Everyone else is far more wary.

Consistency

Trust can be built up over time if behavior is consistent. Since we all work to reduce uncertainty, we scrutinize the behavior of others to determine the degree to which we need to be on our guard around them. Those individuals whom we see as behaving in a consistent manner are easy to relate to, even if their behavior is consistently aggressive. At least we know what to expect and can act appropriately. Those individuals who cause us the greatest concern, however, are the ones whose behavior we cannot predict. We have to be alert all the time to sense what is going to happen next. We can't *trust* them to do certain things.

When we are invited (or told) to venture into a change situation, with all its unknowns, the uncertainty is increased by having the initiators of the change behave unpredictably. When top management says they want to realign jobs so as to delegate responsibility to lower levels, but they have tightly controlled all decisions in the past, it is difficult to believe them. The changees sit back and wait to see if delegation is for real or if it is just a hoax to catch them off guard. It takes time and continued effort for the top management group to prove that they have changed their minds about how to operate.

Often organizations send managers away on training courses where they are subjected to a change process. They return to their organizations with different ideas, attitudes and skills, all ready and excited to try them out. One of the problems they encounter is that the organization is the same as when they left it. They have changed; it hasn't. However, the "new, improved" manager gets down to work to apply what he has learned on his course. Perhaps he has decided to change his style, or perhaps he has learned how to apply behavior modification techniques. What he encounters, though, is this sort of reaction: "Harry has just got back from one of those courses where they spend three weeks at a resort. They always act funny when they get back from those. Just ignore him for a month or so, and he'll get back to normal." So poor Harry tries his new behavior for a month, gets no response, and finally gets so frustrated that he screams and yells at everybody and reverts to his old autocratic style. "There," say his subordinates, "Didn't we say he'd come back to normal after about a month?"

Unfreezing

We have talked about unfreezing as the first stage of the change process, but it is often overlooked in practice. Management by Objectives (MBO) is a system whereby each individual in an organization sets, or has set for him, performance objectives against which he is measured at the end of the year. The emphasis in MBO is on outputs, results, achievements. It's not what you *do* that counts in MBO, but what you *achieve*. The whole focus of the organization is flipped around from rewarding people on the basis of their *behavior* and *attitudes*—keen, diligent, always on time, senior, and so on—to rewarding them on their *accomplishments*. The change is profound.

Early Success

A common fear associated with any change is "Will it work?" As we saw when we looked at the individual's development of his self-concept, he tends to experiment with the environment and then repeat that behavior that works for him. Success breeds further success. Failure results in more tentative behavior next time.

The same type of thing happens in organizational change. The question is still "Will it work?" The changees all tend to be from Missouri: "Show me."

The goal of the initiator of change should be to provide a success experience

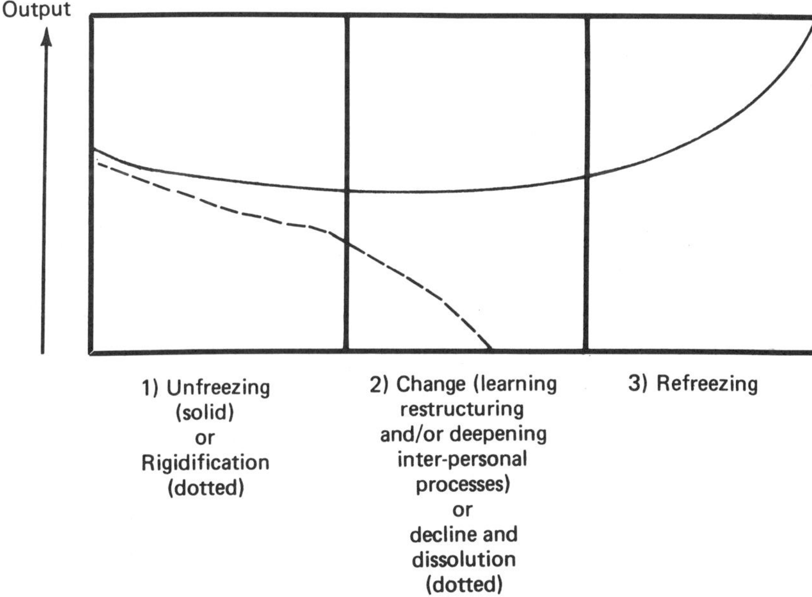

FIGURE 11-6: EFFECTS OF MAJOR CHANGE ON ORGANIZATIONAL OUTPUT. FROM: *BEHAVIOR IN ORGANIZATIONS, 2ND ED.*, R.E. COFFEY, A.G. ATHOS, AND P.A. RAYNOLDS, ENGLEWOOD CLIFFS, N.J.: PRENTICE-HALL, INC., 1975.

as soon as possible. Show them it works; show them it is pleasant, not painful; show them they can do it. And keep showing them, until they build some confidence in the change, because, unfortunately, as Coffee et al. (1975) point out, output tends to *decrease* during major change (Figure 11-6).

Adaptation

Because change involves the unknown, it is naive to think that it can be planned in detail to begin with. Certainly a major change effort should be thought out as carefully as possible before it is begun, but the designers of the program should be sensitive to specific needs and specific problems which reveal themselves along the way. Rather than having a detailed and fixed blueprint for change, an organization would be wiser to have a plan which is subjected to constant evaluation and review.

A committee, representative of different levels and different divisions or departments of the organization is often a useful vehicle for performing this evaluation and review procedure. Inputs can be made from people with different perspectives on the problem, and the discussion in the committee can help to enlighten the group as a whole about the specific problems or benefits of the change to certain levels or functions.

Reinforcement

Behavior modification is change. It is based on the principle of reinforcing acceptable, desired behavior and not reinforcing undesirable behavior. What difference is there between a program of behavior modification aimed at *specific individuals* in their jobs and organizational change aimed at *everyone* in their jobs? The principle of positive reinforcement still stands. Somewhere along the line, change has to be linked to rewards. Those that change in the desired direction should be recognized and rewarded. That is proof that the initiators of the change are serious about it; they are serious enough to reward the behavior they say they want exhibited. If we want someone to change their behavior, let's not ignore them when they do or else we'll see the example of old Harry repeated over and over again.

Resistance Interpretation

We often resist change without really knowing why we do. Others may be able to interpret our resistance and thereby be in a position to help us. The Johari window in Chapter 5 illustrates this well. The more we understand about our behavior, the better we are equipped to handle situations. If others can help us interpret our resistance to change, we are in a better position to work it through, evaluate it, and decide whether to maintain our defenses or lower them.

Assistance in resistance interpretation for those people and groups in the organization who are blocking the progress of change may be of considerable help. If it can be done in a non-threatening manner, allowing them to work through the problems themselves, the potential for positive change is greatly enhanced.

SUMMARY

Our systems model included, as some of the major elements of the organizational system,

- Rewards and punishments
- Structure
- Goals/priorities
- Communications
- Change/development

These are the things that must be maintained and changed for the overall organization to function. We have already talked about all of them as we have proceeded through the book.

Rewards and punishments are an intrinsic part of motivation and leadership. We have discussed identifying and satisfying needs (i.e., finding out how to reward people); we've discussed the leadership styles that are most likely to get them to work best; and we've seen how rewards (reinforcements) are used to get them to alter their behavior.

We've seen the demands that an organization's structure places on the behavior of people in it; how it affects their roles, their status, their communication patterns, their leadership styles.

We've seen that the goals and priorities of the organization are reflected in how it manages people. It can reflect either a concern for task and production or a concern for people and relationships. We are all familiar with a number of organizations and we all have opinions about the importance attached to various types of behavior. An organization's goals don't have to be written down to be understood.

We've seen how communications affect the way people behave; how they can be actively involved and motivated, or excluded and demotivated; how they can be controlled; how they can be stimulated.

And, of course, we've spent some time looking at how all these factors are manipulated as we try to get the members of organizations to adapt their behavior to suit the changing environment.

The process of change provides a good focus for the examination of all of these elements in the organizational system. At the top, where the "climate" is set, change is the name of the game. Sensitivity to the environment and a constant desire to improve effectiveness are manifested in efforts to get a group (and sometimes a very large group) of people to adapt their behavior in a consistent, controlled manner. The situation facing a top-level manager is like that of the captain of a super-tanker. The controls must be handled smoothly, slowly, surely, and sensitively, because it takes a long time to get the ship turned around or stopped.

Every manager is concerned with change. It is the major challenge of his job. It should be the major basis for rewards given him: not just to bring about change for change's sake, but to change *appropriately*, when the time is right.

Being able to manage change effectively requires two skills. First, the manager must understand what's going on around him—must be sensitive to the situation (the environment). And secondly, he must be able to understand behavior—why the people around him (and he himself) act as they do. If he understands *why* certain behavior occurs, then he is far more likely to be able to understand how to change that behavior. He will have a grasp of the roots of the problem and can treat it at that level, rather than involving himself in a trial-and-error attempt at solutions based on little or no understanding of its causes.

THE CHAPTER (AND HOVEY AND BEARD) CONCLUDED

The focus of this chapter is both the bottom part of our systems model of the organization and the top. All organizations are, or should be, concerned with the improvement of productivity, profits, efficiency, growth and development, stability, and satisfaction *(the required system)*.

In order to achieve this improvement, the organization sets certain goals and priorities, structures itself appropriately, implements a system of rewards and punishments that reinforces the performance it requires, makes information available in such a way as to facilitate the accomplishment of jobs and to reinforce the power and authority differences in the structure, and decides on the direction and means of change required to meet is goals *(the organization system)*.

And if the needs of the individuals in the organization are met, their perceptions of the system are positive. Their values and expectations are reinforced *(the individual system)*, while at the same time, behavioral norms, attitudes, and roles are developed informally within the work groups of the organization, and appropriate leadership and support is given these groups *(the work group system)*. Then, it is hoped that the organization's goals and priorities reflected in its *required* system become translated into actuality and turn out as hoped for *(the emergent system)*.

A pretty complicated business! It's not surprising that there is quite often a real discrepancy between what an organization *wants* to achieve (*required* results) and what it actually *does* achieve (*emergent* results). There are a lot of factors that have to be handled in the middle somewhere.

One way to think of the organizational system is to view it as a *framework* within which individuals and groups function. The objective of the organization is to achieve the results that we summarize in the *output system*—productivity, profits, efficiency, growth, stability, satisfaction. In order to do so, it sets goals and priorities. It structures roles and relationships. It builds a system of rewards and punishments that try to channel behavior in an appropriate manner. It manipulates the communication process to reinforce power, authority, motivation, job satisfaction, challenge, growth, and leadership. And it is constantly twiddling the knobs, either changing dramatically, or fine-tuning! The life of every organism is change. There is *no* status quo. The only unchanging thing is a dead thing. Individuals, groups and organizations are constantly adapting themselves to their environments. In the final analysis, all life is change.

In this chapter we have looked at the mechanism of introducing change into an organization. We have tended to talk about rather large-scale changes, but the same principles apply to change at almost any level. One has to be concerned with trust, objectives, communication, support, and so on, in any change situation. While we maintain that in essence all life is change, we are also aware of the fact that if we didn't *have to* change, we'd probably prefer to stay put. Change requires doing something new and untried. It implies risk. How do you know it will work? You *do* know how the old system worked, and even if it wasn't the greatest, at least you knew what to expect.

We talked very early in the book about the need to reduce uncertainty. Life is chancy enough as it is—what we need is less of the unexpected and more of the familiar. But change is the unknown (or at least unfamiliar), and so we are naturally resistant to it to some degree.

We believe that managing change effectively is the major challenge of management. When we say *effectively*, we are implying that the individuals involved find it acceptable, motivating, and reinforcing to their self-concepts. We are also implying that work groups find it congruent with their goals and values. In short, the best organizational change is one where everybody is happy—where the organization gets the results it wants, where the people involved get what they want, and where the Seven Dwarfs syndrome results: people whistle on their way to work.

Let's see how the girls at Hovey and Beard found the change process to which they were subjected. It has been a while since we last looked at Hovey and Beard. You made some predictions at the end of Chapter 7. Before you read Part 5 of the case and the subsequent discussion, would you go back to Chapter 7 and reread Part 4. Review the predictions you made at that time concerning productivity, job satisfaction, and so on. Take a few minutes to consider them in the light of the material we have discussed since then. Would you change anything? If so, what? Why?

HOVEY AND BEARD COMPANY PART 5

The girls were delighted, and spent many lunch hours deciding how the speed of the belt should be varied from hour to hour throughout the day. Within a week the pattern had settled down to one in which the first half hour of the shift was run on what the girls called a medium speed (a dial setting slightly above the point marked "medium"). The next two and one-half hours were run at high speed; the half hour before lunch and the half hour after lunch were run at low speed. The rest of the afternoon was run at high speed with the exception of the last forty-five minutes of the shift, which was run at medium.

In view of the girls' reports of satisfaction and ease in their work, it is interesting to note that the constant speed at which the engineers had originally set the belt was slightly below medium on the dial of the control that had been given the girls. The average speed at which the girls were running the best was on the high side of the dial. Few if any, empty hooks entered the oven, and the inspection showed no increase of rejects from the paint room.

Production increased, and within three weeks (some two months before the scheduled ending of the learning bonus) the girls were operating at 30 to 50 percent above the level that had been expected under the original arrangement. Naturally the girls' earnings were correspondingly higher than anticipated. They were collecting their base pay, a considerable piece rate bonus and the learning bonus which, it will be remembered, had been set to decrease with time and not as a function of current productivity. The girls were earning more now than many skilled workers in other parts of the plant.

It appears at last as if the management in Hovey and Beard had hit on the solution to implementing the change. All the "output system" factors seemed to be improving—productivity, profits, efficiency, job satisfaction, etc. What did they do right? What did they do wrong?

This case involves pretty well everything we have been talking about in this book. The original job allowed the girls some control over the pace of their work.

They had a chance to chat and ''socialize'' while they worked, which made the job more pleasant, and they were also able to get a greater sense of achievement from painting an entire toy (they could judge quality and workmanship and derive some pride from a job well done).

The change took these things away. The conveyor belt controlled the pace of work; the girls were isolated from one another a bit more; the social aspect of the job was reduced; and they only painted part of a doll, which was then whisked away into the oven. On top of it all, the girls had no control over the way in which the change was implemented. Management simply installed the equipment, estimated production speeds, calculated a bonus rate, and told the girls to start operating under the new system. The treatment is rather reminiscent of how little children are handled—the adult makes the decisions and the child does what he is told. Adults placed in this sort of situation often do not experience it as a boost to their self-concepts.

Herzberg and Maslow would both argue that the motivational needs of the girls center around such things as belonging, esteem, achievement and recognition. We would also see their self-concepts calling for reinforcement of their value as human beings and as employees in the company. In many ways, the manner in which the change was implemented was degrading to the girls; it implied that they had no useful input to make on how to get the system to work properly.

From a group point of view, we see management emerging in an adversary role. The group of girls closes ranks in the face of the enemy, and they decide on the amount of work they are prepared to give in exchange for the treatment and the rewards they receive.

In terms of change strategy, a number of factors may have been overlooked. Did the girls see the necessity for change? How *unfrozen* were they? Did they see the old behavior and methods as being inappropriate? What would make them accept management's version of the need for change? To what degree did they trust management? Was there a basis for this trust or mistrust? How was the change communicated? Did the girls get a chance to voice their opinions? (It is interesting to note that the turning point in this situation came when the communication channels between management and the girls were opened with a series of meetings.)

We don't have to go any further into the reasons why the change originally failed, and why it subsequently succeeded. You have read the whole book by now, and you know the reasons yourself. However, it might be useful for you to go back to Part 1 of Hovey and Beard and follow it through from the beginning, reviewing each time you made predictions about the case, and analyzing why you said what you did, when you did.

Postscript

We said at the beginning of the book that the test of theory was whether it helped to describe, understand and explain behavior in organizations. Ultimately, since the book is written to help *you* gain an understanding of organizational behavior, *you* must be the judge. Did what we talked about help you understand and explain things, or didn't it? If it did, we are absolutely delighted, and if it didn't, then it's back to the drawing board for us! We certainly hope it did.

One other thing should be mentioned at this point. This book is an *introduction* to organizational behavior only. There is a lot more to the field than we have talked about. Our hope is that we have been able to explain some of the basic concepts clearly enough to make them useful, and palatable enough to make you want to learn some more. But please don't think that this has been the whole meal. For better or worse, it's really only the hors d'oeuvre.

Chapter Summary

1 There are a number of environmental forces at work which put pressure on organizations to change. These include basic economic forces, competitor's actions and strategies, governmental policies, and the changing social values of our culture.

2 Change can be viewed as a three-part process—unfreezing, change and refreezing. It is as important to *prepare* people and systems for change, and to *support* them when they have changed, as it is to introduce the changes themselves.

3 The change process can also be viewed as a force field, where various forces push *for* the change, and corresponding forces spring up to *resist* the change. Identification of these forces on either side of the status quo allows a clearer and more specific plan of action to be developed.

4 There are a number of critical elements that must be considered in any change effort. A number are listed and discussed. There is no set manner in which to deal with these issues, but they must be examined and dealt with in some fashion for change to take place effectively.

5 The change process provides a good focus for the examination of all the elements in the total organizational system. In order to move the system from A to B, all the subsystems have to be considered, analyzed and dealt with, and their interrelationships have to be borne in mind.

A FINAL NOTE—HOVEY AND BEARD, AND ORGANIZATIONAL BEHAVIOR, REVISITED

One more thing before we finish.

All through the book we have talked about the organization as a system. We have constantly presented a systems model of organizational behavior. We have said, time and time again, that all the sub-parts of the system interract with one another. Change, as we have just been discussing, in one part of the system, brings about changes (sometimes unexpected) in other parts of the system.

Just so that the point is really clear, here is Part 6 of Hovey and Beard. It is a sad story, but true. Oh to be able to recognize that an organization really *is* a system!

THE HOVEY AND BEARD COMPANY PART 6

Management was beseiged by demands that this inequity be taken care of. With growing irritation between superintendent and foreman, engineers and foreman, superintendent and engineers, the situation came to a head when the superintendent revoked the learning bonus and returned the painting operation to its original status; the hooks moved again at their constant, time-studied designated speed, production dropped again, and within a month all but two of the eight girls had quit. The foreman himself stayed on for several months, but, feeling aggrieved, then left for another job.

Appendix:

The Origins of Organizational Behavior

It is often useful to take a brief glance backwards to see where we have come from. One of the expressions used to describe someone who "has it all together" is that "he knows where he's from." The grammar ain't great, but we get the idea. You should know where you are from before you can decide where you want to go. There is an ancient story about a New England farmer who, when asked directions to a nearby town by a tourist, remarked "You can't get there from here." There is more depth to that remark than meets the eye.

One of the reasons why we might want to take time out briefly for a backwards glance is that we may want to retrace our steps at some time. It would also be useful to know if we have inadvertently come full circle and are simply covering old territory. Indians travelling through unfamiliar country used the technique of having one of their group constantly look backwards to see where they had been. That way, when they wanted to return to their original base, at least one of them would recognize the terrain. Things look quite different from the other side.

FROM TRADITIONAL ORGANIZATION TO SITUATIONAL THEORY

Typologies of organization and management are abundant. People talk about "schools" of management thought, and about management theory "jungles" (Koontz, 1961). There are dozens of category systems which differentiate between areas of thought and emphasis in management writing. Kast and Rosenzweig (1974) talk about *three* categories: (1) traditional organization and management concepts; (2) the behavioral and management science revolutions; and (3) the modern view (which is concerned with systems and situation).

TRADITIONAL ORGANIZATION THEORY

In talking about traditional organization theory, we are really talking about three quite different theories. What makes them "traditional" may be that they are old, and that they are, as a result, more formal than modern theories. But the major characteristic of the traditional theories is their *impersonality*. All of them assume a rational model of man. All of them see man as a capital resource of some kind, a machine or a commodity. While this last remark may be a trifle harsh, none of the traditional theories are concerned with the behavior of people as we think of it today. They see man as being driven solely by economic motives and "rational" thinking.

Bureaucracy: Max Weber

To talk about these three traditional theories means to talk about three men with whom they are identified. The starting point for classical organization theory is the writing of Max Weber, a German academic. Weber was interested in why people responded to authority, why they were willing to do what they were told. He saw people in organizations obeying different kinds of leaders. There were those leaders who were highly *charismatic*—that is, who were able to attract followers on the basis of some exceptional quality (Christ was a charismatic leader). There were also *traditional* leaders. Traditional because their authority was defined by custom and tradition.

Weber saw great weaknesses in both types of leaders and the types of organizations which they headed. The *charismatic* leader is fine while he is alive, but when he dies or leaves there are monumental problems of succession, and the organization and its members undergo massive upheaval. Think of Christ, or Lenin, or Howard Hughes, or Jim Slater. The major weakness of the *traditional* organization is that everything is rooted in precedent; things are done because they have always been done. The leader and his organization are inflexible and they tend to be washed away as change overtakes them. The Ford Motor Company almost went under because of Henry Ford's inflexibility about producing nothing but black Model T's.

Weber saw the ideal form of organization as a *bureaucracy*. The term bureaucracy nowadays conjures up images of reams of red tape, detailed procedures, lack of empathy, and staggering inefficiency, but Weber saw it as the fairest, most rational and logical form of organization possible. Weber's Germany was run very much on a "traditional" basis. Jobs were handed out on the basis of who you were related to and knew, or how much influence you had. In the light of this type of system, it is easy to understand why he preferred a more "rational" and impersonal system of organization.

Bureaucratic organization is heavily dependent on rules, procedures, and clearly defined functions and relationships. Weber wanted competitive exams for jobs, clear job descriptions, and rules and procedures to cover almost every eventuality. Nowadays, government departments are run on the bureaucratic model, and we can see why. It is the same reasoning that made it look attractive to Weber. He wanted to get away from favoritism, cliquishness, nepotism and arbitrary and often unfair decisions. Governments, the representatives of the people (or at least they tell us that) must also try to avoid these things. When the bureaucratic system breaks down and we get patronage, kickbacks, influence peddling, and so on, we naturally get upset and prosecute the offenders in the courts.

While bureaucracy may appear to have the effect of making things "fair and aboveboard," it often has other unfortunate consequences. Robert Merton (1940) notes that the tight structure of the bureaucratic process places pressure on the individuals involved to act methodically, carefully, and cautiously. Adherence to rules and procedures "may be exaggerated to the point that primary concern with conformity to the rules interferes with the achievement of the purposes of the organization, in which case we have the familiar phenomenon of technicism or red tape of the official.'' Box A-1 encapsulates the woes of the bureaucracy.

BOX A-1

Ernest Dale (1965) quotes an anonymously written poem which illustrates the unfortunate reversal of ends and means that often occurs in bureaucratic organizations.

The Bureaucrat's Prayer

Oh Thou, who seest all things below,
Grant that Thy servants may go slow;
That we may study to comply
With regulations till we die.

Teach us, O Lord, to reverence,
Committees more than common-sense;
Impress our minds to make no plan
And pass the baby when we can.

And when the Tempter seems to give,
Us feelings of initiative,
Or when, alone, we go too far
Recall us with a circular.

Mid fire and tumult, war and storms,
Sustain us, Blessed Lord, with forms,
Thus may Thy servants ever be,
A flock of perfect sheep for Thee.

Scientific Management: F.W. Taylor

Frederick Taylor was an American engineer who worked for Bethlehem Steel and one of its predecessor companies. His background as an engineer naturally disposed him towards science and the scientific method of analyzing problems. Taylor saw science making great strides on the technological side of business, but saw little or no change taking place on the people side. He reasoned that there had to be a ''best'' way of doing anything. What was required was a ''scientific'' analysis of the problem.

Taylor's first application of ''scientific management'' took place at the Midvale Steel Works where he addressed himself to the problem of increasing the amount of pig iron loaded on flatcars for shipment. The job was done manually, with men lifting the 92 pound pigs, walking up an inclined plank and placing them on the flatcar. Taylor applied the four steps of his "scientific management" approach to this job (Taylor, 1911):

1 ". . . the development of a science to replace the old rule-of-thumb knowledge of the workmen."
2 ". . . the scientific selection and then the progressive development of the workmen."
3 the bringing together of the "scientifically selected workman and the science" through the *inspiration* of some individual.
4 the "deliberate division of the work which was formerly done by the workmen into two sections, one of which is handed over to management."

In other words, he decided how to do the job most efficiently, chose workmen who would accept his instructions and could handle the job physically, gave them a pep talk to get them interested and excited about the work (mainly on the basis that they would earn more money), and then carefully supervised the work to see that it was done according to his plan.

Taylor's results were incredible. In the pig iron job, he increased the amount loaded by a gang of laborers from 12 1/2 tons per man day to 47 tons per man day. At Bethlehem Steel he reduced the number of men laboring in the yard, shovelling and the like, from 600 to 140, with no drop in output. He was able to increase the output of the machine shop at the Midvale Steel Works by between 2 1/2 and 9 times what it had been on every machine. The field of work study and time and motion study owes its beginnings to Taylor. His contributions, and those of his followers, increased productivity and efficiency immensely. He has been called the "Father of Modern Management." But scientific management has had some unfortunate consequences as well.

The reason that Taylor's approach worked so well was that his two basic assumptions concerning people were correct at the time. Workers did not know the best way to do their jobs, and they were quite willing to accept direction in order to get more pay. The major weakness of scientific management springs directly from these two assumptions; as soon as they become invalid, the theory no longer holds. Values have changed considerably since Taylor's time at the beginning of the century. Workers and managers are now much better educated and trained, and money is no longer the major motivational force. Today, people are also concerned with such things as job satisfaction, a sense of achievement, and a need for recognition.

Unions have reacted violently to the institution of "Taylorism" and are still highly sensitive to time and motion studies which aim to determine optimum levels for production, and therefore levels of pay for workers. These matters are negotiated with the utmost care on both sides. There are still plants where any non-worker who stands with his hands in his pockets will cause all work to come to a standstill; he is suspected of timing jobs with a hidden stop-watch. This legacy of mistrust has been the most costly aspect of Taylorism.

The "Principles of Management": Henri Fayol

The third major contributor to the traditional school of organization theory was Henri Fayol, a French mining engineer who spent his life working for a large mining organization, taking it from the brink of disaster to one of the largest firms of its kind. Since Fayol spent much of his working life as a senior executive, his view of management and organization is a sort of top-down one. He was concerned with the *functions* of a manager; what he should do to be effective. Fayol listed five key functions which a manager has to perform:

- Plan
- Organize
- Direct
- Coordinate
- Control

If you look at most of the basic management textbooks of today, they still address themselves to these five functions. In addition to outlining these five functions of management, Fayol went on to prescribe a set of ''principles'' for structuring an organization. He talked about such things as division of work, authority and responsibility, discipline, one-man-one-boss, setting organizational objectives, and the hierarchical chain-of-command with which anyone who has ever been in the armed forces is familiar. He did not intend his ''principles'' to become fixed rules, but saw them as guidelines which management should consider. Unfortunately, they have not always been taken that way.

The major weakness of Fayol's principles stem from taking them as hard and fast rules. When this is done, they overlook situational differences. While they may be appropriate in one setting, they may fail in another. A second criticism that can be levelled at this approach to management is that it largely overlooks the human side of organization. Fayol's focus was on *structural* issues; how to set the organization up so that it functioned smoothly. To some extent, people are seen as simply being parts of the organizational machine, which, if designed well, and with these ''parts'' properly in place, will function efficiently.

MODERN ORGANIZATIONAL THEORIES

The Human Relations Movement: Elton Mayo

The break from Taylor's Scientific Management was first made as a result of a series of research studies done in the Hawthorne Plant of the Western Electric Company over the period 1927-1932. Elton Mayo, a sociologist from Harvard, headed a team which conducted follow-up studies on work done by industrial engineers at Hawthorne on the effects of illumination on productivity. Mayo and his colleagues expanded the study to include a number of other physical variables.

Mayo's team selected, as their experimental group, six female workers from the Relay Assembly Department, placed them in a separate room, with the same type of production facilities as in the main department, and proceeded to vary their working conditions. Box A-2 contains a summary of some of the changes made by the experimenters and concurrent changes in productivity.

The startling outcome of this study was that, whatever the experimenters did, production steadily increased. Mayo and his team were forced to conclude (after a great deal of puzzlement) that the increase in production was the result, *not* of the experimental changes in incentives and working conditions, *but of the changed social situation of the workers*.

Stuart Chase (1941) remarks of the Relay Assembly Test Room Experiments that:

> By asking their help and cooperation, the investigators had made the girls feel important. Their whole attitude had changed from that of separate cogs in a machine to that of a congenial group trying to help the company solve a problem. They had found stability, a place where they belonged, and work whose purpose they could clearly see. And so they worked faster and better than they ever had in their lives.

A second stage of the Hawthorne studies involved the interviewing of over 21,000 employees over a three-year period.

The following is a simplified summary of the conclusions drawn from these interviews:

1. Complaints do not always mean what they say. They are a *symptom* of some personal disturbance. The "real" cause for dissatisfaction may be something quite different and much deeper than the voiced complaint.
2. All actions in an organization are given a social meaning. Employees perceive events from their own standpoint, and make interpretations about their "meanings." The perceived meaning of an action and its intended meaning may differ sharply.
3. The behavior of an individual on the job is a composite of his individual personality, values and attitudes, and the values and attitudes expressed by the people working around him. His perceptual reference point is based on past experience as well as the present situation.
4. The position or status of an employee is an important determinant in how he perceives his working environment and the events that surround him.
5. There is an "informal" organization within any formal organization. This is made up of the relationships which form between individuals at work, and represents a strong base for perceptions about the organization, the job, leadership, etc. The informal work group acts as a powerful controlling force over the behavior of its members.

BOX A-2

Lists of some of the changes made by the experimenters during the Relay Assembly Test Room studies at Hawthorne.

SCHEDULE OF TEST PERIODS
RELAY ASSEMBLY TEST ROOM

Period Number	*Special Feature*	*Dates Included*	*Duration in Weeks*	*A.M.*	*Times of Rest Pauses*	*P.M.*
I	In regular department	4-25-27 to 5-10-27	Approx. 2		None	
II	Introduction to test room	5-10-27 to 6-11-27	5		None	
III	Special group rate	6-13-27 to 8-6-27	8		None	
IV	Two 5-min. rests	8-8-27 to 9-10-27	5	10:00		2:00
V	Two 10-min. rests	9-12-27 to 10-8-27	4	10:00		2:00
VI	Six 5-min. rests	10-10-27 to 11-5-27	4	8:45, 10:00, 11:20		2:00, 3:15, 4:30
VII	15-min. A.M. lunch and 10-min. P.M. rest	11-7-27 to 1-21-28	11	9:30	2:30	9:30
VIII	Same as VII but 4:30 stop	1-23-28 to 3-10-28	7	9:30		2:30
IX	Same as VII but 4:00 stop	3-12-28 to 4-7-28	4	9:30		2:30
X	Same as VII	4-9-28 to 6-30-28	12	9:30		2:30
XI	Same as VII but Sat. A.M. off	7-2-28 to 9-1-28	9	9:30		2:30
XII	Same as III (no lunch or rests)	9-3-28 to 11-24-28	12		None	
XIII	Same as VII but operators furnish own lunch, company furnishes beverage	11-26-28 to 6-29-29	31	9:30		2:30

BOX A-2 CONTINUED

LUNCHES SERVED DURING FIRST TWO WEEKS OF PERIOD VII
RELAY ASSEMBLY TEST ROOM

	First Week	*Second Week*
Monday	Postum, tomato sandwich (whole wheat bread) Apple (raw)	Coffee, tongue sandwich (rye bread) Sliced pineapple
Tuesday	Coffee, tongue sandwich (rye bread) Orange	Postum, tomato sandwich (whole wheat bread) Rice pudding
Wednesday	Tea, peanut butter and jelly sandwich (whole wheat bread) Sliced pineapple	Vegetable soup Apple (raw)
Thursday	Vegetable soup Stewed prunes	Orange juice, peanut butter and jelly sandwich (whole wheat bread) Banana
Friday	Orange juice, marmalade sandwich (whole wheat bread) Banana	Tea, egg salad sandwich (whole wheat bread) Orange
Saturday	Oatmeal with cream Apple (raw)	Oatmeal with cream Stewed prunes

From: F.J. Roethlisberger and W.J. Dickson, *Management and the Worker*, Cambridge, Mass: Harvard University Press, 1939.

A third stage of the research looked at the behavior of fourteen men working in what was known as the Bank Wiring Room. What the researchers found was once again novel and surprising. They discovered that the workers limited their output to a certain level decided on by the group as a whole; that individual workers did not exceed this group-imposed output standard; that the company's financial incentive program which offered bonuses for group production above certain levels had no effect on performance; that, in essence, the group formed a pact of solidarity, and that they decided on what represented a fair day's work for a fair day's pay, and maintained production at that level. As David Ashton remarks (1970):

> Here was a coherent, informal, social group, with its natural leaders, complete in attitudes to work, management, and level of production—i.e., with its own full group culture. The clash between the aims of the company and the aims of this group became obvious, as did the ineffectiveness of purely financial incentive to maximize production. For one

> reason or another, the group had established its rates of work. The chief function of the informal organization was to resist all changes to its standards; it was, therefore, necessarily, at variance with the company's aims.

No single study has had the effect on subsequent management thought and practice that the Hawthorne research has. It represents a cataclysmic break from the traditional theory. For the first time, man's social and individual nature was seen as important to the functioning of organizations. Hawthorne drove a strong nail into the coffin of "rational, economic man." All of a sudden it was discovered that people worked for something other than just money. Man's emotional and social side were seen as major determinants of his organizational behavior. The summary of the research presented here is very brief and very sketchy and does not do justice to its monumental nature. But we can make the point that after Hawthorne, things have never been the same; the management and understanding of *people* has become a top priority.

HUMAN RELATIONS TO BEHAVIORAL SCIENCE

The Hawthorne research stimulated a human relations fever. Management and management writers went off in a flurry of excitement after the New Holy Grail. The assumption was that happy people made an effective organization—the "contented cow" approach. As Malcolm McNair remarked in 1957, "the very avidity with which people prone to fashionable thinking in business have seized on the fad of human relations itself suggests the presence of a considerable guilt complex in the minds of businessmen in regard to their dealings with people." Human relations became a *fad*. It was seen as *the* answer by many. McNair (1957), among others, helped put things in perspective:

> Most great advances are made by individuals. Devoting too much effort in business to trying to keep everybody happy results in conformity, in failure to build individuals. It has become the fashion to decry friction, but friction has its uses; without friction it is possible to go too far in the direction of sweetness and light, harmony, and the avoidance of all irritation. The present day emphasis on "bringing everybody along" can easily lead to a deadly level of mediocrity.

"Human Relations" has given way to "Behavioral Science." The behavioral science movement is interested in investigating the nature and determinants of people's behavior at work. The techniques used are those of anthropology, sociology, and psychology. There is an emphasis on controlled experiments and the scientific process. Studies are more systematic and organized. We are building up a body of "scientific" knowledge about the behavior of people in organizations.

While behavioral scientists work from a sounder methodological base than the early human relations proponents, however, many still exhibit one major drawback. Some of the research into organizational behavior demonstrates what may be termed the "normative error." That is, the researchers begin their work with an idea of what *should* be. They make the unjustified assumption that one thing is better than another. For instance, they assume that a democratic, participative approach to management is "better" than a more autocratic-directive approach. While we all have values that show through in most of our actions, these sorts of preferences do not have a place in scientific investigation.

As Reddin (1970) remarks, "Managerial theory cannot be normative. It cannot be a thinly veiled justification for the way the theorist would like to see the world."

MANAGEMENT SCIENCE

As the behavioral sciences have grown in importance in the understanding of organizational operation, and psychologists and sociologists have applied many of their methods and findings to managerial problems, a second thrust has occurred which has examined management and organizations from a quantitative viewpoint. This second modern wave of inquiry has been labelled the "management science" movement. Its objective is to apply mathematical techniques to the solution of organizational problems. Elwood Buffa (1968) has expressed the optimism of the field,

> The growth of science in management since the end of World War II is one of the most exciting developments ever to come on the business and industrial scene. It has produced managerial obsolescence in many functions of business, and at a minimum has created a feeling of uneasiness in the hearts of men who see the developing power of analytical techniques applied to management problems. It has hastened the development of professionalism in management.

Unfortunately, this forecasted rapid takeover has not materialized. The slowdown in the advance of management science may be partly attributed to the direct conflicts in the values and approaches of its proponents versus those on the behavioral side of the fence. As Buffa's remarks indicate, management scientists have displayed some lack of sensitivity to human problems. The fact that he can revel in the delights of making many managerial functions obsolete and striking fear in the hearts of men may go a long way towards explaining the resistance to these new ideas and techniques.

Management science has, however, developed a number of highly useful analytical tools such as linear programming, queuing theory, game theory, simulation, Monte Carlo techniques, Markov analysis, etc., all of which have made the management of many types of businesses more efficient, effective and reliable. For instance, many oil refineries are now run on sophisticated linear programming models which automatically make decisions as to product mix, given such factors as costs and price.

There can be little argument with a movement towards greater precision in describing, explaining, and predicting behavior in organizations. We still know a pitifully small amount about the determinants of behavior, and much of what we categorize as knowledge in the field is vague and extremely general. However, there is a danger in quantifying variables which are not yet quantifiable. For instance, we "measure" personality by certain tests which produce numerical scores on various dimensions. But what does a score of 23 mean on the trait of ascendance? Is it simply a reference point, indicating that individuals who obtain a score of less than 23 are less ascendant and more than 23 are more ascendant than the comparison subject? Unfortunately, other, stronger, conclusions that may be quite unwarranted are reached from numerical data of this sort. The designers of psychological tests constantly warn users about the difficulties of interpretation, but once the test is scored and we are confronted with a set of numbers, the temptation is often overwhelming. We understand numbers, or at least think we do. We all have a basic idea of arithmetic, and can add, subtract, multiply, divide and compare. But the numerical form of data tends to screen out the fact that the numbers may not apply to the same sorts of things. Two barrels of fruit may contain 46 and 24 units respectively, but it is important to know whether they are both apples or whether one is apples and the other grapefruit. The bias of the behavioralist is that he is afraid of quantifying too many variables before he is sure of what those variables are. What is personality? There are hundreds of conflicting definitions and measures. What is motivation? We are equally unsure. Quantification of these concepts is not what is needed; the issue is first of all *clarification*.

IN SUMMARY

This has been a brief, and very limited summary of the origins of organizational behavior as a field of study. As has been pointed out, a concern for people as differentiated from machines and other factors of production is a relatively recent phenomenon. Mayo and his fellow researchers mark the beginnings of the study of how people behave in organizations. We are still in the early days. There is a great deal we don't know, but, on the other hand, there is a lot that we *do* know about organizational behavior.

Cases

ATTITUDES TO WORK: SHUCKING SCALLOPS—A REPETITIVE TASK

I drove out to a place I'll call Duffy's, where shuckers remove the meat from scallops, for delivery to restaurants and fish markets. Duffy's consists of a couple of small, unpainted one-story buildings on a sandy hill of scrub pine. At nine in the morning, there were about a dozen cars in the gravel parking lot. A steady clattering noise came from the open doors of the larger building; it sounded like a waterfall, but not of water—crockery perhaps. I approached the building—a powerful smell extended into the parking lot—and looked in through a door. The walls were white tile. In the center of the room, a dozen plump burlap bags sat on a duckboard platform. Around the room, waist-high, ran a varnished wooden counter. Seventeen people, of all sorts and ages—young women, longhairs, old geezers—stood elbow to elbow at the counter, working rapidly. In front of each was a pile of scallops; next to it was a shallow white plastic pail; below were a big garbage can and a larger white plastic pail. The workers wore rubber boots, rubber aprons, rubber gloves, and something—a bandanna, a cap—to keep their hair back. Each held a short-bladed knife with its handle wrapped in tape. The noise was thunderous and continuous.

I watched a pretty, dark-haired girl of about twenty. She would grab a scallop in her left hand and insert the blade of the knife between the shells; flip the scallop open and send the top shell flying into the garbage can; insert the blade under the black edging of tiny tentacles that encircle the bottom shell; scoop the tentacles and the attached entrails out in one sweep and into the garbage can, leaving the white adductor muscle—the edible "meat," or "eye"—which she flicked a foot and a half through the air into the plastic pail on the counter. The whole process took a little over a second, and then she grabbed the next scallop. When the pile of scallops on the counter was gone, she walked to the center of the room, picked up a new sixty-pound bag, walked back, flung it up onto the counter, dumped the scallops out, and started in again. When the pail was full, she poured it into the larger pail under the counter and resumed her work.

By nine-thirty, the last bag on the duckboard was gone—the shuckers had been shucking since six-thirty that morning—and it was time for the weigh-in. The workers dumped their garbage pails into bins outside and carried their large white pails to the adjacent building, where a young man waited by a scale that hung from the ceiling. The shuckers stood in line, laughing and talking, and each in turn poured his pail into a larger pail that the young man then hooked onto the bottom of the scale. "Forty-four pounds," he might announce, and a woman with a pad and pencil would write it down. The next boatload of scallops would not arrive until the afternoon, a worker told me, so the shuckers would now be paid—they get forty-five cents a pound—and would have time to go away for a while. Waiting for their money, they sat on the fenders of cars, smoking cigarettes and talking.

I saw the dark-haired girl, and asked her how long she had been working at Duffy's.

"A couple of months," she said. I remarked that it must be pretty tiring.

"You get used to it," she said. "At first, I didn't know so many things could hurt. Your back kills you; your neck is stiff; your legs ache; it feels like your whole body is falling apart. You wake up in the middle of the night with your knuckles throbbing. And you've got blisters, of course, on all your fingers and along your palm. But that comes partly from gripping your knife too tight."

I told her I admired her speed.

"The point is to go as fast as you can," she said. "A lot of us sing to ourselves to keep a rhythm. I prefer 'Rockin' Robin' and 'Yakety-Yak—Don't Talk Back.' They work best for me. Also, everything has to be just right—the placement of your garbage can, the meat bucket, how close the pile of scallops is to you. You should never have to look. The faster you are, the more money you get and the more admired you are. The person with the most pounds is the 'high-liner' of the day. There's no prize—just admiration. There's the challenge of competition, and you feel especially good if you beat out some guy who's been doing it all his life. Of course, he'll always say, 'I got a bad back,' or 'I came in late,' or 'I got a bad bag,' which means he had to throw away a lot."

The girl laughed, and went on, "You try to stay ahead of your neighbors, and if they're ahead you watch and try to figure out why. When you're first starting out, they'll show you how to do it, but they'll show you really fast—to impress you. Once you get going, it's hard to slow the process down and explain it to somebody else, it becomes so smooth."

I asked her how she liked the work.

"I like it," she said. "One thing is, you get paid in cash. So you always have money in your pocket when you leave, no matter how little. If you want more money, you just try to work more and faster, but you can only work when the boats come in. You feel independent, and it's a skill. There's an art to it, so you can feel proud of it. You get to know people, and build friendships. Some of the shuckers are townies, some are drifters, some are old lobstermen or clammers or fishermen. Sometimes, there are people who are too weird to do anything else—but they're accepted here. You can be a person of very few words and be a shucker; nobody bothers you. You eventually become buddies with quite a few people, because you've all been through the lousy work together. There's a lot of banter and joking around; that's nice. And a real community spirit. People help each other lift bags, share bags, carry buckets, and so on. Camaraderie."

I mentioned the continuous noise.

"It's better than the slamming of a hydraulic press on an assembly line," the girl said. "And, at least, scallops are half alive. They don't have much personality, but you get somewhat acquainted with them. There's the surprise of opening the bag. The shells have subtle colors and variations of design. And sometimes you find sea urchins and starfish and a big array of slimy creatures. The worst is the sea cucumber. There is nothing more disgusting. It has no head, no tail, no top, no bottom—no identity at all. Just purple-and-pink mush. You don't know what it is, but you know it's alive!"

She laughed again, and said, "I like living here, too. I like the quiet and the water all around, and the early-morning hours when only you and decent, hardworking people are up. I admire the shuckers and the fishermen—they're people who put their bodies and themselves on the line, doing hard physical work. Also, the people are loose. It's 'Hey, hey!' around here, instead of 'Is Pierson getting his raise before I get mine?' They always ask if you're hung over. The harder you work the harder you play, and this is a small town with not much to do. So people get incredibly drunk at night. But after spending the night passed out in a telephone booth or something they turn up for work the next morning."

The word went around that it was pay time, and the shuckers filed into the larger building. The girl jumped off the car. "One thing about shucking is you get into a kind of meditation," she said. "You look at what's come out of the bag, and daydream about what's under the ocean. You get a great sense of peace." She went into the building to pick up her pay. In a few minutes, she was out again, tucking money into the pocket of her jeans and grinning. "Twenty bucks," she said. The soft sound of guitar music came across the parking lot; a girl was sitting on the hood of a car playing a guitar, and others stood around listening. A light rain began to fall.

ALAN BARKER

During the four months prior to graduating from college, Alan Barker spent a lot of time choosing his first full-time job. He arranged interviews with 26 firms, in a selection of industries. He made it a point to read about each industry and to find out about each company in advance of his interviews. Thus he was well prepared, and was able to ask a number of questions which clarified certain key points for him in each situation. Some of these questions are listed below:

1 What is the hiring policy of your company?
   - What sort of educational standards do you require?
   - Do you hire primarily at lower levels and train your own people, or do you bring in people at all levels of experience?
   - Do you have a stated manpower policy with regards to hiring?
   - What are your expectations concerning the length of time a newly hired graduate will stay with you?
   - What sort of turnover do you experience with new graduates?

2 What sort of training do you offer your new employees?
   - Is training primarily "on-the-job," by experience?
   - Is it formalized, in the sense of having specific courses for new employees?
   - What are the aims of your training program for new graduates?
   - What sort of time span is involved?
   - What are the opportunities available to those who complete the company training program?

3 What are salary levels in your company?
   - What is the average figure for new college graduates?
   - For managers with five years' experience?
   - For departmental managers?
   - For vice-presidents?

4 What are the criteria for salary increments in your firm?
   - Do you have a stated policy for merit increases?
   - What sort of performance review procedure do you have for employees? How often is it conducted?

5 If I were to come up to your expectations, where would I be in the company in five years? In ten years?

6 Will I get experience in a number of different functional areas of the business, or will I remain primarily in one area?
   - Is there a stated policy concerning job rotation?
   - What is the policy on geographical moves?

Barker also asked questions about such things as benefit plans, vacations, and other things of immediate interest to him. He inquired about the company's standing in the industry, its market share, its goals, its current performance. When he had finished an interview he felt he had learned enough about a company to make a decision as to whether he would work for them or not, provided they made him an offer of employment.

When the college year ended, Barker had a number of job offers. After some consideration he decided to enter the finance industry, and accepted a position with a large trust company. He had been impressed by the knowledge of the interviewers from this firm, and by the answers they had given him to his series of questions. What interested him most was their statement that they sought only college graduates for management positions and that they trained their own people from the bottom up, and seldom hired people from outside in senior positions. Training, they told him, was a combination of on-the-job experience under the supervision of a trust and investment officer, and a series of formal courses put on by the company.

Six months after joining the company, however, Alan felt disillusioned. His initial experience on the job had been to spend a full day filling out forms in the personnel department, and then, on the second day, to be assigned to a "group". The group head had talked with him for about fifteen minutes and then had given him a stack of manuals and files about three feet high to read over during the next week. He had not talked to his boss for another two weeks, and had gone over the material in a somewhat bewildered fashion. It was concerned with detailed procedures for administering trusts and estates and for managing trustee investments. At the beginning of his second week on the job, Alan was given some small jobs, mainly concerned with filling in certain forms in a prescribed manner, and performing certain routine administrative tasks, all of which were well documented. By the end of his sixth month on the job it seemed to him that the complexity of the tasks had not increased to any significant extent.

At his six-month review, Alan met with a personnel officer who told him he had received a good rating from his supervisor, that he would receive a raise as a result, and that he would begin to attend a weekly training session on Monday mornings.

The training course proved to be less than Alan had expected. It consisted of a series of managers from various departments in the company talking about their functions. These lectures were set against a background of the company's history, which took the first three weeks. Alan felt he learned very little that would enable him to improve the way he did his own job.

He constantly asked his supervisor for more work, finding that the tasks allotted him were routine, and easily completed. He felt ill at ease since he never seemed to have enough work to do. All the work he did was checked first by the assistant supervisor and then by the supervisor. All letters were sent out over the supervisor's signature, and much of Alan's time was spent rephrasing letters to meet his boss's preferences.

After ten months on the job, Alan's frustrations came to a head one day when he submitted a routine letter for his supervisor's signature. Several minutes later the supervisor appeared at Alan's desk with the letter, heavily pencilled over. In Alan's opinion there was very little difference in the content as a result of the editing, and he was sure his grammar had been faultless.He took the point up rather strongly with his boss.

"Listen", said the supervisor, "you college boys don't know how to write proper English. Letters in this company have to be written in a certain way, and if you don't want to learn our way, it's just going to take you that much longer to go anywhere in here."

That afternoon Alan handed in his resignation.

ATLANTIC GENERAL INSURANCE COMPANY

In July, 1960, Mr. R. Taylor, the fire insurance manager of the Atlantic Insurance Company of Montreal, was killed in an automobile accident.

Mr. Taylor, a man in his late fifties, had been with the company since its founding in 1938. Under him, the fire insurance department had grown from two to over twenty-eight inspectors, underwriters, stenographers and clerks. Taylor, an employee recalled, encouraged the office to run with as little direction from him as possible. To almost any question he would reply, "Well what do you think?" and would frequently allow suggestions that he did not entirely agree with, to be implemented. He took a keen interest in his staff and always had a word for anyone. No office get-together was complete without his presence, and at Christmas and on his birthday his staff always presented him with a small gift financed through a staff collection. While salaries in his department were by no means competitive with other departments in the company, or other companies, Taylor always had on file a great number of applicants for the positions that become available. Such vacancies were quite rare and most of his staff had above five years' service in his department.

Taylor's two assistants were Ellen Robichaud, a married woman in her early forties, and Jack Carr. Mrs. Robichaud was in charge of the stenographers and clerks in the department. She was a very quiet person who tried to keep all her subordinates as happy as possible. She was well liked by everyone. Carr supervised the activities of the underwriters.

Mr. Fisher, the general manager, chose as Taylor's successor Mr. Harold Weston, a man of twenty years seniority with the company, and who for the past ten years had managed a small branch office in Toronto. During his ten-year stay there, he had increased premium income in that area from practically nothing to nearly $500,000 per year. Fisher attributed this success to the fact that, unlike many branch managers, Weston had made a point of visiting regularly all the company agents and successfully cultivating their confidence and friendship.

Soon after this new appointment was made, the company moved its headquarters from the city to a building in a rapidly developing commercial area about two miles away. The third floor of this new building was occupied by the Atlantic General. Unlike the previous building where the company was spread over four floors, the new building was large enough so that one floor could hold all departments of the company—fire, automobile, casualty and claims—totalling more than 250 persons.

In due course, Weston settled into the fire manager's job. The staff, although somewhat apprehensive at first, were soon reassured by their new manager's easygoing manner. He was a friendly, soft-spoken, approachable man who always did his best to put his employees at their ease when they were talking to him. Soon after the move, Weston made it apparent to his department that he wanted to introduce an open door policy, and staff members began to consult him with increasing frequency, particularly on personal matters such as pay, holidays, and promotions. Most of these matters had previously been taken up with Robichaud and Carr, although a staff member said, "Taylor would have been pleased to listen if we had ever wanted to go to him."

Many of the department employees usually found in the course of a day, some problem which required the attention of the manager. Consequently, Weston had an almost constant stream of people moving to and from his office. In order to get time to do his own work, Weston started to stay late at night and even come early in the morning. Nonetheless, he took no action to discourage these practices, believing that things would settle down after a few months.

Mrs. Robichaud reacted strangely. After moving to a new building, she found it increasingly necessary to visit other departments; she occasionally came in late, which she had never done before; and she started to experience sickness which often necessitated her staying at home for a day. While things settled quickly to normal in most departments in the new location, a somewhat different spirit seemed to prevail in the fire department. Several of the staff habitually reported late for work and extended both their coffee breaks and lunch hours. Both Robichaud and Carr, at Weston's request, tried to do something about this development, but met with little success. Less work seemed to be accomplished in the department and many employees became several days behind in their work, although many worked voluntarily through their lunch hours to try and bring their work up to date. More ominous as far as Weston was concerned was the fact that several of his agents complained that they were receiving policies that were incorrectly typed. About four months after being made manager, Weston was called into the general manager's office and asked why several employees of his department had been coming to work with the executives of the company about fifteen minutes after the normal starting time. Immediately after this meeting,

Weston called a meeting of his staff, read them the following notice, explained that he wanted more cooperation and then posted the notice on the department bulletin board.

> TO THE FIRE INSURANCE DEPARTMENT
>
> This office opens for business at 8:30 a.m.
> All staff will be present at this time or
> will see me when they arrive.
> H. Weston,
> Fire Manager.

The notice had an immediate effect. For several weeks no lateness occurred. The situation soon began to deteriorate, however, and after two more months lateness had again developed. Weston was very disturbed by this state of affairs and realized that some action would have to be taken, but was uncertain as to how he should proceed.

BOB KNOWLTON

Bob Knowlton was sitting alone in the conference room of the laboratory. The rest of the group had gone. One of the secretaries had stopped and talked for a while about her husband's coming induction into the Army, and had finally left. Bob, alone in the laboratory, slid a little further down in his chair, looking with satisfaction at the results of the first test run of the new photon unit.

He liked to stay after the others had gone. His appointment as project head was still new enough to give him a deep sense of pleasure. His eyes were on the graphs before him, but in his mind he could hear Dr. Jerrold, the project head, saying again, "There's one thing about this place that you can bank on. The sky is the limit for a man who can produce!" Knowlton felt again the tingle of happiness and embarrassment. Well, dammit, he said to himself, he had produced. He wasn't kidding anybody. He had come to the Simmons Laboratories two years ago. During a routine testing of some rejected Clanson components he had stumbled on the idea of the photon correlator, and the rest just happened. Jerrold had been enthusiastic: a separate project had been set up for further research and development of the device, and he had gotten the job of running it. The whole sequence of events still seemed a little miraculous to Knowlton.

He shrugged out of the reverie and bent determinedly over the sheets when he heard someone come into the room behind him. He looked up expectantly; Jerrold often stayed late himself, and now and then dropped in for a chat. This always made the day's end especially pleasant for Bob. It wasn't Jerrold. The man who had come in was a stranger. He was tall, thin, and rather dark. He wore steel-rimmed glasses and had on a very wide leather belt with a large brass buckle. Lucy remarked later that it was the kind of belt the Pilgrims must have worn.

The stranger smiled and introduced himself. "I'm Simon Fester. Are you Bob Knowlton?" Bob said yes, and they shook hands. "Doctor Jerrold said I might find you in. We were talking about your work, and I'm very much interested in what you are doing." Bob waved to a chair.

Fester didn't seem to belong in any of the standard categories of visitors: customer, visiting fireman, stockholder. Bob pointed to the sheets on the table. "There are the preliminary results of a test we're running. We've got a new gadget by the tail and we're trying to understand it. It's not finished, but I can show you the section that we're testing."He stood up, but Fester was deep in the graphs. After a moment, he looked up with an odd grin. "These look like plots of a Jennings surface. I've been playing around with some autocorrelation functions of surfaces—you know that stuff." Bob who had no idea what he was referring to, grinned back and nodded, and immediately felt uncomfortable. "Let me show you the monster," he said and led the way to the work room.

After Fester left, Knowlton slowly put the graphs away, feeling vaguely annoyed. Then, as if he had made a decision, he quickly locked up and took the long way out so that he would pass Jerrold's office. But the office was locked. Knowlton wondered whether Jerrold and Fester had left together.

The next morning, Knowlton dropped into Jerrold's office, mentioned that he had talked with Fester, and asked who he was.

"Sit down for a minute," Jerrold said. "I want to talk to you about him. What do you think of him?" Knowlton replied truthfully that he thought Fester was very bright and probably very competent. Jerrold looked pleased.

"We're taking him on," he said. "He's had a very good background in a number of laboratories, and he seems to have ideas about the problems we're tackling here." Knowlton nodded in agreement, instantly wishing that Fester would not be placed with him.

"I don't know yet where he will finally land," Jerrold continued, "but he seems interested in what you are doing. I thought he might spend a little time with you by way of getting started." Knowlton nodded thoughtfully. "If his interest in your work continues, you can add him to your group."

"Well, he seemed to have some good ideas even without knowing exactly what we are doing," Knowlton answered. "I hope he stays; we'd be glad to have him."

Knowlton walked back to the lab with mixed feelings. He told himself that Fester would be good for the group. He was no dunce, he'd produce.

Knowlton thought again of Jerrold's promise when he had promoted him—"the man who produces gets ahead in this outfit." The words seemed to carry the overtones of a threat now.

That day Fester didn't appear until mid-afternoon. He explained that he had had a long lunch with Jerrold, discussing his place in the lab. "Yes," said Knowlton, "I talked with Jerry this morning about it, and we both thought you might work with us for awhile."

Fester smiled in the same knowing way that he had smiled when he mentioned the Jennings surfaces. "I'd like to," he said.

Knowlton introduced Fester to the other members of the lab. Fester and Link, the mathematician of the group, hit it off well together, and spent the rest of the afternoon discussing a method of analysis of patterns that Link had been worrying over for the last month.

It was 6:30 when Knowlton finally left the lab that night. He had waited almost eagerly for the end of the day to come—when they would all be gone and he could sit in the quiet rooms, relax, and think it over. "Think what over?" he asked himself. He didn't know. Shortly after 5:00 P.M. they had all gone except Fester, and what followed was almost a duel. Knowlton was annoyed that he was being cheated out of his quiet period, and finally resentfully determined that Fester should leave first.

Fester was sitting at the conference table reading, and Knowlton was sitting at his desk in the little glass-enclosed cubby that he used during the day when he needed to be undisturbed. Fester had gotten the last year's progress reports out and was studying them carefully. The time dragged. Knowlton doodled on a pad, the tension growing inside him. What the hell did Fester think he was going to find in the reports?

Knowlton finally gave up and they left the lab together. Fester took several of the reports with him to study in the evening. Knowlton asked him if he thought the reports gave a clear picture of the lab's activities.

"They're excellent," Fester answered with obvious sincerity. "They're not only good reports; what they report is damn good, too!" Knowlton was surprised at the relief he felt, and grew almost jovial as he said goodnight.

Driving home, Knowlton felt more optimistic about Fester's presence in the lab. He had never fully understood the analysis that Link was attempting. If there was anything wrong with Link's approach, Fester would probably spot it. "And if I'm any judge," he murmured, "he won't be especially diplomatic about it."

He described Fester to his wife, who was amused by the broad leather belt and the brass buckle.

"It's the kind of belt that Pilgrims must have worn," she laughed.

"I'm not worried about how he holds his pants up," he laughed with her. "I'm afraid that he's the kind that just has to make like a genius twice each day. And that can be pretty rough on the group."

Knowlton had been asleep for several hours when he was jerked awake by the telephone. He realized it had rung several times. He swung off the bed muttering about damn fools and telephones. It was Fester. Without any excuses, apparently oblivious of the time, he plunged into an excited recital of how Link's patterning problem could be solved.

Knowlton covered the mouthpiece to answer his wife's stage-whispered "Who is it?" "It's the genius," replied Knowlton.

Fester, completely ignoring the fact that it was 2:00 in the morning, proceeded in a very excited way to start in the middle of an explanation of a completely new approach to certain of the photon lab problems that he had stumbled on while analyzing past experiments. Knowlton managed to put some enthusiasm in his own voice and stood there, half-dazed and very uncomfortable, listening to Fester talk endlessly about what he had discovered. It was probably not only a new approach, but also an analysis which showed the inherent weakness of the previous experiment and how experimentation along that line would certainly have been inconclusive. The following day Knowlton spent the entire morning with Fester and Link, the mathematician, the customary morning meeting of Bob's group having been called off so that Fester's work of the previous night could be gone over intensively. Fester was very anxious that this be done and Knowlton was not too unhappy to call the meeting off for reasons of his own.

For the next several days Fester sat in the back office that had been turned over to him and did nothing but read the progress reports of the work that had been done in the last six months. Knowlton caught himself feeling apprehensive about the reaction that Fester might have to some of his work. He was a little surprised at his own feelings. He had always been proud—although he had put on a convincingly modest face—of the way in which new ground in the study of photon measuring devices had been broken in his group. Now he wasn't sure, and it seemed to him that Fester might easily show that the line of research they had been following was unsound or even unimaginative.

The next morning, as was the custom, the members of the lab, including the girls, sat around a conference table. Bob always prided himself on the fact that the work of the lab was guided and evaluated by the group as a whole and he was fond of repeating that it was not a waste of time to include secretaries in such meetings. Often, what started out as a boring recital of fundamental assumptions, to a naive listener, uncovered new ways of regarding these assumptions that would not have occurred to the researcher who had long ago accepted them as a necessary basis for his work.

These group meetings also served Bob in another sense. He admitted to himself that he would have felt far less secure if he had had to direct the work out of his own mind, so to speak. With the group-meeting as the principle of leadership, it was always possible to justify the exploration of blind alleys because of the general educative effect on the team. Fester was there; Lucy and Martha were there; Link was sitting next to Fester, their conversation concerning Link's mathematical study apparently continuing from yesterday. The other members, Bob Davenport, George Thurlow and Arthur Oliver, were waiting quietly.

Knowlton, for reasons that he didn't quite understand, proposed for discussion this morning a problem that all of them had spent a great deal of time on previously, with the conclusion that a solution was impossible, that there was no feasible way of treating it in an experimental fashion. When Knowlton proposed the problem, Davenport remarked that there was hardly any use of going over it again, that he was satisfied that there was no way of approaching the problem with the equipment and the physical capacities of the lab.

This statement had the effect of a shot of adrenalin on Fester. He said he would like to know what the problem was in detail and, walking to the blackboard, began setting down the "factors" as various members of the group began discussing the problem and simultaneously listing the reasons why it had been abandoned.

Very early in the description of the problem if was evident that Fester was going to disagree about the impossibility of attacking it. The group realized this and finally the descriptive materials and their recounting of the reasoning that had led to its abandonment dwindled away. Fester began his statement which, as it proceeded, might well have been prepared the previous night although Knowlton knew this was impossible. He couldn't help being impressed with the organized and logical way that Fester was presenting ideas that must have occurred to him only a few minutes before.

Fester had some things to say, however, which left Knowlton with a mixture of annoyance, irritation, and, at the same time, a rather smug feeling of superiority over Fester in at least one area. Fester was of the opinion that the way that the problem had been analyzed was really typical of group-thinking and, with an air of sophistication which made it difficult for a listener to dissent, he proceeded to comment on the American emphasis on team ideas, satirically describing the ways in which they led to a "high level of mediocrity."

During this time, Knowlton observed that Link stared studiously at the floor, and he was very conscious of George Thurlow's and Bob Davenport's glances toward him at several points of Fester's little speech. Inwardly, Knowlton couldn't help feeling that this was one point at least in which Fester was off on the wrong foot. The whole lab, following Jerry's lead, talked if not practiced the theory of small research teams as the basic organization for effective research. Fester insisted that the problem could be approached and that he would like to study it for a while himself.

Knowlton ended the morning session by remarking that the meetings would continue and that the very fact that a supposedly insoluble experimental problem was now going to get another chance was another indication of the value of such meetings. Fester immediately remarked that he was not at all adverse to meetings for the purpose of informing the group of the progress of its members—that the point he wanted to make was that creative advances were seldom accomplished in such meetings, that they were made by the individual "living with" the problem closely and continuously, a sort of personal relationship to it.

Knowlton went on to say to Fester that he was very glad that Fester had raised these points and that he was sure the group would profit by reexamining the basis on which they had been operating. Knowlton agreed that individual effort was probably the basis for making the major advances, but that he considered the group meetings useful primarily because of the effect they had on keeping the group together and on helping the weaker members of the group keep up with the ones who were able to advance more easily and quickly in the analysis of problems.

It was clear as days went by and meetings continued that Fester came to enjoy them because of the pattern which the meetings assumed. It became typical for Fester to hold forth and it was unquestionably clear that he was more brilliant, better prepared on the various subjects which were germane to the problems being studied, and that he was more capable of going ahead than anyone there. Knowlton grew increasingly disturbed as he realized that his leadership of the group had been, in fact, taken over.

Whenever the subject of Fester was mentioned, in occasional meetings with Dr. Jerrold, Knowlton would comment only on the ability and obvious capacity for work that Fester had. Somehow he never felt that he could mention his own discomforts, not only because they revealed a weakness on his own part, but also because it was quite clear that Jerrold himself was considerably impressed with Fester's work and with the contacts he had with him outside the photon laboratory.

Knowlton now began to feel that perhaps the intellectual advantages that Fester had brought to the group did not quite compensate for what he felt were evidences of a breakdown in the cooperative spirit he had seen in the group before Fester's coming. More and more of the morning meetings were skipped. Fester's opinion concerning the abilities of others of the group, with the exception of Link, was obviously low. At times, during morning meetings or in smaller discussions, he had been on the point of rudeness, refusing to pursue an argument when he claimed it was based on the other person's ignorance of the facts involved. His impatience of others led him to also make similar remarks to Dr. Jerrold. Knowlton inferred this from a conversation with Jerrold in which Jerrold asked whether Davenport and Oliver were going to be continued on; and his failure to mention Link, the mathematician, led Knowlton to feel that this was the result of private conversations between Fester and Jerrold.

It was not difficult for Knowlton to make a quite convincing case on whether the brilliance of Fester was sufficient recompense for the beginning of this breaking up of the group. He took the opportunity to speak privately with Davenport and with Oliver and it was quite clear that both of them were uncomfortable because of Fester. Knowlton didn't press the discussion beyond the point of hearing them in one way or another say that they did feel awkward and that it was sometimes difficult for them to understand the arguments he advanced, but often embarrassing to ask him to fill in the background on which his arguments were based. Knowlton did not interview Link in this manner.

About six months after Fester's coming into the photon lab, a meeting was scheduled in which the sponsors of the research were coming in to get some idea of the work and its progress. It was customary at these meetings for project heads to present the research being conducted in their groups. The members of each group were invited to other meetings which were held later in the day and open to all, but the special meetings were usually made up only of project heads, the head of the laboratory, and the sponsors.

As the time for the special meeting approached, it seemed to Knowlton that he must avoid the presentation at all cost. His reasons for this were that he could not trust himself to present the ideas and work that Fester had advanced, because of his apprehension as to whether he could present them in sufficient detail and answer such questions about them as might be asked. On the other hand, he did not feel he could ignore these newer lines of work and present only the material that he had done or that had been started before Fester's arrival. He felt also that it would not be beyond Fester at all, in his blunt and undiplomatic way—if he were present at the meeting, that is—to make comments on his [Knowlton's] presentation and reveal Knowlton's inadequacy. It also seemed quite clear that it would not be easy to keep Fester from attending the meeting, even though he was not on the administrative level of those invited.

Knowlton found an opportunity to speak to Jerrold and raised the question. He remarked to Jerrold that, with the meetings coming up and with the interest in the work and with the contributions that Fester had been making, he would probably like to come to these meetings, but there was a question of the feelings of the others in the group if Fester alone were invited. Jerrold passed this over very lightly by saying that he didn't think the group would fail to understand Fester's rather different position and that he thought that Fester by all means should be invited. Knowlton then immediately said he had thought so, too; that Fester should present the work because much of it was work he had done; and, as Knowlton put it, that this would be a nice way to recognize Fester's contributions and to reward him, as he was eager to be recognized as a productive member of the lab. Jerrold agreed, and so the matter was decided.

Fester's presentation was very successful and in some ways dominated the meeting. He attracted the interest and attention of many of those who had come, and a long discussion followed his presentation. Later in the evening—with the entire laboratory staff present—in the cocktail period before the dinner, a little circle of people formed about Fester. One of them was Jerrold himself, and a lively discussion took place concerning the application of Fester's theory. All of this disturbed Knowlton, and his reaction and behavior were characteristic. He joined the circle, praised Fester to Jerrold and to others, and remarked on the brilliance of the work.

Knowlton, without consulting anyone, began at this time to take some interest in the possibility of a job elsewhere. After a few weeks he found that a new laboratory of considerable size was being organized in a nearby city, and that the kind of training he had would enable him to get a project head job equivalent to the one he had at the lab, with slightly more money.

He immediately accepted it and notified Jerrold by a letter, which he mailed on a Friday night to Jerrold's home. The letter was quite brief, and Jerrold was stunned. The letter merely said that he had found a better position; that there were personal reasons why he didn't want to appear at the lab any more; that he would be glad to come back at a later time from where he would be, some forty miles away, to assist if there was any mixup at all in the past work; that he felt sure that Fester could, however, supply any leadership that was required for the group; and that his decision to leave so suddenly was based on some personal problems—he hinted at problems of health in his family, his mother and father. All of this was fictitious, of course. Jerrold took it at face value but still felt that this was very strange behavior and quite unaccountable, for he had always felt his relationship with Knowlton had been warm and that Knowlton was satisfied and, as a matter of fact, quite happy and productive.

Jerrold was considerably disturbed, because he had already decided to place Fester in charge of another project that was going to be set up very soon. He had been wondering how to explain this to Knowlton, in view of the obvious help Knowlton was getting from Fester and the high regard in which he held him. Jerrold had, as a matter of fact, considered the possibility that Knowlton could add to his staff another person with the kind of background and training that had been unique in Fester and had proved so valuable.

Jerrold did not make any attempt to meet Knowlton. In a way, he felt aggrieved about the whole thing. Fester, too, was surprised at the suddenness of Knowlton's departure and when Jerrold, in talking to him, asked him whether he had reasons to prefer to stay with the photon group instead of the project for the Air Force which was being organized, he chose the Air Force project and went on to that job the following week. The photon lab was hard hit. The leadership of the lab was given to Link with the understanding that this would be temporary until someone could come in to take over.

THE BREWSTER-SEAVIEW LANDSCAPING CO.*

PART I

During the summer of my freshman year in college, I worked for a small private landscaping company planting shrubs, seeding new lawns, cutting grass, and tending flower gardens. The company was located in my home

*Note: Please do not read ahead in this case until requested to do so by the instructor.

town of Seaview, N.J., which is a rural community on the coast about 80 miles from Philadelphia. The company was owned and run by Joe Brewster, a 45-year-old man who had lived in Seaview all his life. He had started the company some years ago and not only handled the paper work (payroll, bills, estimates, etc.) but also worked along with the crew six days a week.

The crew consisted of five guys ranging in age from 17 to 20 years. We all lived in towns around Seaview and had gone to the regional high school which was physically located in Seaview. Only two of us were attending college, but all had been hired personally by Joe following a short, informal interview. I can't be completely certain about the others, but I think all of us, and several others, sought the job because we needed work, enjoyed the outdoors, and had heard that Joe paid well and was an OK guy to work for. Working hours were from 8:00 A.M. to 4:30 P.M., with an hour off for lunch, Monday through Saturday. Once in a while we'd work overtime to help out some customer who had an urgent need. Each worker began at the same wage with the understanding that hard workers would be rehired the next summer at a higher wage. Several of the crew I was part of had been rehired under this policy.

Most of the customers we serviced lived in Seaview, knew Joe personally and seemed to respect him.

Joe owned one truck, which he used to transport all of us, and necessary supplies and equipment, from job to job. Each morning, Joe, as we called him, would read off a list of houses that had to be completed that day. He would then leave it up to us to decide among ourselves who would do what task at a particular house. We also were the ones who determined how long we would spend at each house by our work pace.

In doing the work itself, we were able to use our own ideas and methods. If we did a good job, Joe would always compliment us. If we lacked the necessary know-how or did a poor job, Joe was right there willing to help us.

At each house, Joe worked along with us doing basically the same work we did. He dressed the same as we did and was always very open and friendly towards us. He seldom "showed his authority" and treated us as equals. Although our work day was scheduled to begin at 8:00, Joe never became upset nor penalized us if we were ten or fifteen minutes late. Our lunch hour was usually an hour long starting anytime between 11:30 and 12:30 depending on what time we, the crew, felt like eating. Each member brought his own lunch to work and anytime during the day could take time off to go to the truck for a snack.

The crew itself became very well acquainted and we were always free to talk and joke with each other at any time and did so. We enjoyed each other's company, although we did not socialize after hours.

We also became very friendly with the customers. They were always eager to talk to us as we worked and Joe never objected. All in all, the job had a very relaxed, easy-going atmosphere. I, for one, felt little pressure to hurry, and like the others respected and liked Joe very much.

Prediction Questions

1. What will be the productivity, in terms of quantity and quality, of the work crew? Why?

PART II

The attitude we had toward the job was very high. We sometimes talked among ourselves about how we felt a sense of responsibility toward the job. While we talked and joked a lot while working, little horseplay occurred, and the talking and joking did not interfere with the work. We were always working steadily and efficiently, seeking to keep ahead of schedule. The days seemed to go fairly quickly and a lot seemed to get done. I know Joe said that our output was 15 percent above that which other landscaping companies experienced with summer crews.

We also took a lot of pride in our work. Feeling responsible for the job we did, we were constantly checking and re-checking every job to be sure it was perfect. We were always willing to work overtime for Joe when he needed us to do so.

Discussion Question

1. What elements in the situation contributed to these positive results? Can you think of things which, if present, might have led to very different results? Explain how.

PART III

I returned the following summer to work for Joe because of the strong satisfaction I had with the job the summer before. So did the others. However, we were in for a surprise. Many things had changed. Joe had increased the number of workers to 10, hired another truck, and hired two young college graduates from Philadelphia as crew supervisors. His plan was to concentrate on the paper work and on lining up new customers, leaving the direct guidance of the two work crews to the new supervisors.

Joe had hired the two supervisors during the early spring, after interviewing a number of applicants. Both were young (23 and 24), from the city, and had degrees in agricultural management from Penn State, but had not known each other previously.

We "oldtimers" were assigned to one crew and five new workers were hired for the other crew. These new workers had little experience in landscaping. Except for the working hours, which were the same as during the previous summer, the two supervisors were told that they could run their crew in any manner they wished, as long as they kept to the schedule prepared by Joe.

No one on the crew had known the supervisors before. Joe had found them through ads in the paper. The supervisors didn't dress quite as informally as Joe did, perhaps because they didn't do as much actual physical work, but they did dress casually in dungarees and shirts, the same as the crew. Though we called the supervisors by their first names, they did some nit-picky things. For example, Joe never cared who drove the truck or who did what job; sometimes a crew member would drive and Joe would talk with the rest of us. But the supervisors always drove the truck and decided when we would eat. Nor did the supervisors help us unload the tools as Joe had done. They stood around and watched us.

Both supervisors refused to tolerate tardiness in the morning, and immediately set up a scheduled lunch hour which would remain the same throughout the summer. We were no longer allowed to go to the truck for a snack during the day and were constantly being watched over by our supervisor. The supervisors assigned us to specific tasks to be done at each job and told us how "they" wanted them to be completed. They also told us how much time we were to spend doing each job. They refused to let us talk to each other or to the customers (except about business) saying that it "only wasted time and interfered with our work." It was a more structured, more formal atmosphere than the summer before.

Prediction Questions

1. What kind of issues or problems are likely to develop during the second summer? Why?
2. How will productivity compare with that of the previous summer in terms of quantity and quality. Why?
3. What would have been your advice to the two supervisors about how they could best approach their new role?

PART IV

I was disappointed at the new set-up and a little bit surprised that Joe hadn't hired one of the more experienced members of the old crew as supervisor. But I figured it was necessary because of the increased volume of business so I tried to make the best of it. However, very soon my attitude and that of the rest of the old crew fell significantly. We began to hate the new supervisors and soon developed a great disinterest in the work itself. While I'm a person who usually is very conscientious and responsible, I have to admit that before long I, along with the others, began to put little care or concern into my work. The supervisors soon found it very difficult to get anyone to work overtime.

The new employees didn't react as strongly as we did, but I could tell that they weren't working with much enthusiasm, either.

I thought about talking to the supervisors but didn't because I'd only worked there the one year and figured that it was not my place to. The others were older than I and had worked there longer so I figured that they should, but no one did. Instead, we talked among ourselves and individually griped to Joe.

Joe didn't seem to know how to deal with our complaints. He passed them off by saying "Oh . . . I'll talk to the supervisors and straighten it out with them." But nothing changed, and in fact they seemed to clamp down more and push even harder. This only made us madder. Our work rate continued to fall.

Incidentally, throughout this period we had little social interaction with the supervisors but I noticed that they became more and more friendly with each other.

Meanwhile, the new crew's difficulties increased. Being new and inexperienced they couldn't do the work as easily as we could. Also the supervisors didn't, or couldn't, give them any adequate training. Their productivity went lower and lower. The supervisors were very upset and yelled at them, pushing them to get out their quota. We felt sorry for them and tried to help them; but we concentrated on reluctantly meeting our own quota.

I don't think Joe realized that the supervisors were not teaching the new crewmen. He was very busy and not around much, and I think he assumed that they were training the new men. I think he began to put pressure on the supervisors as the work rate fell, because things continued to get worse. We couldn't talk to customers, which surprised them. We couldn't even accept drinks. Production lagged greatly as compared to the previous summer and the two supervisors struggled to meet the schedule and deal with customer complaints about quality. By July 15th the overall productivity of the company was 5 percent below "normal" and way below the previous summer.

As Joe became aware of this huge decrease in production he became very concerned and wondered what to do about it.

Discussion Questions

1. What caused the poor production condition during the second summer?
2. How might this situation have been avoided from the beginning?
3. What should Joe do now?
4. Do you think the supervisors could have effectively adopted Joe's style of leadership? What kind of problems might they have had if they did? How should they have conducted themselves?

From: Allan R. Cohen, Stephen L. Fink, Herman Gadon, and Robin D. Willits, *Effective Behavior in Organizations* (Homewood, Ill.: Richard D. Irwin, 1976), pp. 346–50.

CARTER STEEL COMPANY *

PART I

The Carter Steel Company's Industrial Engineering (IE) Department employed approximately 65 people. The department was subdivided into three sections, one specializing in standard costs, one in incentives and one

**Note:* Please do not read ahead in this case until requested to do so by the instructor.

in methods. Each section performed its special function for all of the manufacturing departments. However, since the work of any one section usually created work for another, each line department (Open Hearth, Sheet Mill, Tin Mill, Wire Mill, Rolling Mill, Maintenance and Transportation) was assigned a "departmental IE" who acted as liaison between all of the IE sections and his particular operating department. This form of organization had existed for many years. Each engineer had become highly specialized in his skills and point of view. This tendency toward specialization had been reinforced by Carter Steel's gradual growth and the relatively stable technology in the steel industry.

The IE sections were physically separated from each other by seven-foot partitions. There was little formal contact between members of the various sections except at the start and completion of a project. Customarily, one and sometimes two men from each section were assigned to a project. They would usually have little contact with anyone within the section but their supervisor during the course of a project.

Procedures and rules within the department were relatively informal. Coffee and lunch breaks were left to the men's discretion. Supervisory pressure was not heavy except when projects fell behind schedule.

All of the men in the department were college graduates and had general industrial engineering training and experience. Most were married, had children, and commuted from the suburbs surrounding the town in which Carter Steel was located. Although the ages of these men varied from 23 to 60 and experience from one to 25 years, the great majority of the men were between 25 and 40 years old with from 5 to 15 years experience. Supervisory status and pay grade correlated closely with age and experience. Promotion depended upon vacancies in superior grades. Salaries were competitive for Carter Steel's region.

Prediction. The reader should answer the following questions on the basis of the above case situation. From what I know of the operations of the IE department described in Part I, I would predict that:

- **a** productivity of the IE department would be (high) (standard) (below standard). Why?
- **b** members of the IE department would be (highly) (moderately) (dis-) satisfied with their job. Why?
- **c** members of the IE department (would) (would not) engage in group activities (inside) (outside) the department. Why?

PART II

The productivity of the IE Department was considered adequate by Carter management, generally. However, some of the line departments complained that IE projects seemed to drag along slowly at times and that they had to ride herd on the IEs to be sure that various phases of projects were carried through. A few men in line management asserted that most of the IEs were rather conservative in their solutions to manufacturing problems and that they resisted ideas for improvement which were originated by production men.

The IEs, themselves, were relatively satisfied with their jobs. Some who were qualified for promotion, particularly those who had at first risen rapidly through the ranks, were frustrated because their progress had slowed or stopped.

The social organization of the department took several forms. Most men commuted in car pools whose membership was dictated more by suburban geography than by IE subsection assignments. Members of the car pools and their families engaged in extra-company social activities. At work, however, the sections were usually the focus of nonwork activities such as "flips" to see who paid for coffee and a number of card game groups which met during lunch.

The members of the department generally liked their supervisors, though some were more highly respected than others. There were strong values particularly among the younger men, for dealing assertively with the line department, for avoiding "pickiness" over details and for "modern" methods.

PART III

Early in June a rumor spread through the department that a reorganization was about to take place. Supervisors would comment only that such rumors had cropped up from time to time but nothing had ever happened. Nevertheless, the productivity of the department declined, any project requiring more than a few days' work being put off until "after the reorganization."

In late July, after the weekly Friday afternoon supervisors' meeting, the supervisors informed their sections that beginning the next Monday the department would begin reorganizing its sections so that each would correspond to one or more of the manufacturing units. Each line department was to have a corresponding IE section to which former specialists in standard cost, incentive and methods were to be assigned. However, the men were now expected to be able to deal with all aspects of a department's project, since each man was by now assumed to be familiar with the established systems and procedures by which the department functioned. It was hoped that the new organization would allow new men to become familiar with all aspects of the department's work. A few senior specialists were to be assigned to a staff group under the chief IE to be of service to the departmental sections. Because of the new staff group and the greater number of IE sections under the new organization, a certain number of promotions were necessary.

The reorganization required physical relocation of IEs so that all men assigned to one department would have desks together. The operation of the move was left to the IEs themselves, although plans called for nearly every man to move. Few of the old spatial relations were to remain unchanged. However, no renovation of office facilities was planned.

PREDICTION

From what I know of the operations of the IE department and the reorganization described in Part III, I would predict that:

- **a** department members would (welcome) (tolerate) (oppose) the reorganization. Why?
- **b** the eventual outcome of the reorganization would be (an increase) (no change) (a decrease) in the productivity of the IE department. Why?
- **c** group activities inside and outside the department would (remain as before) (change). Why?

PART IV

During the first few weeks after the reorganization, there was constant friction among the men over possession and location of desks, chairs, and filing cabinets. Since many of these items had been shared by men who were now to work in different areas, the problems were slow in working themselves out. However, they finally subsided.

Some imbalance in work load soon became evident. A few sections found themselves overstaffed and underworked. No section was found to be undermanned, although no new personnel had been hired. The overstaffed groups became frustrated by their lack of work. Management expected that normal attrition would solve this problem.

Social reorganization was often awkward and slow. Most of the card-playing groups disintegrated and were reformed with new members. Car pool groups, however, remained unchanged. After several months, a new set of social relationships had become established around the departmental sections. These appeared to be somewhat more intensive than those which had existed in the specialty sections.

The new work sections displayed an autonomy which was formerly lacking. The problems of communication between specialities on a project disappeared. The chief IE and his assistant were called on less frequently to solve coordinative difficulties, but were often asked to evaluate and approve innovations in departmental operation. Line department complaints became less frequent. The men in each section appeared to be taking renewed interest in their work. Management interpreted the increased productivity of the IE Department as a sign of the reorganization's success.

CLEVIT CHEMICAL CO. OF CANADA LTD.

". . . and I say, Bob, that he is to be fired! I don't care what you told him; it doesn't make any difference anyway. This is our decision; I'm passing it on to you. It overrides anything you've said or my name isn't Johnston!"

One year after the new Clevit Chemical plant had been completed in southern Ontario, the clerk in charge of the works stores reported missing parts. The works stores contained miscellaneous material and spare parts for maintenance and repair work. At first there had been little supervision over its inventory and workers would help themselves to needed material. After the company had expanded the works stores, a clerk was placed in charge. Later the stores were fully enclosed by a steel fence and kept locked so that parts and material could only be obtained from the clerk during the day. The superintendent of stores then posted instructions that no worker was to enter the works stores and obtain parts and material on his own; he should obtain them from the clerk in charge. Superintendents and foremen also informed the men under their supervision of this new regulation.

Soon after, the assistant personnel manager reported to the superintendent of stores that Marvin Fletcher, an instrument mechanic, had been seen breaking into works stores. This violation of the new regulation was then discussed at an executive committee meeting of the plant. At the meeting were four men: Walter Purvis, the Clevit plant manager; his assistant, Simon Johnston, who was also the technical manager; Sandy Jennings, maintenance engineer; and Bob Denton, instrument engineer and Fletcher's supervisor. They had a report on Marvin Fletcher; he had broken into stores for a file which he had used to make a special wrench. The four men at the meeting all agreed that he should be severely reprimanded or punished; no one suggested discharging him. Then Purvis asked Jennings and Denton if they would make the final decision on Fletcher's case and take whatever action was necessary. Jennings and Denton agreed, and the meeting ended. The company had no policy with regard to the action to be taken in the case of any employee caught stealing.

Marvin Fletcher, originally from Chilliwack, B.C., had been hired by the company and sent to one of the plants of the parent company in the United States where he received special training in instrument maintenance and repair. After six months' training, he was sent to the Canadian plant in Ontario.

"Fletcher will become a good mechanic," Denton had said, "he's just immature—only a youngster, you know, just 22 years old. This is his first permanent job as far as I know and he's a valuable mechanic with that special training he's had. We've had a little trouble with him before but no doubts about his ability. I think he's pretty keen, impetuously so, and acts sometimes without thinking. When he's repairing instruments, for instance, he tends to be a bit heavy handed. Occasionally he breaks parts while he's working on an instrument."

Denton felt the company had a responsibility to Fletcher because he had been sent so far from home. Furthermore, Fletcher had just returned from Chilliwack after marrying his girl friend there. Denton discussed the matter with Jennings and they both agreed to give Fletcher only a severe reprimand.

Denton then called Fletcher into his office. He knew that Fletcher was an expert locksmith and had often been employed by management to pick locks whenever keys had been lost. On being questioned, Fletcher admitted breaking into stores but denied picking the lock; he had used a method developed by the other workers of reaching through a hole and shifting the bolt fastener. When Denton asked him the reason for his action, Fletcher explained he had taken a file to make a wrench which he intended to use on his car. Denton was quite surprised; he had assumed the wrench was for maintenance work in the plant. Denton impressed Fletcher with the seriousness of his action. Fletcher then said that he wanted to resign, but Denton advised him not to do so because he believed Fletcher would become a valuable mechanic. Fletcher then explained that he had talked the matter over with Larry Bates, the shop steward, when he had learned that he had been reported. Bates, an older man and an instrument mechanic, had told Fletcher that the management would probably fire him and advised him to resign before this happened. Fletcher accepted Denton's reprimand penitently and vowed he would refuse to pick locks for anyone in the future.

After the interview Denton learned that some of the workers had lost tools from their work kits, and they had accused Fletcher because they knew he could pick locks. One of Denton's foremen reported a rumor that one of the men had told personnel about Fletcher breaking into stores to get even with him.

Following company policy, Denton wrote up the interview with Marvin Fletcher, reporting what Fletcher had told him and his own subsequent action, and then sent the report to Jennings, Johnston, and Purvis.

A week later Jennings called Denton in and said Fletcher was to be fired. Denton disagreed strongly with his proposed action. He felt it was quite possible that they had made a mistake in just reprimanding Fletcher after they had learned he had taken a file from stores for his own use, but he felt that the company decision handed down to Fletcher should not be reversed. Jennings agreed with Denton; both then went to see Johnston to tell him their opinion.

Johnston rejected their opinion. He said the decision was final, and that Denton had to discharge Fletcher. Johnston pointed out that if they didn't fire him they would be setting a precedent and the man caught breaking into stores could not be fired. Denton, however, felt this decision was all wrong; that once a man had been given a verdict by his supervisor, a man higher up in the company could not come and tell the supervisor to reverse it unless new facts had come to light that completely altered the picture and had not been known to the supervisor. Otherwise, Denton felt such action would completely destroy the supervisor's authority.

Johnston replied that any decision could be reviewed by a superior in the company and be reversed in the same way that a lower court decision could be reversed by a higher court. This was the policy of the Clevit Chemical Company; therefore Denton must do as he had been told.

After arguing heatedly with Johnston, Denton finally returned to his office, called in Fletcher, told him top management had reviewed his situation and had decided he must be fired. Upon hearing Denton's statement, Fletcher ejaculated: "What a dirty trick! You talked me out of resigning and now you're firing me. You're just a tool here. Why did I ever listen to you!" With that, Fletcher left.

After Fletcher had been discharged, Bates, the shop steward, went to Johnston to ask the company to take Fletcher back, having him lose only his seniority. Bates explained that Fletcher had been married recently and had brought his wife out from the west. Bates felt that Fletcher had learned his lesson and could be trusted in the future. Johnston agreed to consult with Purvis and tell Bates of his decision by five o'clock that afternoon.

COLUMBIUM MINING CO. LTD.

With the advent of the jet air age, columbium metal, also known as niobium (Nb), increased in value as an alloying agent in high temperature and corrosion-resistant metals. An important deposit of columbium was located at Beverly Lake in Northern Canada in 1946 by a team of geologists under contract to Canadian Metals Ltd., a firm that specialized in the mining and milling of rare metals. By 1949 Canadian Metals had determined that the Beverly Lake deposit was economically recoverable, had worked out a method for concentration of the columbian pentoxide (Nb_2O_5) on a pilot plant basis, and had set up a subsidiary, Columbium Mining Co. Ltd., to mine and mill the ore. Construction at the mine site was begun during the summer of 1949.

Beverly Lake is located about 175 miles west of Hudson's Bay and just south of 65 degrees north latitude. Access to the lake is primarily by air. There are two flights a week from Winnipeg. During the winter, planes land on the lake adjacent to the mine site. During the summer months planes land about five miles east of the mine site on a sandy strip, a narrow winding road permits completion of the trip by a four-wheel-drive truck. Water transport to Beverly Lake is open for about five weeks each year starting in mid-July when most of the ice has melted. Ships, traveling via Hudson's Bay, Chesterfield Inlet, Baker Lake, and the Thelon River, bring in as much equipment and supplies as possible—heavy mining and milling equipment, fuel oil, chemicals, and nonperishable supplies. Perishable foods, personnel, and their personal effects are moved by air.

The terrain around Beverly Lake is hilly. The mining camp itself is located on the side of a hill that rises over one hundred feet above the normal level of the lake. There are no trees or green grass since the camp is built on solid rock. Trees do grow in nearby areas where there is sufficient soil to provide the necessary nourishment and to permit growth of roots. Tree growth is stunted, however, by the northern climate which provides only a short season for growth. The climate during the winters is frequently severe, with temperatures ranging down to −50° Fahrenheit.

Because of its isolation the Beverly Lake Mine is in effect a self-contained community. Dormitories house the 250 men who work in the mine, the mill, the office, and the kitchen. The company charges each man one dollar a day for his room; there are two men in a room, nine feet square. Multifamily apartments house twenty-five of the staff who have brought their families, including children, along. Single staff employees are housed in the staff building, which also accommodates visitors. In addition there are fourteen unmarried female employees—waitresses, nurses, stenographers, and a school teacher—who are housed in a separate dormitory. The buildings are of frame construction, situated on the rocky hillside over the mine itself, and connected by stairways and wooden walkways. There, steam heated viaducts run above the ground. Water pipes run parallel to the steam pipes and are prevented from freezing by the heat transfer from the steam pipes.

Columbium Mining operates a mess hall in which the men eat in two shifts. A separate dining room, known as the Hunt Room, is maintained for the staff. The company charges each employee one dollar per day for the three meals; total cost to the company is about $2.50 per day. Management feels that this is a worthwhile expenditure, however, since good food is of great importance to the men and it is desirable to minimize their dissatisfaction with it. As a result both meat and fish are served at many meals and a man can get as many servings as he wants. Fresh meat and vegetables are flown in every week. Any number of sandwiches a man requests are put in his lunch box. Admittedly the waste of food is great, but this is believed better than skimping on food, which might give rise to grumbling and dissatisfaction. Nevertheless, there always is some grumbling about the "same old food" from the men after they have been at Beverly Lake a few months. Some complain about the lack of milk. A limited quanity of fresh milk is flown in, but only enough to give each child in camp two quarts a week.

The Beverly Lake mining community is similar to many others that have grown up since the end of the war in the Northwest Territories, though the isolation requires some services that mines close to a town do not need. For example, the company operates a hospital and provides the men with banking facilities. As with other mining camps, however, Columbium Mining operates a commissary which stocks clothing, candy, tobacco, pocket books, and other sundry items at prices much the same as in the major Canadian cities; a post office; a curling rink; a recreation hall with a pool room, bowling alleys, snack bar, and a library and reading room. The recreation hall is operated by a committee elected by the employees. This committee employs a janitor, a coffee bar attendant, and bowling pin setters who are paid out of earnings from bowling and pool.

The company offers movies twice a week. It also arranges a dance once a month, though the ratio of men to women causes the dance floor to be turned into somewhat of a "rat race".

Outdoor activities are limited by the climate. Hunting, skiing, and snowshoeing are popular with about twenty men in winter. A few men go skijoring behind a truck across the lake. The few Finns in the camp have built a *sauna,* and its use has become popular with others. Boating and fishing are very popular during the short summer although the swarms of black flies deter some from these sports. In order to stimulate interest the company offers a prize to the person who catches the largest fish each summer. There is a camera club. Some men have developed an interest in collecting rocks. The company also sponsors an annual outing when prizes are offered for tug-of-war, greasy pole, and mucking contests.

The men have developed hobbies of their own. Some have become hi fidelity enthusiasts or amateur radio hams. A few take correspondence courses. Others undertake what is commonly known as "rabbiting"; they obtain by-product silver ore from the mill and clay crucibles from the assay office by "midnight requisitioning", melt out the silver content in the forge shop, and fashion the silver in the machine and pipe shops. Drinking has also become a pastime for some, though when it caused too many men to miss their shifts the liquor was rationed to two bottles per man a month.

Stanley Bracken, general manager of Columbium Mining, considers that the company has progressed fairly well during the first four years of operation. The grade of ore is holding up well, no major trouble has been encountered in concentrating the ore, and operations are being conducted at a small profit. Bracken is concerned, however, whether he is doing enough to attract and keep workers. This concern is heightened by comments from the company doctor that outlets for recreation are inadequate and that those available are not being used sufficiently.

Employee turnover is also a matter of concern to Bracken. It is running about thirteen per cent a month—somewhat lower for staff (engineers, geologists, chemists, superintendents, foremen) and somewhat higher for wage earners. He feels that this rate is not out of line with other mining companies, especially considering the isolation of Beverly Lake. However, the competition for miners and mill men is severe in 1953 and the mining companies generally are trying to make employment as attractive as possible by offering fringe benefits—recreation halls, commissaries, low cost room and board. The Beverly Lake camp has been built with the primary aim of getting into production quickly. The facilities for the men are therefore quite simple.

Bracken recognizes that employee turnover is costly to the company for it requires transportation of men and their personal effects over a thousand miles as well as the expense of training them. Columbium Mining is still not sufficiently well known with mine and mill workers to attract voluntary job inquiries. Nor do job seekers casually drop in to Columbium's Winnipeg employment office which is located at the company's storage depot.

When job vacancies occur, Bracken sends a requisition to Winnipeg. This specifies job titles, e.g., machinist, electrician, pipe fitter, stope miner, driftman, timberman, lab assistant. The employment manager than advertises or personally visits employment offices as far away as Quebec and British Columbia in search of men to fill these jobs. He has not yet been able to develop a file of potential employees on which to draw. Because the company is generally short of men, few references are checked and the information supplied by applicants is usually accepted. As a result, some of the men employed are not adequately qualified, and this in turn increases the rate of turnover.

Bracken has tried to make the rates of pay and fringe benefits as attractive as possible, but he is under continuous pressure to keep his costs down. He relies on the Winnipeg employment manager for information on what other mines are paying. The following paragraphs outline the wages, hours, and fringe benefits.

Wages. The base pay for miners and mill men is at least as high as they can obtain with less isolated mines. Miners are on incentive pay and many earn a bonus larger than their base pay. Mill men are on straight hourly wages. Rates for tradesmen, e.g., carpenters, pipe fitters are about 25 cents above basic union rates, but are still slightly below those offered on construction jobs elsewhere. A five-cent an hour premium is offered wage earners who return for a second year.

Hours. Miners work eight hours a day six days a week. Mill men work twelve-hour shifts six days a week, and thereby increase their gross earnings by 50 per cent as compared to men in other plants on eight-hour shifts. Tradesmen are frequently offered overtime, though their schedule is less regular.

Transportation. Columbium Mining pays each new employee's transportation from point of hire to Winnipeg. It then charges $180 plane fare for the round trip from Winnipeg to Beverly Lake. This is paid by deduction of $30 a month from each man's pay during his first six months. Upon completion of 200 shifts the man is refunded $90. After 300 shifts he is refunded the remaining $90. Thus, an employee pays for at least half his transportation if he quits before working 300 shifts. If he is fired, however, the company pays for it.

Leaves. Each wage earner qualifies for five weeks' leave without pay upon completion of 300 shifts. Transportation is provided to point of hire, not just to Winnipeg. If a man contracts for another 300 shifts within the five weeks, he retains his seniority and obtains the five-cent premium indicated above. Otherwise, he is hired as a new employee. (Salaried personnel receive five weeks' leave also, but with pay.)

Leaves of absence. These are seldom granted. They are approved only in cases of "compassionate demand"—serious illness or death in a man's family. Columbium Mining pays for the transportation.

Medical benefits. Satisfactory medical and x-ray examinations are required as a condition of employment. All employees participate in a compulsory group plan for medical, hospitalization, and surgical benefits. The total cost is $8.20 per month for a single man (slightly higher for men with families), of which the company contributes 50 percent.

Grade school. Columbium Mining employs a teacher who operates a one-room school for fourteen youngsters in grades one to eight. She also operates a kindergarten once a week to give parents with younger children some free time.

Services and equipment supplies. Charges for room and board are one dollar a day each. Each man is issued a bed roll when first employed for which he is charged $65. Deductions are made from pay for this, and he receives a refund at the end of 300 shifts if he turns it in undamaged; normal wear is allowed for. The company does each man's laundry for three dollars a month. The supply of working clothes is the responsibility of each man.

Most of the employees attracted to Beverly Lake are single and in their middle or late twenties. A primary attraction for some is the opportunity to save and invest money. Several individuals have accumulated sums of $25,000 to $50,000. The company has tried to help these men by inviting to the mine two salesmen representing mutual investment funds and savings plans. Other men have set goals of saving sufficient to buy a house or start a small business later when they settle elsewhere. Still others set a savings goal of a few thousand dollars which they plan to "blow" in one grand spree.

Among the staff personnel the attraction for employment is the opportunity for responsibility which they could not gain as quickly with larger companies in other areas. For the ambitious, incentive to stay beyond one year is enhanced by the chance for promotion due to the rate of personnel turnover. This applies to a lesser degree to some of the wage earners who show promise of becoming shift bosses after a few years.

Bracken employs no personnel manager. In one of his weekly staff meetings he raised the problem of attracting and keeping qualified men and asked for suggestions from his supervisors. He pointed out that any changes suggested would have to be considered with a view to costs.

GRAY DRAKE AIRLINES CASE

Tim Botz was a student at Eastern State University in Dover, New Hampshire. He was 21 years of age and a native of Kellte, Maine, a small town right across the New Hampshire state line.

Tim's major was business administration. During the fall quarter of his senior year at Eastern State, he signed up for a nine-credit transportation course, which was to continue over the remainder of his senior year. As a part of this course, he was assigned to do research for Gray Drake Airlines, a small independent company that operated scheduled flights linking the main cities of the New England States. Gray Drake had flights connecting New York; Boston; Portland, Maine; Dover and Portsmouth, New Hampshire; Derby and New Haven, Connecticut; Middlebury, Vermont; Lexington, Massachusetts; and Concord, New Hampshire. They had 20 planes in use. The crews consisted of flight attendants and pilots. There were 50 of the former working for the company and 30 pilots (see Figure 1). The company's home office was in Dover.

The directors of Gray Drake Airlines interviewed Tim at a board meeting

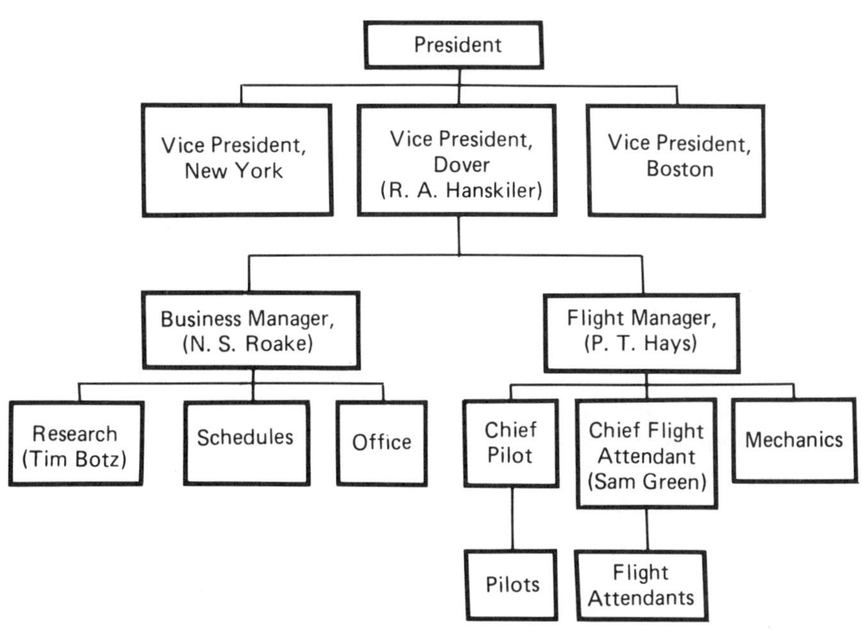

FIGURE 1 GRAY DRAKE AIRLINES ORGANIZATION CHART

and expressed pleasure at having a student from the University do research for them. Consequently, they created a nonsalaried position, director of research, for Tim. He was to be given full access to company files, office space, telephone, mimeograph work, etc. The board of directors recommended that Tim work on the problems of publicity and passenger comfort.

In September, when Tim started to work for the company, he was taken around by Mr. N. S. Roake, his immediate superior (see Figure 1), and introduced to the department heads. It was made clear at this time that anything that Tim suggested, if it had the approval of Mr. Roake, was to be followed. An interoffice memo was also sent around explaining Tim's position and asking that cooperation be accorded him. By October, Tim had decided that the best way to gain the information he needed would be to distribute questionnaires to the passengers. Tim felt that the speediest way to do this would entail having the chief flight attendant distribute the questionnaires on his periodic rounds of checks on the flight attendants.[1] The flight attendants would distribute the questionnaires to the passengers as they embarked on their trip and collect them at the end of the flight. The flight attendant could then either mail the completed questionnaires to Dover or give them to the chief flight attendant on his next trip. This plan was approved of by Mr. Roake, as were the questionnaires. Tim then personally made a pretesting by going on several flights and administering the questionnaires. By the middle of November, he felt that he was actually ready to begin work.

Tim then went to the chief flight attendant to explain the procedure to him. He was surprised to find that he had had previous contact with the chief flight attendant, Sam Green. Tim had first met Mr. Green in the summer of 1953 when, in connection with a sociology class at Eastern State, he had done a project on personality research. Among those on his list to interview, a list of names of volunteers furnished by the instructor, Green's name occurred. Consequently, Tim had two personal interviews with Green during that summer. During the interviews, Sam was quite agreeable and furnished Tim with much helpful information about himself and his background.

Sam Green was 26 years old. In 1945 when he graduated from a Maine high school, he entered the service for three years. Upon returning, he started at Eastern State University. He majored in architecture and also pledged a fraternity. After three years of college, during which he received many low grades, he went to work as a flight attendant for Gray Drake Airlines. Two years later, because of his leadership ability, he was offered the job of chief flight attendant. He had held this job about six months when Tim first started doing survey work for the company.

When Tim entered Green's office to discuss his current research for the airlines, Tim felt that Green was distant or cool compared with what Tim expected, and he decided that perhaps, for some reason, Green did not wish to remember their previous encounter. Hence Tim did not mention it but

[1]On Gray Drake Airlines, because the flights were so short, there were no stewardesses. The flight attendant undertook the necessary duties concerning the passengers, baggage, mail, etc.

merely presented his plan concerning the distribution and collection of the questionnaires. Tim was aware of the interoffice letter sent out to all the men explaining his position with the airlines and the fact that all the personnel were to cooperate with him. He mentioned this to Green and received only a grunt of recognition. During the interview, Green talked very little and seemed to focus his attention elsewhere. Tim left the interview without a feeling of accomplishment but did feel that he had tried his best.

At the beginning of the first week in December, Tim left 1000 questionnaires[2] with the secretary in Green's office (Green was not in then). Tim attached a memo reminding Green of the procedure to be followed. Tim felt that this was a good time to start distribution, as the Christmas rush was nearing. He mentioned this in his note to Green. The following day Tim checked with the secretary and learned that she had personally given the materials to Green the previous afternoon. She commented that Green had read the memo and shrugged his shoulders. But she did see that when he left for his weekly trip he stuffed over half of the questionnaires into his brief case. This seemed like a good omen to Tim. During the two weeks that followed, Tim expected to receive some of the completed questionnaires either by mail or personally from Green; but none came in. As Green did not return to home base, Tim concluded that everything was tied up by the Christmas rush. As the end of the school quarter neared and he was busy with tests, Tim decided to let things rest until January.

The second week of January, Tim returned to his office at Gray Drake Airlines expecting to find many completed questionnaires. However, none were there; and, in checking with the secretary, he learned that Green had left no message for him. Tim then went to see Mr. Roake and explained what had happened. Roake was busy gathering material to take to an airlines convention the following day in New York. His only suggestion was that Tim see Green and get to the bottom of the situation. Tim returned to the office, picked up another batch of questionnaires, and went into Green's office. After an exchange of pleasantries, the following discussion took place:

Tim: Well, Sam, I've been waiting for a report on my questionnaires, but as yet have received no information, nor have I received any completed questionnaires. So, I concluded that you brought them back with you. Do you have them?

Sam: Yes, some were completed. I stuck them somewhere. Let's see now. [He rummaged through several desk drawers and finally pulled out about seventy-five and handed them to Tim.]

Tim: [Tim glanced over them for a moment and noted that they were correctly filled out.] But Sam, what about the rest? You know during the Christmas rush, both Mr. Roake and I agreed, was an ideal time to query our

[2]A copy of this questionnaire appears at the end of this case.

passengers. And you were fully indoctrinated with the policies of distribution and the importance of this survey. What happened?

Sam: Well, we were pretty busy. I did what I could. [Pause.] Excuse me, but I have a luncheon date and must be going.

Tim: Before you go, here are some more questionnaires. Please try to get them completed and back by your next trip. You'll be back in about two weeks, won't you?

Sam: Sure, sure, kid, I'll see you in a couple of weeks.

Tim felt discouraged, but he felt that a start could be made with the seventy-five completed ones he had. He could begin coding them at any rate.

During the next two weeks, no questionnaires were returned, and Tim began to worry. He personally contacted seven flight attendants who came into Dover during his hours at the office. From four of the seven he learned that they had not received any questionnaires to distribute from Green, and three said they had been handed a few by Green who mumbled something about "some college kid's scheme." As a result, Tim felt they were completely ignorant of the whole research project. Tim explained fully to each of them what the project was aimed at, his part in it, what their share of the job was, and also showed them a copy of the interoffice memo written by Roake authorizing utmost cooperation for the project. The men all seemed interested and Tim left fifty questionnaires with each of them to distribute that day. They promised to return them promptly.

Within the next week all but 100 of these were returned completed and with requests for more. However, as yet there was no word from Green. Tim felt that the project was definitely under way. He concluded that perhaps he had been wrong in giving the job to Green to take care of. But as Tim had only been able to contact ten flight attendants personally at Dover, he saw no other way to distribute the questionnaires except through the fieldman, Green. In repeated attempts to see Green during his next few days at the home office, Tim met with no success. Green was either too busy to be disturbed or he was out. As Tim felt that he had almost exhausted the supply of new passengers coming to and going from Dover (most of the planes flying from Dover carried the same passengers on business trips to and from New York, Boston, and Portland), he felt that in order to get a well-rounded and unbiased survey it was mandatory that he reach the opinion of passengers in the six other outlying cities where Gray Drake planes flew. Consequently, he wrote an interoffice memo (shown at the end of this case), to Green and also sent copies to Mr. Roake, Mr. Hays (Green's boss), and Mr. Hanskiler, the vice-president in charge of the Dover port. Eight days passed and Tim received neither an answer from Green nor any completed questionnaires. He wondered what to do.

Gray Drake Airlines Survey Questionnaire

To improve Gray Drake Airlines' service to you, we would appreciate your completing the following questionnaire (sealing it if you wish) and returning it to your flight attendant. You may omit any question that you do not wish to answer.

At what town did you board? ______

At what town will you get off? ______

About how many times have you flown by commercial, scheduled airlines in the past year? ______

About how many times have you flown by Gray Drake Airlines in the past year? ______

Please rate the ground personnel that served you before this flight:

Below average *Average* *Excellent*

Courtesy ______
Appearance ______
Efficiency ______
Willingness to cooperate ______
Comments: ______

Please rate the flight attendant now on duty regarding:

Below average *Average* *Excellent*

Courtesy ______
Appearance ______
Efficiency ______
Willingness to cooperate ______

Comments: ______

What is the purpose of your trip today?

______Business only______Recreation only ______ Business and recreation ______Vacation ______I live there ______Visit to my family

Other ______

If the purpose of your trip is business, what type of business are you engaged in?______

What has influenced you most in choosing to fly Gray Drake Airlines?

______ Newspaper advertising ______Radio advertising ______Friends ______Mail addressed to me ______News item ______Other

If Gray Drake Airlines' service had not been available, how would you have made this trip?

______Automobile ______Train ______Bus ______Another airline ______Uncertain

If Gray Drake Airlines' service were discontinued:

Would you, as an individual, be inconvenienced? ______Yes ______No
Would it impair the efficiency of your business? ______Yes ______No
Would it place your organization at a disadvantage? ______Yes ______No

Do you have any comments regarding this aircraft? ______

______

Is your annual income under $5000 ______over $5000?______
Would you mind giving us your name and home address?
Name: ______Mr. ______ Mrs. ______Miss
Address______________________________
Would you mind giving us your approximate age?
Additional remarks regarding service, schedules, personnel, etc.

Thank you very much,

TIMOTHY JONAS BOTZ, *Director*
Gray Drake Airlines Research
Eastern State University

Interoffice Memorandum

February 10, 1954

To: Sam Green
From: Tim Botz
Subject: Questionnaire Distribution

I have found it extremely difficult to work out a method whereby the inflight questionnaires can be distributed to flight attendant personnel. My many attempts to discuss this project with you have met with disinterest and abruptness, which I am at a loss to comprehend. I do lack the necessary instructions from your office in order to execute this portion of the project.

As it is my understanding that you were to cooperate with me in this endeavor, I am therefore making this final attempt to solicit your help. I naturally desire to get this work under way as soon as possible, and my memorandum of the eleventh[3] sufficiently covered the implements necessary to the project.

Your response at the earliest possible date will be greatly appreciated.

Respectfully,

TIMOTHY JONAS BOTZ

cc: N. S. Roake
P. T. Hays
R. A. Hanskiler

---

[3] This refers to the first memo Tim sent to Green, accompanying the first group of questionnaires left in Green's office.

JACK DOBBINS' PROBLEM
—DAVID R. KENERSON

Jack Dobbins left the vice-president's office feeling elated as well as concerned about the new responsibilities he was about to assume. Ralph Barnes, State College's vice-president and comptroller, had just told Jack of the Executive Committee's decision to appoint him superintendent of buildings. Jack was concerned because Mr. Barnes had gone into considerably more detail about the many management and morale problems among the college's custodial workers and their supervisors than in any previous interviews.

THE SITUATION

State College was located in a rural area just outside St. Louis, Missouri. It was one of several universities run by the state and was less than ten years old. In this short time it had grown rapidly to 9,500 students, the majority of whom lived off campus and commuted to school each day.

The superintendent's major function was to plan, organize, direct, and control the activities of about eighty employees and supervisors involved in keeping all college buildings except for the dormitories, in clean and orderly condition. There were ten major buildings ranging in size from 24,000 square feet to 137,000 square feet. Total square footage under the jurisdiction of the superintendent amounted to 1,025,000. This space included classrooms, faculty offices, administration and library buildings, student center, and so on.

Of the eighty employees in the department, sixteen were women, and sixty-four were men, including the four supervisors who reported to the superintendent. Starting wages for maids had just been raised to $2,580 per year from $2,300. By some quirk of the state's budgeting system, starting wage for male janitors had just been lowered to $2,700 per year from $2,900. Employees could receive only one raise per year, usually on July 1st at the beginning of the fiscal year. It was within the superintendent's authority to grant raises up to a maximum of 10 percent the first year, 7 percent the second year, and 5 percent the third year. In order to qualify for the maximum, however, employees had to receive a rating of "outstanding." The work week was forty hours. Vacation leave of ten working days was allowed while sick leave was accrued at the rate of one day per month to a maximum of thirty days. Group life insurance, Blue Cross & Blue Shield hospitalization were available by payroll deduction at employee expense. State employees were not covered under Social Security but did participate in the state retirement system under which both the state and the employee contributed. The total budget for the department amounted to about $280,000, with $250,000 for wages and salaries and $30,000 for supplies and materials.

Turnover among employees was unusually high. In July and August of 1967, Turnover amounted to 15 percent and 20 percent. Typically in this type of work in universities, turnover normally runs 100 percent per year. Most of the employees were Negroes, and the majority of them were holding down other full-time jobs outside the college.

DEPARTMENTAL WORK ORGANIZATION

There was no organization chart for the department; but Jack Dobbins felt it would look pretty much like the chart shown in Figure 1. Work was organized on the basis of special tasks. Although supervisors were assigned responsibility for different buildings, work was specialized into floor-mopping crews, followed up by waxing and buffing crews. Supervisors decided when particular floors were mopped, waxed and buffed and coordinated and scheduled the different crews in proper sequence. The day crews worked largely on rest-room detail in all buildings with special groups assigned for carpet cleaning, window washing, and straightening and cleaning up meeting rooms before and after meetings.

JACK DOBBINS' BACKGROUND

Jack Dobbins was a retired military man with twenty years service in various posts as management analyst and operations and training officer. As a young man, he had graduated from a midwestern engineering school. On resigning from the military, he had enrolled as a student in a Chicago College of Business Administration in order to earn a second degree in management and business administration. At forty-five he was looking forward to a new career in a new environment in a field where he felt his experience, knowledge, and training could be most effectively used.

During the last hour and one-half in his talk with Mr. Barnes, he had learned much about the current problems of the department. Harry Kraft, the man he was replacing, had come to State College when the first students were admitted. He was about fifty years old, of limited education, and with a varied background as foreman or supervisor in construction firms. When the college was small with only a few buildings and few employees, he was reasonably successful. However, four months previously, Harry had fired one of the supervisors, with rather disastrous results. Rank-and-file employees were indignant and had sent a petition all the way to the state capital in an attempt to get Harry's decision reversed. Some were threatening not to come to work. Morale was low, turnover high, and top officials of the college as well as the department itself were being deluged with complaints about the lack of good housekeeping in all buildings. Toilets were not adequately serviced, classrooms and offices frequently went untouched for a week at a time.

Although Jack was concerned, he was not dismayed because he felt strongly that his recent exposure to a wide variety of management courses

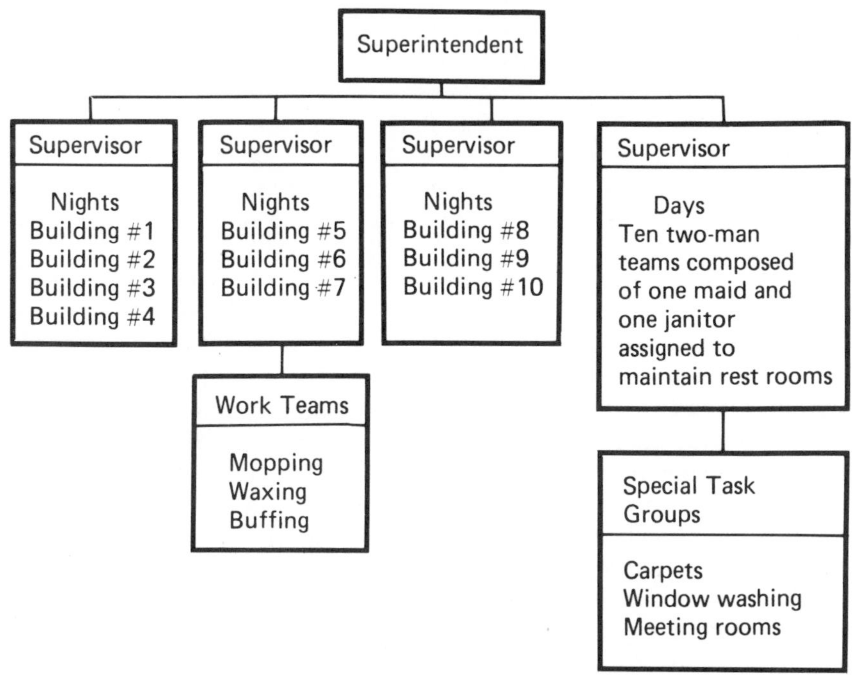

would make it relatively easy to show substantial improvements in this department, even despite the fact that no raises could be given to any employees before the next fiscal year eleven months away.

JOHN ANDERSON

John Anderson was a man of fifty-four. He had spent much of his working life as a personnel specialist with a number of large companies, usually in the area of training and development. His experience included jobs on both sides of the Atlantic, and he was familiar with many of the latest approaches to training and development in both the United States and Britain.

Anderson had returned to North America in 1971, after a four-year stay in England with a major manufacturing firm where he had occupied the post of Training Director. He had returned to accept a job with the Potterton

Corporation, a large consumer durables manufacturer, as Manager of Management and Organizational Development for the Stag division.

Stag employed some 45,000 people and stretched across the country. Plants were either located near sources of supply, or close to major customers, and varied in size from 2,000 to 8,000 employees.

There were three levels of organization in the company. At the corporate level, Anderson reported to a vice-president of Manpower Development and Industrial Relations. There was a small corporate staff of eight specialists in the areas of management and organizational development.

At the divisional level, each division in turn had its own staffs. At Stag, Management and Organizational Development, under Anderson, consisted of twenty specialists.

And finally, each plant had training and development people within the personnel function. These managers reported directly to the Plant Personnel Director, but also worked closely with the divisional staff. Their loyalties were often torn between the two. In the larger plants they tended to make themselves more independent of divisional influence, while in the smaller plants they were often loaded down with several other jobs and felt that the demands placed on them by divisional people were unrealistic.

When John Anderson took over as head of the Stag division training and development staff, morale was low. Of the twenty staff specialists, four were senior "career" people who had a broad range of experience in the training field. There were seven younger persons who had university degrees and who saw themselves as "professional" trainers. The remaining nine staff positions were filled with persons between the ages of 35 and 60 who had been moved into the management training function from other areas, for a variety of reasons. Several had been line managers in plants which had been reorganized, moved, or closed; a number had been timestudy men and skill trainers in the plants (that is, they had been involved in teaching workers how to use machines, etc.); and two were ex-sergeants whose training experience had been in teaching trades or specific combat skills. There was little sense of cohesion among these groups. This problem was magnified by the fact that, with the exception of two older men, none of the training staff in the Stag division had been in their present jobs for longer than four years. Fifty percent had less than two years service with Stag.

Anderson called a meeting of the entire training and development staff of the Stag division on his third day on the job. At the meeting he introduced himself and gave a short resume of his background and experience. He asked each of the people at the meeting to introduce themselves and to describe their activities in training to date. Anderson then talked about his views on management and organizational development for about twenty minutes, and put forward his conception of the goals of the divisional staff. He then asked for comments and there was a discussion for another half hour. At the close of the meeting, Anderson said that his prime goal was to build an effective team within the Stag division. He stressed that he would be available for consultation at all times, and he encouraged every member of the staff to visit him in his office to discuss any problems they might be encountering.

Within the next few days, Anderson circulated a memo to all staff, listing his objectives for the group, and asking for comments, changes, additions or deletions, from anyone. He also converted an open area of the office into a lounge by bringing a number of coffee tables and easy chairs in. He made a point of appearing regularly at 10:45 a.m. and 3:15 p.m. for coffee, and usually stayed for about twenty minutes, chatting with whoever happened along. Within a week, almost everyone in the office came for coffee at these times. After a month on the job, Anderson invited the staff for a barbecue one Saturday evening at his home. The party was informal and friendly and everyone seemed to enjoy themselves.

Three months after he had taken over, Anderson moved the divisional training staff to its own quarters, which included facilities for various training activities, and had a regular dining room, lounge and small bar. The site also contained living accommodation for 25 people, and became used for a number of residential training activities. The daily coffee meetings continued, the staff all had lunch together in the dining room, and most of them stayed for a drink at 6:00 P.M., as the bar opened for people on residential courses. A number of social gatherings were organized by various members of the staff. Sometimes these were held at private homes, and sometimes the facilities of the training center were used if no training activities were scheduled. At the suggestion of one staff member, a club tie was designed with the figure of a stag leaping in the air emblazoned on it. This became the "Stag Club" tie. It could be worn by members of the divisional training staff or by individuals who had attended training activities at the center and was a good seller at the bar. On any given day, 60 percent of the divisional staff could be seen wearing the "club" tie.

At the end of his first year as Manager of Management and Organization Development at Stag, John Anderson felt he had improved morale tremendously. He also felt he had increased the level of motivation and achievement of his staff. He noted that there was now a constant flow of ideas and suggestions from the staff on a wide variety of problems. They seemed to have organized themselves informally into a number of groups with common professional interests. Membership in these groups often overlapped. There was a great deal of informal communication on problems; suggestions and help were freely solicited and offered. The dichotomies of old/young, professional/nonprofessional, management training/skill training, management development/organization development, and so on, all appeared to have been broken down. Anderson felt that he had, in fact, created a "team" at Stag.

However, problems began to occur in divisional relationships with both the plants and the corporate staff. The corporate group, in an attempt to unify management development and organizational development policy throughout the company, began to set goals and objectives for adoption at all levels. The changes required were significant, and called into question much of what had been done in the company before. Corporate staff spent a large amount of time visiting the divisions, attempting to get agreement on the new policies. In a number of cases they reported back to the corporate vice-president that they were meeting with marked resistance from Stag. They felt that Anderson was blocking them on many occasions, and that he was being "uncooperative." The vice-president met with Anderson and talked the matter over with him. Anderson stated that he had no intention of being uncooperative, but that the corporate people expected too much too soon. He made the point that he had a very full program of activities on his own slate and that his people were overworked already. As soon as they could manage it, he said, they would begin to integrate their activities with the new corporate policy.

Late in 1972, the corporate vice-president was informed that the Stag division had not compiled the data for a government grant for training of minority groups. The potential loss to the company was approximately $500,000, as many of the Stag plants were located in areas where the labor force contained a high percentage of minority groups, and the company had been active in training and employing people from all these groups. Without data to back up their claim for assistance, they would not receive the government grants available for these activities. The vice-president immediately contacted Anderson, who admitted it had been an oversight on the part of his staff.

Ten days later the data was on the vice-president's desk, and two of his own staff were in his office maintaining that the figures represented only about 60 percent of the actual training that had been done. They argued that there was another $200,000 of grant money not being claimed. As a result, the vice-president sent the two men into Stag to see if they could gather the missing data in the little time left. They managed to recover another $125,000.

This issue brought to light a number of complaints from the corporate staff. They maintained that Anderson was building an empire for himself at Stag and that he wanted to "go it alone" without the aid of the central staffs. The plants also began to complain. Several of the Plant Personnel Directors contacted the vice-president and complained that various training and development packages were being shoved down their throats. They said they wanted their own plant people to have more autonomy, and questioned the usefulness of divisional staff. The vice-president pointed out that the reason for having divisional staffs was to try to unify the training and development program across plants, and to spread the overhead of specialists in a number of areas.

Privately, the vice-president was worried. While he could not be sure of the accuracy of the figure, he was informed by members of his own staff that

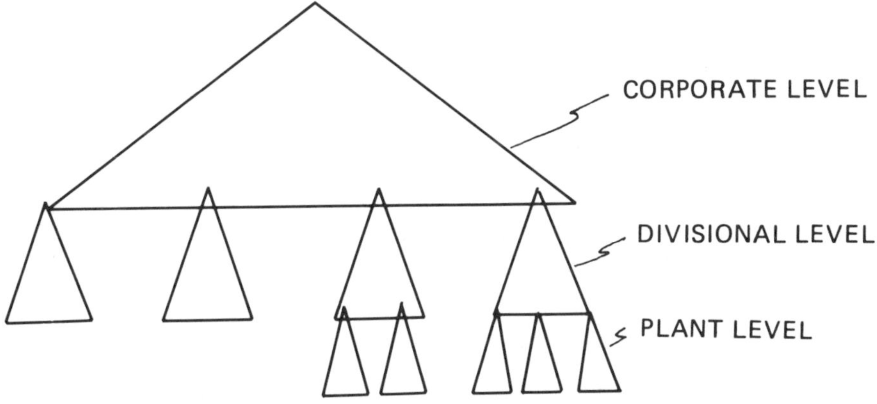

FIGURE ONE "LINKING PINS" (INDIVIDUALS MEETING WITH TWO LEVELS OF GROUPS)

Stag had lost about $75,000 of federal grant money by poor administration and control procedures. He was also disturbed by the "club" atmosphere at Stag's training center. He wondered if it served as a unifying or divisive force for the company as a whole. And he noted that while Anderson had a very close rapport with his subordinates, and they were very loyal to him, he adopted a very protective attitude towards them, and effectively screened them from other parts of the corporation. This had resulted in a number of other administrative problems, none quite as serious as the government grant, but otherwise annoying to the corporate group, and, to some extent, to the plants.

The vice-president decided that a tighter integration of the three levels of the company was needed. He saw the system of overall goals and objectives providing part of this linkage, but also decided to explore the idea of building interlocking teams within each functional area, using Likert's "linking pin" approach. His basic idea is demonstrated by Figure 1, below, showing the linkage between the corporate level, divisional level, and plant level in the company.

In order to explore the idea more carefully, the vice-president arranged for a workshop where representatives from each level could learn about team building and could discuss its benefits and weaknesses in the light of the actual situation within the company. He asked that each division choose several representatives to attend the two-day meeting, and that some of the larger plants be represented by one or two people as well. The workshop was limited to training and development personnel, since they would ultimately be involved in any implementation of a program of team building within the company.

Stag division was represented by Anderson and one of his senior subordinates. It seemed to the vice-president that they stayed out of the discussions as much as possible for most of the two days, contributing very little overall. During the final session, however, which was centered on sketching preliminary outlines for a plan of implementation, they both vigorously attacked the idea. It seemed to the vice-president that their arguments were not aimed at attacking the concept of team building, but rather that they were against the idea of the teams being built from the top level, downwards. They maintained that each division should maintain autonomy over how its training and development programs were designed and implemented. The workshop ended on a confused note, with some divisional people expressing interest in a corporate-initiated team building program, and others either remaining neutral, or going against the idea.

In the light of the developments at the workshop, the vice-president came to the conclusion that Anderson was building his own empire at Stag, to the detriment of the corporation as a whole. Within two months the vice-president submitted a plan to the Executive Committee for the reorganization of the Manpower Development and Industrial Relations function. The plan called for the break-up of the divisional groups; the manpower and industrial relations function was to be handled on a regional basis, with policy being set at the corporate, rather than the divisional level. It was argued that this approach would result in a unified approach to manpower problems over the entire firm.

The proposal was accepted by the Executive Committee for immediate implementation. Anderson was promoted to Corporate Manager of Employee Benefit Systems. The vice-president moved his corporate staff into the quarters of the now-defunct Stag divisional group. The center was renamed the Corporate Management Training Center. The "Stag Club" passed out of existence.

THE KINGSTON COMPANY

The Kingston Company, located in Ontario, was a medium-sized man ufacturing firm which made a line of machine parts and marketed them to plants in the southeastern section of the province. Harold Kingston, the president and majority shareholder in the company held a Master of Business Administration degree from an American university, and was a vigorous supporter of the usefulness and value of a graduate business education. As a result, he had on his staff a group of four young MBA's to whom he referred as "the think group" or "the troubleshooters."

The four members of the group ranged in age from the youngest at 23 to the oldest at 35, with the two intermediate members being 27. They were all from different universities, and had different academic backgrounds. Their areas of interest were Marketing, Organizational Behavior, Operations Research, and Finance. All had been hired simultaneously and placed together in the "think group" by Mr. Kingston because, as he put it, "With their diverse knowledge and intelligence they ought to be able to solve any of this company's problems."

For their first month on the job, the "Big Four," as they became known in the firm, familiarized themselves with the company's operations and employees. They spent a half-day every week in conference with Mr. Kingston and his executive committee, discussing the goals and objectives of the company, and going over the history of the major policy decisions made by the firm over the years. While the process of familiarization was a continuing one, the group decided after four weeks that it had uncovered some of the firm's problems and that it would begin to set out recommendations for the solution of these problems.

From the beginning, the members of the group had worked long hours and could usually be found in the office, well after the plant had closed, discussing their findings and trading opinions and ideas. The approach to problem solving which they adopted was to attack each problem as a group and to pool their ideas. This seemed to give a number of different slants to the problems, and many times helped clear away the bias which inevitably crept into each member's analyses.

Mike Norton, the finance specialist, and the youngest member of the group, and Jim Thorne and Dave Knight, the operations research man and the behavior management man, respectively, spent a lot of time together outside the work environment. They seemed to have similar interests, playing tennis and golf together, and generally having a keen interest in sports. They managed to get tickets together to watch the local professional football games, and ice-hockey tickets, etc. The fourth and oldest member of the group, Cy Gittinger did not share these interests. The only "sports" he played were shuffleboard and croquet, and he didn't join the other three too often after work for a beer in a local bar, since he also abstained from alcohol.

The group, from the beginning, was purposely unstructured. All the members agreed to consider themselves equals. They occupied one large office, each having a desk in an opposite corner, with the middle of the room acting as a "common." Basic decisions were usually made with the four men pacing about in the open area, leaning against the walls and desks, and either squeezing or bouncing "worry balls" of a rubber-putty substance, used for cleaning typewriters, off the walls. The atmosphere was completely informal, and the rest of the firm kidded the members of the group about the inordinately large amount of typewriter cleaner used in the room when there were no typewriters to be seen.

While consensus was not required, the group found that they were able to agree on a course of action most of the time. When they were unable to do so, they presented their differing opinions to Mr. Kingston, in whose hands the final decision rested. They acted in a purely staff capacity, and unless requested to help a particular manager, and authorized to do so by Mr. Kingston, they confined their reports to the president and his executive committee. Reports were usually presented in written form, with all four members of the group present and contributing verbal support and summation.

The group realized that working in close contact would result in strained relations on occasion, and they agreed to attempt to express their feelings accurately and try to understand issues from the other members' point of view. Jokes about "happiness boys," "peddlers," and formula babies" were bandied about, and each of the four made a conscious effort to see the biases introduced by his field of interest. Attempts at controlling the discussion and establishing a leadership position were handled by pointing out the behavior to the individual involved.

However, as the months passed, there seemed to be a growing uneasiness in the relationship between Norton, Thorne and Knight, and the fourth member, Gittinger. The three brought their feelings out one day when they were playing golf. At the nineteenth hole, over a drink, Thorne commented on the amount of time Gittinger spent talking to Mr. Kingston in his office. They all spent a great deal of time out of their office talking to managers and workers all through the plant, gathering data on various problems, but, Thorne remarked, Gittinger seemed to confine his activities to the upper levels of management far more than the others did. The other two had made the same observation, but felt that it was really hard to put a finger on anything "wrong" about consulting with the president continually. They agreed that their fact finding did not generally require as much time at higher levels as Gittinger was devoting, but when the point was brought up in subsequent discussion at the office, Cy explained that in order to get information from Mr. Kingston, he found an "indirect" approach, which entailed a certain amount of small talk, was most successful.

After the group had been functioning for ten months, Kingston called them in to a meeting with his executive committee and went through an appraisal of their performance. He was, he said, tremendously pleased that his "think group" had performed so well, and he felt vindicated in his belief in the potency of applying the skills learned in graduate business school. His executives added their words of praise. Then Mr. Kingston brought up a suggestion he said he and Cy Gittinger had been discussing for the past month and a half, to appoint one of the group members as a coordinator. The coordinator's job would be to form a liaison between Kingston and the executive committee on the one hand, and the group on the other, and also to guide the group, as a result of the closer ties of the coordinator with the management team, in establishing a set of priorities for different problem areas. When Kingston had finished describing the proposal, which, it seemed, met with his and the committee's approval, Jim Thorne remarked that this procedure seemed to be unnecessary in the light of the previous smooth functioning of the group, and began to explain that such a change would upset the structure and goals of the group. He was interrupted by Mr. Kingston who said he had an important engagement. "We'll leave the working out of all the details to you men," he said. "We don't want to impose anything on you, and we have all agreed that you should be the ones to work out just how this new plan can be implemented." At this point, the meeting ended.

As the group walked back to their office, Gittinger was the only one who talked. He wondered aloud who would be the most suitable man for the coordinator's job, and repeated Kingston's words, citing the advantages that would accrue to the company with the creation of such a position. Since it was 4:45 P.M., they all cleared their desks and left the plant together, splitting up outside to go home.

At 6:00 P.M., Thorne called Norton to ask him what he thought about the developments of the afternoon. The latter expressed surprise, anger, and resentment that the decision had been made without the consultation of the group, and remarked that Knight, to whom he had just been talking, felt the same way. The trio made arrangements to meet for dinner at their downtown athletic club at 7:00 P.M. that evening to discuss the situation.

MARTIN JOHNSTON, INC.

Kay Halloran was a long-time employee of Martin Johnston, Inc., a large Canadian investment dealer. She worked in the accounting department, but had a job which brought her into close contact with the bond traders and salesmen in the firm. Essentially, her job was to keep track of the inventory of bonds held by the firm and to circulate a list of these holdings, twice a day, to everyone involved in selling or trading.

Martin Johnston, Inc. had its head office in Montreal, and branches across Canada, in the United States and Europe. One of its major activities was trading bonds, primarily in the Canadian market, but often internationally as well. Unlike the equity side of the investment business, which is dominated by trading on large exchanges where prices are posted openly and trades are made on the floor and recorded immediately, the bond market operates as a network of firms who buy and sell from one another, both for clients and for their own accounts. When a firm wishes to buy or sell certain bonds, its traders must call a number of other firms to establish the going price. This may vary between dealers. While the "spreads" (the differences between the price offered by one dealer versus other) are not usually wide, the volume of trading (often in the millions of dollars at a time) makes these differences critical.

Typically, a trading operation is set up with a staff of traders sitting around a large desk, each with a panel in front of him of fifty to a hundred direct telephone lines to other traders around the world. At the touch of a button the telephone will ring in another dealer's office and the process of buying or selling may take place. The trader's function is primarily to know who is willing to, or has to, buy or sell certain bonds.

The bond market is very much an open trading situation where timing, knowledge and skill are crucial. All trades are made verbally, and a trade, once made, is never reneged on. Among other things, it is essential that traders know what bonds their firm owns, or does not own, and what they are prepared to buy or sell. To aid them, each dealer compiles "position sheets" which reflect the holdings of the firm, and the average prices at which each type of bond was purchased (or sold, if sold short). These sheets are kept as current as possible and are circulated to all traders.

Kay Halloran's job was to compile these "position sheets" every morning, and make sure that they were on all the necessary desks prior to the commencement of work. During the day, as records of trades were made available to her she updated the sheets and issued new ones after lunch. Since trading could often be hectic, with several people making trades with other dealers simultaneously, the accuracy of these position sheets was crucial. If, for instance, one of the traders had sold all of the holdings of a particular issue without a second trader being aware of it, the same bonds could be sold a second time. This, of course, meant that the firm would have to purchase enough of the bonds elsewhere in order to fulfill its second sale. Should the price of the bonds rise in the interim, this could be a costly error.

All of the traders worked in one room so that as they completed transactions they shouted the details to their colleagues or passed notes to one another. The trading desk at Martin Johnston, Inc. was made up of specialists in various types of bonds who mainly traded only in their segment of the market—e.g., long-term government bonds, provincial bonds, municipal bonds, corporate bonds, etc. While it might appear on the surface that these segments were different enough to prevent overlap, there was in fact a close relationship in the prices of bonds between segments. For instance, if long-term government bonds changed in price, short-term governments often moved to maintain some sort of relationship as did bonds in all other segments of the market. Thus, if a large trade occurred in one segment, the various other segments of the market could also change. The bond traders therefore operated closely together, and spent a lot of time discussing strategy and forecasts for the market.

In 1964 Kay Halloran had been with Martin Johnston, Inc. for twenty-four years. She had completed two years of high school, was married and had two grown children. She was well liked by the bond traders at Martin Johnston. She had a happy disposition and she was able to laugh at the constant joking and teasing that was directed at any women who entered this all-male domain. Her arrival was always greeted with enthusiasm by the traders, not only because they liked her, but because she brought the all-important position sheets with her. She usually stopped to talk with various people for a half hour or so every time she made an appearance in the trading room.

During 1964 the company had begun a study of the application of computer systems to the investment banking business. Because of the large numbers of transactions in both stocks and bonds, the first application was in the billing area. Contracts could be dispatched with greater speed and accuracy and client accounts kept up to date more easily with machine accounting. However, the cost of a computer was such that other applications would have to be found if the firm were to begin to break even or save money from its application.

A team of systems analysts spent the spring and summer of 1964 examining possible avenues for extending the use of the computer. One of these uses became apparent rather quickly. With a simple program, the computer could print up to date position sheets for the bond trading operation every hour or two. The accuracy of these sheets would represent a major advantage for the traders who previously had to rely on their own hurried changes as they heard announcements of trades being made around them. It was customary to find one or more errors in the figures on the old morning position sheets after the traders had pencilled in several changes. If machine-tabulated sheets could be distributed hourly there would be less pressure on the traders to keep their own sheets current, and the likelihood of errors in trading as a result of incorrect data would be greatly decreased.

In September of 1964 the new system was introduced to the bond traders. Each time they made a trade they marked out the basic details on a small sheet of carbonized paper, placed one copy in a vacuum tube which transported it to the computer room one floor below, and kept one copy for themselves, to be used to amend the current position sheet they were using. Upon notification of a trade the data was immediately punched into the computer, and once an hour revised sheets were issued.

Kay Halloran was assigned the job of checking the computer output. She visited the trading room hourly, collected the carbon copies of all trading slips, made her own calculations and then checked these against the position sheet printed out by the machine. Since she had to do all her calculations by hand, she ran two hours behind the machine. If she detected an error she immediately notified the computer room and the trading desk, and adjustments were made by hand on the traders' sheets. The reason for the error was traced by the systems staff, and corrective measures taken. After the first few days relatively few errors occurred.

After six weeks the new system seemed to be running well. Kay was assigned a new job handling customer billings in the accounting department. She began to lose weight and was off work sick for ten days in November. In December she became ill again and spent four weeks in the hospital and another three months convalescing. In April, 1965, she returned to work for half-days, three days a week, while she slowly recovered her strength.

THE PARADOXICAL TWINS: ACME AND OMEGA ELECTRONICS*

PART I

In 1955, Technological Products of Erie, Pa. was bought out by a Cleveland manufacturer. The Cleveland firm had no interest in the electronics division of Technological Products and subsequently sold to different investors two plants which manufactured printed circuit boards. One of the plants, located in nearby Waterford, Pa., was renamed Acme Electronics and the other plant, within the city limits of Erie, was renamed Omega Electronics, Inc. Acme retained its original management and upgraded its general manager to president. Omega hired a new president, who had been a director of a large electronics research laboratory, and upgraded several of the existing personnel within the plant.

Acme and Omega often competed for the same contracts. As subcontractors, both firms benefited from the electronics boom of the early 1960s and both looked forward to future growth and expansion. Acme had annual sales of $10 million and employed 550 people. Omega had annual sales of $8 million and employed 480 people. Acme was consistently more effective than Omega and regularly achieved greater net profits, much to the chagrin of Omega's management.

Inside Acme

The president of Acme, John Tyler, credited his firm's greater effectiveness to his manager's abilities to run a "tight ship." He explained that he had retained the basic structure developed by Technological Products because it was most efficient for high volume manufacture of printed circuits and their subsequent assembly. Tyler was confident that had the demand not been so great, its competitor would not have survived. "In fact," he said, "we have been able to beat Omega regularly for the most profitable contracts thereby

*Note: Please do not read ahead in this case until requested to do so by the instructor.

increasing our profits." Acme's basic organization structure is shown in Figure 1. People were generally satisfied with their work at Acme; however, some of the managers voiced the desire to have a little more latitude in their

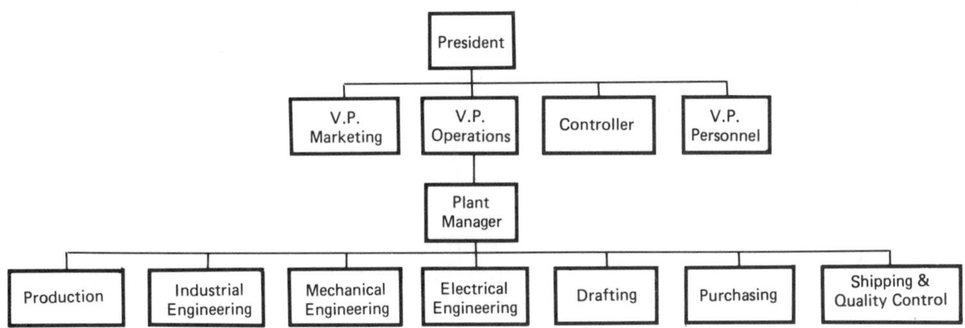

FIGURE 1 ACME ELECTRONICS ORGANIZATION CHART

jobs. One manager characterized the president as a "one man band." He said, "while I respect John's ability, there are times when I wish I had a little more information about what is going on."

Inside Omega

Omega's president, Jim Rawls, did not believe in organization charts. He felt that his organization had departments similar to Acme's, but he thought the plant was small enough that things such as organization charts just put artificial barriers between specialists who should be working together. Written memos were not allowed since, as Jim expressed it: "The plant is small enough that if people want to communicate they can just drop by and talk things over." Other members of Omega complained that too much time was wasted "filling in" people who could not contribute to problems and solutions. As the Head of the Mechanical Engineering Department expressed it: "Jim spends too much of his time and mine making sure everyone understands what we're doing and listening to suggestions." A newer member of the Industrial Engineering Department said, "When I first got here, I wasn't sure what I was supposed to do. One day I worked with some mechanical engineers and the next day I helped the shipping department design some packing cartons. The first months on the job were hectic but at least I got a real feel for what makes Omega tick." Most decisions of any significance were made by the management team at Omega.

Analysis Questions

1. How would you describe the management systems utilized by Omega and Acme? What factors led you to this conclusion?

2. How can you explain Acme's effectiveness in contrast to Omega's? What factors might change it?

PART II

In 1966, the integrated circuits began to cut deeply into the demand for printed circuit boards. The integrated circuits (I.C.) or "chips" were the first step into micro-miniaturization in the electronics industry. Because the manufacturing process for I.C.'s was a closely guarded secret, both Acme and Omega realized the potential threat to their futures and both began to seek new customers aggressively. In July 1966, one of the major photo-copy manufacturers was looking for a subcontractor to assemble the memory unit for their new experimental copier. The projected contract for the job was estimated to be $5 to $7 million in annual sales. Both Acme and Omega were geographically close to this manufacturer and both had submitted highly competitive bids for the production of one hundred prototypes. Acme's bid was slightly lower than Omega's; however, both firms were asked to produce one hundred units. The photo-copy manufacturer told both firms that speed was critical because their president had boasted to other manufacturers that they would have a finished copier available by Christmas. This boast, much to the designer's dismay, required pressure on all subcontractors to begin prototype production before final design of the copier was complete. This meant that Acme and Omega would have at most two weeks to produce the prototypes or delay the final copier production.

Analysis Question

1. Which firm do you think will produce the best results? Why?

PART III

As soon as John Tyler was given the blueprints (Monday, July 11, 1966), he sent a memo to the Purchasing Department requesting them to move forward on the purchase of all necessary materials. At the same time, he sent the blueprints to the Drafting Department and asked that they prepare manufacturing prints. The Industrial Engineering Department was told to begin methods design work for use by the Production Department foremen. Tyler also sent a memo to all department heads and executives indicating the critical time constraints of this job and how he expected that everyone would perform as efficiently as they had in the past. On Wednesday, July 13, Purchasing discovered that a particular component used in the memory unit could not be purchased or shipped for two weeks because the manufacturer had shut down for summer vacations. The Head of Purchasing was not overly concerned by this obstacle because he knew that Omega would face the same problem. He advised Tyler of this predicament and he in turn decided that Acme would build the memory unit except for the one component and then add that component in two weeks. Industrial Engineering was told to build this constraint into their assembly methods. On Friday, July 15, Industrial Engineering notified Tyler that the missing component would substantially increase the assembly time if it was not available from the start of assembly. Mr. Tyler, anxious to get started, suggested he would live with that problem and gave the signal to go forward on the assembly plans. Mechanical Engineering received manufacturing prints on Tuesday, July 12, and evaluated their capabilities for making the chassis required for the memory unit. Because their procedure for prototypes was to get estimates from outside vendors on all sheet metal work before they authorized in-house personnel to do the job, the Head of Mechanical Engineering sent a memo to the Head of Drafting requesting vendor prints be drawn up on the chassis and that these prints then be forwarded to Purchasing who would obtain vendor bids. On Friday, July 15, Mr. Tyler called the Head of Mechanical Engineering and asked for a progress report on the chassis. He was advised that Mechanical Engineering was waiting for vendor estimates before they moved forward.

Mr. Tyler was shocked by the lack of progress and demanded that Mechanical Engineering begin building those "damn chassis." On Monday, July 18, Mr. Tyler received word from the Shipping Department that most of the components had arrived. The first chassis were sent to the Head of Production who began immediately to set up an assembly area. On Tuesday, July 19, two Methods Engineers from Industrial Engineering went out to the production floor to set up the methods to be used in assembly. In his haste to get things going, the Production Foreman ignored the normal procedure of contacting the Methods Engineers and set up what he thought would be an efficient assembly process. The Methods Engineers were very upset to see assembly begin before they had a chance to do a proper layout. They told the foreman they had spent the entire weekend analyzing the motions needed and that his process was very inefficient and not well-balanced. The Methods Engineers ordered that work be stopped until they could rearrange the assembly process. The Production Foreman refused to stop work. He said, "I have to have these units produced by Friday and already I'm behind schedule."

The Methods Engineers reported back to the Head of Industrial Engineering who immediately complained to the plant manager. The Plant Manager sided with the Production Foreman and said, "John Tyler wants these units by Friday. Don't bother me with methods details now. Once we get the prototypes out and go into full production then your boys can do their thing." As the Head of Industrial Engineering got off the phone with the Plant Manager, he turned to his subordinates and said, "If my boss doesn't think our output is needed, to hell with him! You fellows must have other jobs to worry about, forget this one." As the two Methods Engineers left the Head Industrial Engineer's office, one of them said to the other, "Just wait until they try to install those missing components. Without our methods, they'll have to tear down the units almost completely."

On Thursday, July 21, the final units were being assembled although the process was delayed several times as Production waited for chassis from Mechanical Engineering to be completed. On Friday, July 22, the last units were finished while John Tyler paced around the plant. Late that afternoon, Tyler received a phone call from the head designer of the photo-copier manufacturer who told Tyler that he had received a call on Wednesday from Jim Rawls of Omega. He explained that Rawl's boys had found an error in the design of the connector cable and taken corrective action on their prototypes. He told Tyler that he checked out the design error and that Omega was right. Tyler, a bit overwhelmed by this information told the designer that he had all the memory units ready for shipment and that as soon as they received the missing component, on Monday or Tuesday, they would be able to deliver the final units. The designer explained that the design error would be rectified in a new blueprint he was sending over by messenger and that he would hold Acme to the delivery date on Tuesday.

When the blueprint arrived, Tyler called the Production Foreman in to assess the damages. The alterations in the design would call for total disassembly and the unsoldering of several connections. Tyler told the foreman to put extra people on the alterations first thing on Monday morning and try to finish the job by Tuesday. Late Tuesday afternoon the alterations were finished and the missing components were delivered. Wednesday morning, the Production Foreman discovered that the units would have to be torn apart again to install the missing components. When John Tyler was told this he "hit the roof." He called Industrial Engineering and asked if they could help out. The Head of Industrial Engineering told Tyler that his people would study the situation and get back to him first thing in the morning. Tyler decided to wait for their study because he was concerned that tearing apart the units again could weaken several of the soldered contacts and increase their potential rejection. Thursday, after several heated debates between the Production Foreman and the Methods Engineers, John Tyler settled the argument by ordering that all units be taken apart again and the missing component installed. He told Shipping to prepare cartons for delivery on Friday afternoon. On Friday, July 29, fifty prototypes were shipped from Acme without final inspection. John Tyler was concered about his firm's reputation so he waived the final inspection after he personally tested one unit and found it operation. On Tuesday, August 2, Acme shipped the last fifty units.

Inside Omega

Jim Rawls called a meeting on Friday, July 8, that included department heads to tell them about the potential contract they were to receive. He told them that as soon as he received the blueprints, work could begin. On Monday, July 11, the prints arrived and again the department heads met to discuss the project. At the end of the meeting, Drafting had agreed to prepare manufacturing prints while Industrial Engineering and Production would begin methods design. On Wednesday, July 13, at a progress report session, Purchasing indicated a particular component would not be available for two weeks until the manufacturer reopened from summer vacation shutdown. The Head of Electrical Engineering suggested using a possible substitute component, which was made in Japan, containing all the necessary characteristics. The Head of Industrial Engineering promised to have the Methods Engineers study the assembly to see if the unit could be produced in such a way that the missing component could be installed last.

The Head of Mechanical Engineering raised the concern that the chassis would be an obstacle if they waited for vendor estimates and advised the group that his people would begin production even though it might cost more. On Friday, July 15, at a progress report session, Industrial Engineering reported that the missing component would increase the assembly time substantially. The Head of Electrical Engineering offered to have one of his engineers examine the missing component specifications and said he was confident that the Japanese component would work. At the end of the meeting, Purchasing was told to order the Japanese components.

On Monday, July 18, a Methods Engineer and the Production Foreman formulated the assembly plans and production was set to begin on Tuesday morning. On Monday afternoon, people from Mechanical Engineering, Electrical Engineering, Production, and Industrial Engineering got together to produce a prototype just to insure that there would be no snags in production. While they were building the unit, they discovered an error in the connector cable design. All of the engineers agreed after checking and rechecking the blueprints, that the cable was erroneously designed. People from Mechanical Engineering and Electrical Engineering spent Monday night redesigning the cable and on Tuesday morning, the Drafting Department finalized the changes in the manufacturing prints. On Tuesday morning, Jim Rawls was a bit apprehensive about the design changes and decided to get formal approval. Rawls received word on Wednesday from the head designer of the photocopier firm that he could proceed with the design changes as discussed on the phone. On Friday, July 22, the final units were inspected by Quality Control and then they were shipped.

Analysis Questions

1. *How can you explain the differences between what happened at Acme and Omega?*
2. *What do you predict will happen to the final contract? Why?*

THE SLADE COMPANY

Ralph Porter, production manager of the Slade Company, was concerned by reports of dishonesty among some employees in the plating department. From reliable sources, he had learned that a few men were punching the timecards of a number of their workmates who had left early. Porter had only recently joined the Slade organization. He judged from conversations with the previous production manager and other fellow managers that they were, in general, pleased with the overall performance of the plating department.

The Slade Company was a prosperous manufacturer of metal products designed for industrial application. Its manufacturing plant, located in central Michigan, employed nearly five hundred workers, who were engaged in producing a large variety of clamps, inserts, knobs, and similar items. Orders for these products were usually large and on a recurrent basis. The volume of orders fluctuated in response to business conditions in the primary industries which the company served. At the time of this case, sales volume had been high for over a year. The bases upon which the Slade Company secured orders, in rank of importance, were quality, delivery, and reasonable price.

The organization of manufacturing operations at the Slade plant is shown in Figure 1. The departments listed there are, from left to right, approximately in the order in which material flowed through the plant. The diemaking and setup operations required the greatest degree of skill, supplied by highly

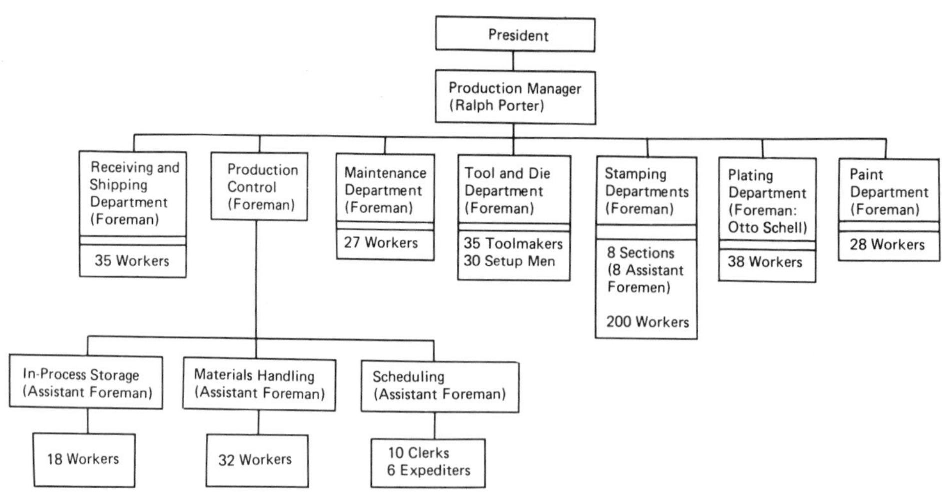

FIGURE 1 MANUFACTURING ORGANIZATION

paid, long-service craftsmen. The finishing departments, divided operationally and geographically between plating and painting, attracted less highly trained but relatively skilled workers, some of whom had been employed by the company for many years. The remaining operations were largely unskilled in nature and were characterized by relatively low pay and high rate of turnover of personnel.

The plating room was the sole occupant of the top floor of the plant. Figure 2 shows the floor plan, the disposition of workers, and the flow of work throughout the department. Thirty-eight men and women worked in the department, plating or oxidizing the metal parts or preparing parts for the application of paint at another location in the plant. The department's work occurred in response to orders communicated by production schedules, which were revised daily. Schedule revisions, caused by last-minute order in-

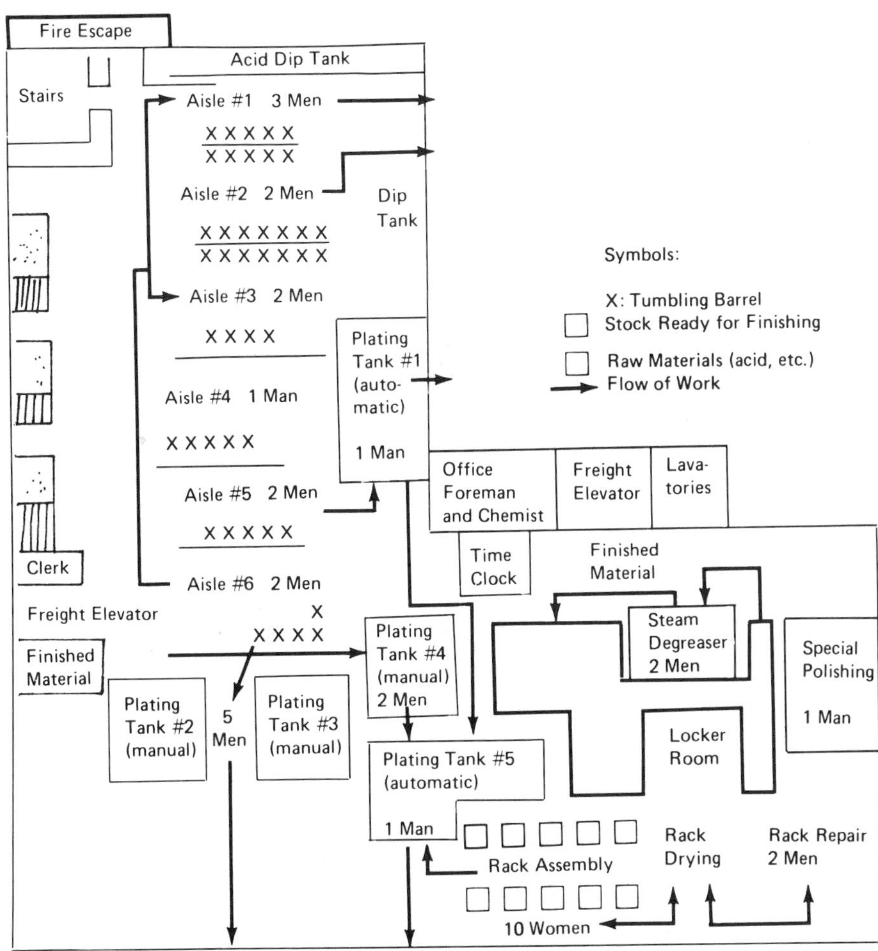

FIGURE 2 PLATING ROOM LAYOUT

creases or rush requests from customers, resulted in short-term volume fluctuations, particularly in the plating, painting, and shipping departments. Figure 3 outlines the activities of the various jobs, their interrelationships, and the type of work in which each specialized. Figure 4 rates the various types of jobs in terms of the technical skill, physical effort, discomfort, and training time associated with their performance.

The activities which took place in the plating room were of three main types:

1. Acid dipping, in which parts were etched by being placed in baskets which were manually immersed and agitated in an acid solution.
2. Barrel tumbling, in which parts were roughened or smoothed by being loaded into machine-powered revolving drums containing abrasive, caustic, or corrosive solutions.
3. Plating, either manual, in which parts were loaded on racks and were immersed by hand through the plating sequence, or automatic, in which racks or baskets were manually loaded with parts which were then carried by a conveyor system through the plating sequence.

Within these main divisions, there were a number of variables, such as cycle times, chemical formulas, abrasive mixtures, and so forth, which distinguished particular jobs as they have been categorized in Figure 3.

The work of the plating room was received in batch lots whose size averaged a thousand pieces. The clerk moved each batch, which was accompanied by a routing slip, to its first operation. This routing slip indicated the operations to be performed and when each major operation on the batch was scheduled to be completed, so that the finished product could be shipped on time. From the accumulation of orders before him, each man was to organize his own work schedule so as to make optimal use of equipment, materials, and time. Upon completion of an order, each man moved the lot to its next work position or to the finished material location near the freight elevator.

The plating room was under the direct supervision of the foreman, Otto Schell, who worked a regular 8:00-to-5:00 day, five days a week. The foreman spent a good deal of his working time attending to maintenance and repair of equipment, procuring supplies, handling late schedule charges, and seeing that his people were at their proper work locations.

Working conditions in the plating room varied considerably. That part of the department containing the tumbling barrels and the plating machines was constantly awash, alternately with cold water, steaming acid, or caustic soda. Men working in this part of the room wore knee boots, long rubber aprons, and high-gauntlet rubber gloves. This uniform, consistent with the general atmosphere of the "wet" part of the room, was hot in summer, cold in winter. In contrast, the remainder of the room was dry, was relatively odor-free, and provided reasonably stable temperature and humidity conditions for those who worked there.

Aisle 1:	Worked closely with Aisle 3 in preparation of parts by barrel tumbling and acid dipping for high-quality* plating in Tanks 4 and 5. Also did a considerable quantity of highly specialized, high-quality acid-etching work not requiring further processing.
Aisle 2:	Tumbled items of regular quality and design in preparation for painting. Less frequently, did oxidation dipping work of regular quality, but sometimes of special design, not requiring further processing.
Aisle 3:	Worked closely with Aisle 1 on high-quality tumbling work for Tanks 4 and 5.
Aisles 4 and 5:	Produced regular tumbling work for Tank 1.
Aisle 6:	Did high-quality tumbling work for special products plated in Tanks 2 and 3.
Tank 1:	Worked on standard, automated plating of regular quality not further processed in plating room, and regular work further processed in Tank 5.
Tanks 2 and 3:	Produced special, high-quality plating work not requiring further processing.
Tank 4:	Did special, high-quality plating work further plated in Tank 5.
Tank 5:	Automated production of high- and regular-quality, special- and regular-design plated parts sent directly to shipping.
Rack Assembly:	Placed parts to be plated in Tank 5 on racks.
Rack Repair:	Performed routine replacement and repair of racks used in Tank 5.
Polishing:	Processed, by manual or semimanual methods, odd-lot special orders which were sent directly to shipping. Also, sorted and reclaimed parts rejected by inspectors in the shipping department.
Degreasing:	Took incoming raw stock, processed it through caustic solution, and placed clean stock in storage ready for processing elsewhere in the plating room.

FIGURE 3 OUTLINE OF WORK FLOW, PLATING ROOM

*Definition of terms: *High or regular quality:* The quality of finishes could broadly be distinguished by the thickness of plate and/or care in preparation. *Regular or special work:* The complexity of work depended on the routine or special character of design and finish specifications.

The men and women employed in the plating room are listed in Figure 5. This figure provides certain personal data on each department member, including a productivity-skill rating (based on subjective and objective appraisals of potential performance), as reported by the members of the department.

Jobs	Technical Skill Required	Physical Effort Required	Degree of Discomfort Involved	Degree of Training Required†
Aisle 1	1	1	1	1
Tanks 2-4	3	2	1	2
Aisles 2-6	5	1	1	5
Tank 5	1	5	7	2
Tank 1	8	5	5	7
Degreasing	9	3	7	10
Polishing	6	9	9	7
Rack assembly and repair	10	10	10	10

FIGURE 4 SKILL INDICES BY JOB GROUP*

*Rated on scales of 1 (the greatest) to 10 (the least) in each category.
†The amount of experience required to assume complete responsibility for the job.

The pay scale implied by Figure 5 was low for the central Michigan area. The average starting wage for factory work in the community was about $1.25. However, working hours for the plating room were long (from 60 hours to a possible and frequently available 76 hours per week). The first 60 hours (the normal five-day week) were paid for on straight-time rates. Saturday work was paid for at time and one half; Sunday pay was calculated on a double-time basis.

As Figure 5 indicates, Philip Kirk, a worker in Aisle 2, provided the data for this case. After he had been a member of the department for several months, Kirk noted that certain members of the department tended to seek each other out during free time on and off the job. He then observed that these informal associations were enduring, built upon common activities and shared ideas about what was and what was not legitimate behavior in the department. His estimate of the pattern of these associations id diagrammed in Figure 6.

The Sarto group, so named because Tony Sarto was its most respected member and the one who acted as arbiter between the other members, was the largest in the department. The group, except for Louis Patrici, Al Bartolo, and Frank Bonzani (who spelled each other during break periods), invariably ate lunch together on the fire escape near Aisle 1. On those Saturdays and Sundays when overtime work was required, the Sarto group operated as a team, regardless of weekday work assignments, to get overtime work completed as quickly as possible. (Few department members not affiliated with either the Sarto or the Clark groups worked on weekends.) Off the job, Sarto group members often joined in parties or weekend trips. Sarto's summer camp was a frequent rendezvous.

Sarto's group was also the most cohesive one in the department in terms of its organized punch-in and punch-out system. Since the men were

Location	Name	Age	Marital Status	Company Seniority	Department Seniority	Pay	Education	Familial Relationships	Productivity-Skill Rating*
Aisle 1	Tony Sarto	30	M	13 yrs.	13 yrs.	1.50	High school	Louis Patrici, uncle Pete Facelli, cousin	1
	Pete Facelli	26	M	8 yrs.	8 yrs.	1.30	High school	Louis Patrici, uncle Tony Sarto, cousin	2
	Joe Iambi	31	M	5 yrs.	5 yrs.	1.20	2 yrs. high school		2
Aisle 2	Herman Schell	48	S	26 yrs.	26 yrs.	1.45	Grade school	Otto Schell, brother	8
	Philip Kirk	23	M	1 yr.	1 yr.	0.90	College		†
Aisle 3	Dom Pantaleoni	31	M	10 yrs.	10 yrs.	1.30	1 yr. high school		2
	Sal Maletta	32	M	12 yrs.	12 yrs.	1.30	3 yrs. high school		3
Aisle 4	Bob Pearson	22	S	4 yrs.	4 yrs.	1.15	High school	Father in tool and die dept.	1
Aisle 5	Charlie Malone	44	M	22 yrs.	8 yrs.	1.25	Grade school		7
	John Lacey	41	S	9 yrs.	5 yrs.	1.20	1 yr. high school	Brother in paint dept.	7
Aisle 6	Jim Martin	30	S	7 yrs.	7 yrs.	1.25	High school		4
	Bill Mensch	41	M	6 yrs.	2 yrs.	1.10	Grade school		4

FIGURE 5 PLATING ROOM PERSONNEL

*On a potential scale of 1 (top) to 10 (bottom), as evaluated by the men in the department.
†Kirk was the source of data for this case and, as such, was in a biased position to report accurately perceptions about himself.

Location	Name	Age	Marital Status	Company Seniority	Department Seniority	Pay	Education	Familial Relationships	Productivity-Skill Rating*
Tank 1	Henry La Forte	38	M	14 yrs.	6 yrs.	$1.25	High school		6
Tanks 2-3	Ralph Parker	25	S	7 yrs.	7 yrs.	1.20	High school		4
	Ed Harding	27	S	8 yrs.	8 yrs.	1.20	High school		4
	George Flood	22	S	5 yrs.	5 yrs.	1.15	High school		5
	Harry Clark	29	M	8 yrs.	8 yrs.	1.20	High school		3
	Tom Bond	25	S	6 yrs.	6 yrs.	1.20	High school		4
Tank 4	Frank Bonzani	27	M	9 yrs.	9 yrs.	1.25	High school		2
	Al Bartolo	24	M	6 yrs.	6 yrs.	1.25	High school		3
Tank 5	Louis Patrici	47	S	14 yrs.	14 yrs.	1.45	2 yrs. college	Tony Sarto, nephew Pete Facelli, nephew	1
Rack Assembly	10 women	30-40	9M,1S	10 yrs. (av.)	10 yrs. (av.)	1.05	Grade school (av.)	6 with husbands in company	4 (av.)
Rack Maintenance	Will Partridge	57	M	14 yrs.	2 yrs.	1.20	Grade school		7
	Lloyd Swan	62	M	3 yrs.	3 yrs.	1.10	Grade school		7
Degreasing	Dave Susi	45	S	1 yr.	1 yr.	1.05	High school		5
	Mike Maher	41	M	4 yrs.	4 yrs.	1.05	Grade school		6
Polishing	Russ Perkins	49	M	12 yrs.	2 yrs.	1.20	High school		4
Foreman	Otto Schell	56	M	35 yrs.	35 yrs.	(not available)	High school	Herman Schell, brother	3
Clerk	Bill Pierce	32	M	10 yrs.	4 yrs.	1.15	High school		4
Chemist	Frank Rutlage	24	S	2 yrs.	2 yrs.	(not available)	2 yrs. college		6

FIGURE 5 *(continued)*

*On a potential scale of 1 (top to 10 (bottom), as evaluated by the men in the department.

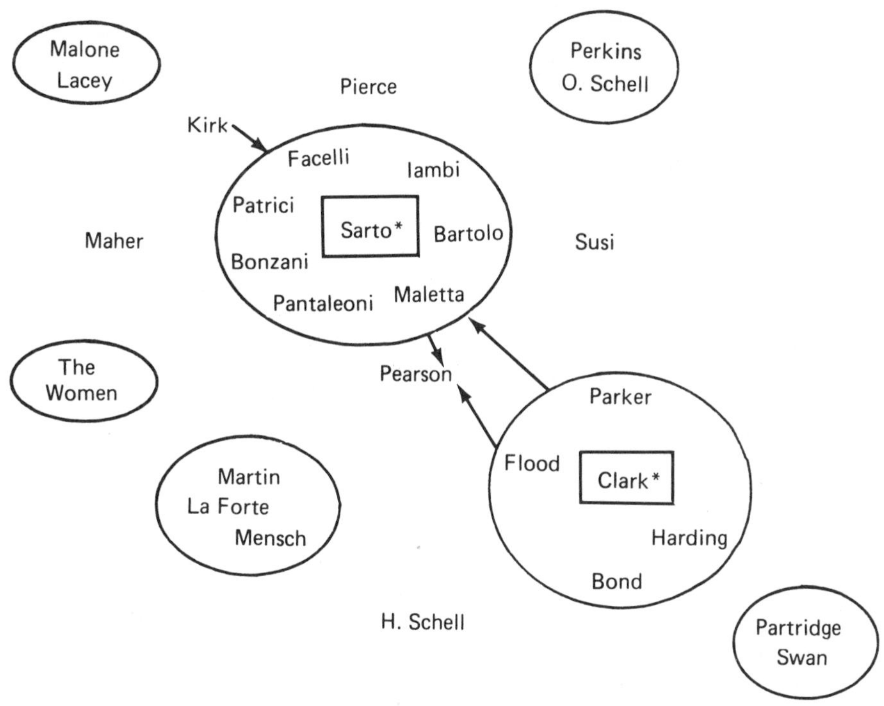

FIGURE 6 INFORMAL GROUPINGS IN THE PLATING ROOM

*The boxes indicate those men who clearly demonstrated leadership behavior (most closely personified the values shared by their groups, were often sought for help, arbitration, and so forth).

†While the two-and three-man groupings had little informal contact outside their own boundaries, the five-man group did seek to join the largest group in extra plant social affairs. These were relatively infrequent.

‡Though not an active member of any group, Bob Pearson was regarded with affection by the two large groups.

regularly scheduled to work from 7:00 A.M. to 7:00 P.M. weekdays, and since all supervision was removed at 5:00 P.M., it was possible almost every day to finish a "day's work" by 5:30 and leave the plant. What is more, if one man were to stay until 7:00 P.M., he could punch the timecards of a number of men and help them gain free time without pay loss. (This system operated on weekends, also, at which times members of supervision were present, if at all, only for short periods.) In Sarto's group the duty of staying late rotated, so that no man did so more than once a week. In addition, the group members would punch a man in in the morning if he were unavoidably delayed. However, such a practice never occurred without prior notice from the man who expected to be late and never if the tardiness was expected to lay beyond 8:00 A.M., the start of the day for the foreman.

Sarto explained the logic behind the system to Kirk:

> You know that our hourly pay rate is quite low, compared to other companies. What makes this the best place to work is the feeling of security you get. No one ever gets laid off in this department. With all the hours in the week, all the company ever has to do is shorten the workweek when orders fall off. We have to tighten our belts, but we can all get along. When things are going well, as they are now, the company is only interested in getting out the work. It doesn't help to get it out faster than it's really needed—so we go home a little early whenever we can. Of course, some guys abuse this sort of thing—like Herman—but others work even harder, and it averages out.
>
> Whenever an extra order has to be pushed through, naturally I work until 7:00. So do a lot of the others. I believe that if I stay until my work is caught up and my equipment is in good shape, that's all the company wants of me. They leave us alone and expect us to produce—and we do.

When Kirk asked Sarto if he would not rather work shorter hours at higher pay in a union shop (Slade employees were not organized), he just laughed and said: "It wouldn't come close to an even trade."

The members of Sarto's group were explicit about what constituted a fair day's work. Customarily, they cited Herman Schell, Kirk's work partner and the foreman's brother, as a man who consistently produced below that level. Kirk received an informal orientation from Herman during his first days on the job. As Herman put it:

> I've worked at this job for a good many years, and I expect to stay here a good many more. You're just starting out, and you don't know which end is up yet. We spend a lot of time in here; and no matter how hard we work, the pile of work never goes down. There's always more to take its place. And I think you've found out by now that this isn't light work. You can wear yourself out fast if you're not smart. Look at Pearson up in Aisle 4. There's a kid who's just going to burn himself out. He won't last long. If he thinks he's going to get somewhere working like that, he's nuts. They'll give him all the work he can take. He makes it tough on everybody else and on himself, too.

Kirk reported further on his observations of the department:

> As nearly as I could tell, two things seemed to determine whether or not Sarto's group or any others came in for weekend work on Saturday or Sunday. It seemed usually to be caused by rush orders that were received late in the week, although I suspect

it was sometimes caused by the men having spent insufficient time on the job during the previous week.

Tony and his group couldn't understand Herman. While Herman arrived late, Tony was always half an hour early. If there was a push to get out an extra amount of work, almost everyone but Herman would work that much harder. Herman never worked overtime on weekends, while Tony's group and the men on the manual tanks almost always did. When the first, exploratory time study of the department was made, no one in the aisles slowed down, except Herman, with the possible exception, to a lesser degree, of Charlie Malone. I did hear that the men in the dry end of the room slowed down so much you could hardly see them move; but we had little to do with them, anyway. While the men I knew best seemed to find a rather full life in their work, Herman never really got involved. No wonder they couldn't understand each other.

There was quite a different feeling about Bobby Pearson. Without the slightest doubt, Bob worked harder than anyone else in the room. Because of the tremendous variety of work produced, it was hard to make output comparisons, but I'm sure I wouldn't be far wrong in saying that Bob put out twice as much as Herman and 50 percent more than almost anyone else in the aisles. No one but Herman and a few old-timers at the dry end ever criticized Bobby for his efforts. Tony and his group seemed to feel a distant affection for Bob, but the only contact they or anyone else had with him consisted of brief greetings.

To the men in Tony's group the most severe penalty that could be inflicted on a man was exclusion. This they did to both Pearson and Herman. Pearson, however, was tolerated; Herman was not. Evidently, Herman felt his exclusion keenly, though he answered it with derision and aggression. Herman kept up a steady stream of stories concerning his attempts to gain acceptance outside the company. He wrote popular music which was always rejected by publishers. He attempted to join several social and athletic clubs, mostly without success. His favorite pastime was fishing. He told me that fisherman were friendly, and he enjoyed meeting new people whenever he went fishing. But he was particularly quick to explain that he preferred to keep his distance from the men in the department.

Tony's group emphasized more than just quantity in judging a man's work. Among them had grown a confidence that they could master and even improve upon any known finishing technique. Tony himself symbolized this skill. Before him, Tony's father had operated Aisle 1 and had trained Tony to take his place. Tony in his turn was training his cousin Pete. When a new finishing problem arose from a change in customer specifications, the foreman, the department chemist, or any of the men directly involved would come to Tony for help, and Tony would give it willingly. For example, when a part with a special plastic embossing was designed, Tony was the only one who could discover how to treat the metal without damaging the plastic. To a lesser degree, the other members of the group were also inventive about the problems which arose in their own sections.

Herman, for his part, talked incessantly about his feats in design and finish creations. As far as I could tell during the year I worked in the department, the objects of these stories were obsolete or of minor importance. What's more, I never saw any department member seek Herman's help.

Willingness to be of help was a trait Sarto's group prized. The most valued help of all was of a personal kind, though work help was also important. The members of Sarto's group were constantly lending and borrowing money, cars, clothing, and tools among themselves and, less frequently, with other members of the department. Their daily lunch bag procedure typified the "common property" feeling among them. Everyone's lunch was opened and added to a common pile, from which each member of the group chose his meal.

On the other hand, Herman refused to help others in any way. He never left his aisle to aid those near him who were in the midst of a rush of work or a machine failure, though this was customary throughout most of the department. I can distinctly recall the picture of Herman leaning on the hot and cold water faucets which were located directly above each tumbling barrel. He would stand gazing into the tumbling pieces for hours. To the passing, casual visitor, he looked busy; and as he told me, that's just what he wanted. He, of course, expected me to act this same way, and it was this enforced boredom that I found virtually intolerable.

More than this, Herman took no responsibility for breaking in his assigned helpers as they first entered the department, or thereafter. He had had four helpers in the space of little more than a year. Each had asked for a transfer to another department, publicly citing the work as cause, privately blaming Herman. Tony was the one who taught me the ropes when I first entered the department.

The men who congregated around Harry Clark tended to talk like and copy the behavior of the Sarto group, though they never approached the degree of inventive skill or the amount of helping activities that Tony's group did. They sought outside social contact with the Sarto group; and several times a year, the two groups went "on the town" together. Clark's group did maintain a high level of performance in the volume of work they turned out.

The remainder of the people in the department stayed pretty much to themselves or associated in pairs or triplets. None of these people were as inventive, as helpful, or as productive as Sarto's or Clark's groups, but most of them gave verbal support to the same values as those groups held.

The distinction between the two organized groups and the rest of the department was clearest in the punching-out routine. The women could not work past 3:00 P.M., so they were not involved. Malone and Lacey, Partridge and Swan, and Martin, La Forte, and Mensch arranged within their small groups for punch-outs, or they remained beyond 5:00 and slept or read when they finished their work. Perkins and Pierce went home when the foreman did. Herman Schell, Susi, and Maher had no punch-out organization to rely upon. Susi and Maher invariably stayed in the department until 7:00 P.M. Herman was reported to have established an arrangement with Partridge whereby the latter punched Herman out for a fee. Such a practice was unthinkable from the point of view of Sarto's group. It evidently did not occur often because Herman usually went to sleep behind piles of work when his brother left or, particularly during the fishing season, punched himself out early. He constantly railed against the dishonesty of other men in the department, yet urged me to punch him out on several "emergency occasions."

Just before I left the Slade Company to return to school after 14 months on the job, I had a casual conversation with Mr. Porter, the production manager, in which he asked me how I had enjoyed my experience with the organization. During the conversation, I learned that he knew of the punch-out system in the plating department. What's more, he told me, he was wondering if he ought to "blow the lid off the whole mess."

TRAVERS BOTTLING CO.

Lou Travers was the president of a small, independent softdrink bottling company that employed about one hundred people. Most of the employees had been with the company for fifteen years or more, and Lou knew everyone in the plant and on the salesforce by name. Travers was a man of forty-seven, very energetic, outgoing, articulate, and keenly competitive. He worked long hours and lived for his business. He kept a notepad next to his bed so that if he woke up during the night with a good idea, he could write it down and act on it in the morning. He also kept detailed records in his office of sales, production, maintenance costs, and other measures of performance, and prided himself on having "a better record system than the rest of the firm put together."

He had been known to fire a man on the spot for an infringement of the rules which he happened to observe, but had also, on several occasions, hired the man back to work the following day. He showed no hesitation in criticizing employees for what he considered poor decisions or actions. In meetings he was very outspoken and tended to get his way on most points.

Travers Bottling was highly successful. It maintained a large market share, competing against bottlers many times its size. Lou's personality reflected itself in the organization which maintained a close touch with the market, was aggressive, competitive and flexible.

Pay throughout the company was low in comparison with other firms in the area. Nor did employees, management or hourly paid workers, work in splendid facilities. Offices and plant were functional, clean and sparse. Lou's own office was no exception.

Of the four managers who reported directly to Lou Travers, three had been with the company for over fifteen years, and one for eleven. All had worked their way up the organization. They were all competent, knowledgeable, hard working, and devoted to the company.

Recently, Travers had decided to diversify his interests and was looking at acquiring another business. He realized, however, that he would have to start spending less time and energy at the bottling company, and that much of the work he was presently doing would have to be done by his managers. Unfortunately, when he tried delegating decisions, he discovered that somehow they ended back up on his desk, and he made them. It seemed that the more he railed at his managers, the less they were willing to make decisions by themselves.

WORK GROUP OWNERSHIP OF AN IMPROVED TOOL

The Whirlwind Aircraft Corporation was a leader in its field and especially noted for its development of the modern supercharger. Work in connection with the latter mechanism called for special skill and ability. Every detail of the supercharger had to be perfect to satisfy the exacting requirements of the aircraft industry.

In 1941 (before Pearl Harbor), Lathe Department 15-D was turning out three types of impeller, each countered to within 0.002 inch and machined to a mirrorlike finish. The impellers were made from an aluminum alloy and finished on a cam-back lathe.

The work was carried on in four shifts, two men on each. The personnel in the finishing section were as follows:

1. *First Shift*—7 A.M. to 3 P.M. Sunday and Monday off.
   a. Jean Latour, master mechanic, French Canadian, forty-five years of age. Latour had set up the job and trained the men who worked with him on the first shift.
   b. Pierre DuFresne, master mechanic, French Canadian, thirty-six years of age. Both these men have trained the workers needed for the other shifts.

2. *Second Shift*—3 P.M. to 11 P.M. Friday and Saturday off.
   a. Albert Durand, master mechanic, French Canadian, thirty-two years of age; trained by Latour and using his lathe.
   b. Robert Benet, master mechanic, French Canadian, thirty-one years of age; trained by DuFresne and using his lathe.
3. *Third Shift*—11 P.M. to 7 A.M. Tuesday and Wednesday off.
   a. Philippe Doret, master mechanic, French Canadian, thirty-one years of age; trained by Latour and using his lathe.
   b. Henri Barbet, master mechanic, French Canadian, thirty years of age; trained by DuFresne and using his lathe.
4. *Stagger Shift*—Monday, 7 A.M. to 3 P.M.; Tuesday, 11 P.M. to 7 A.M. Wednesday, 11 P.M. to 7 A.M.; Thursday, off; Friday, 3 P.M. to 11 P.M.; Saturday, 3 P.M. to 11 P.M.; Sunday, off.
   a. George MacNair, master mechanic, Scotch, thirty-two years of age; trained by Latour and using his lathe.
   b. William Reader, master mechanic, English, thirty years of age; trained by DuFresne and using his lathe.

Owing to various factors (such as the small number of workers involved, the preponderance of one nationality, and the fact that Latour and DuFresne had trained the other workers), these eight men considered themselves as members of one work group. Such a feeling of solidarity is unusual among workers on different shifts, despite the fact that they use the same machines.

The men received a base rate of $1.03 an hour and worked on incentive. Each man usually turned out 22 units a shift, thus earning an average of $1.19 an hour. Management supplied Rex 95 High-Speed Tool-Bits, which workers ground to suit themselves. Two tools were used: one square bit with a slight radius for recess cutting, the other bit with a 45-degree angle for chamfering and smooth finish. When used, both tools were set close together, the worker adjusting the lathe from one operation to the other. The difficulty with this setup was that during the rotation of the lathe, the aluminum waste would melt and fuse between the two toolbits. Periodically the lathe had to be stopped so that the toolbits could be freed from the welded aluminum and reground.

At the request of the supervisor of Lathe Department 15-D, the methods department had been working on his tool problem. Up to the time of this case, no solution had been found. To make a firsthand study of the difficulty, the methods department had recently assigned one of its staff, Mr. MacBride, to investigate the problem in the lathe department itself. Mr. MacBride's working hours covered parts of both the first and second shifts. MacBride was a young man, twenty-six years of age, and a newcomer to the methods department. For the three months prior to this assignment, he had held the post of "suggestion man," a position which enabled newcomers to the methods department to familiarize themselves with the plant setup. The job consisted in collecting, from boxes in departments throughout the plant, suggestions submitted by employees and making a preliminary evaluation of these ideas. The current assignment of studying the tool situation in Lathe Department 15-D, with a view to cutting costs, was his first special task. He devoted himself to this problem with great zeal but did not succeed in winning the confidence of the workers. In pursuance of their usual philosphy: "Keep your mouth shut if you see anyone with a suit on," they volunteered no information and took the stand that, since the methods man had been given this assignment, it was up to him to carry it out.

While MacBride was working on this problem, Pierre DuFresne hit upon a solution. One day he successfully contrived a tool which combined the two bits into one. This eliminated the space between the two toolbits which in the past had caught the molten aluminum waste and allowed it to become welded to the cutting edges. The new toolbit had two advantages: it eliminated the frequent machine stoppage for cleaning and regrinding the old-type tools; and it enabled the operator to run the lathe at a high speed. These advantages made it possible for the operator to increase his efficiency 50 percent.

DuFresne tried to make copies of the new tool, but was unable to do so. Apparently the new development had been a "lucky accident" during grinding which he could not duplicate. After several unsuccessful attempts, he took the new tool to his former teacher, Jean Latour. The latter succeeded in making a drawing and turning out duplicate toolbits on a small grinding wheel in the shop. At first the two men decided to keep the new tool to themselves. Later, however, they shared the improvement with their fellow workers on the second shift. Similarly it was passed on to the other shifts. But all these men kept the new development a closely guarded secret as far as "outsiders" were concerned. At the end of the shift, each locked the improved toolbit securely in his toolchest.

Both DuFrense, the originator of the new tool, and Latour, its draftsman and designer, decided not to submit the idea as a suggestion but to keep it as the property of their group. Why was this decision made? The answer lies partly in the suggestion system and partly in the attitude of Latour and DuFresne toward the other features of company work life and toward their group.

According to an information bulletin issued by the company, the purpose of the suggestion system was to "provide an orderly method of submitting and considering ideas and recommendations of employees to management; to provide a means for recognizing and rewarding individual ingenuity; and to promote cooperation." Awards for accepted suggestions were made in the following manner: "After checking the savings and expense involved in an adopted suggestion [the suggestion committee] determined the amount of the award to be paid, based upon the savings predicted upon a year's use of the suggestion." "It is the intention of the committee . . . to be liberal in the awards, which are expected to adequately compensate for the interest shown in presenting suggestions." In pursuance of this policy, it was customary to grant the suggestor an award equivalent to the savings of an entire month.

As a monetary return, both DuFresne and Latour considered an award based on one month's saving as inadequate. They also argued that such awards were really taken out of the worker's pockets. Their reasoning was as follows: All awards for adopted suggestions were paid out of undistributed profits. Since the company also had a profit-sharing plan, the money was taken from a fund that would be given to the workers anyway, which merely meant robbing Peter to pay Paul. In any case, the payment was not likely to be large and probably would be less than they could accumulate if increased incentive payments could be maintained over an extended period without discovery. Thus there was little in favor of submitting the new tool as a suggestion.

Latour and DuFresne also felt that there were definite hazards to the group if their secret were disclosed. They feared that once the tool became company property, its efficiency might lead to layoff of some members in their group, or at least make work less tolerable by leading to an increased quota at a lower price per unit. They also feared that there might be a change in scheduled work assignments. For instance, the lathe department worked on three different types of impeller. One type was a routine job and aside from the difficulty caused by the old-type tool, presented no problem. For certain technical reasons, the other two types were more difficult to make. Even Latour, an exceptionally skilled craftsman, had sometimes found it hard to make the expected quota before the new tool was developed. Unless the work load was carefully balanced by scheduling easier and more difficult types, some of the operators were unable to make standard time.

The decision to keep the tool for their own group was in keeping with Latour's work philosphy. He had a strong feeling of loyalty to his own group and had demonstrated this in the past by offering for their use several improvements of his own. For example, he made available to all workers in his group a set of special gauge blocks which were used in aligning work on lathes. To protect himself in case mistakes were traced to these gauges, he wrote on them: "Personnel *(sic)* Property—Do not use. Jean Latour."

Through informal agreement with their fellow workers, Latour and DuFresne "pegged production" at an efficiency rate that in their opinion would not arouse management's suspicion or lead to a restudy of the job, with possible cutting of the rate. This enabled them to earn an extra 10 percent incentive earnings. The other 40 percent in additional efficiency was used as follows: The operators established a reputation for a high degree of accuracy and finish. They set a record for no spoilage and were able to apply the time gained on the easier type of impeller to work on the other types which required greater care and more expert workmanship.

The foreman of the lathe department learned about the new tool soon after it was put into use but was satisfied to let the men handle the situation in their own way. He reasoned that at little expense he was able to get out production of high quality. There was no defective work, and the men were contented.

Mr. MacBride was left in a very unsatisfactory position. He had not succeeded in working out a solution of his own. Like the foreman, he got wind of the fact that the men had devised a new tool. He urged them to submit a drawing of it through the suggestion system, but this advice was not taken, and the men made it plain that they did not care to discuss with him the reasons for this position.

Having no success in his direct contact with the workers, Mr. MacBride appealed to the foreman, asking him to secure a copy of the new tool. The foreman replied that the men would certainly decline to give him a copy and would resent as an injustice any effort on his part to force them to submit a drawing. Instead he suggested that MacBride should persuade DuFresne to show him the tool. This MacBride attempted to do, but met with no success in his efforts to ingratiate himself with DuFresne. When he persisted in his attempts, DuFresne decided to throw him off the track. He left in his lathe a toolbit which was an unsuccessful copy of the original discovery. At shift change, MacBride was delighted to find what he supposed to be the improved tool. He hastily copied it and submitted a drawing to the tool department. When a tool was made up according to these specifications it naturally failed to do what was expected of it. The workers, when they heard of this through the "grapevine," were delighted. DuFresne did not hesitate to crow over MacBride, pointing out that his underhanded methods had met with their just reward.

The foreman did not take any official notice of the conflict between DuFresne and MacBride. Then MacBride complained to the foreman that DuFresne was openly boasting of his trick and ridiculing him before other workers. Thereupon, the foreman talked to DuFresne, but the latter insisted that his ruse had been justified as a means of self-protection.

When he was rebuffed by DuFresne, the foreman felt that he had lost control of the situation. He could no longer conceal from himself that he was confronted by a more complex situation than what initially he had defined as a "tool problem." His attention was drawn to the fact that the state of affairs in his department was a tangle of several interrelated problems. Each problem urgently called for a decision that involved understanding and practical judgement. But having for so long failed to see the situation as a whole, he now found himself in a dilemma.

He wished to keep the goodwill of the work group, but he could not countenance the continued friction between DuFresne and MacBride. Certainly, he could not openly abet his operators in obstructing the work of a methods man. His superintendent would now certainly hear of it and would be displeased to learn that a foreman had failed to tell him of such an important technical improvement. Furthermore, he knew that the aircraft industry was expanding at this time and that the demand for impellers had increased to such an extent that management was planning to set up an entire new plant unit devoted to this product.

Bibliography

Asch, S. E. "Effects of group pressure upon the modification and distortion of judgments," in *Basic Studies in Social Psychology*, eds. H. Proshansky and B. Swidenberg. New York: Holt, Rinehart and Winston, 1965.

Ashton, D. "Elton Mayo and the empirical study of social groups," in *Management Thinkers*, eds. A. Tillett, T. Kempner, and G. Wills. Harmondsworth, England: Penguin, 1970.

Bales, R. F., et al. "Channels of communication in small groups," *American Sociological Review*, 16 (1951), 461–68.

Beme, E. *Games People Play*. New York: Grove Press, 1964.

Bott, Elizabeth. "The concept of class as a reference group," *Human Relations*, VII (1954), 259–85.

Brown, W. *Explorations in Management*. London: Heinemann, 1960.

Buffa, E. S. *Operations Management: Problems and Models*, 2nd ed. New York: Wiley, 1968.

Carter, L., et al. "The relation of categories and ratings in the observation of group behavior," *Human Relations*, 4 (1951), 239–54.

Chase, S. *Men at Work*. New York: Harcourt, Brace & World, 1941.

Churchman, C. W.; R. L. Ackoff; and E. L. Arnoff. *Introduction to Operations Research*. New York: Wiley, 1957.

Coffey, R. E.; A. G. Athos; and P. A. Raynolds. *Behavior in Organizations*, 2nd ed. Englewood Cliffs, N.J.: Prentice-Hall, 1975.

Croy, H. *Wheels West.* New York: Hastings House, 1955.

Dale, E. *Readings in Management.* New York: McGraw-Hill, 1965.

Drucker, P. F. *The Age of Discontinuity.* New York: Harper and Row, 1968.

____________. *The New Society.* New York: Harper and Row, 1950.

____________. *The Practice of Management.* New York: Harper Brothers, 1954.

Economic Council of Canada, *First Annual Review.* Ottawa: The Queen's Printer, 1964.

Fayol, H. *General and Industrial Management.* London: Pitman, 1949.

Festinger, L. "A theory of social comparison processes," *Human Relations,* 7 (1954), 117–40.

Fiedler, F. E., and M. M. Chemers. *Leadership and Effective Management.* Glenview, Ill.: Scott, Foresman, 1974.

Ford, H., and S. Crowther. *My Life and Work.* New York: Arno, 1973.

Gellerman, S. W. *Motivation and Productivity.* New York: American Management Association, 1963.

Georgopoulus, B. S.; G. M. Mahoney; and N. W. Jones. "A path-goal approach to productivity," *Journal of Applied Psychology,* 41 (1957), 345–53.

Gibb, J. R. "The effects of group size and of threat reduction upon creativity in problem solving," *American Psychologist,* 6 (1951), 324.

Goffman, E. *The Presentation of Self in Everyday Life.* New York: Doubleday, 1959.

Harris, T. A. *I'm OK–You're OK.* London: Pan, 1969.

Henderson, L. J. *Pareto's General Sociology.* Cambridge, Mass: Harvard University Press, 1935.

Hersey, P., and K. H. Blanchard. *Management of Organizational Behavior,* 3rd ed. Englewood Cliffs, N.J.: Prentice-Hall, 1977.

Homans, G. C. *The Human Group.* New York: Harcourt, Brace & World, 1950.

____________. *Social Behavior: Its Elementary Forms.* New York: Harcourt, Brace & World, 1961.

Jay, A. *Corporation Man.* New York: Random House, 1971.

____________ . "General systems theory: Applications for organization and management," *Academy of Management Journal* (1972), 447-65.

____________. *Organization and Management: A Systems Approach,* 2nd ed. New York: McGraw-Hill, 1974.

Katz, D., and R. L. Kahn. *The Social Psychology of Organizations.* New York: Wiley, 1966.

Kellman, H. C. "Compliance, identification, and internalization: Three processes of attitude change," *Journal of Conflict Resolution,* 2 (1958).

Kelly, J. *Organizational Behavior,* rev. ed. Homewood, Ill.: Irwin, 1974.

Koontz, H. "The management theory jungle," *Academy of Management Journal,* 4, 3 (1961), 174–88.

Kriesberg, M. "Executives evaluate administrative conferences." *Advanced Management,* 15, 3 (1950), 15–17.

Lawrence, P. R., and J. W. Lorsch. *Developing Organizations: Diagnosis and Action*. Reading, Mass.: Addison-Wesley, 1969.

Leavitt, H. J. *Managerial Psychology*, rev. ed. Chicago: University of Chicago Press, 1964.

Levin, K. *Field Theory in Social Science: Selected Theoretical Papers*, ed. Dorwin Cartwright. New York: Harper & Row, 1951.

Likert, R. *The Human Organization*. New York: McGraw-Hill, 1967.

____________. *New Patterns of Management*. New York: McGraw-Hill, 1961.

Lorenz, K. *On Aggression*. New York: Harcourt, Brace & World, 1966.

Maslow, A. H. *Motivation and Personality*. New York: Harper & Row, 1954.

McClelland, D.C. *The Achieving Society*. Princeton, N.J.: Van Nostrand, 1961.

____________. "Business drive and national achievement," *Harvard Business Review*, July–August (1962), 99–112.

____________. "Money as a motivator: Some research insights," *The McKinsey Quarterly*, Fall (1967), 10–21.

____________. "That urge to achieve," *Think*, Nov.-Dec. (1966), 19–23.

Merton, R. K. "Bureaucratic structure and personality," *Social Forces*, 18 (1940), 560–68.

Milgram, S. "Behavioral study of obedience," *Journal of Abnormal and Social Psychology*, 67 (1963), 371–78.

____________. "Group pressures and action against a person," *Journal of Abnormal and Social Psychology*, 69 (1964), 137–43.

Miller, D. C., and W. H. Form. *Industrial Sociology*. New York: Harper and Row, 1951.

Mooney, J. D., and A. C. Reiley. *Onward Industry*. New York: Harper and Row, 1931.

Morris, D. *The Naked Ape*. New York: McGraw-Hill, 1967.

Newman, P. L. "Wild man behavior in a New Guinea Highlands community," *American Anthropologist*, 66 (1964), 1, 16–19.

Packard, V. *The Status Seekers*. New York: Longmans, Green & Co., 1959.

Potter, S. *The Theory and Practice of Gamesmanship*. London: Rupert Hart-Davis, 1947.

"Power is the great motivator," *Harvard Business Review*, 54, 2 March-April (1976), 100–10.

Rapoport, Roger. "Life on the line," *The Wall Street Journal*, July 24, 1967.

Read, P. P. *Alive: The Story of the Andes Survivors*. New York: Lippincott, 1974.

Reddin, W. J. *Managerial Effectiveness*. New York: McGraw-Hill, 1970.

____________, and R. Stuart-Kotze. "Toward situational management," *Cost and Management*, May-June (1973).

Richards, M. D., and P. S. Greenlaw. *Management: Decisions and Behavior*, rev. ed. Homewood, Ill.: Irwin, 1972.

Roethlisberger, F. J., and W. J. Dickson. *Management and the Worker*. Cambridge, Mass.: Harvard University Press, 1939.

Rogers, C. R. *Client-Centered Therapy*. Boston: Houghton Mifflin, 1951.

__________, and R. E. Farson. *Active Listening*. Industrial Relations Center, University of Chicago.

Rosen, N. "Supervisory behavior as perceived by subordinates: Cause or consequence of performance and group cohesion?" eds. B. M. Bass, R. Cooper, and J. A. Haas. *Managing for Accomplishment*. Lexington, Mass.: D. C. Heath, 1970.

Schein, E. H. "Interpersonal communication, group solidarity, and social influence," *Sociometry*, 23 (1960), 148–61.

Scott, W. G., and T. R. Mitchell. *Organization Theory: A Structural and Behavioral Analysis*, rev. ed. Homewood, Illinois: Irwin-Dorsey, 1972.

Seiler, J. A. *Systems Analysis in Organizational Behavior*. Homewood, Ill.: Irwin-Dorsey, 1967.

Shibutani, T. *Society and Personality*. Englewood Cliffs, N.J.: Prentice-Hall, 1961.

Simon, H. A. *The New Science of Management Decision*. New York: Harper and Row, 1960.

Smith, P. B. *Groups Within Organizations*. New York: Harper and Row, 1973.

Sprott, W. J. H. *Human Groups*. Harmondsworth, England: Penguin, 1958.

Stewart, R. *The Reality of Management*. London: Heinemann, 1963.

Taylor, F. W. *Scientific Management*. New York: Harper and Row, 1911.

Thompson, V. *Modern Organization: A General Theory*. New York: Knopf, 1961.

Urwick, L. F., and L. Gulick. (eds.) *Papers on the Science of Administration*. New York: Institute of the Public Administration, Columbia University, 1937.

Vroom, V. *Work and Motivation*. New York: John Wiley & Sons, 1964.

Weber, M. *The Theory of Social and Economic Organization*. Oxford: Oxford University Press, 1947.

White, R. F. "Motivation reconsidered: The concept of competence," *Psychological Review*, 66, 5 (1959).

Whyte, W. F. "An interaction approach to the theory of organization," *Modern Organization Theory*, ed. Mason Haire. New York: Wiley, 1959.

__________. *The Organization Man*. New York: Simon and Schuster, 1956.

__________. *Organizational Behavior*. Homewood, Ill.: Irwin-Dorsey, 1969.

Wickesberg, A. K. "Communications networks in the business organization structure," *Academy of Management Journal*, 11 (1968), 253–62.

Young, S. "Organization as a total system," *California Management Review*, 10 (1968), 21–32.

Index